REINTERPRETING MENOPAUSE

M

REINTERPRETING MENOPAUSE

Cultural and Philosophical Issues

Edited by
**Paul A. Komesaroff, Philipa Rothfield,
and Jeanne Daly**

Routledge
New York & London

Published in 1997 by
Routledge
29 West 35th Street
New York, NY 10001

Published in Great Britain by
Routledge
11 New Fetter Lane
London EC4P 4EE

Library of Congress Cataloging-in-Publication Data

Reinterpreting menopause : cultural and philosophical issues / edited
  by Paul A. Komesaroff, Philipa Rothfield, and Jeanne Daly.
      p.   cm.
    Includes bibliographical references.
    ISBN 0-415-91564-3 (cloth). — ISBN 0-415-91565-1 (paper)
    1. Menopause.   2. Middle aged women—Health and hygiene.
  3. Middle aged women—Psychology.   I. Komesaroff, Paul A.
  II. Rothfield, Philipa.   III. Daly, Jeanne.
    [DNLM: 1. Menopause.   2. Women.   WP 580 R374 1996]
  RG186.R36   1996
  612.6'65—dc20
  DNLM/DLC
  for Library of Congress   96-28892
                                                                          CIP

Contents

Discursive Strategies

Metaphors and Mutations

INTRODUCTION

1

Mapping Menopause
Objectivity or Multiplicity?

Paul A. Komesaroff, Philipa Rothfield, and Jeanne Daly

Does "the menopause" exist? Certainly, from a point of view widely adopted within medicine, it does. For many practitioners and researchers, menopause is to be understood as a purely *technical* phenomenon. From this viewpoint, it can be satisfactorily described in terms of hormonal changes and their accompanying effects. In particular, according to a popular view, a decline in the circulating levels of the female hormone estrogen is responsible for most of the acute symptoms of menopause and for the epidemiologically defined increase in the risk of certain conditions. Menopause is therefore considered a "deficiency disease" for which a cure is needed—the logical remedy taking the form of hormonal supplementation or "replacement."

This account of menopause, which constitutes one of the orthodoxies of modern medicine, is widely familiar today. It is not, however, uncontested. Informally, many women in midlife have sought other explanations for the changes they experience. In recent years a substantial body of writing has developed that takes issue, both implicitly and explicitly, with the medical view of menopause. The factual bases for the claims about the physical and other changes associated with menopause and the effects of the various available hormonal treatments are matters of continuing controversy. The limitations of approaches that conceptualize complex fields of experience and behavior exclusively in biological terms are increasingly being recognized. The social presuppositions and political outcomes of these and other reductionist theories are today subjected to vigorous criticism.

This process of questioning has drawn on a variety of theoretical traditions and perspectives, including feminist theory, politics, philosophy, sociology, psychology, and anthropology. One of the major strategies of feminist discussions of menopause has been to shift the analysis from a form of technical knowledge to understandings that issue from women's perspectives, whether experiential, theoretical, cultural, or political. These have shown that there are several ways of seeing menopause, and that these perspectives may be contradictory and even incommensurable. Other critical analyses have also contested the character of biomedical models and their exclusions, attempting to revise and supplement the technical picture in social, cultural, and political terms. These differing accounts can be understood in relation to the cultural and the conceptual origins of menopause, biomedical knowledge, and practice.[1] In other words, the critical examination of menopause has exposed to investigation not only the contents of discourses about menopause but also the various metadiscursive contexts within which they operate. As a consequence of these engagements, women in midlife are able to strategically avail themselves of these multiple perspectives that contest the apparent singularity of the biomedical model.

Science, Knowledge, Culture

How does the biomedical rendition of menopause manage to maintain such a position of influence? The cogency of science resides in part in its adherence to facts, the "stuff" of the objective world. This applies to all objects of scientific study, whether, for example, elementary particles, plants, or women's bodies. Yet one of the main insights of recent philosophy of science has been the recognition that science is a cultural practice. The cultural character of science pertains to the epistemology with which it operates (the kinds of knowledge it practices) and the social functions it performs. This has implications regarding that which can be known—the object of scientific knowledge. By recognizing the cultural aspects at work here, scientific discourses themselves can be seen as strategies for the *construction* of objects of investigation, producing techniques for studying them, and the criteria for successful research. Accordingly, they entail the establishment of particular notions of objectivity and truth. They also entail comprehensive evaluative apparatuses, usually codified within ethical systems.

The scientific and medical discourses involving women's bodies are no exception here. In this volume, Emily Martin argues that throughout most of the twentieth century, women's bodies have been conceptualized as machines designed to produce products. Medicine's mechanistic body has been traced to scientific elaborations upon Descartes' distinction between the mind and the body, otherwise known as Cartesian dualism.[2] The sexual specificity of the *female* body adds something more to the mechanistic metaphor. The element of productivity is doubly emphasized with respect to the feminine body such that not only is the machine conceived in terms of human activity (productivity), it is also expected to reproduce (to produce other machines) smoothly and consistently. In line with these metaphors, menstruation will tend to be seen as a breakdown of continuous functioning—more precisely, as the moment of failure to produce a baby. Likewise, menopause comes to be seen as a breakdown of the machine's reproductive capacity, inaugurating an inexorable slide into uselessness and disrepair.

Metaphors of Female Corporeality

One way of contesting dominant discourses of women's bodies is to produce other metaphors of feminine corporeality. Alternative descriptions of the female body are able to yield different understandings, which need not rely upon the machine, its products, and its moments of breakdown. Alongside the view of the body as a machine, a number of sharply divergent sets of metaphors have recently arisen that are challenging accepted ways of understanding physiological functioning. Among these are forms of systems theory such as chaos theory, nonlinear dynamics, and complexity theory. Such conceptual models have already been applied with suggestive outcomes in some areas of clinical research, including cardiology, oncology, and immunology. Martin argues that it is possible also to regard menopause, and the female reproductive system in general, in terms of these paradigms. When one does so, the aspect that, from the mechanical view, is described as breakdown and failure, presents itself instead as a discontinuous change of state. The singularity of reproduction as the mode of production and teleology of feminine corporeality no longer follows according to some essential bodily logic. The transitions associated with menopause appear not as moves from order into disorder, but as moves from one kind of order to another. It is arguable that the full development of these novel theoretical perspectives could have an important practical impact on the medical treatment of meno-pause, as well as on the ways in which individual women experience it.

Kwok Wei Leng argues for another kind of corporeal metaphor, one developed by Donna Haraway, that of the *cyborg*. As a figure that resists binary opposition—here, that between nature and culture—the cyborg is said to enable a politics and practice of menopause that is neither wholly pro- nor wholly antimedicine and its attendant technologies. According to cyborg thinking, there is no natural body that experiences menopause. Rather, the lived menopausal body is itself an intricate admixture of organism and machine, a more complex, ambivalent entity that therefore resists any simple framework of solution to be automatically applied to menopausal women.

Narrative and Necessity

Metaphors also have a history. The ways of understanding bodies, and especially women's bodies, within medicine represent the outcomes of complex historical processes of development. These processes, which also generated the structures and the practices of the modern clinic, can be shown to have been dependent upon deep philosophical, social, and ethical assumptions.[3] The development of the contemporary conceptions of menopause in particular has been characterized by significant moments of exchange between scientific, philosophical, ethical, and aesthetic themes. The ways in which the figure of the aging woman has been demonized and pathologized have been charted. Less well studied is the more subtle rhetorical feminization of larger processes of decline and degeneration in the nineteenth century. Robyn Gardner traces the ways in which biology, social theory, and history of the late eighteenth- and nineteenth-centuries were preoccupied with processes of decline. Invoking a much older ideal of the whole, the pure, and the timeless, an ideal of the feminine was developed in opposition to what it was thought not to be—the diseased, the deformed, the disfigured, and the non-European. The menopausal woman (who is clearly the subject of temporal processes) was seen according to the image of darker, disfigured, and degenerate historical and cultural forms of decline.

The power of the increasingly sophisticated physiological models of the body that have developed during the course of the twentieth century has derived substantially from the ability of these models to accommodate and to redefine the most persistent and persuasive narratives of the classical and of the religious traditions. On the one hand, the biological narratives represent the most impressive accomplishments of contemporary science; on the other, these very representations perform the narrative role that religious traditions have occupied in times past. The contemporary images of the body as a hormonal system articulate a sense of complexity and of mystery, while at the same time holding a promise of final revelation and a possibility of unimagined opportunities for strategic interventions. It is not often recognized that the invention and development of the hormonal body was contemporaneous with, and in many ways parallel to, the development of psychoanalysis. For Gardner, their histories are interrelated. Similar anxieties and preoccupations are apparent, as are some important differences: both systems, for example, are informed by images and structures derived from *fin de siècle* racial and biological anxieties; and both aestheticize complexity in terms of the "textual."

Issues of textuality also govern cultural representations and images of female bodies and of aging women. Mia Campioni shows the way in which the psychoanalytic figure of the oedipal mother is caught up with the model of the reproductive female, that is, the figure of the maternal. Freud's oedipal triangle is posed in the familial field of the mother, father, and infant, at a time when the woman is involved in a certain phase of reproductive femininity. Her temporality is that of the mother of the newborn infant. The figure of woman in this scenario operates within an economy of reproductive femininity that *excludes* the older woman, rendering her either a threat or a problem, to be dealt with or to be cured. This provides a symbolic setting for the pathologization of the menopausal woman that is at the same time *unable* to incorporate and to embody the historical processes and meanings of life, death, and aging. Campioni revisits the oedipal myth to produce another narrative of older femininity, one liable to political revolt and resistance.

Another means of challenging biomedicine's grip upon the definition of menopause is to question its reliance upon a certain distinction between the mind and the body. The notion of a physiological body and its contrast with the emotions and psyche mirrors the mind/body split and is utilized within menopausal accounts that explain women's experience as psychological symptoms produced by physical, hormonal causes. Philipa Rothfield points out the dualism that underlies menopausal discourses that attribute hormonal activities to the physical realm and experiential perspectives to the psychological. If the distinction upon which such an explanation rests is *destabilized*, then the whole edifice becomes insecure. The fixity of the distinction between the interior and exterior of a bodily subject has been called into question by a number of contemporary thinkers such as Foucault, Deleuze, and Grosz. The notion of a psychical interior as distinct from a bodily exterior or material objectivity has been undermined via the figures of the Möbius strip, the fold, the pleat, or the surface.[4] In each of these, the one dimension continually threatens to become the other: for example, the Möbius strip is a shape whose external facade becomes an internal surface, which then becomes an external facade and so on; similarly, pleats or folds are formed by what was originally an external aspect of material becoming an internal aspect via the folding process.

Each of these metaphors implies a process of mutation from one state to another. Merleau-Ponty also works to destabilize mind/body dualism, by analyzing experience and materiality in overlapping rather than distinct terms. In the spirit of Merleau-Ponty, Rothfield discusses the experiences of pregnancy as a form of play that cannot be divided into mental and physical realms. Although different in many respects, there are affinities between pregnancy and menopause; these concern biomedical emphases upon hormonal activity. Rothfield argues that, from the point of view of experience, materiality has a certain give— an openness to experience and to interpretation—that resists any simplified notion of hormonal causality. This means that, while the finer nuances of hormonal mappings are valid in their own technical terms, they do not suffice as explanations of lived bodies of experience.

As a result of such questioning, the objectivity of the body and its contrast with the mental realm of experience is seen to be not so fixed. The body's opposition to the psyche is unhinged, undermining its ability to be scientifically quantified independent of considerations of subjectivity, experience, representation, and discourse. Neither is the body able to be sustained as an "it," that is, as an object that transcends history and culture. The historical constitution of menopausal bodies implicates relations of power, knowledge, and the attainment of particular forms of biomedical hegemony. These elements of power and their ability to produce bodies and bodily experience pertain both to the bodies of women who experience menopause and to the bodies of biomedical knowledge that are able to define and to treat menopause. The development of counter-strategies on the part of menopausal women can be assisted by the analysis and exposure of the processes that have led to a particular form of biomedical and corporeal hegemony. In other words, once a particular form of objectivity is exposed as a vicissitude of history—that is, contingent—room is made for the promotion and politicization of *other* contingencies—in Foucauldian terms, counterstrategies.

Roe Sybylla analyzes menopause across three periods in time: the mid-nineteenth century, the mid-twentieth century, and the present day. In distinct ways across this period of time, menopause has been seen differently, changing as the social context changes. Menopause, she argues, has been a site of contesting strategies, a network of power relations. Domination of the field of knowledge about menopause by the medical profession has conferred the power to define menopause as a disease and to define the changing nature of the disease. Women have not so much lost their power or capacities but have had these captured for the use of others. Kwok Wei Leng makes a different discursive point. She examines discursive identities between biomedical and particular feminist analyses of menopause. On the surface, these two discourses are oppositional; however, at a deeper level, there is a fundamental structural similarity: both are dependent upon a logocentric metaphysics of truth. That is, each form of analysis claims a truth of the menopausal body: one, a truth of science; the other, a truth of feminism; both, *the* truth of some natural body.

The Popular Imaginary

In terms of popular culture, contemporary constructions of menopause have narrowed rather than multiplied. According to Margaret Morganroth Gullette, a "menoboom" has occurred via proliferating discourses in society, politics, and feminism. Although this upsurge of interest in menopause in the popular literature addresses issues of considerable complexity, a substantial part of the reportage of putative medical "breakthroughs" leaves the dominant paradigm unexamined. The construction of menopause as a drastic, universal sexual and biological health event breaks the continuity of a woman's life in the middle. Gullette sees menopause as a "magic marker" that divides such a woman both from women at other ages and from men. The public discourse is one in which the menopausal woman is seen as aging, as infirm, as socially contaminated. These perceptions are reinforced through the marketing of health, fitness, youth, sexuality, and medicine itself, and through deeply entrenched cultural biases against older women. Women have participated in these representations. Indeed, these negative accounts of menopause are now so culturally intrusive that it is difficult for women to resist them. Gullette favors a strategy that focuses on women's diversity (against biological determinism) and portrays the continuities in women's lives so that menopause becomes a change women manage with competence.

The lack of popular representations of menopause that emphasize diversity is reflected in popular films and novels.[5] These representations of menopause pose no simple solutions, unless it is of the need for women to take stock of their lives and rebel against oppression. E. Ann Kaplan notes the absence of positive Hollywood images of older women. Unlike a number of films concerned with the aging male's potency, older women are at best supposed to cede ground to younger women (for example, to their daughters) to relinquish the privileges accorded to youthful femininity. Privilege is the subject of the two films of independent women directors that Kaplan examines: Pam Tom's *Two Lies* and Yvonne Rainer's *Privilege*. Each of these films reminds us that youth is not the only form of privilege, for they also both look at the privileges associated with being white and middle class as created through modes of racism and western ethnocentrism. Tom's film is concerned with plastic surgery, its aesthetic Caucasian norm, and the ambivalences of approaching assimilation through surgical alteration. A particular focus of this film is the shape of eyes and that which constitutes the desired norm. The cost of such assimilation—both desirable and not—is the effacement of difference. Rainer's film, *Privilege*, explicitly addresses menopause, a site of female corporeality already intersected by other forms of marginalization, effected through axes of racist and capitalist oppression. Kaplan notes the resonance between "restoring" a western youthful norm via plastic surgery and "replacing" a hormonal decline by means of hormonal therapy. In both instances, nonwestern and menopausal bodies are pathologized. Kaplan neither idealizes nor demonizes bodily alterations *per se*, for she acknowledges the equivocations that surround the lived subjectivities of women within a patriarchal, Eurocentric culture such as that of the United States.

One strategy of supplementation and subversion is to focus upon that which is substantially missing in medical and other texts: accounts of what women themselves say about their experience. Jeanne Daly's contribution to the debate is an empirical, sociological analysis of 150 women's accounts of what Daly prefers to call midlife. On the one hand, this study reinforces the image of competence and resistance suggested by Gullette. On the other, some of the women in this study did experience debilitating problems, often associated with depression. It was a common experience of these women that medical treatment was either denied them or that it had only a minimal effect in dealing with the complex interaction of problems they faced in midlife. This diversity of experience and the complex interactive nature of the problems led the women to have a high regard for support from other women in midlife.

Menopausal Meanings

For an individual woman, menopause can be associated with a great variety of meanings and theoretical constructions. There is the physiological interpretation of menopause, discussed at the beginning of this introduction, which is associated with certain notions about the nature of truth, science, and the body. There are the competing ways of understanding biological systems, which emphasize complexity and equilibrium rather than control and order. There are the cultural interpretations that view menopause as a social construction, arising in relation to systems of discourse and communication. There are interpretations that fall within mainstream conceptions, and there are those that do not. Each perspective gives rise to sets of personal meanings for individual women. Each is embedded in its own way in the spaces of lived experience. Each must provide answers to questions about the nature of corporeality, about the end of fertility, about the experience of change, about the meaning of aging, illness, and death.

The sources and dynamics of personal meanings are always complex. They depend on the symbolic and imaginary constructions of bodies in relation to specific cultural settings and practices. As indicated by Campioni, in the case of the older woman, corporeal presence takes on a powerful, disturbing, and sometimes threatening character. The menopausal woman becomes the personification of all that opposes or destabilizes the existing order. Her presence and her speech appear to signify that she knows otherwise. Viewed in terms of what Campioni calls the psychoanalytic fairy tale, the menopausal woman's anger and perversity signify a return of the repressed. The older woman is thereby killed off in order to prevent her testifying to her sexuality. This symbolic image may affect the older woman directly, threatening to leave her with a profoundly negative view of herself rather than to invite the tendencies of resistance and lucidity that may also arise.

The ambiguities of the images of menopause, however, also lead to an irreducible subversive moment. The menopausal woman acquires a variety of social and psychological meanings: she may be "wise woman," "oracle," "priestess," or "healer"; but she is also "monster," "harbinger of man's fate," "evil force," "destroyer," "avenger," "bitter and twisted hag," "witch," or "castrating bitch." The menopausal woman is the personification of the "abject." She embodies the repressed, unacknowledged, and feared parts of both personal identity and societies. She disturbs identity, system, order. She arises out of, and passes back into, repression, control, exclusion, and ritualization of all that we fear.

Wendy Rogers discusses menopause in terms of abjection, drawing upon a concept and process theorized by Julia Kristeva. Abjection is explicated as something that both establishes the human subject's identity and embodies that which is feared, repressed, and expelled. This operates in bodily terms (for example, via menstruation and defecation) and through social processes via rituals of pollution and purification (the sacred and the profane). Rogers looks at menopause in terms of abjection—its existence as a boundary between female fertility and nonfertility, its ambiguity, its social repression and pathologization, its attempted control via the biomedical application of drugs and definitions, and, finally, its threat in terms of its tendency to represent aging and death.

It is arguable that, for all this complexity, in modern western culture it is no longer possible to experience the transitions associated with menopause as meaningful life events. Fiona Mackie posits that—despite the subversiveness of the abject moment of menopausal embodiment—the insertion of the female body into networks of gender ascription, systems of knowledge, and commodification has been so comprehensive and uncompromising that it has been robbed of its private, inner dimension and rendered defenseless against the structures of power and the medical gaze. To fit the capitalist world of commodities, bodies have come to be perceived as things that are solid, excluding all qualities relating to fluidity and flow. The subjects of these bodies are understood to be isolated and atomized, defined by their separation from others rather than by their connections to them. People are thereby marked off from one another via the boundaries of the individual body.

Political Ramifications

As has been argued in a variety of ways, understanding menopause is critically dependent upon social, cultural, historical, and corporeal variables. The fact that these variables are contingent means that alternative theoretical strategies are able to be developed, utilized, and promoted by menopausal women themselves. The cultural imaginary of the menopausal woman as *lacking* is not unassailable, nor are the negative connotations of aging femininity necessary. Any challenge to these supposed negative inevitabilities is likely to involve challenging the epistemological dominance of certain menopausal paradigms, their correlative practices (treatments, diagnoses, etiologies), and their underlying cultural symbolic. These contestatory productions are thus not purely abstract exercises in theory, lacking any impact on the lives of ordinary women. On the contrary, they carry the potential to be utilized for personal and political ends, to generate other experiences, other manifestations. As Campioni puts it, menopause embodies the possibility of revolt.

Today, with the benefits of the theoretical achievements of feminism and postmodernism, we can understand how the body is subjected to a wide range of strategies of power, how it is organized, disciplined, and put under comprehensive techniques of surveillance. The separation and isolation of bodies from each other, which in part arise out of the polarity between solidity and fluidity, cut the links between bodies and culture, and between bodies and space and time. The recognition of these structures of culture and knowledge raises the possibility of a more dynamic and fluid understanding of menopause, one that would be capable of generating new meanings and new possibilities for experience. From this perspective, and at Mackie's invitation, menopause can be seen as the experience of transition, as a "body-induced invitation to rebalance one's energy around an altering bloodtide." Menopause—at least potentially—offers access to shifting modalities of subjectivity, released from the fixity of dominant unified subject positions.

From One to Many Discourses

One of the more important outcomes of the modern critiques of medicine and its institutions has been the reassessment and reinterpretation of menopause. Out of these critiques many different perspectives have developed regarding medicine, the female body, femininity, aging, and temporality. Indeed, it is not an exaggeration to say that menopause has today become a major site, or battleground, for radical and innovative reflections on medicine, culture, and society. The cultural representations of menopause and aging, the assumptions about the roles of women and experiences of embodiment, the analyses of the effects and ill effects of hormonal and other medical therapies, the interpretation of the roles of the institutions of power, are all subject to critique and to contestation. A potential space thus emerges for other forms of subjectivity and of lived experience.

Of course, the entrenched relationships of power are not easily overcome. On the contrary, the political structures that characterize the construction, understanding, and experience of menopause are deeply enmeshed with those of society at large. The patriarchal power of doctors, the development of elaborate cultural institutions to contain and to sanitize the physical functioning of women's bodies, the use of both medicine and culture to create huge profits from the sale of pharmaceutical agents, the pressures to submit to experimental procedures and treatments—all these are merely facets of a comprehensive system of domination and control that pervades all aspects of contemporary life. Indeed, as Sybylla maintains, the quest for scientific truth itself, taken for granted in medical discourses about menopause, presupposes decisions about why the particular aspects of knowledge that are searched for today are valued at all.

If much of the contemporary practice of medicine has become identified with a social project characterized by biological reductionism and the protection of the entrenched institutions of power, it does not follow that medicine as such is inevitably tainted. Indeed, as Paul Komesaroff shows, clinical practice has always contained a moment within which the complexity of corporeal experience and the ambiguities and limitations of the scientific formulations are recognized. Komesaroff argues that this moment—which should be extended and deepened—arises out of a fundamental concern of medicine with ethical questions, with the problem of otherness, and with the vicissitudes of bodily meanings. Viewed from this perspective, with respect to menopause, medicine has much to offer both as an instrument of knowledge and as a locus of therapeutic practice. Menopause can be understood not merely in terms of physiological processes but also in conjunction with the motifs of disruption that often characterize the experiences of women at midlife. These disruptions, at the levels of biology, social relationships, sexuality, and values, can be negotiated in manifold ways that depend upon the particularity of the circumstances of individual women. Stripped of ideological distortions, and limited to a field of application properly within its competence, medicine can assist in the passages between the universal and the particular and heighten the appreciation of the complexity of the issues that arise at this time.

Despite certain hegemonies of explanation and understanding, there is no single discourse of menopause. The concept of "menopause" itself is now a complex one, referring to a multiplicity of theoretical and cultural perspectives on a variety of issues, from the biology of aging to the philosophical understanding of death. Discussions of menopause may refer to biology or politics, hormones or feminism, psychoanalysis or social control; when it comes to individual experiences, a similar range of variation is found. It is impossible to consider the meaning and experience of menopause without exploring the cultural, historical, sexual, epistemological, and ethical contexts within which bodies are shaped and experiences of menopause are deemed to occur—or are prevented from occurring.

The breaking of the hegemony of the old paradigms of knowledge, culture, and power will not, it is to be hoped, lead seamlessly to the institution of a new one. Indeed, if any of the claims of postmodern theories of society are correct, consensus paradigms are now obsolete. This, of course, does not mean that political power is obsolete, or that specific discourse systems do not have powerful implications, both positive and negative. Indeed, the old discourses of power have not lost their sway, and the new techniques of science if anything carry with them enhanced capacities for surveillance and management. But they also provide new possibilities for resistance.

This book is offered both as a reflection on the expanding discourses around menopause and as a contribution to attempts to use the understanding of the operation of the existing structures of culture and power to fashion such new and creative strategies of resistance. If there were to be a single thesis that emerges from these pages, it would be that there is no such thing as *the* menopause. There are menopausal experiences. The menopause can be a time of biological disruption, of physical change, of social transformation, of philosophical reflection. The various components do not fit together in a single, well definable whole, nor should they. This does not mean that women do not experience discomfort, perplexity, turmoil, or pain. It does mean that menopause is more complex and interesting than its public facade has hitherto suggested.

Notes

1. See, e.g., Barbara Ehrenreich and Dierdre English, *Complaints and Disorders: The Sexual Politics of Sickness* (London: Readers and Writers Publ. Coop. 1973); John Ehrenreich, ed., *The Cultural Crisis of Modern Medicine* (New York: Monthly Review Press, 1976); G. Greer, *The Change: Women, Ageing and the Menopause* (London: Hamish Hamilton, 1991); Sandra Coney, *The Menopause Industry: A Guide to Medicine's "Discovery" of the Mid-life Woman* (Melbourne: Spinifex, 1993); Ruth Formanek, ed., *The Meanings of Menopause: Historical, Medical and Clinical Perspectives*

(Hillsdale, NJ: The Atlantic Press, 1990); J. Weeks, *Sex, Politics and Society: The Regulation of Sexuality since 1800* (London: Longman, 1981).

2. See D. Leder, ed., *The Body in Medical Thought and Practice* (Dordrecht: Kluwer Publishers, 1992); F. Capra, *The Turning Point: Science, Society and the Rising Culture* (London: Fontana, 1982).

3. See M. Foucault, *The Birth of the Clinic, an Archeology of Medical Perception*, trans. A. Smith (New York: Vintage Books, 1975).

4. The Möbius strip has been utilized by Grosz, the fold or pleat by Deleuze. See E. Grosz, *Volatile Bodies* (Sydney: Allen and Unwin, 1995); G. Deleuze, *The Fold, Leibniz and the Baroque*, trans. T. Conley (Minneapolis, University of Minnesota Press, 1993); *Foucault*, trans. S. Hand (Minneapolis: University of Minnesota Press, 1988).

5. *Shirley Valentine*, as play and film, has given women an image of a woman who responds to a range of problems in midlife by deserting an ungrateful family to seek adventure on a Greek island. Menopause is presented merely as a dismissive epithet that Shirley Valentine's husband invokes to explain her rebellion. Evelyn Crouch, in Fannie Flagg's book, *Fried Green Tomatoes at the Whistle Stop Cafe*, has a "bad menopause" that she negotiates with humor, hormones, and the wise advice of an older woman. Fay Weldon's *Lives and Loves of a She-Devil* has the heroine remaking herself, changing form, and coming back as a she-devil to take revenge on the husband who rejected her. See W. E. Russell, *Shirley Valentine* (London: Methuen, 1988); F. Flagg, *Fried Green Tomatoes at the Whistle Stop Cafe* (London: Vintage, 1987).

MENOPAUSAL BODIES

2

The Left Hand of the Goddess

The Silencing of Menopause as a Bodily Experience of Transition

Fiona Mackie

Embodiment in Modernity

The governing code in modernity has been tied to a gridlike relationship, perfected across centuries in the construction of the person as subject. To trace the silencing of menopause, its constriction in dread and silence, it is necessary to uncover this subjection as a positioning that architects the experience of bodiliness toward imprisonment. Despite the proclaimed freedom and privilege of western forms, the prevailing experience of bodiliness approximates to Weber's "iron cage,"[1] especially, perhaps, in the case of woman.[2] It is thus impossible to consider the meaning and experience of menopause, without first exploring this sociohistorical context that shapes body as a particular form in which the experience of menopause is deemed to occur, or is prevented from occurring.

From the moment of birth, a child of modernity imbibes an externalized form of knowledge and control deemed objective and associated with "mind." Thus begins the long progression in which "mind" becomes detached from "body" and installed as emperor over all that lies below the neck. This panoptic "head"[3] governs each bodiliness toward a self-enacted control, premised on a form of "rationality" marked profoundly by its separation from "nature."[4] "Body," deemed part of "nature," is thus relatively put out of play. Spontaneous emanations of bodiliness enter the "brain," now under the dominance of a particular form of "reason," only as disturbances, distractions; and it is ensured that the idea that hand, womb, body might "think" will present itself only as illusion. Head-brain, in its decreed monopoly, becomes the repository and receptor of a mode of "knowledge" considered as coming from outside the body.[5]

As if such silencing and robbery of an ongoing experience of embodiment were not enough, this governing mechanism is annexed to another separation. "Subjective" knowledge, arising from personal experience and insight, is marked as the lesser in the polarized pair objective/subjective. This closure, too, becomes etched into the body from a very young age in all those haunting cries from the schoolroom: "We're not interested in *your* opinion" but in what you have taken in from an externalized knowledge-mode.[6] At many phases of life, it is pertinent to wonder how much is left of the person's unique experience base, his or her unique "embodiedness," through this subjugating regime. To ask this is particularly relevant at menopause, because its construction, *as* experience, is the outcome of all these inheritances, accrued across half a century. If you have behaved *properly*,[7] you will have little awareness that, or how, this has been done, and menopause, in the particular form of its occurrence in modernity, will present simply as a fait accompli rather than as a particular, and alterable, sociocultural form.

Perhaps the policing of the perimenopausal transition is so strident and severe because, like "adolescence," it provides a powerful possibility of insight into all this robbery. In this chapter, I shall attempt to speak through and against that silencing, using broad brushstrokes to sketch the vast terrain of relevance so often excised when menopause is treated as an isolated event, relevant only to old women.

To fit the capitalist world of commodities,[8] with a technologized form of "science" that has emphasized solids to the exclusion of fluid and flow,[9] "body" has come to be perceived as a "thing." If not a mechanism for transporting the disembodied self, it is a kind of house the self inhabits, which, like all commodities, needs servicing so as to go on functioning effectively for "the self." The subject of this construction, as individual, is thought and enacted as atomized,[10] defined in its separation from others, not its interflow with and as them.[11] The skin of the thing-ized body is perceived as and acts like walls. Given the marginalization of flow, as concept and experience, no outflow nor inflow penetrates the skin cells. Through this deactivated body, the subject becomes boxed off from space, and if you perceive yourself and others as flowing beyond their body walls, if you mingle with others' surrounding space, best you not speak this. It is not part of "the normal."

This outcome of the tyranny of the normal is dire in its consequences for menopause. The severance from spacetime, in its many facets both within and beyond the socially constructed body walls, operates to disenable an experience of menopause as transition. Crucial to this disenabling mechanism are the intricate interlinkings of the internal/external barrier, which operate both as a linchpin of the polarizing mechanisms across which self and body are ongoingly crucified, and as the policing operation that each person endlessly enacts, thus subjecting him or herself to the governing code. "Dare I say this, do that, move my leg now . . . or not?" Must one hold it in, or dare one let it out?

The Crucified Body "in" Space; Its Resurrection *as* Space

Hung, drawn, and quartered, the body of modernity is crucified upon a cross that ensures both its ongoing commodification and the breakdown of its potential as flow. Governing directional codes carve into the psyche and bodily experience, partitioning it into sectors, broken off according to up/down, top/bottom, right side/left side.[12] Thus partitioned and tied to the cross of this cleavage, body is endlessly evoked, in social action, according to these directional codes, while simultaneously balancing across the outer/inner divide, haunting psyche's every action and thought.

In each of those interlocking polarities, one half is denigrated, silenced, exiled, and put out of play. That lost side, as Derrida has so eloquently conveyed,[13] serves only to effect the elevation of the preferred pole, at the exiled's expense—up over down, high over low, right over left, outer over inner. The consequences of this in embodiment are drastic. Yet voices have always cried out against such "freezing of being," reminding us that "our body is not primarily *in* space: it is of it," "inhabits space."[14] Thus, for Merleau-Ponty, color is a field. One enters each color differently, recovering one's senses and bodily experience from the domination by a particular and limiting form that exiles this wider mode of sensation, as "co-existence and communion."[15] Instead of phenomena being externalized, they think themselves within me.[16] I become a field of interblended senses, no longer carved between inside and outside: "I see sounds or hear colors," where the bundling of senses apportioned to different "parts" of the body no longer applies.[17] "My body is the fabric into which all objects are woven."[18] I inhabit a depth of space, in oscillation, not the mere emptiness of space as modernity has constructed it—mere background, not living, not there, and *certainly* not an aspect of one's embodiment.[19]

In this wider mode, thingness of body is breached. The external refuses to remain outside, nor I within. Beyond the broken portcullis of the internal/external divide, "the landscape thinks itself in me, . . . and I am its consciousness."[20] As for the body, far from being frozen out of space, "it applies itself to space like a hand to an instrument."[21] From subjectivity, one's mode of personness expands toward intersubjectivity and interconnectivity with one's surrounding world. Instead of an atomized separation, housed behind body walls and sealed in the deadened internal, my consciousness "slips spontaneously into the other person's," we are able to intermingle with and as space—resurrected from our crucifixion as object, in a world of separated objects.

Irigaray begs us not to draw ourselves back "up" to fit the erect and head-controlled embodiment that tears us apart from each other and our surrounding world and seals our bodies against interflow and communion. "Erection," she claims, "is no business of ours." "We have so much space to share," "so many dimensions." In trying to speak the different voices of menopause, her assurance is helpful: "don't worry about the 'right' word. There isn't any." But to find words that are not already colonized, one must walk away from the "proper" and avoid prevailing body effects whereby "you pull yourself in, you become narrower as you rise. Stretching upward, reaching higher, you pull yourself away from the limitless realm of your body. Don't make yourself erect, you'll leave us. The sky isn't up there: it's between us."[22]

Menopause in the Governing Code

In the intricate web of polarizations that haunt thought, language, experience, and bodiliness, the governing evaluations are etched into inequalities and hierarchies that can present to us as if they were natural, hiding the force of their operations. "Woman" is already excluded from language, where "he" reigns in the name of all;[23] and the exclusion of women for so many centuries from the arenas where culture is formed means, as Dorothy Smith traces,[24] that the private realms, to which woman's largely home-based terrain has been limited, are locked out of a prevailing definition of "culture" that has been tied to the public realm, largely reserved for men.

Tracing the interlocking patterns, one sees a dominant form of rationality that emphasizes externalized knowledge cut off from the subjective sphere, from inner emotions, from nature (externalized as a raw material for technological and scientific advance), and from body. All the attributes attached to rationality are also those deemed to be more accessible to and appropriate to men. Women, by contrast, are deemed more emotional, more subjective, more tied to their bodies; associated with the inner, the private, and nature. In this dominant construction of gender, which has attributed qualities according to sexual difference, a hierarchy is ensured, since the valued qualities in each case are assigned to males. Religion, at the same time, is based on a thoroughly male notion of God, Spirit, Trinity;[25] and a long history of persecution has eliminated all significant traces of any Goddess.[26]

Meanwhile, in a culture emphasizing youth over age, and an embodiment where all have been heavily forced toward right-handedness over left-handedness, any attempt to speak of menopause as having importance beyond its source as a market for medicaments for old women has had about as much currency as trying to articulate the left hand of the goddess. Where women are already marginalized, where inner and bodily knowledge are not deemed an important component of the governing rationality, and where subjective experience is treated as the paltry cousin of quantifiable analysis, where the subjective represents a sample of a mere one person, influenced, to boot, by her own emotional views, it becomes a hard line to hoe to suggest that there lies within the uniquely personal experience of menopause a vast fund of vital human insight. Even the language

that might speak has to carve its way between words as they have been constructed, since language is imbued with the polarities and values alluded to above,
which leave the speaking of such a menopausal experience in a marginalized and
disabling silence.

Added to this, care must be taken in seeking to speak a more joyous
menopausal experience. Social constructions create a situation where very few
women will be enabled to experience a joyous transition at this phase of their
life, where midlife pressures from job and family make huge demands on male
and female alike. Pressures of class, race, and ethnic background will intersect in
such ways as to generate huge disadvantages for many women. And since it is
generally agreed that the menopausal transition will be easier if you feel satisfied
with your life-situation as it has thus far unfolded—therefore perhaps easier if
you are educated, have a job you enjoy, are happy about your family circumstances[27]—it can readily become the case that those thus privileged, in speaking
in positive ways about the transition, become used as condemnation of those
whose circumstances ensnare them in the powerful prevailing construction of
menopause as misery.

Misery is certainly the governing picture in modernity. As the age approaches
when menopause may occur, one is regaled with social expectations that speak
only of loss—loss of womanliness, of childbearing, perhaps of sexuality; "death"
of the womb, the ovaries; loss of menstruation and of youth. One is beckoned
toward portals that mark one's passage toward a kind of crone, a purposeless old
woman, where both those terms reach one already thoroughly steeped in nega-
tivity and constructed as the negative poles of all that is deemed worthy and
good.

Apart from the outrageousness of this situation, it is also interesting. Such
heavy preponderances of dread, exile, silencing, and doom collected around a
moment of human transition may indeed be read as indicating that only horror
lies ahead. But it would be silly to accept this surface analysis, in a context where
it has become so clear, through the now pervasive critiques of modernity generated by phenomenological, hermeneutic, and especially feminist and postmodern
approaches, that dominant codes operate as mechanisms of power and thus need
to be unmasked. Looking from this viewpoint, the very force with which dread,
horror, death mark the menopausal portals might suggest that something of
worth lies here, from which the mechanisms of the dominant code strive desper-
ately to point people away. It is clearly the case that the medical profession,
which has had the biggest stake in the characterization of what menopause
means, has had much to gain from a negative interpretation. The pervasive pressure toward hormone replacement treatment, as a way of basically avoiding the
whole change, would not have been nearly as powerful, were it not that such
negative interpretations prevail.[28]

I shall leave it to other chapters of the book to present both the positive and
negative aspects of "hormone replacement therapy" (HRT).[29] Instead of focusing

on powerful elements within the medical profession and among drug manufacturers as the constructors and beneficiaries of these negative constructions of
menopause, I shall bypass this level of analysis in favor of an engagement that
seeks, at least a little, to displace those more foundational levels of the culture of
modernity to which I have alluded above. Having sketched how women in
modernity, as menopause approaches, confront an entire governing code that
decrees their placement according to prevailing values operating greatly to their
disfavor, I shall spend the rest of this chapter seeking to displace those evaluations. My aim is to speak (from a personal perimenopausal transition) a
language that emanates from experiences of bodiliness, bespeaks a very different
universe, and does not proceed according to symptoms but rather experiences
those as offshoots of something much deeper. Something joyous is screened
out, exiled, and given no space for its articulation if the dominant characterization of menopause is used as the frame of analysis. In writing in this "other"
mode, I take a risk; but the risk of failing to carve out a language for this voice
is much greater. Without such voices, we remain condemned to a crucifixion
that, because it architects our embodiment and characterizes the whole experience of a surrounding world and its interpretive frame, will tend to bring about
its definitions as reality, where *my* reality, if I allow it credence against the tide
of "the normal," does not fit this governing code but presents as profoundly different.

It is not in the language of an essentialism of the body that this other voice
speaks. Rather, the voice emerges through a displacement of the governing
polarizing mechanisms, where body is rendered almost insensate; and where
mind dominates, with a language of thought that is actively part of the silencing
of bodily sensations *as* thoughts. What the transitional experience of menopause
can enable is an alteration in this univocity, this domination that operates within
thought.

I do not attribute the multiplicity of voices that can emerge, the balance of
this polyphony that is enabled, to some biological quality of body. Rather, the
voices that speak convey both many accumulated effects of the very specific
social constructions of bodiliness induced as modernity, and the lost experiential
histories silenced through this exiling. Since the silencings effected have thus
been highly sociohistorical, so the voices and insights are similarly socially
located. The voices would clearly be quite variable in different cultures, experiencing different constructions of bodiliness and different mechanisms of bodily
control, requiring different displacements. Thus, no universal language emerges
from this engagement and no essentialist claims are made. Rather than essentialism, the frame from which this language speaks is phenomenological,
emerging as a lived experiential critique of the governing frames of world, body,
self in modernity—a critique that allows subjective experience a more worthy
place than its denigration and subjugation under the posturing claims of objectivity have allowed.

Menopause as Spacetide

The general robbery of subjective, internal, and bodily knowledge can deeply affect the overall menopausal transition because its first, perimenopausal phase is liable to creep in, unannounced and without an easy label to define and declare its presence. Only if you are prepared to take yourself seriously enough to begin to scribble notes as you feel the early harbingers of change will you be able to track its course, both for yourself and as a means to begin to contribute to the stories we need to share. At age forty-three, a note that presages much tells me "My body is so tired it simply refuses to bother about worrying, or rushing about preparing." Already, that early, the needs of a new rootedness asserted themselves; and a reversal in the decreed direction of knowledge. Exhausted from brain directing body, body began to declare to brain; and my voice could be heard demanding, in the face of everyday pressures, "I *have to* find a new way of balancing my energy." Old ways no longer worked.

The whole bodytide was changing. Within two years I could feel the moon alter its pull upon the bloodtide. The first tangled traces of hormone slippage, as a period lurches, misses, then realigns with the full moon—needing the stronger pull, now that the blood flow has started to alter, shifting from its endless centering on the ovaries, the womb, in its monthly cycle. Far from being ghastly, deathlike, and doom-laden, the experience is, for me, one of increasing awe, delight, rejuvenation—an awakening to bodiliness, asserting itself through difference, as it did at adolescence, and with that same sense that one could never be sure who one was, what was happening. For me, a deep sense of adventure, but one that the governing code, with its endless pressures of time and its obsession with fixed identity militate powerfully against, determined to make one fearful, to make one resist the assertion of flow: in terror, to impose a tautness full of nostalgia for what is departing. But I personally do not regret a cracking in what I see, not as my "femininity," but as the governing code's destructive demand for the myth of the unified subjectivity that, through the imposition of endless habit, has been made to seem like "me" rather than a decreed aspect of modernity.

If you have resisted becoming a junkie of the fixed and unified self, with its frozen and paralyzed body, then the organism's resistance, diffusion, quiet seepage across the fixed lines of its enclosure is delicious, a delight—an ally in the serious game of that refusal. Like a trace, in silver slippers, the process arrives with a smile. The energy flow shifts across centers, between limbs, and I know that something is coming. Brain gently invaded with body's demands for the right to move more slowly, more gently, to let the wind blow, and move with it, spreading one's roots toward a new and different strength.

And so, the struggle is engaged, for whose world will allow them to shift toward *being*, against the endless pressures to *do*, push, rush; annihilating bodily sensations as one races forward, bound to a linear time, frozen in the face of the future, through the teeth of rage? Whatever had been one's praxes toward preserving life, against this deathdrive of "the normal," they are joined now by a companion:[30] body asserting itself within language, against its exile. Instead of consciously reining myself in, I need now only listen to the shifting tide of the blood's circulation in the depth of the cells, calling me toward different patterns of living. Perimenopause announces a new balance: its journey, an engagement toward its bodily discovery and articulation. A sister within, smiling, beckons toward and enables rest; no longer as something promised, put off, never arrived at, but as the demand for rest as an inbuilt and ongoing quality of bodiliness, which I have never achieved before.

The everyday world acts powerfully against this, as do a lifetime of inbuilt habits that have architected and maintained the governing closure, named as subject positioning. Part of the exploding perimenopausal demand to realign one's energies emerged, for me, through noticing an enormously swollen goiter, which had pushed my windpipe far to the right of my neck and would ultimately have strangled me. So, as well as giving oneself the right to record one's changes at this time, to write with dignity, one also needs to evolve one's own meditative curing relationship to one's bodiliness, and to have found people within the medical profession who will concur in and support one's right to a major role in one's own curing and health.[31] From my point of view, an operation to remove the growth would have been totally counterproductive. Aghast that I could have almost strangled myself without noticing, I needed to find my own ways to reverse what had brought this about. So, I kept my goiter and, through the language I listened to from the body, I found how to empty it of its tight and fistlike torsion, a result of massive and long-term overwork, and of a lifetime of swallowing what must not be spoken, on pain of survival, so that one could keep it alive, against the taboos, and in silence. To displace this, an organismic voice and senses found their speech. I began to notice, differently.

Subtly, like seasons through undergrowth, the body is changing its scent, where only those among the grasses would notice, who smell as Nature gave our other senses, on the lost side of what we now think we know. The last blood of each periodic flow is dark—dark like the good earth, deep from the center: full and full of feeling. It is a vast robbery that we have been trained not to look at it, to see it, to smell its earthiness through the pores. Taught that it's dirty, to hide it. Across the centuries, a terror-laden treachery toward "woman": more deeply, a crime against life. It is worth displacing this sacrilege.

To effect such a displacement is an engagement also with language. By *feeling* the body, one can come to know not just that, but *how* prevailing pressures, etched into bodiliness, have effected, over years, the closure of pores, the constriction of vessels and circuits, the stifling and poisoning of flow. But the governing codes work from the shadows against this excavation of the body's feelings, insights, knowledge. There is no language for the connectedness with, dispersal *as* spacetime that is the context of this banished text, and all the words you go to use will already have been colonized by inhibiting labels that will seem "mad," "emotional," "superstitious," "witchy": anything but wise.[32] A wisdom tied to body and nature is what the particular governing form of "rationality" in modernity had to slay to set up its global throne. So it will not lightly let you speak, or even believe your silent voices; and it certainly will not give you the time, which might explode its governing linearity.[33]

Oddly, the strategies for overcoming these taboos are very simple, and the time needed is tiny to effect a change in one's orientation to time. I am forever indebted to my sister, Liz Mackie, for the key that unlocked my access in such ongoing realms: through what she called "a starfish."[34] I talk to her one day by phone, from the midst of the everyday whirlwind, about the ridiculous pressures, pace, the harm one can feel it is doing. "Fiona," she says, "just take five minutes, whenever you can in the day, and lie flat on your back, with legs and arms slightly apart. It's wonderful what it can do." That is all it has taken to find access to the meditative process, though it is always ridiculously difficult to claim that space, even for so short a time.

The body's energy sinks into the earth, even through floorboards and concrete. One grounds oneself, and begins to find the body's natural capacity for this, its major points from which such rooting can continuously flow. And I found that all my circuits had been blocked by the governing construction of body as "thing," its closure from space, from earthing. Sometimes, the arms, legs, or back would suddenly lift from the ground, jerk, shake, and fall back, spontaneously releasing vast funds of tension I had been holding in, carrying around, without knowing it, especially around the shoulders, the jaw, the neck. Once these released, slowly, over many starfishes, I learned how every center— breastbone, belly, elbows, knees—was all dammed up, like fetid pools that could now release. Breath could move and nourish, heart could beat again without being armored into relative closure.

As the energy roots itself into the earth, so, behind closed eyes and with another vision, one sees the canopy of one's space re-open as a surrounding glow, encircling one all around. This capacity of the body to flow into space is a phenomenal inheritance that has been heavily occluded through the "terrorism of the governing code."[35] In my experience, bodiliness is an aspect of space, but this aspect of our inherited capacities is disallowed, unrecognized, and tyrannized in modernity. Body as solid, sealed behind walls, is cruelly forced to forego this aspect of itself—to repel its surrounding space as outside it.

As the canopy of one's spatiality re-forms in meditative vision, one can see the wounds within one's energy-body that have been specifically effected through the rigidifying, partializing, and enchainment that have characterized the enclosure of body-thing. Vibration, oscillation, depth in space, and shifting colors increase as aspects of living, as the canopy of one's space becomes inhabited, lived instead of exiled.

Not only an aspect of meditative vision, this healing of the torn helix of one's spatial embodiment increases the degree of one's connectedness, mutuality, and merging within and *as* space in a more general way. Space calls to space, and once one reclaims one's right to reinhabit spatiality, one is summoned, as active attraction, by surrounding nature, people, and other living forms. A dancing sparrow delights with its feathery excitement, a flower, a tree—all weave themselves within your vision. No longer screened out as separate and irrelevant objects, sealed in an outside, living phenomena enter one, even before one sees them, through a spatial language that needs no words. I *feel* a kangaroo on the air, spin round, almost on instinct, and see it only *after* and *because* I have first felt it on the airwaves. I *feel* my mother's sorrow across half the globe, so I ring her and find that in that exact moment she was, indeed feeling that sorrow.[36]

There is a language of the air that my cells can sing, that sings between cells, "mine" and those of "others." As inner, so outer: as the flow of my spatiality is released through the humble starfish, I regain a language known in childhood, which needs no spoken words and which *connects* me, as an intersubjective, inter-connective mode of person, rather than the severed, cut-off, numbed, and thing-ized separation to which it has been in capitalism's and modernity's interests to condemn us all. Released to flow as an element of the "within" of me, this spatial extendedness immediately finds itself not alone—as if it were the nature of this capacity that it is a language of myriad voices, both part of me and different, vastly increasing the dimensions of my personness in this dance of difference, where neither loses its uniqueness, but each can enter the other's difference.[37] In this sharing of beingnesses, the language of the bird, flower, tree speaks itself in me and different life-forms can share the language of a mutual mutation.

Such interconnectivity, simultaneity, communication across distance, and the apparent "consciousness"—not only of cells but of other elements considered even more inanimate in the governing code—have all been discovered within the realms of what is called "new science." Yet, while much of this now circulates as popular reading,[38] its implications are not readily acknowledged within ongoing everyday life or in our social theories. The "self" presumed in social theory is almost always that isolated self, as perfected under modernity, that makes social theory, even in its critical variants, ridiculously complicit with the power operations that constitute and maintain "modernity" as a social form. The Eurocentrism inherent in this view makes the language of mutuality and inter-connectivity seem "childish," "primitive"; definitely not "objective"; but this cultural imperialism is at last being eroded by different cultural voices that bespeak alternatives to the isolated atom as "subject."[39]

The surge of perimenopause-menopause blurs the boundedness, the borders of that enclosed subjectivity to which a particular culture has confined us. Where one has had one's long-tested methods of keeping one's wider spatiality alive, both the manners of doing this, and the capacity to see how the power mechanisms of everyday modernity militate against this, alter and increase. As at adolescence (and many times before and since), the legendary nature of the transition is this discovery that one's old, tried shields and protections against the onslaughts of these operations of power, while excellent before and what one's survival depended upon, no longer hold and have to change. That is both terrifying and exciting.[40] The challenge is to live this discovery of a new self-ing, rather than tighten yet more to impede and avoid it at enormous cost. Perimenopause-menopause is, for me, this invitation to flow yet more fully into one's surrounding space, *as* a part of one's self—to reclaim one's aspect *as* spacetime.

Through these new bodily insights, I found that I had survived by, as it were, hanging up my body's energy as if on a coat hanger, across shoulders and neck. This at least allowed a freedom of flow much greater than one is "normally" expected to experience in the rest of the body, which, on the wings of that support, could commune with space in ways normally taboo. But now, the silencing involved could no longer be sustained, nor the deep-level gathering at the base of the neck, torturing the thyroid gland, skewing, compressing the windpipe, and pulling the shoulders taut, like steel, so that the energy could not flow down, nor root itself in the earth that one dangerously skimmed across, rather than the feet communing with it, as with a mother. The windpipe, not like a sweet vibrator of air, but a rigid pole, needed now to be loved, relaxed, gentled; not forever holding the armored edifice erect. Yet its poisedness has been etched like my psychic signature, since childhood: the changing is more fascinating than terrifying. In that mutation, I trace earlier times and events when these psychic stances were taken on: all those swallowed words, to take the strain, all that holding in of space flow. Now I chisel gaps through the language, to cry out their voice with joy, in the face of half a century, finding the sensitivities they protected still alive.

The continuing journey of perimenopause-menopause is into a realization and actualization of an orchestration, which constitutes the body in lived balance. One discovers thereby that the soul, far from being divorced from bodiliness, rather is hidden in that organismic language, cell deep. As alchemy, sufism, and other modes of spirituality damned as "primitive" at the rise of western "rationality," this kind of soul-nature link, carried as a capacity deep within the body cells, depends vitally on the moment-by-moment permeability of "inner" and "outer," "outer" and "inner." As the decreed internal/external divisions remerge from their constructed break, so "creativity," "conscious," "unconscious," and "dreaming" burst from their sealed categories and infuse a different thinking.[41] Awareness grows with the shifting symphony that is the perimenopausal-menopausal transition—so different from the governing models of wound, disease, disgust, and dread. Exhaustion can be one gateway toward these realizations, releasings, displacements; the needs of a bone-weariness asserting itself, a weeping exhaustion of the muscles, root tired, like an aching tree, requiring different rhythms, no longer able to hold all the energy in.

As the transition moves toward these new realizations, releasings, displacements, a new restfulness imbues the body, so that it is not inertia, but an equal energy, differently deployed that comes as the reward. Body loves it, and smiles. But we are mostly denied the space to find it.

The way each body has been carved into separate sides, a top, and a bottom, and tied to the governing frames, is both different and the same. Each of our praxes of resisting this has been different, according to different histories; and each embodiment is unique. Thus the journey, the stories of each transition, will be unique. But there are patterns and insights to be shared among the journeys and discoveries.

The hot flushes and night sweats are, for me, fascinating, bespeaking so much of the shifting circulatory tides, as the blood flow reorients itself away from its cycling centeredness on the womb. They are awkward, too, like the calcifications that appeared in a breast and, avoiding biopsy, resolved themselves as benign. And the faithful intrauterine device that has through most of my life ensured a joyous sexuality without fear of a motherhood I chose against (given the current state of the world) becomes more subject to infection, now that the blood no longer sweeps regularly through the womb. This long pattern must also alter.

So, there are many aspects in the change that can present as symptoms if one is unable to engage with a deeper process of which they are facets. It is my choice to avoid, as much as possible, having these interpreted as "symptoms" and separately dealt with according to the governing medical canon. The risks seem even greater that again, as the body is dealt with as unconnected parts and problems that the overall transition will be obscured, as will the chance to relate to its capacities, possibilities, invitations. So I always need a physician who respects my own relation to my organism and who will offer me the space to gear any medical intervention to my own overall engagement and my sense of the ongoing process. My so-called symptoms are often part of the process of healing I am engaged in. They are wounds of a past containment, revealing themselves because a deeper healing is in train. Left alone, they resolve themselves; they reveal themselves as part of the changing.

When you want medical guidance, I would urge you to find a person who will listen, can understand, and will support this multifaceted experience you are engaged in, who will respect your own understanding of the relevance of a particular symptom, and who will support you where you wish to *avoid* medical intervention. Try massage, acupressure, herbal baths, aromas—anything that restfully aids your reconnectedness in a changing body. And most of all, believe your own emerging stories, the language of your reawakened bodiliness. Activate that voice and listen to it against the distorted pictures generated by modernity, so often geared to keep us enchained. Allowed and enabled in these ways to actually *experience* the phenomenon of perimenopause-menopause, with the joyous gradual release it is offering me from the monthly discomfort of periods, with all their hormonal torment, fog, and moodiness, I can only concur with Germaine Greer that "I wouldn't have missed it for the world."[42] The last thing I feel I'll want is to be pumped with doses of artificial estrogen. Released from the slightly paranoia-inducing effect of my natural estrogen-menstruation cycle, I neither mourn nor regret its passing. Nor would I relinquish this chance, for the first time, to realize its influence and to experience the contrast of its passing, which releases me into another aspect of myself. Why give away half the world to stay the same, especially when the sameness was so heavily an imposed form? I would rather grab the chance for both release and insight. An insight that, through my own reactivated bodiliness, brings deeper gifts to enhance the more "mental" praxes of understanding I had previously tried to build.

Like a left hand allowed at last to show its competence, like a goddess speaking from the universe of her exile from the cold and drafty temples of the gods, I welcome this transition as my companion, I live it with fascination, and I quietly spit on all those creeds and canons that would seek to make it wither in my hand or would drive me from it in fear of death. In my experience, it offers life, abundantly and with a difference that awakens my awareness, so that life cannot so easily be stolen away, wrapped in a thousand habits, numbnesses, and torpors: a life that sees more clearly what has been done to it in the names of power, and that speaks with a voice of difference into that hidden place of our construction where, if we are not careful, we are endlessly stolen away from ourselves, without even noticing that we are gone.

Notes

1. M. Weber, *The Protestant Ethic and the Spirit of Capitalism*, trans. T. Parsons (London: Unwin University Books, 1968).
2. A. Howe, *Punish And Critique: Towards A Feminist Analysis of Penality* (London and New York: Routledge, 1994). Note especially pages 157–68 and 199–207, where Howe cogently suggests that the model on which the development of the prison system in the nineteenth century was based was the imprisonment of women's bodies, which had already been so pervasively effected. She rightly observes that this analysis is missing from the androcentric texts that have dominated the understanding of penality.
3. M. Foucault, *Power/Knowledge: Selected Interviews & Other Writings 1972–1977*, ed. C. Gordon (New York: Pantheon, 1980); and M. Foucault, "The Subject and Power," *Critical Inquiry* 8 (Summer 1982): pp. 777–95.
4. Weber, *Protestant Ethic*.
5. For contrasting critiques, see N. O. Brown, *Love's Body* (New York: Random House, 1966), on the body; and Koestler's argument that the governing model of how creative breakthroughs occur does not reflect the lived modes of creativity often experienced, which are masked by and exiled from the mode of rationality through which they are reported (A. Koestler, *The Ghost In The Machine* [London: Hutchinson, 1967]; and A. Koestler, *The Roots of Coincidence* [London: Hutchinson, 1972]).
6. F. Mackie, "The Crisis of Self-Reflection and the Uncritical Foundations of Our System of Early Childhood Education," in *Australian Educational Policy: Issues and Critique*, ed. R. Young, M. Pusey, R. Bates, pp. 39–59 (Melbourne: Deakin University Press, 1982); and F. Mackie, "A Study In Some Central Misrecognitions

of the Education Process," in *Sociology of Education*, ed. R. K. Browne and L. E. Foster, pp. 314–21 (Melbourne: Macmillan, 1983).

7. J. Derrida, *Margins of Philosophy*, trans. A. Bass (Sussex, UK: Harvester Press Ltd, 1982).

8. K. Marx, *Capital: A Critical Analysis of Capitalist Production*, trans. S. Moore and E. Aveling, ed. F. Engels (London: S. Sonnenschein, 1918).

9. L. Irigaray, *This Sex which Is Not One*, trans. C. Porter with C. Burke (Ithaca, NY: Cornell University Press, 1985).

10. F. Mackie, *The Status of Everyday Life: A Sociological Excavation of the Prevailing Framework of Perception* (London, Boston, Melbourne, Henley: Routledge and Kegan Paul, 1985).

11. J. Benjamin, *The Bonds of Love: Psychoanalysis, Feminism and the Problem of Domination* (New York: Pantheon Books, 1988); E. Bloch, *A Philosophy of the Future*, trans. J. Cumming (New York: Herder & Herder, 1970); and F. Mackie, "Intersubjectivity: Extended Forms of Personness," *Arena Journal*, New Series (1994), No. 3; pp. 219–45.

12. Mackie, *The Status of Everyday Life*.

13. J. Derrida, *Margins of Philosophy*. See especially pp. 329–30, and "The Supplement of Copula: Philosophy Before Linguistics," "Différance," "Tympan," "Signature Event Context."

14. M. Merleau-Ponty, *Phenomenology of Perception*, trans. C. Smith (London: Routledge and Kegan Paul, 1962), pp. 54, 148, 102.

15. Ibid., pp. 153, 213.

16. Ibid., p. 214.

17. Ibid., pp. 255, 229, 234.

18. Ibid., p. 235.

19. F. Mackie, *The Hounddogs of Reason: Spacetime and Social Theory* (forthcoming); and F. Mackie, *Spacetime and the Social* (forthcoming).

20. M. Merleau-Ponty, *Sense and Non-sense*, trans. H. L. and P. A. Dreyfus (Evanston: Northwestern University Press, 1964), p. 17.

21. Ibid., p. 5

22. L. Irigaray, *This Sex*, p. 213.

23. C. Miller and K. Swift, *Words and Women: Language and The Sexes* (Garden City, NY: Anchor Press, 1976).

24. D. E. Smith, *The Everday World as Problematic: A Feminist Sociology* (Boston: Northwestern University Press, 1987).

25. J. Kristeva, *Tales Of Love*, trans. L. S. Roudiez (New York, Guildford, Surrey: Columbia University Press, 1987).

26. R. Eisler, *The Chalice and the Blade: Our History, Our Future* (London, Boston, Sydney, Wellington: Mandala, Unwin Paperbacks, 1987).

27. G. Greer, *The Change: Women, Ageing and the Menopause* (London: Hamish Hamilton, 1991), p. 114.

28. G. Sheehy, "The Silent Passage: Manopause," *Vanity Fair*, October (1991), pp. 118–57.

29. S. Coney, *The Menopause Industry: A Guide to Medicine's "Discovery" of the Mid-Life Woman* (Auckland, N.Z.: Penguin, 1991), pp. 179–216; and G. Greer, *The Change*, index, p. 466.

30. V. Sackville-West, *All Passion Spent* (London: L. & V. Woolf, 1931), p. 194.

31. In this respect I am extremely grateful to Dr. Champak Rana, Director of the Health Service, La Trobe University, Bundoora, and to its Medical Officer, Dr. Vicky Cocotis, as well as to Dr. Lyndall Whitecross, previously a Medical Officer there, currently Medical Educator, Family Medicine Program, Royal Australian College of General Practice.

32. G. Greer, *The Change*, pp. 390–412.

33. B. Adam, *Time and Social Theory* (Cambridge: Polity Press, 1990); and B. Adam, *Time-Watch: The Social Analysis of Time* (Cambridge: Polity Press, 1995).

34. Mackie, *The Status of Everyday Life*.

35. J. Baudrillard, *The Mirror of Production*, trans. M. Poster (St. Louis: Telos Press, 1975).

36. Mackie, *Hounddogs*.

37. N. Sharp, "Stars of Tagai: The Torres Strait Islanders," *Aboriginal Studies Press*, Canberra, 1993; and Mackie 1994, *op. cit.*

38. P. Davies, *The Mind Of God: The Scientific Basis for a Rational World* (New York, London, Toronto, Sydney, Tokyo, Singapore: Simon & Schuster, 1992); G. Zukav, *The Dancing Wu Li Masters: An Overview of the New Physics* (Suffolk, UK: Flamingo, Fontana, 1986); D. Bohm, *Wholeness and the Implicate Order* (London, Boston, Melbourne, Henley: Routledge and Kegan Paul, 1980); R. Sheldrake, *A New Science of Life: The Hypothesis of Formative Causation* (London: Blond and Briggs, 1985); R. Sheldrake, *The Presence of the Past: Morphic Resonance and the Habits of Nature* (London: Collins, 1988); R. Sheldrake, *The Rebirth of Nature: The Greening of Science and God* (London: Century, 1990); D. Zohar, *The Quantum Self: A Revolutionary View of Human Nature and Consciousness Rooted in the New Physics* (London: Bloomsbury Publishing Ltd., 1990).

39. G. Tawadros, "Beyond the Boundary: The Work of Three Black Women Artists in Britain," *Third Text*, 8/9 (Autumn/Winter 1989); pp. 121–50; C. Fusco, "The Border Art Workshop: Interview with Guillermo Gomez-Pena and Emily Hicks," *Third Text* (Summer 1989); pp. 53–76; N. Richard, "Postmodernism and Periphery," *Third Text*, 2 (Winter 1987/88); pp. 5–12; G. G. Márquez, *One Hundred Years Of Solitude*, trans. G. Rabassa (London: Cape, 1970); B. Okri, *The Famished Road* (London: Vintage, 1992); B. Okri, *Songs Of Enchantment* (London, Sydney, Auckland, Bergvlei: Random House, 1993).

40. M. Berman, *All That Is Solid Melts into Air: The Experience of Modernity* (New York: Simon & Schuster, 1982), pp. 15–36.

41. G. Bachelard, *The Poetics of Space*, trans. M. Jolas (Boston: Beacon Press, 1969); G. Bachelard, *The Poetics of Reverie: Childhood, Language and the Cosmos*, trans. D. Russell (Boston: Beacon Press, 1971); G. Bachelard, *Water and Dreams: An Essay on the Imagination of Matter*, trans. E. R. Farrell (Dallas: The Bachelard Translations, The Dallas Institute of Humanities & Culture, The Pegasus Foundation, 1983); H. J. and H. A. Frankfort, *Before Philosophy: The Intellectual Adventures of Ancient Man. An Essay on Speculative Thought in the Ancient Near East* (Chicago: Chicago University Press, 1949).

42. G. Greer, *The Change*, Introduction, p. 9.

3

Menopausal Embodiment

Philipa Rothfield

> *Her critics, the critics, will accuse her, the woman who writes in this way, of confession.*
> *As if the "I" on the page should have known better than to let slip a messy reminder of*
> *the body that holds the pen. As if there weren't in any case gaps and fissures between*
> *that "I," that body, that pen. As if confession was a transparent term.*
> —Drusilla Modjeska, *The Orchard*[1]

Phenomenology, Hormones, and Experience

The aim of this chapter is to look at menopause in corporeal terms. Although very much an experience of the body, the *kind* of body imputed to menopausal experiences belongs to biomedical science. My aim is to discuss the menopausal body in terms familiar to another kind of body, one closer to phenomenology's notion of lived embodiment. Phenomenology's body differs from biomedicine's by virtue of its emphasis upon the *subjectivity* of the body. This differs from biomedicine's stress upon the *objectivity* of the body, where the body functions primarily as an object of knowledge and of treatment. Although biomedicine does acknowledge human subjectivity, it says that the mind is the seat of subjectivity. By contrast, phenomenology attempts to locate experience within the *bodily* subject. Although our bodily experience is clearly in some sense objective and real, there are differences if we see that site as the province of science (object of analysis) or of phenomenological philosophy (embodied subject of experience). The significance of phenomenology's approach is that it looks to bodily experience as the site of subjectivity and not merely to the mind. In the case of a body-centered experience such as menopause,[2] the potential exists to seek out a richer sense of bodily experience for the subject herself.

⋅ I have chosen to contrast biomedicine and phenomenology by taking two interconnected terms that can be aligned with objectivity and subjectivity, respectively: hormones and experience. The differences between biomedicine and phenomenology will emerge via a discussion of these two terms. Why hormones and experience? As several chapters in this collection indicate, hormonal explanations have come to dominate contemporary menopausal discourses, both technical and popular. This is especially the case in biomedical approaches to menopause, which tend to cite hormonal activity as the basis of most, if not all, menopausal phenomena. Feminists have endeavored to point out that biomedical narratives that appeal to hormonal causation construct menopausal women in terms of lack, whereby they suffer hormonal deficiencies that ideally can be remedied by hormonal therapy. These critics proffer women's experience as an *antidote* to the biomedical story to find out what "really goes on" in menopause. Women's experiences of menopause may conflict or tally with explanations that cite the hormonal changes occurring in a body. There is no necessary relation of harmony or disharmony in this regard. What interests me here is the way in which we conceive of the relations between hormonal forms of materiality and experience.

By materiality, I mean that complex of matter that constitutes our sensuous, cultural, kinetic, and physical place in the world. There are many elements that combine to form the material bases of our bodily selves. In this menopausal context, I shall select just one element of that complex: hormones. To suggest that hormones can fully represent the materiality of the human subject would be to distort their interaction with other factors—discursive, cultural, as well as fleshy. It is a moot point whether hormones can be raised independently of cultural and other matters. I discuss the role that hormones play in their own right because of their prominence in nearly all discourses about menopause—whether biomedical or feminist—not to suggest that they play an independent, determining role within menopause.

It would be quite easy to regard hormonal activity as the underlying physical part of menopause and women's experience of it as the psychological part. Such a distinction reflects a dualism of mind and body. I propose to resist this tendency by looking at hormones and experience in relation to *embodied subjectivity*, a term that does not suggest a separation of mind and body. My approach is informed by the philosophical phenomenology of Merleau-Ponty, whose criticisms of dualist modes of thinking can be felt in his utilization of the notion of embodiment.

Phenomenology's emphasis upon embodiment is an attempt to say that we humans are both material and sentient creatures, and that we cannot consider one of these aspects without implicating the other. The term, the *lived body*, has been formulated to make the point that it isn't just a question of having a body as if it were a thing operated or controlled by the mind. Rather, what matters is how we live our bodies, including the kinds of experiences we have in living as bodily beings in the world. Here, instead of being a thing, the body is the linchpin of subjectivity, the site and source of our having a world and living in it.[3] It is the site of human agency. Yet at the same time, we are material beings. We are physical selves who exist in a world of other physical selves and things. Hence, we are neither wholly subjective nor exclusively objective, but an existential "cocktail" moving between the two.

If we were to transpose some of these ideas to the topic of menopause, a shift in understanding and emphasis would occur. Menopausal bodies would not be analyzed in purely objective terms. Their lived subjectivity would be taken to be simultaneously relevant. Yet, to speak of subjectivity would not be a purely psychological matter. A phenomenologically informed emphasis upon the corporeality of menopausal experience attempts to take on board subjectivity and materiality together. How this intricacy might be spelled out in relation to menopause, its material and lived dimensions, is to be considered below.

As regards my own orientation, rather than speak from the perspective of a menopausal woman, I propose to begin with another position, that of pregnant embodiment. Although pregnancy could seem to occupy the other end of the scale in relation to a woman's reproductive life, it need not be constructed in opposition. My recent experience of pregnancy has led me to reflect upon a number of matters that are also relevant to menopause. The sphere of relevance has to do with what it feels like to supposedly experience massive hormonal changes in one's body. So, although there are many factors to distinguish pregnancy from menopause, *especially* since a woman's reproductive status is deemed so central, this very emphasis on the reproductive female body and its hormonal antecedents also yields a common ground (as well as a ground of difference).

What inspires me to make the connection between pregnancy and menopause are some thoughts that developed out of my own experience of pregnancy. As a philosopher and a dancer with an interest in the body, I lived my pregnant state with a great deal of corporeal curiosity. The most notable thing I encountered was that there wasn't one kind of experience to be had in relation to any particular phase of the pregnancy. I found the embodied experiences of pregnancy were much more mutable than I had expected. This mutability, which was intensified in the nausea of morning sickness, led me to the following view: that, on the one hand, a lot was going on in my body due to the pregnancy but, on the other, I didn't always experience these goings on *in the same way*. Somehow, a given material condition, a radical condition of material, bodily change, seemed to embody a range of possibilities rather than to dictate a particular form of experience. That play between possibilities has led me to speculate in philosophical terms upon the lived character of hormonal changes, a play that could be said to operate betwixt and between hormones and experience, materiality and subjectivity.

I draw upon my own lived bodily experience, not to speak for the experiences of others but to use it as a springboard for discussing the perceptual character of a period of hormonal upheaval. As Merleau-Ponty has argued in "The Child's Relations with Others," we only have a sense of our own bodies in virtue of their connectedness with others.[4] So, while no one can say what other people experience, we may try to say something about the character of that experience in philosophical terms.[5] This is not to suggest that to be pregnant means one knows everything there is to know about it. The lived body is not a transparent object, neither for the subject of experience herself nor for the doctor's gaze. Indeed, the very *opacity* of experience is the reason why it is the subject of philosophical investigation. Embodiment is a complex (and therefore a rich) matter, from the perspective both of the subject herself and of those who interact with her. It allows us to ask the following questions: How do we come to know a condition such as menopause? Who is in a position to know? The subject herself? Objective science? Do symptoms lie on the surface of experience? Are our experiences veridical, distorted, constructed? If we have a set of bodily experiences, when can we say that they are due to hormonal activities rather than to something else? That is, when can an experience be attributed to hormonal causes? How do we know about the body, how do we know about hormones, and how do we know about menopause?

Pregnancy and menopause are similar in some respects. Each is experienced by women. They are both culturally and biomedically defined in relation to notions of reproductive femininity. Both are medically managed in industrialized countries, and both are commonly described in hormonal terms. Thus, by speaking through and about some experiences of pregnant embodiment, I propose to shed some light on the ways in which we might conceive of the activity of hormones and the ways in which such activities are thought to be experienced.

I will begin by discussing the ways in which hormones feature in matters menopausal as described from a biomedically informed point of view. These considerations will then form the background for the shift to a phenomenological discussion of pregnancy, and the place of hormones and experience within lived bodies. I will conclude with a few general remarks on hormones, experience, lived corporeality, and menopause.

Hormones, by Definition

What follows is an account of hormones framed according to the terms of conventional biomedical discourse. It is by no means the only way in which we could come to understand or to explain hormonal activities, but it is commonly invoked as a means of explanation. What is a hormone? According to Speroff, *et al.*:

> The classical definition of a hormone is a substance which travels from a special tissue where it is released into the bloodstream to distant responsive cells where the hormone exerts its characteristic effect.[6]

Hormones are "chemical messengers."[7] They travel the body, providing "information" or producing typical effects. Glands that secrete substances directly into circulating blood are called *endocrine glands*, and their secretions are hormones. Hormones are also released by the hypothalamus and the pituitary gland. The responsive cells to which hormonal molecules travel include *receptors*, which enable them to respond to the hormone in question. Gail Vines writes:

> The fusion of hormone and receptor in turn sets off a chemical chain, a cascade of biochemical events, which may activate certain genes and eventually lead to changes in what particular cells do.[8]

The one hormonal substance may travel to several receptor sites, producing many kinds of effect. A "target site" may in turn alter the hormone as part of its metabolism. It may also participate in "feedback loops," which connect to the site where the hormone was produced, perhaps an endocrine gland, an organ, the brain, or pituitary gland.[9] Feedback loops provide "information" on hormonal activities in so-called distant sites. The information is provided by the passage of hormones themselves. An example of feedback loops might involve the passage of hormones to a part of the brain (hypothalamus) that in turn incites further hormonal activities—whether the cessation, inauguration, or alteration of hormonal excretions. Feedback systems are said to operate between the hypothalamus, pituitary, and endocrine glands and may include neural influences from the central nervous system.[10]

An example of this can be found in menstruation, which is said to involve a number of circulating hormones, the hypothalamus, the pituitary gland (in particular, the adenohypophysis), ovaries, breasts, skin, uterus, and other bodily sites. Some moments of the event involve the stimulation of certain processes (e.g., maturation of ova); others the movement of a hormone to the brain, which may trigger the end of a particular menstrual phase (such as building the uterine lining) through further hormonal changes operating as signals. In these matters, hormones are said to effect the transmission of messages and actions between elements of the brain and the reproductive organs (e.g., ovaries, uterus), among other sites. Although the brain is seen to be the site of control, flows of information move between brain sites (hypothalamus, pituitary gland) and distant sites (ovaries, uterus) and vice versa.

Some of the terms of this account are metaphors commonly invoked to explain hormonal activities—messengers, signals, flows of information, command, control, feedback loops. These terms derive from paradigms of information processing. They locate the brain at the apex of an informational hierarchy, issuing commands to peripheral sites.[11] As Emily Martin's contribution to this collection indicates, it is perfectly possible to utilize other metaphors in explaining hormonal processes (yielding potentially different perspectives on pregnancy, menstruation, and menopause).

Hormonal Effects, Both Great and Small

Even though hormonal processes are by no means confined to activities associated with female reproduction, in everyday discourse they are renowned for their participation in these matters. It is as if their activities and effectivity are at their strongest with respect to the female body.[12] To speak of hormonal effects in this way is to move between distinct kinds of effect and different realms of discourse. That is to say, although hormones can be specified in carefully defined biochemical terms, they can be, and often are, deemed *causally responsible* for a much wider sphere of human effect.[13] For example, aggressive behavior in males is often linked to testosterone, emotional upset in women to impeding menstruation, cravings in pregnant women to the hormones of pregnancy, and, closer to home, a plethora of experiential vicissitudes in midlife women to the cessation of estrogen in menopause. These effects are not limited to biochemical changes but involve the behaviors and experiences of the whole person. Here, the typical effects of a hormone—considered biochemically—are also taken to have *other* typical effects, namely of an experiential and behavioral kind. Hormones are thus seen to have two spheres of influence and therefore two kinds of effect—one within the biochemical body, the other in regard to the person who is the subject of experience and the agent of activity.

Although the links between hormones and behavior, the biological and the social, have always been contentious, especially in the eyes of feminists, this has not diminished the zeal of the psychobiologist's "will to explain." To illustrate, in a collection entitled *Hormones and Behavior* Richard Whalen explains the influence of several hormones on animal behaviors, listing a number of their various effects in a table.[14] Prolactin, for instance, is included as having the mammaries as its target site, and "lactation and parental behavior" as its rather wide sphere of effect.[15] For Whalen:

> Hormone secretions control behavior, and behavior controls the secretion of hormones. Hormones control behavior through their actions on the brain and on peripheral structures, while behavior controls hormone secretion by producing stimuli that alter the neural activity of the brain.[16]

Notice the way in which Whalen inserts behavior within the metaphors of control, central and peripheral structures, stimuli and neural registration. Although originally describing animal behavior, human behavior is taken to be a form of extension of this model (rather than constituting a difference in kind). By extending the model, human activity (a complex form of movement, experience, and intentionality) is refracted through a certain kind of discourse of the biomedical body.

Although much of the experimental work referred to by Whalen has been conducted upon animals—most notably, upon rodents, monkeys, birds, and fish—research has also been conducted in regard to the human species of the animal kingdom. For example, John Money worked in the 1960s with patients who had a variety of hormonal conditions and genital structures. Money speculated about the influences of hormonal flows upon the sexuality of his patients on the basis of their physical conditions and reported sexual lives.[17] Vines refers to numerous research projects that, over the years, have attempted to associate and to correlate human behaviors with hormonal fluctuations, presences, and absences. These behaviors include sex, eating, sleeping, stress, and violence. Vines is rather skeptical with respect to the assertions and findings of some of these projects. Indeed, the very nexus between behavior and hormones has been the subject of much argument, especially on questions of sexual difference.[18] Without entering into the finer points of such arguments, there are some general features of those who assert a causal link between hormones and behavior.[19] This has to do with the meaning and function of biology for these authors.

Biology, Reduction, and Causation

Psychobiologists and sociobiologists of the 1970s, such as E. O. Wilson, Whalen, and Money, appeal to biology as the means of explaining a wide range of human behaviors, social and sexual differences. Biology performs a kind of legitimating function for these supposed forms of social knowledge, giving them a scientific imprimatur. Thus conceived, biology is utilized to explain, and even to justify, social orders such as patriarchy, kinship relations, racism, and sexual behaviors. In response, the figure of biology has been criticized for functioning in reductive and essentialist ways.[20] By being essentialist, changes in the social order would seem to be ruled out. By being reductive, all the complexities of society and the vicissitudes of history become a derivative instance of the biological.[21] One complaint of feminist critics has been that hormonal explanations reductively appeal to biological causes when accounting for a complex life process.[22] By basing an account of the social on the biological, human meaning is reduced to an effect of a very narrow conception of the body.

Apart from being reductive and essentialist, biology is also taken to be *analytically distinct*. This is important for sociobiological explanation, for if biology were not separable from the social, it could not be posited as a causal power in its own right. As a distinct factor, biology is able to be causally operative and combine with other factors, or simply be causally determining on its own. Hormonal causes are a particular instance of this framework of explanation, for they appeal to a biology that is said to underlie a range of behaviors, experiences, or symptoms.

There are further reasons why hormones so readily adhere to a causal framework. First, hormones themselves are *defined* in terms of their having effects— hormones are chemicals that enter the bloodstream and provoke certain results.

Second, the biomedical discourse within which they feature is wedded to a framework of symptom, etiology, and treatment. Experience easily becomes symptom or clinical manifestation, physiological structures easily become causal factors (etiologies), and pharmacological substances become remedies. Such is the teleology and logic of contemporary western medicine. The notion of effect, originally biochemically defined, is thus readily extended to a whole life-experience such as menopause. What begins as something defined in hormonal terms gets extended, thus producing a *slippage* between an endocrinal definition of menopause and a broader sense of menopause that includes experiences otherwise attributed to the midlife, climacteric, or life experiences of women.

For example, in a recent article on endocrinological aspects of menopause, Al-Azzawi writes:

> The menopause is a consequence of oestrogen deficiency due to the depletion, or relative absence, of primordial follicles responsive to the rising level of gonadotrophins. This deficiency results in target organ failure, e.g. failure to induce endometrial proliferation and subsequent menstrual bleeding. . . . A greater understanding of the mechanisms of oestrogen action, and deficiency is therefore vital to understand and logically target pharmacological manipulations of the hypo-oestrogenic woman.[23]

In the above, Al-Azzawi begins by positing menopause as a *consequence* of dwindling estrogen levels—from a narrow endocrinological point of view, perhaps an uncontentious point. But the endocrinological definition then comes to appropriate the explanatory field. By the end of this section, menopausal women are now "hypo-estrogenic" women, whom it is "logical" to manipulate with drugs. Furthermore, Al-Azzawi continues by discussing the various "clinical manifestations of the climacteric."[24] Once women enter the clinic, the medical perception of their experiences dubs them manifestations, that is, manifest to the gaze of the clinician. By taking endocrine changes as first base, women's experiences of menopause (and perhaps *beyond* menopause) are appropriated to the sphere of the clinic and its symptoms. This seemingly uncontroversial tendency results in the ascription of experiences (*qua* symptoms) to hormonal causes or at least in a research agenda oriented toward the establishment of such an end. Once an event is described as consequent upon hormonal changes, the desire is formed to causally explain phenomena in terms of these changes.

The desire to explain in causal, hormonal terms is also mirrored in potentially critical reviews of menopausal science. For example, Linda Gannon has written a comprehensive review on the research literature on endocrinological approaches to menopause until 1990.[25] Her article presents and evaluates the literature and research on the endocrinal bases and treatment of menopause. Because its own structure replicates that of the research literature and clinical appraisals, it is also an example of the standardized categories and means by which endocrinal understandings are applied to menopause: menopausal symptom, hormonal cause, appeal to biology as explanation, physical materialism, and psychological *sequelae*.

To illustrate, Gannon begins by depicting menopause in relation to its *characteristic hormonal changes*. She enumerates the kinds of *menopausal symptoms* said to be felt by or observed in women. These include hot flashes, sweating, headaches, weight gain, dryness and thinning of vaginal walls, irritability, depression, insomnia, and osteoporosis.[26] How are these symptoms to be understood? Gannon notes:

> The primary theoretical model for conceptualizing menopausal symptoms has been a biomedical one, which states that both physical and psychological symptoms are the direct result of estrogen withdrawal or the result of biochemical changes concomitant with estrogen withdrawal.[27]

In evaluating the research literature, Gannon points out the problems encountered in establishing the etiology of menopausal symptoms. In her view, some symptoms are best viewed "from a biological perspective."[28] She believes that hot flashes, vaginitis, and osteoporosis are the most likely candidates for having hormonal causes and thus a biological origin. Other symptoms such as depression, anxiety, and fatigue require the incorporation of cultural and stress factors associated with social attitudes to menopause and to aging. According to Gannon, such symptoms probably have "multiple, interacting etiologies."[29]

Gannon critically remarks upon the way in which the "physiological event" of menopause has been accentuated at the expense of sociological perspectives. Her solution is to posit an *interaction* of cause (multiple etiology), a series of distinct, interacting factors. Gannon has the merit of attempting to recognize a range of factors—biology, society, psychology—but each is spoken of in distinct terms as differentiated causal factors, working together to produce menopause. By speaking of menopause as a physiological event, and its manifestations as either physical or psychological,[30] her analysis buys into a mind/body dualism. Gannon is by no means singularly responsible for these distinctions. They underlie much medical discourse and popular representations of the mind and the body.[31]

Hormonal Dualism

Mind/body dualism also underlies some feminist approaches to menopause. Consider the following discussion of the differences between British and North American feminists. Vines writes that most U.S. feminists reject hormonal therapy, whereas some U.K. feminists argue for its availability.[32] For Vines, the reasoning behind the U.K. feminists' position is that rejection of hormonal therapy involves a denial of the hormonal causes of menopausal experiences. And if hormonal causes do not exist, then women's (troubling) experiences of menopause are "in the mind."[33] Hence, hormonal therapy is recommended so as to legitimate women's midlife experiences. According to this argument, experience is deemed psychological—materially lacking—in need of the legitimating activity of physical, biological causes. To have a physical cause thereby confers reality on an experience that it would not otherwise have. Hormonal causes are taken to stand for the entire field of physical cause such that if a hormonal cause does not exist, women's experience is physically bereft. Hence, the legitimating need for hormonal therapy. In a similar fashion, books on menopause, written for menopausal women, raise the question of whether women's midlife experiences are just "in the head."[34] Grimwade writes: "Whilst the majority of women are relieved by the loss of their fertility, some women do truly grieve over this loss. This should not be confused with depression, it is a real sadness."[35] Kahn and Holt cite Phyllis Perlman: "I believe mood swings, including depression and manic feelings are about half-hormonal and half-psychological."[36]

What is at stake in asking the question is whether the experiences are somehow justified by a distinct physical cause or exist as psychological phenomena without a material basis. Accordingly, either an experience has a physical basis (= real) or not (= psychological).

The dualist's body, with its hormonal flows and physical structures, is evacuated of all manner of human subjectivity. The mind, as the proper site of experience, is kept apart, correspondingly evacuated of all physical happening. Activity in one of these two levels may produce activity in the other of these two levels. They are perhaps connected in causal terms but are at the very least conceptually distinct.[37] The mind does one thing, the body another. Thus, it is possible to isolate the body without implicating the mind. This enables a certain kind of medical practice, one that takes the body as its object. Such an attitude has been roundly criticized by a number of authors, both feminist and phenomenological.[38]

Phenomenological Reformulations of Mind and Body

Phenomenology rejects the dualist distinction between mind and body. Its starting point is the philosophical problematic of embodied subjectivity. The problem is not put as how do we connect mind and body, but rather, how to articulate the fact that we are both material selves (sensible) and the subjects of experience (sentient).[39] Note that mind and body have become reformulated away from terms that make it difficult to resist a split way of talking (mind/body) to other means of understanding the various bodily and experiential aspects of human subjectivity (sensibility/sentience). Our sensibility refers to the fact that we are material beings in a material world. We are able to be sensed, as are other objects in the world. Our sentience refers to the fact that we actively perceive other beings and other objects in the world. I link sensibility with human materiality, and sentience with embodied experience.[40]

And yet, it is impossible to define each of these latter notions without calling upon the other. For example, although sentience is experiential, relating to the subject's perceptual grasp upon the world, it is always an *embodied* perspective. There is no sentience without embodiment. This is because one is a subject through one's body.[41] Yet embodiment is epitomized via sensibility, the fact that we are part of a world of objects. Clearly, there is an overlap of concept here. Merleau-Ponty's later work on the flesh is an attempt to articulate this overlapping complexity. He puts it as the attempt to explain how it is that we are material creatures who are also the subjects of experience; how we are both sensible and sentient. Rather than appeal to dualism or to some reductive monism—all is mind or all is body—Merleau-Ponty writes that there is an abyss, a chiasm between these two aspects of embodied being.[42] The term "chiasm" means an intercrossing, one aspect bridging the other and vice versa with a crossover. An abyss suggests a depth of indeterminate distance. These concepts are attempts to speak of something that is not simply split. Merleau-Ponty's way of putting it is to say, "There is reciprocal insertion and intertwining of one in the other."[43] For Grosz:

> Perception is as it were mid-way between mind and body or subject and object, requiring the terms of both categories to be comprehensible. Neither empiricism nor idealism, neither pure psychology nor pure physiology has been able to provide an adequate explanation on its own, nor in conjunction, for the complex and reciprocal implications of each in its opposite.[44]

The point here is that there is some kind of movement at the heart of embodied corporeality that resists separation into mind or body, or reduction to one term or the other. How might this be felt in the realm of menopause? A phenomenological perspective on menopause would refuse to polarize the physical and the psychological. Instead of dividing menopause into physical, hormonal causes and distinct symptoms that are either physiological or mental, the realm of menopausal embodiment would be taken to be a complex field of experience not easily resolved into its constituent elements. Like sentience and sensibility, the elements of menopause would be taken to overlap in complex ways. What are the elements of menopause? For the purposes of the ensuing discussion, let us associate sentience with experience and sensibility with hormones. Hormones are an aspect of our sensibility, a materiality that can be perceived, tracked, and measured. Although only a partial aspect of our material being, I link hormones with sensibility because of their prominence in menopausal discourse. Experience I take to be shorthand for sentience, our subjective, embodied grasp upon the world. Although one could give a psychologistic reading of experience (it's only in the mind), it is equally amenable to the embodied perspective of phenomenology.

Pregnant Embodiment

A phenomenological treatment of hormones and experience, in the manner of Merleau-Ponty's work on the flesh, would acknowledge their interrelatedness. It would trace the ways in which hormonal moments of materiality exist within experience, and the ways in which experience is inscribed in the materiality of hormones. Since I cannot speak of menopause in subjective bodily terms, this is where I now turn to pregnant embodiment. I propose to sketch a phenomenological approach to hormones and experience in relation to pregnancy, similarly linking its two facets of sensibility and sentience with hormones and experience.[45]

In the following, I discuss pregnancy's morning sickness as an embodied state, like Merleau-Ponty's chiasm, continually moving between mind and body, hormone and experience, sensibility and sentience. I select morning sickness because it is a sensation that strongly characterized my own and many other women's experiences of the early stages of pregnancy. Indeed, the first trimester of pregnancy is often identified in terms of its presence. My discussion of morning sickness will emphasize and analyze its variability as an experience, a variability that I found to have *hermeneutic* and *kinesthetic* roots.

Hermeneutic and Kinesthetic Corporeality

Hermeneutics concerns interpretation. Although usually associated with the interpretation of events, consciousness, literary, and artistic works, here it signifies the interpretation of *bodily experience*. Drew Leder has written that "the phenomenologist of the body is already, and necessarily, a hermeneut. To explore the region of the body most hidden from awareness is merely to extend this hermeneutical approach."[46] The point about hermeneutics is this: although being bodily is integral to our subjectivity, this does not mean we are *fully cognizant* of our bodies' workings.

First, we are not always aware of our bodily workings and feelings. Even setting aside the bodily processes we are unable to feel, those we are able to feel are not always felt. Sometimes we are aware of our arms and legs, sometimes we are not. Sometimes we notice how we use our bodies, sometimes we do not. Some activities lend themselves to a heightened awareness of particular regions or aspects of our corporeality. During a golf lesson we might focus upon the way we swing our torso into action, how we swivel after striking the ball. Leder discusses the example of pain or injury and the ways in which malfunction draws our attention to the body. If I twist my ankle, I am likely to become aware of the way I use it at least while it is sprained.

Second, becoming aware of our bodily feelings does not automatically yield complete perspicuity. There are questions of judgment, interpretation, skill, and facility involved. In other words, being attentive to the body is one thing. It is a further question *what* it is that we feel when we do shift our attention bodywise. Although no one else can tell us what we feel, those feelings are open to investigation and to refinement of judgment. Our own feeling body is not always subjectively transparent. It requires a hermeneutic judgment, a point readily conceded in relation to the mind but less familiar in regard to subjective, bodily experience. Just because subjective embodiment is not culturally familiar—not an everyday aspect of lived corporeality—its nuances may well be neglected. For example, I may not have investigated the feel of my pelvic floor muscles or how my head sits on my neck or the feel of the ground under my walking feet. To suddenly turn my attention to these matters may be to do something I have not done before. These questions of attention, investigation, and understanding are the focus of a number of epistemologically oriented body practices such as the Feldenkrais and Alexander techniques.[47] Although Alexander technique seems to be more wedded to the idea of the objective body (what might be objectively functional for movement), and Feldenkrais to the learning process itself, both approaches place a lot of emphasis upon the subject's own perception and facility of movement. Rather than the biomechanical importance of "getting it right" from an external point of view, these approaches center upon the subject's experience of movement and her ability to learn through doing. This is not to eschew objectivity but to acknowledge the subjectivity of embodiment. The subjective body is thereby deemed central. Though its nuances may not be apparent to the subject herself, they are thought to be accessible to investigation and, moreover, to learning. Hence, the epistemological character of their approach and the hermeneutic quality of such corporeal self-understanding. Both Feldenkrais and Alexander workings spend a lot of time with the person in movement focusing upon what she feels. Often very ordinary movements, such as walking or sitting, are the bases of investigation.

I mention kinesthetics, along with hermeneutics, to underline the fact that we live and move our embodiment. Although a profound explication of embodied subjectivity, Merleau-Ponty's work on the flesh centers upon perception rather than upon action. Kinesthetics indicates that the subject is alive. She moves, she lives her experience. Understanding and experiencing one's own bodily activities are not a matter of fixing them under a lens of investigation. It is rather a question of engaging within the movement of the experience. I cite the kinesthetic practices of dance and movement, especially Feldenkrais and Alexander techniques, because these latter orientations are concerned with the kinds of learning processes made possible by the subject herself *in movement*. A hermeneutics of the body—with the bodily subject as both investigator and subject of the experience—is a practice that the subject engages as part of her life.

Part of the difficulty in conceiving the active participation of the subject in experience is that we tend to view the subject as nonmaterial. Bodies are material, subjects aren't. They're psychical such that to actively engage in experience is to insert the mind's eye. Not so. Once we acknowledge that subjectivity is embodied, that we are subjective, material beings, the subject who investigates is always embodied. Such investigations are not merely psychical. They are predicated upon the embodied experience of a realm. The subject who interprets is also the subject of interpretation. The subject is *actively inscribed* within the interpretative activity.

Feeling Sick

I use the terms hermeneutics and kinesthetics to emphasize a linked, double sense of mobility in relation to morning sickness. One has to do with the mobility of its interpretation (hermeneutics), the other with its *means* of interpretation (kinesthetics). What this means in concrete terms is that I found morning sickness to vary in the context of varying activities lived as part of the pregnancy. The interpretative variations occurred in tandem with a variety of lived, bodily practices. Here, hermeneutics and kinesthetics come together in a joint form of mutability. A few examples:

1. I found that a form of nausea, felt very early on, was in part determined by a sense of uncertainty as to whether I was pregnant. For once confirmed via pathology's objective certitude (by a urine test), the experience of nausea gave way to more specific sensations of pulsation, indigestion, heartburn, and gastric reflux. The confidence of knowing made space for the experience to resolve itself more specifically in terms of the body's geography.

These uncertainties were experienced while participating in a dance workshop held over two weeks. Some dance classes open up an epistemological space for investigating bodies in movement. The sort of class that does this may have a warm-up that brings the mover's attention to her body, dwells upon its regions and actions, gives enough time for the subject to connect with and explore her body, and includes qualities of movement that allow for a nuanced subjective involvement of the dancer in her movement.[48] The focus of these kind of classes upon what's happening at a subjective, embodied level made me quite aware of fluctuating energies, uncertainties of feeling, including questions of pregnancy. These fluctuations were felt in the context of performing choreographic material over several days. I noticed how these indeterminacies shifted once I "knew" I was pregnant, how my movement, in the execution of the choreography, changed along with a shift of feeling, and how the nausea itself resolved into certain constituent elements.

2. Over the next weeks, an ensuing nausea came and went rather differently according to whether anxieties were felt about the possibility of miscarriage, and whether something was felt to be "wrong" or not. The anxieties over miscarriage were not just felt passively (by an inert body) but varied a lot depending upon whether I kept up my dance classes, lay in bed feeling queasy, or turned up to

work. That is, the quality of the nausea depended upon my lived embodiment. I found that by dancing the nausea abated somewhat. I found that by lying in bed, I felt both comforted and yet delicate. The passivity of bedrest—though crucial in relation to fatigue—was akin to lying in a boat at sea, feeling its lurches in response to the waves. By contrast, the activity of dancing was a little more like surfing the waves. The activity of dancing generated a certain corporeal confidence that lying in bed did not. The influence of experiencing activity or passivity on the quality of the nausea was profound. Pregnant women in Australia are now encouraged to exercise for the very reason that to remain (or become) active has positive repercussions for the pregnancy.

In philosophical, phenomenological terms, the nausea itself had aspects of sensibility and sentience. It was definitely there—a feeling of being rendered nauseous—and yet it was also felt: a sense of actively feeling the nausea. The notion of active birth, developed by J. Balaskas, draws upon the active involvement of the woman in labor. Its rejection of giving birth lying down is a literal and symbolic rejection of the passive notion of giving birth, that is, of being delivered rather than birthing one's baby. Having just gone through the birth process, I found in experiential terms that getting up and moving with the contractions felt extremely different from lying in bed having the contractions. The difference was not only in the intensity of the pain (by a factor of about 10) but also qualitatively—by moving with the contractions, I felt like I was having the contraction and its pain. By lying down, I felt like I was being assaulted by the contraction and its pain. Being subjected to the pain made me feel much more like needing to be rescued from it (via pain relief, etc.), whereas moving with it brought with it a sense of managing the situation and not needing rescue. The duality of the birth experience has resonances with the duality I have ascribed to the forms of nausea in morning sickness. In each case, the experience is still there—the pain, the nausea—but its qualities differ, and those differences are tied to a subjective involvement in bodily activities.[49]

Merleau-Ponty discusses a perceptual *reversibility* in his work on the flesh. I touch my hand. It is able to touch me back. A reversibility of touch is immanent in my touching of it. I feel the nausea and am felt by it. To feel the nausea and be felt by it are not wholly distinct experiences. One is struck by nausea. One feels it as if it is "there." Yet, the way in which it is there is not completely fixed. It changes along with changes in the subject herself, changes that are also part of the body-subject who feels. There is no separation here of observer and observed. Hence, the intertwinings of strands of the nausea itself.

Epistemology and Hormonal Play

Morning sickness is not something to be controlled. This is not a discourse of control but of mutability, mobility, and indeterminacy. These shifts of feeling between the various attitudes, feelings, and activities were all played out within the general terrain of nausea and the lived temporality of early pregnancy. After a certain point in time, the feelings ebbed and so did my possibilities of investigation. Such a clear cessation indicates the *material aspect* of the experience.[50] The palpability of that materiality is part of the whole field. Feelings of drowsiness, vomiting, loss of appetite, pulsation, are not bars to the investigation but rather its material means. Hence, I am inclined to acknowledge the play of hormones in morning sickness. Hormonal activity is undoubtedly part of the material field of the experience. But is it causal? Is it determining of the experience? As with all questions of the hormonal determination of experience, this is a link that is hard to prove.[51] One may treat a patient with hormones and alleviate symptoms but, as Gannon points out, this is not a proof of etiology.[52] The establishment of a *causal mechanism* between hormone and experience requires the bridging of an abyss. One cannot "read off" a person's experience from cataloguing their hormones. This is the case even though hormonal shifts may well contribute to the material basis of the field of experience. Materiality becomes emulsified in experience. It exists but not as some distinct substructure that will ultimately be revealed.

From the point of view of experience, the material terrain of experience has a degree of open-endedness, a mobility of interpretation. Such a mobility is not a basis for skepticism, the view that we cannot know. Rather, it is a reformulation of what knowledge in this field consists of. To know one's body through feeling and by incorporating its materiality is to acknowledge a degree of indeterminacy that cannot be bridged. The inability to achieve closure, however, is not bad. One can still do things, take hormones or not, seek other remedies, experiment, weather the changes, fight them, move with them, whatever. The acknowledgment of biomedical researchers that causal links are not all proven does not—even from their own point of view—*nullify* modes of hormonal treatment.[53] It may, however, impact upon the representations made on its behalf.

Rather, the impossibility of epistemological closure—of knowing it all—is embodied in the duality of human subjectivity itself: its intertwining sentience and sensibility. Menopause may be characterized in hormonal terms, a tale of cessation, the promise of replacement, of time frozen. But it is also an experiential play, a field of embodied experiences, lived by women, felt by them in cultural, kinesthetic, and emotional terms. If not causality, materiality. If not pure psychology, embodied subjectivity.

The gap between the causal framework and phenomenological intertwining cannot be bridged. It is a tale told by Derrida of the human sciences and its two notions of interpretation.[54] One sense of interpretation "seeks to decipher . . . an origin which escapes play," the other *affirms* play, moving beyond our need to establish fixity of knowledge, full presence, and solid foundation. For Derrida, it is not a matter of choice, of *choosing* (hormonal) causality over phenomenological mutability. Each has its place. Each contradicts *and* coexists in our approach to knowledge:

> There are more than enough indications today to suggest we might perceive
> that these two interpretations of interpretation—which are absolutely irrecon-
> cilable even if we live them simultaneously and reconcile them in an obscure
> economy—together share the field which we call, in such a problematic fash-
> ion, the social sciences.[55]

Derrida's two modes of interpretation fit the biomedical and phenomenological approaches, respectively. The notion of interpretation as decipherment,
seeking a fixed origin, a solid basis of knowledge, resonates with the biomedical
approach. The ascription of hormonal cause to menopausal experience satisfies
this interpretative demand for a knowledge that escapes play. The second sense
of interpretation revels in its indeterminacy, affirming play. Derrida's point is
that they coexist. There is no point in *expelling* the causal framework. It is what it
is—an objective, externally oriented attempt to find the hormonal origin of
menopausal experience. Whether it can or cannot, its attempts at pharmacological remedy can be seen for what they are.[56] This field of determination and
causality is subject to the shifting sands of phenomenological embodiment.
Where materiality and experience collide, one cannot extract the one without
encountering the other.

Here, the play of materiality within embodied experience does not seek rescue
from its indeterminacy. Play is not pathology but endemic mutability. To juxta-
pose these two senses of interpretation and their two bodies—biomedical and
phenomenological—is to suggest that determination and indeterminacy each need
to acknowledge the Other. If determination and causality has the day with
menopause, then it is time to make space for its Other, the Other of experience
and its material intertwinings. In this way, perhaps further support might be created for women to move with menopausal experience and not simply be moved by it.

The menopausal woman is able to live her experiences through the indeterminacies and epistemological complexities of her changing body. The materiality of
embodiment precludes a purely psychologistic approach to menopausal experience. The question whether an experience is real (hormonal) versus psychological
does not arise within an embodied approach. To enter the field as a menopausal
subject is to partake of its materiality at the same time as to taste its subjective
nuances. It is to experience menopause at ground level rather than to gaze upon it
from afar—via the mind's eye or under the clinician's microscope. The meanings
and nuances of the subject's experience are her province and ground of critical
investigation. They are the site of her subjectivity, the linchpin of her world. This
is a world replete with possibility and challenge. It is a world that acknowledges
hormonal play but that is not fully contained within or by it. Menopausal embodiment is thus a rather complex terrain. It may invite interpretation, present
hardship, suggest classification, and offer treatment, but it is also the potential
ground for the subject of the experience herself to enter the field as one who is
very much part of it rather than merely its object.

Notes

1. D. Modjeska, *The Orchard* (Sydney: Picador, 1995), pp. 31–32.

2. By body-centered, I mean that menopause is one of those experiences *seen* to be of the body. Other experiences such as writing a book or inventing some device are more often attributed to the person's mind than to his/her body.

3. This view is elaborated in the latter part of Merleau-Ponty's *Phenomenology of Perception* (London: Routledge and Kegan Paul, 1962).

4. M. Merleau-Ponty, "The Child's Relations with Others," *The Primacy of Perception* (Evanston: Northwestern University Press, 1964), pp. 96–155. Merleau-Ponty's point is that our own sense of self is in the first instance attached to a sense of others, that we begin with an originary indistinction between self and other upon which is developed the later individuations needed to establish a sense of self. The implication of this view is that our knowledge of other minds cannot proceed via a process of inductive generalization from our own case to that of others.

5. The methodological differences between this approach and those involving scientific generalization are vast. First, there is no attempt to generalize from my own case to that of others as concerns the content of experience. Rather, what interests me is the character of lived bodily experience, one that I glean from the necessarily specific site of my own being. This in part arises from phenomenology itself and its terrain of the subjective, lived body. In other words, if we are to speak of embodied subjectivity, we need in some way to connect with that site of subjective being. This is why a rather particular bodily specificity inflects many phenomenological writings. See, for example, Kay Toombs' discussion of multiple sclerosis and Carol Bigwood's of pregnancy: K. Toombs, "The Body in Multiple Sclerosis, A Patient's Perspective," in *The Body in Medical Thought and Practice*, ed. D. Leder, pp. 127–37 (Dordrecht: Kluwer Academic Publishers, 1992); C. Bigwood, "Renaturalizing the Body (With a Little Help from Merleau-Ponty)," *Hypatia* 6 (3) (Fall 1991); pp. 54–73.

   The question of beginning from one's own bodily situation also has to do with what we think knowledge is. Does knowledge arise from the particular, the universal, the abstract, or the statistical? Philosophers of science have traditionally emphasized universal, lawlike behaviors, although some have recently focused more on the role of the particular. For Rouse, scientific knowledge is essentially embodied in the particular site. It is a *local* knowledge. Rouse claims that the development of scientific knowledge involves the adaptation of knowledge from site to site rather than the instantiation of universal law in the particular. Turnbull similarly writes of the transmission of practices rather than of the operation of universal laws.

   By keeping within the terrain of my own experience, I describe a particular site. But it is a site that may be intersected by other sites and is liable to transmission and adaptation in the above senses. In sum, then, the phenomenological emphasis on the embodied particular is neither solipsism nor the first step of generalization but a necessarily situated perspective on subjectivity. See J. Rouse, *Knowledge and Power* (Ithaca and London: Cornell University Press, 1987); D. Turnbull, "Inside the Gothic Laboratory, Templates, Skills, Geometry and Tradition in the Construction of Gothic Cathedrals and Their Implication for Understanding Technoscience," *Thesis Eleven*, No. 30 (1991); P. Rothfield, "Alternative Epistemologies, Politics and Feminism," *Social Analysis*, No. 30 (December 1991); pp. 54–67; D. Haraway, "Situated Knowledges, The Science Question in Feminism and the Privilege of Partial Perspective," *Feminist Studies*, 13 (3) (1988); pp. 575–99.

6. L. Speroff, R. Glass, and N. Kase, *Clinical Gynecologic Endocrinology*, 2d ed. (Baltimore: Williams and Wilkins Co, 1978), p. 1.

7. J. Grimwade, in collaboration with I. Fraser and E. Farrell, *The Body of Knowledge, Everything You Need to Know about the Female Cycle* (Melbourne: William Heinemann Australia, 1995), p. 45.

8. G. Vines, *Raging Hormones, Do They Rule Our Lives?* (London: Virago Press, 1993), p. 5.

9. Vines, *Raging Hormones*, p. 5.

10. R. F. Schmidt, ed., *Fundamentals of Neurophysiology*, 3d ed. (New York: Springer-Verlag, 1985), p. 259.

11. I have written elsewhere on the brain, suggesting that it need not be located within a hierarchy of command. I argue that, in relation to the coordination of voluntary movements (motor skills), there are grounds for claiming that it *cannot* play such a role. See P. Rothfield, "Beyond the Brain, Towards an Alternative Economy of the Body," *Hysteric, Body, Medicine, Text*, Issue 1 (1995); pp. 33–39. See also Emily Martin's piece in this collection for a thorough depiction of these metaphors as applied to female reproduction.

12. Vines keeps returning to the theme of sexual difference within endocrinological research. She illustrates the desire to utilize such research to explain the existence of sexual difference both historically and in contemporary work:

    One of the central themes that emerges from a look at the science of hormones is the distinctly different ways in which hormonal accounts have been applied to women and to men. Hormones are frequently proffered as explanations of women's everyday experience, but this is rarely the case for men. (Vines, *Raging Hormones*, p. 7)

    Vines notes that deviant activities such as rape are attributed to hormonal influence, but that hormones are taken to be the "essence" of femininity.

13. The desire to causally explain the human sphere in relation to hormones manifested in the 1960s as a form of hormone-behavior determinism. More recent causal research acknowledges a broader perspective than the behavior-hormone dyad while still seeking causal data on hormonal influence. See Vines, *Raging Hormones*, p. 2; and R. Whalen, ed., *Hormones and Behavior* (New York: Van Nostrand Co, 1967).

14. Whalen, *Hormones*, p. 8.

15. Ibid.

16. Ibid., p. 10.

17. See, for example, J. Money, "Components of Eroticism in Man, the Hormones in Relation to Sexual Morphology and Sexual Desire," in Whalen, *Hormones*, pp. 140–58.

18. See, for example, E. O. Wilson, *Sociobiology, A New Synthesis* (Cambridge: Harvard University Press, 1975); A. L. Caplan, ed., *The Sociobiology Debate* (New York: Harper and Rowe, 1978); S. Rose, "Biological Reductionism, its Roots and Social Functions," in *More than the Parts*, ed. L. Birke and J. Silvertown (London: Pluto, 1984); G. Kaplan and L. Rogers, "The Definition of Male and Female, Biological Reductionism and the Sanctions of Normality," in *Feminist Knowledge, Critique and Construct*, ed. S. Gunew (London: Routledge, 1990).

19. In the following, I treat causality as efficient cause, efficient cause being only one of Aristotle's four senses of cause. Efficient cause is a notion of causality common within empiricist philosophy and empirical research. For a discussion of such a notion of

causality in relation to human behavior, see A. Ryan, *The Philosophy of the Social Sciences* (London: Macmillan, 1970), especially chapter 5, "The Causal Explanation of Behaviour." See also, D. Hume, *A Treatise of Human Nature* (London: Dent, 1974) for an eighteenth-century treatment of efficient causality.

20. For a discussion of feminism and biologism, see E. Grosz, "Conclusion, A Note on Essentialism and Difference," in Gunew, *Feminist Knowledge*, pp. 332–44; and L. Birke, "Transforming Biology," in *Knowing Women, Feminism and Knowledge*, ed. H. Crowley and S. Himmelweit, pp. 66–77 (Cambridge: Polity Press and Open University, 1992).

21. I have argued elsewhere that biology need not stand for biomedical science at its most reductive and physicalist. Linda Birke also makes an argument for retaining and transforming the notion of biology. Foucault himself wrote of his interest in the way in which biology *interacts* with history. Once history is paired with biology, it becomes possible to acknowledge biological corporeality without asserting some kind of extrasocial essence. Indeed, from the point of view of history, it is important not to reject biology but to see how bodily matters emerge in particular times and places. Birke claims that the body is liable to be lost in the rejection of biology. Clearly, much is at stake in the meaning and functioning of biology. Its narrow sense may be problematic, but the rejection of a broader sense of biology could have its own problems. For a discussion of biology and the body, see P. Rothfield, "Thinking Embodiment, Practising the Body: Medical Ethics, Foucault, and Feminism," in *Troubled Bodies: Postmodern Perspectives*, ed. P. Komesaroff (Duke University Press, 1995). See also, M. Foucault, *The History of Sexuality*, vol. 1 (Harmondsworth: Penguin, 1978), pp. 151–52, and Birke, "Transforming Biology."

22. Birke and Silverton, *More Than the Parts*, R. Hubbard, R. Henifin, and B. Fried, eds., *Women Look at Biology Looking at Women* (Cambridge: Schenkman, 1979); R. Bleier, *Science and Gender* (New York: Pergamon Press, 1984); Kaplan and Rogers, "Definition."

23. F. Al-Azzawi, "Endocrinological Aspects of the Menopause," *British Medical Bulletin*, 48 (2); p. 262.

24. Ibid.

25. L. Gannon, "Endocrinology of Menopause," in *The Meanings of Menopause, Historical, Medical and Clinical Perspectives*, ed. R. Formanek, pp. 179–237 (New York: The Analytic Press, 1990). See also L. Gannon, *Menstrual Disorders and Menopause* (New York: Praeger, 1985).

26. Gannon, "Endocrinology of Menopause," p. 188.

27. Ibid., p. 190.

28. Ibid., p. 223.

29. Ibid.

30. Ibid., p. 190.

31. See, for example, D. Leder, "A Tale of Two Bodies, the Cartesian Corpse and the Lived Body," in *The Body in Medical Thought and Practice* (Dordrecht, The Netherlands: Kluwer Academic Publishers, 1992) pp. 17–36.

32. Vines, *Raging Hormones*, p. 140.

33. Ibid.

34. See, for example, chapter 9, Kahn and Holt, eds., *Menopause* (London: Bloomsbury, 1987). Gannon refers to the findings of Utian and others that depression, irritability,

insomnia, and palpitations were likely to be of "psychological origin" since they responded to placebo therapy (Gannon, "Endocrinology of Menopause," p. 191).

35. Grimwade, *Body of Knowledge*, p. 112.

36. Kahn and Holt, *Menopause*, p. 147.

37. It is a notorious problem for the dualist to explain the connection between the mind and the body. Although Descartes maintained a form of substance dualism, modern dualists have appealed variously to two-way causality (interactionism), sustained separate spheres (parallelism), and a form of physical causality having psychological effects (epiphenomenalism).

38. See S. Bordo, *The Flight to Objectivity, Essays on Cartesianism and Culture* (New York: SUNY Press, 1987); R. Baron, "Why Aren't More Doctors Phenomenologists?" and D. Leder, "A Tale of Two Bodies: The Cartesian Corpse and the Lived Body," both in *The Body in Medical Thought and Practice*, ed. D. Leder, pp. 37–47 and 17–35, respectively (Dordrecht: Kluwer Academic Publishers, 1992).

39. These two terms arise in Merleau-Ponty's essay, "The Intertwining—The Chiasm," *The Visible and the Invisible*, trans. A. Lingis (Evanston, IL: Northwestern University Press, 1968).

40. In an earlier work, Merleau-Ponty used the terms of phenomenal and objective body to describe our subjective and objective bodily being. See M. Merleau-Ponty, *Phenomenology of Perception*, trans. C. Smith (London: Routledge and Kegan Paul, 1962), especially Part 1, chapter 3. Although he recognized that the two are not separate aspects of the one bodily subject, his later usage of the terms sentience and sensibility was simultaneous with a more explicitly interrelated conceptualization of their interdependence.

41. This is a strong theme of *Phenomenology of Perception*.

42. Merleau-Ponty, *Phenomenology*, p. 137.

43. Ibid., p. 138.

44. E. Grosz, "Merleau-Ponty and Irigaray in the Flesh," *Thesis Eleven*, No. 36 (1993); pp. 38–39.

45. I would like to acknowledge the work of Marion Young and Carol Bigwood on phenomenology and pregnancy. Young develops the theme of pregnancy as a form of alienation from within, as posing questions of the pregnant woman's subjectivity—is she one or two beings? Bigwood intersperses her experience of the latter stages of pregnancy as she writes her paper on renaturalizing the body using Merleau-Ponty's work. See I. M. Young, "Pregnant Embodiment, Subjectivity and Alienation," *Throwing Like a Girl and Other Essays in Feminist Philosophy and Social Theory* (Bloomington and Indianapolis: Indiana University Press, 1990), pp. 160–74; Bigwood, "Renaturalizing the Body (With a Little Help from Merleau-Ponty), *Hypatia*, Vol. 6, No. 3, Fall 1991, pp. 54–73.

46. D. Leder, *The Absent Body* (Chicago: Chicago University Press, 1990), p. 37.

47. See M. Alexander, *The Alexander Technique, Selected and Introduced by Edward Maisel* (New York: Carol Communications, 1967); M. Feldenkrais, *Awareness through Movement* (Harmondsworth: Arkana Books, 1990); A. Olsen, in collaboration with C. McHose, *BodyStories, A Guide to Experiential Anatomy* (New York: Station Hill Press, 1991).

48. I speak here of the general structure of a class and the way in which it can encourage the development and practice of an epistemologically oriented bodily attitude. Not

all students will avail themselves of this orientation, while some dancers take this attitude to whatever movement they do. The faster and more mechanical the class, however, the less likely it is to encourage such learning, focusing perhaps on spectacular display rather than on phenomenal learning.

49. See J. Balaskas, *Active Birth* (London: Unwin Paperbacks, 1984).

50. This is not a sense of materiality that is distinct from its representation within experience. Its implication within experience, rather than outside, renders it part of a complexity rather than an independent substance.

51. Animal experiments are slightly different, for they observe behavior, not experience. Scientists do not concern themselves with the subjectivity of the animal or, if they do, the question of experience is viewed reductively from a behaviorist, external point of view.

52. Gannon, "Endocrinology of Menopause," p. 191.

53. K. T. Khaw, the scientific editor of a special issue of the *British Medical Bulletin* on hormone replacement therapy, writes in conclusion to her own work on the epidemiology of menopause that "the relationship between changes in hormone levels and symptoms is not at all clearcut." For Khaw, although physiological changes (changes in hormonal levels) follow menopause, the variety of symptoms felt by individuals varies so widely within and between populations that she stops short of asserting a causal link between hormonal cause and experiential effect (symptom). See K. T. Khaw, "Epidemiology of the Menopause," *British Medical Bulletin* 48 (2) (1992); 257.

54. J. Derrida, "Structure, Sign and Play in the Discourse of the Human Sciences," *Writing and Difference*, trans. A. Bass (London and Henley: Routledge, 1978), pp. 278–93.

55. Ibid., p. 293.

56. The reformulations of scientific knowledge, developed by Rouse and Turnbull, could be utilized in regard to pharmacological remedy. Rather than developing a position that makes a universal claim regarding HRT, it would be possible to reformulate an approach in terms of adapting knowledge from one site (body) to another (body), or of transmitting practices. These reformulations would allow for the specificity of women, whereas for Khaw, who is wedded to the universality of science, the gap between universal causality and individual symptomology will always be an abyss.

4

Medicine and the Moral Space
of the Menopausal Woman

Paul A. Komesaroff

Ambivalence

Amelia, a forty-seven-year-old lecturer in women's studies, has experienced a variety of symptoms she attributes to menopause—including hot flashes, headaches, tiredness, and irritability—for more than a year. Despite her open mistrust of western medicine and her conviction that hormonal therapy is primarily a device to promote patriarchal power and drug company profits, she now attends a menopause clinic and takes estrogen therapy. Although this is successful in controlling her symptoms, her assessment of medicine and hormonal therapy is unchanged.[1]

Brenda is fifty-nine and also suffers from menopausal symptoms. About five years ago, she attended an open day organized by a local menopause clinic to promote hormonal treatments. She listened to women who described how they had been rejuvenated by "HRT" and subsequently commenced the treatment. Although it provided little relief, she persevered because of alleged beneficial effects for her bones and heart. Last month she was diagnosed as suffering from breast cancer and she has been told that a link between the treatment and the diagnosis cannot be ruled out. She blames the doctor for her cancer and is angry and resentful.

No matter what form it takes, medicine is regarded with ambivalence and suspicion, as are the doctors who practice it. This is hardly surprising: on the one hand, medicine promises relief from pain and disease and the restoration of health and vigor. On the other, the death rates for many diseases, like HIV and cancer, remain unchanged, and there seem to be endless series of reports about the harmful effects of drugs and other medical treatments. On the one hand, the doctor is entrusted with confidences and confessions of a most intimate kind; on the other, the relationship itself is formal and impersonal, with an explicit commercial content. On the one hand, the doctor is appealed to as an ally against the crushing weight of everyday life and the rigors of work; on the other, he or she is clearly a representative of privilege and power and a functionary of an elaborate and ruthlessly efficient system of social control.

Medicine lies on an invisible boundary between the private and the public, between personal freedom and social control, between the intractable demands of nature and the historically conditioned effects of culture. In recent years, the internal tensions within medical practice have been exposed in a series of potent critiques. Feminists, gay activists, philosophers, and cultural theorists have subjected its philosophical and cultural presuppositions and its social origins and outcomes to relentless scrutiny. In particular, the disciplinary functions of medicine have been carefully analyzed, including both the ways in which medicine helps to service the productive apparatus of society directly and the more subtle, indirect means by which it reinforces the complex ideological structures that regulate individual bodies.[2]

As many of the chapters in this book demonstrate, one of the most fruitful outcomes of this critical examination of medicine and its institutions has been the reassessment and reinterpretation of menopause. Indeed, menopause has become an important site for innovative and radical cultural and theoretical reflections on medicine. The analysis of the promotion and effects of hormonal therapies; of the operations, under the guise of mere "technical" decision making; of institutions of power; of the reduction of complex realms of experience and meaning into biological facts or their consequences—all of these reveal as much about medicine as they do about menopause. What is more, they reveal not just the limitations of medicine but also its richness, diversity, and subtlety.

This essay seeks to examine the vicissitudes of clinical communication around menopause and what is thereby revealed about the experiences of menopausal women. It explores the anatomy of the communicative structure of this aspect of medical practice and the role of values in shaping the face-to-face interactions within the clinic and clinical relationships generally. It argues that medicine is in large part a practice of ethics, and that the complexity of the clinical space can be properly appreciated only in relation to its ethical structures. The development of this argument entails a critique of classical conceptions of ethics and detailed reflections on the body, sexuality, and truth within clinical practice.

The Multiple Discourses of Medicine and Menopause

Carli is forty-three and scared of dying. She is unemployed. She can't sleep. All her life she has had to battle against prejudice directed at her racial background. She has never had children and doesn't know if she should regret that. She is tired; she is putting on weight; her marriage is threatened. When she comes to the doctor she says that she cannot understand what is happening to her: her body is out of control. She has tried herbal medicines, but they didn't work. She says that she felt she "needed to nurture (her)self," so she took leave without pay from work—she never went back—and prac-

ticed meditation, yoga, and aromatherapy. That hasn't worked either. She wants "a measure of something," "a way of organizing and controlling" her experiences.

Contrary to the impression sometimes created by its critics, clinical medicine does not consist of a single, unitary discourse. Rather, it is a complex of contending discourses. There are the discourses of science, anatomy, and physiology, and of the pathological theories developed out of them; there are psychological, social, and ethical discourses; and there are those of practical action—technical and moral—and of therapeutic interventions of various kinds. There is not one "medical gaze," but many.

The same can be said of menopause. There is no single discourse of menopause: indeed, as has been argued in the introduction to this collection, the concept of "menopause" is itself a complex one, referring to a multiplicity of theoretical and cultural perspectives on a variety of issues, from the biology of aging to the philosophical understanding of death. Discussions of menopause may refer to biology or politics, hormones or feminism, psychoanalysis or social control, and when it comes to individual experiences, women provide widely varying accounts.

The contending themes of medicine intersect with those of menopause in unpredictable ways. In a particular case, the locus of these intersections is subject to the social and psychological context and to the value systems of patient and doctor. Values are of particular importance, despite the emphasis in medicine on technical, instrumental action. Indeed, interactions between doctors and patients are critically dependent on personal commitment and communication regarding issues of value: the two come together in a moral universe, or, as I shall term it, "moral space," a conception that will be developed in detail presently.

Medicine has an inherent ethical character that manifests itself not so much at the level of decision making about normative rules for action but at the level of practices bearing on questions of interest,[3] practices that encompass the moral world of the clinic and define its structures and temporal development. Although the all-pervasiveness of ethical issues within medicine has been recognized since ancient times, modern discussions about medical ethics have tended to focus on narrower, more technical considerations. This approach has come under challenge from expanding conceptions of ethics and changing views about truth in contemporary western societies.

In modern society, "ethics" and "truth" have undergone profound changes—so profound that these changes are often said to reflect an epochal shift from "modernity" to "postmodernity."[4] The commitment to certain knowledge and the search for an irrefutable foundation for truth, so the argument goes, have been largely displaced by a sensitivity to the production of knowledge and truth as cultural products. "Grand narratives" have been declared historically obsolete—especially the great cultural constructions of "humanity," "the proletariat," "womankind," "beauty," and the project of universal "liberation."[5]

From the point of view of postmodernity, in place of knowledge we now have "discourses," which can proliferate and may be incommensurable. In place of reason, we have reasons.[6] In place of the subject of knowledge, we have a "decentered" construct embedded in a network of social processes. This is the world that Nietzsche was describing when he referred to the "lack of order, arrangement, form, beauty, wisdom, and whatever other names there are for our esthetic anthropomorphisms." It is a world that is free of ethical or esthetic presuppositions. In Nietzsche's words again:

> How could we reproach or praise the universe? Let us beware of attributing to it heartlessness and unreason or their opposites: it is neither perfect not beautiful, nor noble, nor does it wish to become any of these things. . . . None of our esthetic and moral judgements apply to it.[7]

The postmodern world is a place of infinite variety and diversity. There are no fixed, unchallengeable criteria for judgment: only contending perspectives. This world is—at least potentially—a place of radical freedom, in which the existential choices may extend to the nature of one's subjectivity itself. Even the identity of the postmodern person is contingent and context dependent.[8]

The changes in the concept of ethics in postmodern society have been profound. Ethics today is concerned with a wide range of issues regarding values, the nature of the good life, and how one should behave in relation to other people both in general and in specific circumstances. There has been a growing emphasis on the fact that society is a battleground for contending value systems, what Max Weber called "a patchwork of cultural values."[9] Just as in the field of aesthetics there is no single category of beauty that can provide a universally applicable aesthetic norm,[10] so also in ethics there is no longer a single, universally valid, category of the Good. There is not one Good, but an infinity of goods; there is not one method, but a multiplicity of discursive frameworks within which ethical analysis and debate can occur.[11] Great systems are opposed rather than sought, and diversity is promoted and celebrated. The task of ethics is no longer to define the nature of the Good, or duty, or "the ends of man," and much less to derive irrefragable principles for correct action. Rather, it is to uncover the nature of ethical values and the processes of value creation; it is to examine existing concepts and to expose their hidden assumptions; and it is to challenge the hegemony of existing value systems and so to expand the possibilities for ethical action.

This view of ethics as a field of interaction around a multiplicity of values clearly diverges sharply from the classical accounts of ethics and morality and has radical implications for the understanding of ethics within medicine. It stands in opposition to the elaborate constructions of ethical theory in medicine that have been developed over the last twenty-five years or so under the rubrics of "bioethics" and "biomedical ethics." These constructions have been essentially conservative in nature, seeking to preserve the classical ethical commitments of the European Enlightenment. Like the latter, they aim at the elaboration of universally valid principles and norms to guide action and the search for a rational justification of rules for good conduct. Indeed, as in the Enlightenment tradition generally, within them, morality itself became identified with a process of following universally applicable rules. Classical approaches to ethics and morality—which had previously commanded wide acceptance, such as the foundational role of the virtues or the recognition that there are a number of quasi-autonomous goods—were discounted.

There can be no doubt that bioethics has made useful contributions to contemporary debates about medicine. However, like the classical tradition itself, it has also limited these debates and radically restricted the issues that can be considered. The agenda bioethics has set for itself has been largely limited to a few familiar problems that have come to be regarded as the key issues of medical ethics to be discussed. In addition, the general strategy of argument has been severely restricted: a question to be analyzed from the point of view of its ethical content is usually posed as a dilemma—that is, as a problem in a well-demarcated theoretical field that itself specifies the possible form of the solution. Thus, most commonly, it is postulated that particular choices need to be made from a narrow range of possibilities, and the discourse itself is directed toward guiding these choices. The effect of this procedure is invariably that the focus is not on the actual process of clinical judgment but on formalized and abstracted representations of medical practice.[12]

Carli's discourse above contains a miscellany of epistemological styles and questions of moral significance. The world of things and values she inhabits is under threat. Basic questions she has asked or avoided asking throughout her life thrust themselves forward at this time. Her moral space—the region within which she has made her decisions about relationships, work, and children and has interpreted her bodily experiences—is fragmented and disordered. The framework within which she once oriented herself with respect both to morality and truth now appears to her gratuitous and unworkable. In this setting, she seeks the assistance of the doctor. In the medical encounter she exposes herself—the questions, the doubts, the confusions about issues of value—and attempts to come to terms with her predicament.

Although the provision of such assistance is an ancient component of clinical practice, it is almost completely absent from contemporary accounts of the ethical dimensions of medicine. Indeed, despite their popularity and inherent interest, these accounts omit from consideration a large part of the many issues of values that preoccupy individuals in their daily interactions. The precise nature of these issues varies according to the setting. In the context of menopause, these issues include a wide range of questions concerning sexuality, aging, death and the body, the relationship between the individual and society, the social functions of medicine, and the roles of hormonal therapy as possible instances of patriarchal power. Both medical practice and the varieties of menopausal experience, therefore, are complex and multifaceted; to develop further the understanding of both of them, and of their interaction, it is necessary to pass to a closer examination of the moral dimensions of the clinical interaction.

Moral Space, Identity, and Microethics

About a year and a half ago, Diedre, a thirty-four-year-old landscape gardener with two young children, developed severe pelvic pain. Her gynecologist assured her that nothing was wrong, but the pain continued and eventually became much worse, necessitating an emergency operation. It was found that she had benign tumors on both ovaries and that a ruptured cyst had led to the widespread dissemination of tumor material throughout the pelvis and abdomen. A substantial operation was required, involving the removal of both ovaries, the uterus, and other tissue in the pelvis and abdominal cavity. After the operation Diedre was devastated. She had no energy and was unable to work. She experienced intermittent pelvic pain, which always suggested to her the possibility of tumor recurrence. She attempted to contact the gynecologist but was told repeatedly by his secretary that he did not need to see her again. Eighteen months later, Diedre seeks another medical opinion. She still has not returned to work and, indeed, remains largely confined to bed. Her life is limited, isolated, and lonely.

People come to doctors for many different reasons. They may say that they merely seek information and advice about technical questions, for example. Often, as they talk, however, it becomes obvious that there is much more to it than this. The experience of the illness and the operation shattered Diedre's world. They destroyed her confidence in her body and in her relationships with others. She has lost her job, her marriage, the overall direction of her life. For more than a year, she has had no one to turn to, no one with whom to share her pain. As a last, desperate act she is seeking assistance and advice. She puts her objective bluntly: "I want my life back."

Such moral disorientation does not represent a psychiatric condition. Diedre is appropriately despondent about her illness. The fixed points in her world have been destroyed. She has been set adrift in an existential sense: she has no way of recognizing what is of value to her, of establishing or ordering the things that are important. Her lifeworld—once vibrant and joyful—is characterized by uncertainty, fragility, and precariousness. Ironically, although she feels that she was betrayed by medicine in the past, it is to medicine that she turns again. The problem arose in the clinic; she seeks to resolve it there too.

The task of a doctor here is clearly a complex one. He or she must analyze the patient's current physical status, make an assessment about the need for further treatment, and provide the information she seeks. More important, however, and indeed as a precondition for success, it is necessary for the doctor to reestablish the patient's confidence in medicine as a whole. The doctor must engage the patient in a dialogue about her values and aspirations; must stimulate a questioning about her body and its social and biological functioning. In this process, it is the dialogue that is important: the doctor cannot seek to impose his or her own plan upon the patient's world. This does not mean that the task here is to reestablish "autonomy" (as a bioethicist might put it), at least in a narrow sense: it is more about sharing responsibility. Nor is this a case of treating the "whole" patient, as is sometimes said: on the contrary, the doctor has access to no more than a fragment of her life—that part which manifests itself within the horizons of the clinic. The doctor does not know "who" she is, and indeed, does not need to know. Nonetheless, the dialogue is not any ordinary dialogue: it is a therapeutic interchange that is rigorously structured in relation to the discursive forms of the clinic. As a therapeutic dialogue, it is directed toward making use of the destabilization of her existing framework of values to provoke an enhanced self-understanding of both her predicament and the process of questioning itself.

Every individual inhabits a space of questions about what is good or bad, what is worth doing and what is not, what has meaning and importance and what is trivial or secondary[13]—that which is being called here a moral space. Within this region, decisions are made about contending values, about personal priorities and aspirations, about conflicting interests within relationships. Each person constructs a distinctive moral space of his or her own that acquires a sense of coherence and unity. The decision to take up landscape gardening, and the meaning of this activity; the experience of her body as youthful, vigorous, and potent; the quality and significance of her personal relationships, including her relationships with her children; the impact of disease and pain and the imminent threat of death and disability—these and other components of Diedre's experience mark the structures of her moral space. This space forms a dimension of her personal life; it is a component of her lifeworld, that realm of immediate experience and face-to-face interactions. With her, as with others, conflicts may occur with people with different moral perspectives; uncertainty and doubt can also develop, leading to internal conflict or a loss of moral orientation; sometimes both can reach pathological proportions.

The moral space is implicated in clinical medicine in several different ways. It substantially determines the manner of the interaction between doctor and patient; it provides the field of problems or issues that the clinical encounter must address; it contributes to choices that are made regarding the technical aspects of diagnosis and treatment. As in any relationship, the moral spaces of both parties are simultaneously implicated, although the interactions between them are controlled by the larger scale structures of the clinical encounter.

The moral space encompasses a range of questions, problems, values, and purposes. These may refer to a variety of contexts and philosophical perspectives. Although in an individual case there is a sense of coherence or unity, a characteristic "moral style," this is not based on an *a priori* commitment to a particular concept of the good or of the good life. Rather, each person develops a set of values and a set of convictions regarding what is right or important: within the lifeworld, as has already been said, there is no concept of the good, but only multiple goods and values.

The notion of moral space is a version of the idea of moral identity appropriate for the contemporary cultural configuration. It places the moral orientation of an individual at the center of his or her social interactions; indeed, it suggests that relationships only exist in the context of prior moral commitments. This formulation diverges from traditional views of moral identity, in which it is assumed that identities are stabilized around systems of fixed coordinates or universal principles. Indeed, the very notion of a sense of self in the classical accounts was dependent on a sense of the good. The self, or personal identity, provided the means for locating the subject in relation to established systems of belief and value: it defined the link with Reason, God, and History. In other words, as Zygmunt Bauman has put it,

> "Identity" is the name given to the sought escape from . . . uncertainty. . . . Identity is a critical projection of what is demanded and/or sought upon "what is," with an added proviso that it is up to the "what is" to rise, by its own effort, to the "sought/demanded"; or, more exactly still, identity is an oblique assertion of the inadequacy or incompleteness of the "what is."[14]

The *modern* problem of identity was to keep it solid and stable. Under conditions of postmodernity it is impossible to appeal to universal moral coordinates, and this heterogeneity and pluralism is itself regarded as a value. Accordingly, the *postmodern* problem is just the opposite: it is how to avoid fixing the variables and how to keep the options open.[15] No longer can human identity be understood as a transcendence of the individuality and specificity of social and corporeal life. Indeed, it is recognized to be rooted in the present, inseparable from social life and dependent on the modalities of physical and sensory experience. This concept of identity was rendered necessary by the insight—supplied by Nietzsche and Freud at the height of the age of modernity—that it is impossible to understand the individual merely as a worker, consumer, or even as a citizen. They showed (in the words of Alain Touraine) that the individual "has ceased to be a purely social being and has become a being of desire inhabited by impersonal forces and languages, as well as an individual or private being."[16]

The moral spaces of the lifeworlds of both patient and doctor define the terrain of the clinical encounter. Every clinical interaction consists of a multiplicity of events concerning issues of value. Mostly, these are of infinitesimal dimension, inconspicuous to the participants. In the flow of the interaction, decisions about moral value constantly arise and pass away. From the doctor's perspective, a range of questions may arise: How should I palpate the abdomen of this woman who experiences intractable pain? How should this difficult or potentially intrusive question be asked? How shall I communicate my assessment of this patient's illness in a way that is both constructive and convincing?[17] From the patient's viewpoint, an analogous series of decisions must be made: Is my description of my pain sufficiently forceful? Can I entrust this doctor with my confidences? Am I saying too much? In each instance, the character of the response may take a number of forms. For the doctor, it may involve a particular choice of words or manner of delivering those words, or it may be embodied in the pitch of the voice, the length of the pause, or the softness of the touch; for the patient, it may take the form of a verbal or physical response, a facial expression, a cough, a laugh, or a grimace. Whatever the case, it will of course in turn evoke a response, to which a further adjustment will be made.

In the moral lifeworld of the clinic, at the intimate level of the interchange between patient and caregiver, the patient confides his or her story, and the shape of the clinical consultation is fashioned and refashioned. Here, different moral styles compete, and a multiplicity of voices and experiences, ambivalent desires, and uncertain choices contend. The moral space, in other words, is marked by "heteroglossia": in the lived experience of the clinic, moral issues are shaped and individualized, and moral actors find themselves confronted with a "multitude of routes, roads and paths."[18]

The moral space has been described as a region within the lifeworld. It is, however, possible to think of the lifeworld itself as inherently ethical in character. In the philosophy of Emmanual Levinas, for example, the most fundamental fact is taken to be the ethical relation, the quintessential encounter with otherness, which he refers to as "alterity." Ethics is that "putting into question of my spontaneity by the presence of the other,"[19] which fixes the point of alterity. The encounter with the other arises in the primordial relationship of the "face to face relation," which well represents the clinical encounter. The face is the way in which the other presents himself or herself; the face-to-face relation is a confrontation that is open and unfettered but that recognizes irreducible difference.

It is not the job of the clinical encounter to reverse the disruption of Diedre's moral space, to restore some putative, preexisting equilibrium. It is true that the exchanges around values in the interactive field of the clinic can alleviate anxieties or doubts, reassure, or even stimulate processes of questioning. However, in this case, as in any other, the space between the patient and the doctor is marked by the irreducible fact of alterity. This adds to the clinical encounter an intractability and a perplexity that is a major source of its fecundity. The structured alterities of the clinic can provide the background against which Diedre can reconstitute her world of values and relationships. By resolving the technical issues, the clinical interaction can clarify the factual basis of her physical symptoms; through this means, and through the process of the interaction itself, it can facilitate the deep interrogation that has to this point been obstructed.

The identity of an individual subject is secondary to alterity. Indeed, the other in a sense constitutes, and has priority over, the subject. It renders the latter open to others and it opens the world itself to the subject. Ethics is the domain of the response to the other's needs, and it is a responsibility for the other's actions—even if those actions are inflicted on the subject.[20] Herein lies another dimension to the complexity—and the potential richness—of the ethical relationship between Diedre and her physician. It is not the goal of the encounter to establish her autonomy, in the sense of specifying her ethical identity, any more than the existence of such autonomy can be taken as a premise; rather, in the process of the interaction itself, both confront and utilize the intractable and tantalizing *a priori* fact of the autonomy *of the other.*

The Body in the Menopausal Space

Emma is a forty-eight-year-old woman who has been a successful actress and is now a promising painter. She is presently experiencing hormonal changes associated with menopause that are producing a variety of symptoms causing significant discomfort. She experiences hot flashes many times a day and she wakes, drenched in sweat, several times a night. She also complains of, among other things, extreme and debilitating tiredness and lethargy, unpredictable moods and outbursts of anger, and an abiding sense of emptiness.

She speaks eloquently about what she is going through. Her body, she says, is like a stranger to her now; it seems external, separate, a nuisance. Once she took it for granted; now she talks to it and asks it questions. Her world used to be organized, stable, and predictable; now it is confused and chaotic. She was once celebrated for her savoir faire; today, she avoids other people because of her inability to control her impatience with them and her frequent explosions of anger. Her paintings have changed too: whereas five years ago she was painting large, brightly colored canvases, today, the colors are muted, the mood is somber and introverted, and the emphasis is on intricate, carefully executed patterns and designs.

She has an ongoing sexual relationship with a male friend, and this has suffered because of reduced sexual desire and difficulty reaching orgasm. However, she does not cite this as a matter of serious concern. Rather, it is for her just another symptom of the general malaise that has thrown her whole world into question.

Motifs of Disruption

One of the main components of the moral space to which medicine has access is the body. Of course, it is obvious that the body is, in some sense, the "object" of medicine. However, it is not, as earlier medical ideologies tried to portray it, simply an inert object of scientific knowledge or therapeutic action. It is, rather, a complex social construction, deeply infused with questions of values. It is the source of meaning and meaning-creation—and critical reflections on meaning itself. It is the perspective from which we enter the world.

The classical account of the body as the objectivistic target of medical technologies arises from the Cartesian tradition of medicine. Here, the corpse is granted epistemological primacy, and the living body is treated as essentially no more that an elaborate physiological and biochemical apparatus.[21] There can be no doubt that the Cartesian paradigm has yielded impressive results, including some of the most striking technical achievements of contemporary medicine. However, the price of this success has been the omission of a vast field of meaning and experience, an omission that, at least in principle, imposes an internal limit on both the analytical and the therapeutic potentials of medicine. Medicine is in fact concerned with the body not simply as a physiological system but as the site of lived experiences. This "lived body," furthermore, cannot be understood merely as the objectivistic body with some additional conditions: rather, it is itself the condition underlying *all* conditions. As the philosopher Merleau-Ponty once said, the body is "the house we inhabit," the setting within which the world is revealed to us.

The concern of medicine with the manifold of embodied experience is not restricted to the general topography of the latter but extends to the ways in which it can be disrupted. In conditions of disease or illness, the body becomes experienced as a problematic or disharmonious thing, and therefore in some fashion cast into doubt. An example may be given of the experience of pain, which has been analyzed by Drew Leder. As Leder puts it, pain is "ultimately a manner of being-in-the-world." Occurring in a body previously free from it, it "reorganizes our lived space and time, our relations with others and with ourselves";[22] it induces a split between our own sense of reality and the reality of other persons; and it causes a split between the mind and the body.[23] This applies equally to any other process that throws into question modes of bodily being that have been formerly taken for granted—including disease in general, pregnancy, puberty, aging, and menopause. In all these cases, apparently unproblematic modes of corporeality are disrupted, and the subject is led to a reflection on his or her bodily performance. In many cases, the transformation, sometimes abrupt and unexpected, may be unsettling or even threatening; in some others, it may lead to a new closeness to, and an enhanced valuation of, the body.[24] There may be a sense of decay or loss or occasionally even one of renewal or exhilaration. Leder's Heideggerian language aside, this description is consistent with Emma's experience: she too encountered a "novel body" brought into existence through processes that subverted preexisting assumptions and that carried with it new internal spatial and temporal structures.[25]

The tendency to ignore the existential dimension of illness and to treat all physical disturbances as narrowly biological in nature has led to the disruptions that occur at the psychological, social, or moral levels being largely obscured. Despite the widespread critiques of medicine, such "reductionist" paradigms are now deeply embedded in the medical culture; they have become more firmly entrenched than ever with the success of new techniques in biological research such as molecular biology. In the context of menopause, biological reduction-ism—often referred to, inappropriately, as "medicalization"—manifests itself as a conflation of lived experience and the dominant discourses of disease and illness. It thus represents an annulment of the subversive potential of the physical disruptions associated with menopause, a rejection of any possibility that they might give rise to challenges to the constraining influences of ideology and culture.

The Cartesian tradition of a medicine that aims at the normalization of the body is often opposed to the Christian one of redemption through suffering. Neither, however, adequately captures the complexity of or the depth of mean-ing arising out of the experience of the physical transformations that may occur through the life course. This point was made very forcefully by Friedrich Nietzsche, who trenchantly, and in characteristically grandiose terms, attacked both perspectives:

> Our dear pitying friends . . . wish to help [but] have no thought of the personal necessity of distress, although terrors, deprivations, impoverishments, mid-nights, adventures, risks, and blunders are as necessity for me and for you as are their opposites. It never occurs to them that, to put it mystically, the path to one's own heaven always leads through the voluptuousness of one's own hell.[26]

The experiences of the motifs of disruption of menopause are extremely het-erogeneous. As shown by the case of Emma—and indeed, by the others discussed in this essay—these experiences are also highly idiosyncratic, varying with the nature and severity of the processes and contingent internal variables. From a clinical point of view, this means that few generalizations can be made, with even the commonest "symptom" being experienced in widely varying ways. Nonetheless, it frequently occurs—no doubt as a result of the withdrawal of pos-itive values attached to aging at the cultural level and the devaluation of the postmenopausal woman at the social level—that the experiences of menopause become linked to images of deterioration and decay. Often, the raising of the issue of aging provokes reflections on the question of mortality, undoubtedly made more poignant by the deep ambivalence of our culture toward death and dying. Menopause, aging, death: disengaged from global social traditions that supply meaning and purpose, they lose their coherence psychologically and become precipitous and terrifying.[27]

To associate menopause with a narrow tendency to biological reductionism, or with a fear of aging and death, may, in the contemporary climate, seem a pes-simistic interpretation. After all, important changes have occurred, of which the present discussion itself is, at least in part, an outcome. There have been strenu-ous attempts to reverse and challenge at the cultural level the values attached to aging and menopause; hence the proliferation of books with titles like *Journey through Menopause* and *Transformation through Menopause*. In addition, a greater, welcome openness about menopause has developed both in private conversation and in the public media. It is widely argued that women, being free subjects, should be able to make their own decisions about the issues affecting them and about the treatments to which they are to be subjected. The emphasis in the popular literature on women making their own decisions and on exercising their autonomy, however, does little to challenge the narrow conceptions of the body assumed by the dominant medical paradigms. Putting aside the obvious point that much of this literature merely reproduces uncritically the narrow biomedical perspective, the preoccupation with "autonomy," as Rosalyn Diprose has shown,[28] takes for granted that a woman's body is an object of exchange and regulation and that the question to be decided is just who should exercise sovereignty over it: the woman "herself" (that is, considered separately from her body), the biomedical practitioner or perhaps the bioethicist (as representative of the law and the common good). The use—either explicit or implicit—of ethical "principles," according to this argument, actually exacerbates the distancing of the agent from her body and from others and contributes to the enforcement of a covert disciplinary regime. Behind the veil of universal principles and the liberal democratic pretext of enhancing the freedom of the menopausal woman, the reality is that the tendency to control the body and to ensure that it remains compliant and pliable—that is, compatible with the social body—is reinforced.

Medicine contributes to the maintenance of the disciplinary structures by means of which the bodies of individuals are in various ways organized, controlled, and subjugated. These structures are very elaborate, and draw on a variety of sources ranging from the epistemologies of science to universalistic ethical theories. In spite of the complexity of this system of domination, however, the varieties of embodied experience can never be fully contained. They cannot be precisely delineated and organized around a set of principles, no matter how intricate. For this reason, the account given here is not a pessimistic one. As Emma herself shows, the body always retains an irreducible capacity for resistance and subversion.

Indeed, the category of the body itself is unpredictable and heterogeneous; and it is from this that the subversive capacity of embodiment derives. The category of the body embraces irreconcilable and incommensurable elements. There is no monolithic entity, "the body." There are only particular kinds of bodies.[29] There are anatomical and physiological bodies, male and female bodies, imaginary bodies, lived bodies, discursive bodies, and poetic bodies. These bodies can be intertwined, and contain social and cultural as well as physical attributes, and they may be disrupted and diseased. Furthermore these disruptions themselves contain a subversive potential: they may actually expand experience and open up new possibilities. On occasion, because of the embeddedness of embodied experience in moral space, the process of disruption may challenge fundamental assumptions about meaning or values, thus further expanding and obscuring limits and boundaries.[30]

Sexuality and the Body of the Doctor

In the dominant discourses of medicine, a rather narrow concept of sexuality is applied, restricted largely to specific sexual practices. Despite occasional notable exceptions, an emphasis is placed on pathological disruptions of sexuality and on therapeutic techniques to rectify them, which range from hormonal treatments to psychotherapy. While such an approach no doubt answers some kind of need, like many other medical paradigms it entails striking omissions: on the one hand, it excludes from consideration the bodily experiences of the patient under conditions of illness, except in the most fragmented and attenuated sense; and on the other, it omits in its entirety the body of the doctor.

Of course, sexuality can be seen in many different ways: for example, it can be viewed as a purely private affair or as an elaborate device for protecting the established structures of power. Since Freud, we have become accustomed to the possibility that sexuality can be polymorphous, and we have come to accept that it inhabits almost every aspect of our lives. Deep studies of the nature of sexuality have shown its close association with the ways in which networks of intersubjectivity are inscribed within bodies and common languages are developed that permit mutual intelligibility. It is, in Merleau-Ponty's words, a "general presence in the world," which is both subjective and objective, private and social.

This general presence, this intertwining, is the proper field of sexuality. Sexuality is a fundamental fact of human existence; in it is projected our manner of being toward the world, toward time, and toward other people.[31] It can never be transcended nor shown up by representations, either conscious or unconscious; nor can it be understood or interpreted at a purely cognitive level. It is like an atmosphere in which we are immersed, albeit one that is ambiguous and problematic.[32]

An understanding of sexuality expanded in this manner has direct implications for clinical medicine. The illness that brings the patient to a doctor is a component of a corporeal world that is both private and shared. It becomes accessible to the doctor in its fullness because of the nature, and through the medium, of sexuality. The suffering of another cannot be understood through processes that are purely cognitive: what is required is a perception that is sexual in character, in the sense that it aims directly from one body to another. To understand a patient's experience, if that is the doctor's intention, it is not enough merely to theorize it; it must in some way be brought into existence for his or her own body.

To consider again the case of Emma, her "illness," if that is the right word, clearly has a hormonal component and identifiable physical effects. It is also psychological, emotional, and existential. Her field of sexuality (in the broad sense in which I am using the term), which once provided secure and stable coordinates for both physical experience and social meanings, is profoundly disrupted.

From a therapeutic point of view, there are some physical issues to deal with, but these will have little impact on her global predicament. What is the role of the doctor here? What is his or her responsibility, and what are the means available to discharge it?

Medicine is a practice of the body, which stands alongside other practices of the body in a given society. In comparison with sport, dancing, aerobics, and so on, it has some special features. For example, in the relationship with a doctor, many conventional rules of physical relationships are suspended: the bounds of privacy, respected even in intimate relations between lovers, are shifted, and a stranger is granted access to secret recesses of one's body and psychic life. Nonetheless, the rules that do govern the conduct of a doctor are very strict. No doubt transgressions occur, although what is perhaps truly remarkable is that these are, comparatively speaking, rare.

In a case such as the one here, the interventions of the doctor are those neither of a mere technician nor of a disembodied sounding board; instead, he or she acts as an embodied subject who can understand and respond to the suffering of the patient within the order of the body itself. This means that the therapeutic process is multifaceted: it encompasses pharmacological and other physical therapies, language and communication, and, maybe, a contribution from the contact involved in the physical examination.

This last factor—the physical examination—is largely neglected in discussions about medicine, although its complexity and potency is familiar to clinicians. Indeed, it may be for this very reason—and because of the obvious sensitivities associated with it—that it has been so carefully avoided. Intense issues may arise around it. Anxieties may be focused or released. Communication may be obstructed or facilitated. The patient may feel threatened or experience a sense of protection and security. Whatever the details in a particular setting, though, a fundamental point is inescapable: the physical presence of the doctor plays a critical role in the clinical interaction.

As the doctor palpates the patient's body, possibilities for understanding and communication not otherwise available are opened up. This may have an indispensable therapeutic role. Indeed, it may be not too extreme to postulate, using the language of sexuality itself, that the doctor's touch may have some of the qualities of a caress. For, like the sexual caress, aiming at neither person nor thing, the doctor's touch searches, or forages.[33] It seeks to understand but not to dominate. It is sensibility, but beyond sensibility. It respects, but questions, otherness. Occupying the space between biological matter and the construction of meaning, it establishes a deliberate and systematic ambiguity.[34]

The contact between doctor and patient at once presupposes both alterity, the irreducible outsideness of each to the other, and the possibility of proximity, of summoning up an other in answer to a need. The doctor is the proximate other who is open or susceptible to the patient's call. In the medical relationship, as in those that Levinas describes, "it is the absolutely other, the stranger, that I already have in my arms, already bear, according to the Biblical formula, 'in my breast as the nurse bears the nurseling'."[35] The openness of the doctor is not a secondary phenomenon that is merely added to a preexisting relationship: it is itself a precondition of that relationship, "an assignation—an obligation, anachronistically prior to a commitment."[36]

Medicine is concerned immanently with issues of sexuality—that is, with the shared meanings that arise in relation to corporeal existence. Doctors and patients encounter each other as embodied subjects and therefore within an ethical relationship. In the complex ethical topography of the clinic, the ambiguities of the field of sexuality are well represented. The clinical encounter is open, if not completely naked. It inhabits a space that is at once personal and social and that spans the sexual field in which both patient and doctor are immersed. It is diverse and differentiated; it must accommodate different roles and therapeutic strategies and the different stories the patient may tell. Its unifying theme is the ethical presupposition on which it is built.

Conclusions: The Ethical Structures of the Clinic

The clinical space of menopause is complex and multilayered. It includes a variety of discourses deriving from the many facets of medicine on the one hand and from the proliferation of the social formations of power on the other. It also embraces various discourses and voices coming from the women themselves.

I have argued that the clinical space of menopause is a moral space: it is a field of ferment, of negotiation and conflict over values. Like all spaces, real and metaphorical, it has boundaries. In this case, the boundaries are set by the horizons of the clinic itself and by the structures of the relationships that are possible under the general rubric of clinical medicine. These horizons and structures themselves depend upon different cultural and epistemological variables. This is due to both the large-scale social constructions that shape the clinical encounter and the mutual nature of the relationship, which includes the doctor himself or herself, not just as a cipher of social discourses of power but as an embodied subject.

The intricate complexity of the clinical space is especially conspicuous in its ethical structures, which display certain fundamental divergencies in comparison with the classical conceptions of ethics.[37] For example, as I have argued, given the diversification and differentiation of the project of ethics in the "postmodern" world, the field of ethical phenomena cannot be limited to the pursuit of the good life. Rather, evaluative activities that are not specifically oriented toward the good have become equally valid components of the ethical domain. Similarly, interactive behavior with ethical content is not exhausted by theoretical discourse aimed at generating universally valid norms. While moral action may always carry some normative content, this may be only "local," in the sense of being restricted to the immediate context of interaction rather than extending to the social group or the society as a whole.

Recognition of these basic facts may help us to understand the diversity and even contradictoriness of medicine in its intersections with complex fields of experience like menopause and the ambivalence that develops in relation to it. It may make it possible to see how medicine itself can subserve a great variety of tasks and, at the same time, how menopause can manifest itself within its horizons in widely varying ways.

Medical practice—or rather the set of diverse, value-laden practices that constitute medicine—is, as I have sought to show, complex and heterogeneous, but it nonetheless has a definite structure. By way of summary, at least three strata may be identified, which may be described in schematic terms as "global," "regional," and "local."

First, viewed from the broadest perspective, there are *global structures* that are common to every interaction with ethical content. These have the status of conditions of possibility of ethical discourse; they include procedural principles like the categorical imperative, and various premises that might be stated for any interaction.[38]

At the next level, there are the ethical forms that derive from the social groups to which the participating individuals belong. In terms of the interaction, these can be characterized in relation to the specific discursive forms that are deployed in the exchange. In any particular case, there may be several discourses acting simultaneously. Imperatives can be derived at this level, but they are *regional* rather than universal, and their applicability is restricted to the discursive frameworks in which they are embedded. The regional level refers to the specific requirements, distortions, and resistances that emerge from the structures of the particular relationships that are established. This is the level at which the social discourses of power act, and at which many of the excesses so relentlessly attacked in recent critiques of the "medicalization" of menopause are to be found. Here, imperatives arise from any of the particular discourses that are employed in clinical interactions—for example, discourses about the biology of menopause, or about its "social" or "psychological" dimensions. At this level, each discourse may be associated with a set of moral imperatives of its own, which may not all be consistent; accordingly, there is a proliferation of moral values, each with a purely regional sphere of applicability.

The main concern of this essay has been with the third, or *local*, level, which encompasses the interactive practices that occur within the constraints of the lifeworld or, more specifically, within the differentiated field of the moral space that I have sought to describe. This is the level of microethics—in functional terms, the substantive level of the ethical relationship. It is a field of face-to-face relationships, of local responsibility, of the meanings and values associated with sexuality and embodiment. The constitutive principles and the regulative imperatives of the global and the regional structures continue to operate here;

however, at this level, there are no endogenous rules to guide conduct along a predetermined path, and there are no ultimate criteria by which actions can be retrospectively judged. Any "ethic" here can be no more than a local procedural one—for example, along the lines of an "ethic of responsibility"; but it must be remembered that even this will be devoid of teleological content.

The three domains that constitute the ethical structure of medicine are of course interdependent. The global domain is logically prior, in the sense of con-stituting conditions of possibility for any ethical relationship. However, the microethical domain is factually and practically prior, since all ethical behavior passes through this realm and is therefore subject to its structural constraints, including its uncertainties: it is the interface between interpersonal interactions and the remainder of the ethical apparatus; it functions as the domain within which values arise and are tested and within which ethical pathologies manifest themselves.

In any specific clinical interaction, all three levels operate to generate an elab-orate moral configuration. This means that even those aspects of medicine that are, on the face of it, most straightforward can often be very complex. The cases of Emma, Carli, Diedre, Amelia, and Brenda all at first sight involved only rela-tively simple technical questions; on closer analysis, however, a multiplicity of issues, each of great complexity and sedimented at different ethical and episte-mological levels, revealed themselves. These issues cut across discursive boundaries; they embraced the biological, the social, the psychological, the exis-tential, the sexual; they presupposed the existence of imperatives built into cultural systems as elaborate disciplinary structures, and the resistance to them.

In any individual case, all these factors may be visible at one time. To illus-trate this, I give the last word to the woman who, when considering whether to commence hormone treatment, expressed her misgivings with great power and poignancy:

> Why should I take hormonal therapy, with all its unknown side-effects, includ-ing possibly the increased risk of breast cancer, so that I will become dependent on my doctor and the whole medical machine just when I thought I was becoming rid of them, so that my husband will regard me as a "triumph of sci-ence"—and merely in order to live for a few extra months, alone, when I'm eighty?

At the outset of this essay I drew attention to a widely felt ambivalence toward medicine in the community. Among the things that I have hoped to show is that this ambivalence is not generated by either ignorance or *ressentiment:* rather, it is well founded in both the deep structures of medicine and the conditions that put people into contact with it. The clinical encounter is a site where conflicting themes and forces intersect in unpredictable and sometimes disturbing ways.

Similarly, menopause today has emerged as a battleground on which conflicts of various kinds—political, cultural, personal—are fought. This means that many contending descriptions of it are available. Some of these defend medicine for its analytical capacities and technical potency, while others dismiss it for its complicity in the status quo. In a sense, all are right, since medicine is an ill-defined, heterogeneous collection of discourses, practices, tools, and languages: accordingly, both menopause and medicine can be sites for both affirmations of the existing order and for critical reflections on it; each can be a locus of moral action without defined end-points or unequivocal outcomes. This may seem a perplexing diagnosis on which to end, but in reality it merely repeats what on a larger scale has become fundamental for us. Indeed, as Nietzsche put it,

> perhaps this is the most powerful magic of life: it is covered by a veil interwoven with gold, a veil of beautiful possiblities, sparkling with promise, resistance, bashfulness, mockery, pity, and seduction. . . .[39]

Notes

I thank John Wiltshire for his helpful comments and suggestions.

1. The descriptions of women's experiences contained in this essay are based on actual clinical cases. Details have been changed to protect confidentiality. I should like to record how indebted I am to these women for their insights.

2. See, e.g., M. Foucault, *Birth of the Clinic*, trans. A. Sheridan (London: Tavistock, 1973); I. Illich, *Limits to Medicine* (London: Marion Boyars, 1976); J. Ehrenreich, ed., *The Cultural Crisis of Modern Medicine* (London: Monthly Review Press, 1978); C. Dreifus, *Seizing Our Bodies* (New York: Vintage, 1978), and many more recent examples.

3. P. A. Komesaroff, "From Bioethics to Microethics: The Need to Return Medical Ethics to the Clinic," in *Troubled Bodies: Critical Perspective on Postmodernism, Medical Ethics and the Body* (Durham, NC: Duke University Press, 1995).

4. P. A. Komesaroff, "Postmodern Medical Ethics?" *Troubled Bodies*.

5. J-F Lyotard, *The Postmodern Condition: A Report on Knowledge* (Manchester, UK: Manchester University Press, 1986), pp. 31ff.

6. W. van Reijen and D. Veerman, "Interview with Jean-Francois Lyotard," *Theory, Culture and Society* 5(2–3) (1988): 277–311, 278.

7. F. Nietzsche, *The Gay Science*, trans. W. Kaufmann (New York: Random House, 1974), p. 168.

8. A. Heller, "The Contingent Person and the Existential Choice," *The Philosophical Forum* 21 (1–2) (1989–1990).

9. M. Weber, "The Meaning of 'Ethical Neutrality' in Sociology and Economics," in *The Methodology of the Social Sciences* (New York: The Free Press, 1949), pp. 3–4.

10. P. Bürger, *Theory of the Avant-garde* (Manchester, Manchester University Press, 1984).

11. J-F Lyotard, *Postmodern Condition and Just Gaming* (Minneapolis: University of Minnesota Press, 1985), pp. 50–59.

12. Komesaroff, "From Bioethics to Microethics."

13. C. Taylor, *Sources of the Self* (Cambridge, MA: Harvard University Press, 1989), p. 28.

14. Z. Bauman, *Life in Fragments: Essays in Postmodern Morality* (Oxford: Blackwell, 1995), p. 82.

15. Ibid., p. 81.

16. A. Touraine, *Critique of Modernity* (Oxford: Blackwell, 1995), p. 130.

17. Komesaroff, "From Bioethics to Microethics."

18. M. M. Bakhtin, *The Dialogic Imagination: Four Essays* (Austin: University of Texas Press, 1991), p. 278. See also p. 276.

19. E. Levinas, *Totality and Infinity* (Pittsburgh: Duquesne University Press, 1969), p. 43.

20. E. Grosz, *Sexual Subversions* (Sydney: Allen and Unwin, 1989), pp. 142–43.

21. D. Leder, *The Body in Medical Thought and Practice* (Dordrecht: Kluwer Academic Publishers, 1992), pp. 17–37.

22. D. Leder, *The Absent Body* (Chicago: University of Chicago Press, 1990), p. 73.

23. Ibid., pp. 74, 77.

24. Ibid., p. 90; see also S. Gadow, "Body and Self: A Dialectic," in *The Humanity of the Ill*, ed. V. Kestenbaum, pp. 92–99 (Knoxville: University of Tennessee Press, 1982).

25. See F. Mackie, "The Left Hand of the Goddess," in this collection.

26. Nietzsche, *The Gay Science*, p. 269.

27. Cf. M. Heidegger, *Being and Time* (Oxford: Blackwell, 1978), pp. 179–85.

28. R. Diprose, "The Body Medical Ethics Forgets," in Komesaroff, *Troubled Bodies*, chapter 10; and R. Diprose, *The Bodies of Women: Ethics, Embodiment and Sexual Difference* (London: Routledge, 1994).

29. E. Grosz, "Notes towards a Corporeal Feminism," *Australian Feminist Studies*, 1987 (5): 9. Quoted by Philipa Rothfield in Komesaroff, *Troubled Bodies*, p. 175.

30. "Even the determination of what is healthy for your *body* depends on your goal, your horizon, your impulses, your errors, and above all on the ideals and phantasms of your soul. Thus there are innumerable healths of the body; and the more we allow the weak and incomparable to raise its head again, and the more we abjure the dogma of the 'equality of men', the more must the concept of a *normal* health, along with a normal diet and the normal course of an illness, be abandoned by medical men." (Nietzsche, *The Gay Science*, p. 177).

31. M. Merleau-Ponty, *Phenomenology of Perception* (London: Routledge, 1962), p. 158.

32. Ibid., p. 168.

33. Levinas, *Totality and Infinity*, pp. 259, 258.

34. L. Irigaray, *An Ethics of Sexual Difference* (Ithaca, NY: Cornell, 1993), pp. 185ff.

35. E. Levinas, *Otherwise Than Being: Towards Essence*, trans. A. Lingis (The Hague, Martinus Nijhoff, 1981), p. 91.

36. Ibid., pp. 100–101. For emphasis, attention is drawn to the distinction I am making between "sexuality," which is the subject of these comments, and "sexual practices," which is not. It may also be appropriate in this context to stress that, unlike the "authority" of the doctor, there is no place in the clinical encounter for the exercise

of "power"; indeed, the introduction of the latter is directly subversive of the clinical relationship.

37. See P. A. Komesaroff, "The Ethical Conditions of Modernity," in *Ethical Intersections: Research Methods and Ethical Responsibility*, ed. J. Daly (Melbourne: Allen and Unwin, 1996).

38. J. Habermas, *Justification and Application: Remarks on Discourse Ethics* (Cambridge, MA: MIT Press, 1993), chapter 2.

39. Nietzsche, *The Gay Science*, p. 272.

POLITICS OF THE SYMBOLIC

5

Revolting Women
Women in Revolt

Mia Campioni

This chapter will approach the issue of menopause in light of the fact that we are all situated as sexed subjects in a symbolic order, a culture of meaning, which structures our experiences and thoughts about our body, its functions, and its place in the world, among others. These cultural processes of signification, which form our frames of reference, are largely unconscious and primarily center on the meaning of sexual difference for each subject in every human society, which is grounded in the body/sex of women as site of human origin. Rather than taking "real" women as my referents, I am proposing to examine our modern western cultural unconscious whose Symbolic Order produces the meaning of "the menopausal woman" as a corollary of a larger scenario, that of "Woman" in the discourse of "Man," the Subject representing both women and men in all culturally dominant narratives. In a psychoanalytic reading, which I will critically employ, this meaning of "Woman" is inescapably grounded in the imaginary and symbolic significance of the "(M)Other's body" for each and every human subject. The way we experience the so-called menopause and the way in which the culture reads its occurrence in women's bodies/minds appears thus to lead us right back to this problematic foundation in the body/sex of the (M)Other/Woman.

The modern invention of the menopause and a woman's experience of "her menopause" is inscribed (if I can use that word to mean the creation of structural meaning) by various techniques of the body that have reduced this historical event in women's lives as a factor of social cohesion to an ensemble of culturally anomalous and personally problematic processes. I will argue that this modern interpretation of a uniquely female changing body/sex/mind has left us with "menopause" as a purely technical problem of improper hormonal secretion dominated by the dread of aging and of loss of sexual vibrancy, with no concern for its specifically female symbolic meaning in the social order and with a total denial of its potential self-enhancing prospects. Rather than leaving it here (as Germaine Greer did with her book *The Change*),[1] I will attempt to draw some psychoanalytic conclusions from this continual process of cultural denial and historical leveling of woman's morphological aging. By critically examining its symbolic significance in the story of the human subject, whose narrative Freud presented as the drama of Oedipus, I intend to point to an unconscious cultural significance of the appearance of "the menopause" in women. It would appear that the "revolting" (in both senses of the word) presence of the menopausal older woman/(m)other, whose "dying" sex/body genealogically embodies the only living testimony to the origin of each subject in "Woman" remains the archaic unpleasant reminder of the fantasy of the self-engendered and eternally reinvented New Man (or Woman). The central theme of my paper therefore suggests that the meaning of "menopause" cannot be understood without reference to a history of the symbolic function of "Woman" as (M)Other to the Subject, who ceaselessly writes "Her" in the story of each and every culture.

The paper is divided into two main parts: the first addresses the modern approach to women's climacteric and its effects of pathologizing and dehistoricizing of this period in a woman's life; the second deals with a theoretical, largely psychoanalytic, retrieval of the figure of the older (mo)ther/woman from the imaginary and symbolic shadow cast by the birthing/succoring/sexual Woman for Man.

Women's Time

The modern creation of menopause as a problem and a loss/lack rather than a gain of physical maturity and female cultural wisdom, coupled with "suitable treatment" to better label it a misfortune of the female body in need of rejuvenation, has cut the link to the history of each woman's body and to a history of humankind as well. It has replaced a representation of the older woman as culturally approaching the status of oracle, witch, healer, soothsayer, wise woman, harridan, and virago—her sharp tongue emitting "bitter truths" and her behavior unpleasantly devoid of feminine decorum—with that of an unwell woman. "Unwell" to the extent that her body/presence no longer represents the comforting continuity of sexuality/maternality of that normally "unwell" figure: Woman, compared to Man. So, the menopausal woman is doubly unwell, because doubly lacking, she represents decaying female sexuality, while the latter itself is already a poor "other" to male sexuality. Thus the state of "free fall" (as Germaine Greer so aptly termed it) experienced in going through or approaching the onset of menopause is interpreted as even more of an indication of a process of deterioration of the already abnormal nature of female sexuality, rather than as a potentially liberating force.

Though no longer regarded as suffering from a "wandering womb" (wombs are very much out of fashion, except in maternity wards, oncology departments, and reproductive engineering institutes), the modern menopausal woman now "merely" suffers from a "normal" hormonal deficiency. This discovery nonetheless signifies that her body is unbalanced because it is "lacking" something (if not a valued organ—the penis—then estrogen, which makes her a "proper" woman). This renders her prone to all sorts of erratic and disturbing behavior, indicating a dangerously unhinged mental state. This instability in the older/menopausal woman is again supposed to point to a lack, that of rationality, patience, demure behavior, and deference to men and younger people. The boundaries of a proper feminine sense of place appear to be transgressed. This unstable condition can now be "effectively" managed with so-called hormonal replacement therapy ("HRT") providing a "top-up" of what is lacking to make her feminine again, and counteract all possible ravages from what might turn out to be natural female aging plus an exhilarating but unacceptable possibility to undo the effects of an exacting life as a mother/woman in a male-dominated culture. It is said that "our bodies desert us" at the onset of the end of menstruation, which may socially mean that we are supposed to enter a state of horrid sexlessness. This so-called desertion—if it at all occurs to the extent imagined—is never discussed as something positive and liberating, but as a disaster equal to the feared older male impotence. It is certainly never interpreted as a woman's body giving her to understand that there is life after the "proper" female existence of always being reduced to nothing but a body/sex, and that she is "coming to her senses" in going beyond this narrow corporeality to find a knowledge of her own. Such a knowledge might be termed a real "thinking through the body,"[2] which refers not to sex but to a mind/body totality, an embodied knowledge, and in this case an understanding of life/death as a genealogy of the female body as history.

The changing of a woman's body in this profound existential sense may appear no longer to serve a purpose in a culture where individuals measure creativity by the extent to which they can reinvent themselves every day, and where forgetting is the ideal in an endless vertigo of newly manufactured realities. Perhaps in the age of virtual reality it may be enjoyable to imagine menopause as a possibility to leave the (reproductively organized) body behind, leading to all sorts of virtual possibilities in the cyberspace. But we should ask ourselves why this desire to avoid, indeed repress, the identification in/with the body/sex of (M)Other/Woman as potent reminder of the inevitable sexual embodiment of each subject? It is in this sense that I want to explain the scientific desire to reduce menopause to a simple identification of its hormonal "textuality," remaining deaf and blind to its discourse as part of the historical truth of "women's time" in the culture. I am referring here to a psychoanalytic concept of embodied consciousness, where woman's experience of her body/sex as feminine continuity in the life/death of the species involves a specific sense of historical space/time,[3] which is entirely ignored as truth/knowledge in the culture in favor of a masculine-oriented history as discontinuous events authorized solely by their facticity in writing or archival documentation.

Moreover, by creating menopause as nothing but a precise and exclusively endocrine identity in need of "suitable treatment," women are robbed of (and men are shielded from) a deeper understanding of its mind-altering aspects, with their powerfully revolting symbolic connotations in the culture. One of the effects of this procedure of erasing women's embodied history has been the so-called discovery of "early menopause." In fact the construction of the term "early menopause" proves that the modern conception of the menopause involves the leveling if not denial of what I have called above "women's time." It treats the female body as timeless, as without history, consciousness, and knowledge, and consequently as purely determined by the physiological processes of hormonal production. It reduces the female body to that of a male one—which indeed lacks specifically male cyclical processes—with, as sole exception, a peculiar hormonal organization (serving particular limited purposes) added to it. Presenting the discovery of premature cessation of menstruation, absence of ovulation, etc. as proof that menopause is simply hormonal imbalance is then another indication that women's bodies have no lives of their own and can be reduced to nothing but well-oiled or faulty machines. Yet the technical identification of premature menopause in a young woman does not make her an old one. There is no lived-body/consciousness related to a cycle of menstruation, maternality, and sexuality with their female maturing/aging patterns, nor is there a subjectivity perceived as typically menopausal in the culture (unattractive, hysterical, annoying, bitter, shrill, domineering, deranged, etc.) confronting the early menopausal woman, because she simply is not (yet) the type, and no technical early menopausal body will exempt her later from falling victim to such a negative cultural imago. Similarly, naturally menopausal or postmenopausal women who are artificially induced to conceive may serve to bear witness to the wonders of reproductive engineering, but they remain old women giving birth; they do not become suddenly thirty again by the very act of artificial reproduction. They share this problem with very old fathers. Equally, to imagine that "HRT" or any other propping up of a woman's hormonal "balance" will halt her so-called debilitating aging symptoms and make her operate again as if she were thirty—actually dooming her to a prolonged menstrual cycle and thus a real hormonal imbalance—is nothing but an atrocious denial of the totality of her bodily experience, if not a ridiculous fantasy of scientific megalomania. The new strategy appears to be to stress women's right to be free from "symptoms" and to have the freedom to choose to control their lives with "HRT" and/or all sorts of other "cures." If, however, estrogen (or equivalent homeopathic products) has a pacifying effect (apparently its abundance at pregnancy explains its placid, inward-centered female state of mind), then women are offered to "freely" choose their own subjugation (once again?).

Though I am not convinced that all this prescribed estrogen/progesterone management can indeed keep a good menopausal woman down, the cultural myth created by "HRT" as a panacea for a supposedly indispensable reconstruction of the body/sex/mind of menopausal women has important possibilities for the psychological blackmail of women. For example, women have always been denigrated when they revolted against their inferior conditions by references to their "raging hormones" (cf. "premenstrual syndrome"). It is conceivable that not being on "HRT" will have the same connotations for the woman herself and her environment. So that every sign of unease or atypical behavior (such as feeling subject to a "racy consciousness," as Greer termed it) requires a woman to do something about her clear "lack" of proper hormonal balance. Dr. Wilson described his mother's senseless rages as almost demonical and so hurtful to herself and, perhaps more importantly, to his father's and his own image of this previous "angel in the house" that he had to invent a "cure," "HRT."[4] One does not have to be paranoid to see a future where women are given "HRT" as a matter of course to prevent them from being invaded by such dreadful demons, like babies are routinely inoculated against infectious diseases. Already, as a matter of routine, "HRT" is now often prescribed preventatively to premenopausal and middle-aged women with no discernible related symptoms, and women in their 80s are given "HRT" by their doctors for all sorts of entirely unrelated complaints: sleeplessness, arthritis, heart palpitations, etc. These practices appear to be spreading rapidly (it is, after all, a gold-mine industry), but it also shares a general trend in late capitalism that female nature is essentially in need of close medical attention, intervention, and technical adjustment. It is this which differentiates women's bodies culturally from men's bodies, which are regarded as perfect though recently discovered to be vulnerable to dangerous social neglect. Similarly with the menopausal body vis-à-vis the older man's body, the former needs a total reconditioning, the latter just needs better looking after. It indicates that menopause is never just a hormonal event in an individual woman's body (just as menarche or pregnancy/childbirth or the absence of these in a female are) but a culturally significant connotation of the status of the body/sex of Woman/(M)Other in the symbolic order of Man.

The reduction of menopause to nothing but sex and hormones—that is, to a deficiency in/of the female body/sex—may well be an attempt of modern behavior modification serving age-old western attempts to pacify uncontrollable revolting tendencies in older women of speaking their minds and claiming true knowledge, while refusing to do the dominant culture's bidding any longer. Such tendencies are no longer culturally regarded—perhaps ever since the institutionalizing of all forms of patriarchal religion—as signs of socially cohesive and politically useful power, though in medieval witch hunts and eighteenth- and nineteenth-century fairy tales we still find traces of their problematic existence for the rising bourgeois, male/subject culture.

Maybe it is fanciful to present the menopausal woman as a "draft resister," because physically and mentally women approaching menopause in late capitalist culture may feel depressed, confused, ill, prone to uncontrollable sweats, sleeplessness, mood swings, etc. But I am suggesting that this hangs together with the fear instilled in us of our body/sex as the root of the problem, while the negative experience of these bodily symptoms may be an effect of an entirely diminished cultural image of women's "change of life." Apparently Chinese women have no hot flashes, and in African tribes women still look forward to menopause to achieve a measure of social status, though not for long it appears, since the wonders of a globally effective modern patriarchy with the concomitant "HRT" appear to be spreading, successfully captivating women the world over.

Reduced to a hormonal malfunction or depletion, there is no room in "the menopause" for a positive reference to a changed consciousness, to becoming a "different, (even less) knowing woman," which could personally and symbolically be invested with cultural significance. Yet women approaching and going through menopause often report to each other remarkably positive feelings of sudden insight, clarity of vision, heightened perception, intense sensitivity to inner and outer worlds, and not seldom a sense of freedom of thought and action, a loss of shame and guilt feelings in expressing anger and passion, and a sharper sense of the ridiculous. No amount of sympathetic interviewing of menopausal women, built on the patronizing idea of menopause as a state of disease, is going to unearth and give voice to these enriching and empowering feelings. These may be mythical states of consciousness, the expressions of which are harnessed in oral traditions of "wise woman," "oracle," and "speaker of cultural truths," where they perform a function of moral and historical guardianship. The point is not whether they form the real truth of the "menopause," a sort of sociological lost faculty of older women, but that the medical imago of corporeal deterioration in need of rejuvenation, that is, as "lacking" body/sex, helps to undermine and to pathologize the cultural dignity and personal importance of menopause in a woman's life.

Whereas in the traditional culture the acknowledged status of female elder may entail a conserving cultural function, the modern direction of the processes of the climacteric in a woman may propel her toward experiencing "the change" in a radically different way, precisely because she no longer has a significant role to play in the culture. In a society governed by a humanist ideology of freedom and equality, and with a now well-documented history of women's dissatisfaction with their social condition, the potentially subversive aspects of these psychical states of revolt are evident. They can find expression in an increased political awareness about the masculine domination of female existence born from personal experience, and an active creation of a life and meaning outside male-defined parameters of femininity and sexuality. This leads to a search for a community of women as a political goal ("the sisterhood") and is often in previously heterosexual women coupled with a change in erotic relationships in the direction of lesbian sexuality. This specifically menopausal "raised consciousness" may be characterized by little regard for institutionalized power and justice born from a sense of heightened urgency of the need for immediate social change.

Politics of Menopause

Whereas her life in a male-normalized culture has been spent subjected to "being-for-others" and thus in being excluded from cultural discourse as "woman for herself," the menopausal woman in her not seldomly unapologetic strident attitude appears to threaten the social and symbolic sign of the "feminine" by unraveling its "natural function" when she stops being a "real woman." Her existence appears to fuzz the "natural" boundaries between the sexes; neither maternal/virginal nor paternal/masculine, she is the supplement, the in-between. She begins culturally to enter a state of indefinable existence in terms of the dominant parameters of phallic sexuality and reproduction, which renders her redundant in a male-defined paradigm. This impossible condition operates culturally as a freak of nature, because her body/sex is no longer reducible to that of the "natural feminine" state of representing the ageless (m)other, the forever silent center of support for everyone's fragile subjectivity. Nor can her body/sex be easily reduced to that of "all she needs is a good fuck," because she is fast losing her sex appeal and appears to engage instead in lethal brain-fucks of others. The menopausal woman herself may experience this state of affairs in her body/sex/mind as rather scary, but also as an opening of doors to perceptions, which are mind-blowing, felt as uncannily astute, and the embodiment of a new female erotics of power.

It is remarkable that feminists have not exploited this possibility to unpack the culturally repressed, mind-altering aspect of menopause philosophically, by critically analyzing the imaginary and symbolic significance of the figure of the older (m)other/woman in male supremacist culture. They instead appear to have ignored the other voice that appears to confront here the social order. In the sparse texts on menopause, the exclusive concern seems to be to combat over-medicalization and/or to develop more "natural" practices of self-help, diet, and "living through menopause" with a positive frame of mind. As central problem, "the change" thus remains unassailably a personal and corporeal problem. Even Greer's interpretation of menopause, though alone in taking it seriously and devoting an immense body of research to its background, remains in the last analysis a mostly individualistic description of a unique female physical occurrence, at the most providing a chance for a personal "getting in touch with your body" or for rejoicing in playing the eccentric witch/crone in group gatherings or in debates with younger women. In spiritual feminist approaches, confronting "the change" (if it is mentioned at all) appears to involve an appropriation for the purposes of creating a mythical state of the Goddess inside. Alternatively, it is presented, but scarcely with any political historical insight, as emblematic of the archaic omnipotent and all-loving Great Mother, which entirely represses the very real aspects of an overpowering capacity for political disturbance embodied in the figure of the older woman in the culture. These ways of dealing with the threshold to the cessation of the reproductive part of the female body/sex in themselves may be experienced as personally liberating, but amount to mystical individualism and feminine narcissism if they lack an outward-looking political analysis of the symbolic order and the cultural unconscious that supports it.

A politics of menopause, which concentrates on the undoubtedly significant potential for "maintaining the rage" in this period of a woman's life, is virtually absent from so-called postfeminist analyses. Yet, I think it presents great possibilities to wrest the definition of "the change" away from masculinist, medicalized, and New Age individualized frameworks, and to acknowledge that the revolt of our sexed bodies may have a psychologically "revolting" unconscious basis in and effect on the culture. This period of change can contribute to different ways of seeing, with sometimes remarkably productive results, as long as they are employed for a wider political purpose. As women we might have to begin to recognize this "difference" among ourselves and in ourselves, instead of wishing it away or attempting to soften its impacts or turning it into a "getting in touch with nature" experiment with a limited political potential.

For a start, we might decide to reread the work of women theorists as possible menopausal texts, which does not mean they should be glorified as essential manifestos for revolutionary change. Many of the most incisive writings by influential women thinkers appeared in their midlife (Alexandra Kollontai, Margaret Mead, Emma Goldman, Helene Deutsch, Melanie Klein, Hannah Arendt, among others, spring to mind). The objection may be raised that varying ages in the female thinkers mentioned (from forty to sixty years old) do not warrant bundling them into so specific a period as "the menopause." But I maintain that it is only in medical discourse, and in male-normalized public opinion, that "the menopause" is a clear and distinct break-off point. In reality, a woman's body prepares itself over years for the cessation of menstruation and reproductive capacity. But more important, a woman herself starts being aware of a growing sense of freedom to think independently, a pronounced "Will to Power/ Knowledge" (to use a Foucauldian term)—which I think are female midlife signs—at any time over the age of forty when she is culturally regarded, and imagines herself, as "over the hill" (a fascinating term!), becoming uncharacteristically "revolting," "shrill," that is: "menopausal."

As an example, four of the most well-known classic feminist texts were written by women in this midlife period. I am referring to Simone de Beauvoir's *The Second Sex*, Betty Friedan's *The Feminine Mystique*, Adrienne Rich's *Of Woman Born*, and Audre Lorde's *Sister Outsider*. What is remarkable here is that neither by their creators nor by their feminist readers are these four texts (and countless others) signposted as works of their writers' midlife experience. What gets lost in this process is that the appearance of a specific critical consciousness and the influence of a mature philosophical insight are not brought into connection with the menopausal changes in a woman's corporeal and mental experience. This stage in a woman's life can then continue to be denied any specific discursive advantages (and perhaps also disadvantages) because it is dismissed as having any creative aspects and only negative physical connotations, which is precisely why it is repressed in a woman's text in the first place.

The menopause (which is not a "pause" but an "ending") is, however, not simply a physical stage in a woman's life, resulting in a specific mind-state. As I have already started to indicate in the previous sections, the female menopause appears to have special cultural connotations. In what follows I will develop a theoretical, largely psychoanalytic, argument about the symbolic, unconscious function of the menopausal body of Woman in the culture of Man, the Subject. I maintain that the cultural meaning of both this body/sex's physiological characteristics and its experiential ramifications have to be seen in light of the cultural significance of the female body for men (and women) as the always already poor substitute for the imaginary and symbolic archaic (M)Other/Woman of Mankind. Since menopause is corporeally and culturally defined by the physical ending of the female reproductive capacity, it cannot fail to be closely connected to and disturbingly remind us of this cultural imago of the maternal feminine. This changing female body/sex, which appears to painfully represent the finitude of the site of origin of the subject, thus spells a sort of "lifting of the veil," exposing the eternal guarantee sought in the body of the archaic (M)Other/Woman as a fiction of the subject. In what follows I will try to present this idea in a more detailed, theoretical manner.

Subject and its (M)Other

In the psychoanalytic narrative of the birth of the Subject, human beings are subjects of desire, a desire born of an initial imaginary experience of once perfect union/identity of self and (m)other, which has been lost in the process of separation/differentiation from the maternal body. The sense of incompleteness and contingency this brings is psychically covered over by imagining ourselves as creators of our own subjecthood and sexual immortality, and denying thus the power and knowledge embodied in the (m)other/woman, who exists from now on only as our imaginary construct of an always already absent symbolic (M)Other/Woman.[5] There is, however, a problem with this story. As adults we are literally confronted by the reality of the reproductive female body/sex in its maturity and with its slow "death" in menopause, reminding us of our dependency on/in this body, which appears to disturb the ego's reverie of perpetual self-engenderment by threatening the fantasy of the guarantee of infinitude in the forever absent, archetypal ageless, (m)other/woman of infancy. "She" never grows old, and in a sense never existed, because when and how she was there in the dim, barely aware experiences of infancy is irretrievably absent from adult consciousness and completely overshadowed by the culturally constructed and personally significant symbolic meaning of (M)Other/Woman. The Symbolic

Order of western culture supports and augments the imaginary function of this (M)Other/Woman by entirely subordinating women as self-directed beings to a discourse of sacrificial and perpetual maternality. They exist nowhere for themselves, and their cultural meaning is exhausted in their function as Other to the Subject.

This cultural fantasy contrasts sharply with the real existence and presence in the culture of that "other woman," the menopausal (m)other/woman, who appears to destroy or fall short of the constructed image of Mother/Woman. She no longer fits the image of mother-for-the-child, because for the adult subject she emerges in her menopausal persona as the proverbial "bad mother," a poor substitute for the fantasized lost (M)Other/Woman. Her obstinate presence actually blocks the continual view on and deployment of that dim, Minoan creature the (M)Other/Woman/Goddess, who eternally guarantees the subject for her/himself. Her menopausal body/sex also threatens the very existence of the subject with the memory of her/his finitude in this body.

In this sense, the phenomenon of the female menopause lends a painfully real, historical dimension to both the fantasy of the self-engendered immortal subject and to the fantasy of its (m)other, that fiction of the essential, forever young, sexually objectifiable, reproductive Woman, who ceaselessly submits herself to being-for-the subject/child.

Modern psychoanalytic women theorists who invoke/reemphasize the importance of Woman as (M)Other in theories of subjectivity, sexuality, culture, and the body appear invariably also to collapse this figure into the mother-for-the-newborn-child, i.e., this largely fictional eternal (m)other of childhood created by the culture. In the theories of Irigaray, Kristeva, Chodorow, Benjamin, and others,[6] the maternal body/sex remains forever locked in the fairy tale (or horror story) of the young mother/child couple. We never move to an examination of the subject's confrontation with and acceptance of the reality of the older (m)other/woman, both in themselves as theorists and in others as older women/mothers. Yet, it is that woman who confronts the speaking subject/writer, even a feminist one, as the live example of (m)other/woman in the culture, behind whose all too concrete body/sex presence we perhaps fabricate the more appealing self-important imaginary and symbolic image of (M)Other of/for our infancy. Her painfully real aging body/sex/consciousness precisely blocks our view and undermines our grip on this controlled fiction.

The particularly shrill presence of the menopausal woman—that is, the woman who generationally is in the place of every adult (speaking/writing) subject's mother, and whose body/sex exhibits the aging of the maternal feminine—contests the psychical allocation of mute, timeless, and essentially ageless (m)other/woman. She literally threatens to destroy the imaginary relation to that maternal feminine, the forever pre-oedipal mother, in each subject. She represents as such the living embodiment of the abject, the monstrous, the castrating force, and repugnant reminder of the insecurity of the subject, who speaks/writes/represents her/himself by attempting to salvage and to control the imaginary construct of her/his (m)other/woman.

Following Freudian theories of infantile sexuality, which define the adult as product of unconscious childhood identifications of sexual difference in the maternal body, it has been customary to define the eruption and the function of this as horror at the absence of an organ the child once presumed to be present, a sort of "return of the repressed" of childhood. I want to argue against that interpretation, by maintaining that the imaginary construct of the so-called pre-oedipal mother—in which the uncanny, threatening feminine as well as the primary "sexual love object" for the subject is supposed to be based—is always already the fantasy figure in the narrative of the adult subject, who speaks/writes/represents the (m)other/woman as her/his important primary other. The fiction of childhood as the locus of the truth of this narrative of the subject and the function of the (m)other/woman there, is the center and force of the psychoanalytic fairy tale. Even Freud of course operated with this knowledge, when he coined the term "childhood amnesia," cleverly lowering the veil over something he himself as father and husband had put there, but that is really "nothing to be seen." He deployed the exchange of discourse between analyst and analysand as if this "royal road of the unconscious" led back to an incontrovertible truth before the order of culture and language intrudes, including the discourse of psychoanalysis, as a specific historical expression of that order. This "truth" is always and only retrievable via the discourse of the adult signifying subject (including that of Freud himself)—that is, of the adult as bearer/producer of cultural signs of sexual difference. In this way the child inherits the fantasy of the adult, without which the latter could not cope in order to accept his/her sexual identity.

Oedipus Revisited

Perhaps it is then relevant to question seriously the course of events as narrated in the psychoanalytic fairy tale—which, after all, is the response of the Father/Son to the power of the (M)Other—by setting it on its head. Because in reality, contrary to fairy tales, Greek mythology, philosophy, and psychoanalysis, where the birthing mother-of-the-subject is always already and essentially absent, to be spoken about, but never speaking, the mother herself lives on as the older (m)other/woman of the adult, fictionalizing subject. So, who after all, actually confronts as their other the community of men and women as speaking subjects? She is not the fictitious pre-oedipal mother, but this older woman who knows "one or two things about them" and whose body "knows otherwise." Her body/sex/speech testify corporeally and consciously to the subject's (male and female) contingent and finite relation to the sex of and origin in the maternal body.

In the Oedipus myth, the Sphinx represents this knowing older body/woman/ monster, whose riddle deals precisely with this female knowledge about the birth and trajectory of the subject, and it is addressed to the grown Man. The oedipal myth concerns the central role of Jocasta, the older mother/wife of her son/husband, both birthing mother and sexual object of father/son. In this context it is interesting how Freud employs the myth of Oedipus to prop up his belief in the young mother/child couple as innately incestuous, that is, governed by a fully sexual desire that stands in the way of the conjugal rights of the father, while virtually ignoring that the consummation of this wish occurs between an adult son and an older woman, who turns out to be his mother.[7] Freud continues there a tradition as old as mankind, that of the mythical figure of the Great Mother/ Consort, but with an important difference. He no longer revoked the power of the (M)Other as the Matriarch (which is always identified as mythical rule by older women/mothers over adults of both sexes), but in fact substituted that mythical figure with the passive, mutely mirroring forever young mother/consort to the child/man assisting the "birth of the subject" as phallic.

Freud never discusses Jocasta nor analyzes her age,[8] nor the peculiar fact that Oedipus as husband, father/king, became the brother of his children (and of his dead father). That is, both man and child (as Man) are confronted and in struggle with the maternal as sexual in the figure of the always already older (m)other/ woman. And we never hear more in fact than the Father/Man story. (In this context it is perhaps interesting to note that Freud's only analysis of childhood, that of the five-year old famous Little Hans, was entirely conducted in a dialogue between the boy's father and Freud.[9]) Jocasta, in Freud's sexual interpretation of the story of Oedipus, is returned to her eternal shadowy place of already absent and abstract (m)other and thus does not need to be confronted as the older mother/woman, whose presence renders the fantasy of the union with the maternal body (the incestuous wish) truly monstrous and unimaginable. Instead Freud transmogrifies Jocasta into the pre-oedipal mother of the man/child, and this man/child is made to bear/represent the existential angst of the adult man. In other words, we are back in childhood, where the maternal feminine is safely ensconced in the dim Minoan regions, and we have managed to avoid the confrontation with the sexuality and generative knowledge of the older woman/ mother, who can only ever appear as herself when young and gone.

One could interpret the Oedipus myth as the prophecy of the inescapable centrality of the maternal sexual body for the origin of Man, where the father is always already the dead Father, and the living father is actually the mature son of the older woman/mother, whom he impregnates. That is, consort and offspring of the Mother/Woman are one and the same—indeed a very old story, repeated in most matrilineal creation myths—but which in its patriarchal version can only be achieved in the union of the mature male and the older mother/woman's body. It is the one union that is universally repulsive to consciousness and struck by the famous incest-taboo, because sex and origin cannot take place in the one body and need to be kept separate. And the sex of the mother has to be repressed to give primacy to that of the (male-identified) child. (Cf. also the Australian film *Bad Boy Bubby*, where we recoil in utter horror from the vilest act of all: Bubby's enforced "serving" of his hideous middle-aged mother. The abjection of the mother this allows for in the viewer works cathartically, and makes the figure of Bubby almost Christlike. He suffered for all of us.)

His Mother's Voice

The story of the origin of the human sexual being, mostly spoken/written by the male adult subject, thus contains indeed a matricide, but, I maintain, it is as the unthinkable figure of the powerful older woman/mother as sexual being, not as the young, pre-oedipal mother, that she is "killed," to prevent her speaking/testifying to what is "repressed." Her erasure guarantees the continuation of the fantasy of the ageless mother/woman, whose entire function is exhausted in being for-the-man/woman-as-child only, and whose body/sex remains forever displaced onto variations of the virginal "eternal feminine" (m)other/woman.

In *Totem and Taboo* Freud appears to tell the story with the slant of making it the foundation of "culture,"[10] but there again he avoids mentioning that the Sexual Contract, resulting from symbolic murder of the father, incestuous taboo, and rivalry between the sons, originates in the sexual desire of the men/sons of mothers for the older woman/mother. This problem can be solved by Freud in psychoanalysis, making of each child always already a (little) man, the bearer of culture, and thus interpret every child's physical need and affection for its mother as a fully fledged sexual urge connected inescapably to its genital apparatus, the so-called infantile incestuous wish. All this to prove that it all takes place as an innate constitution of childhood and women's early mothering, and has nothing to do with the man/father's jealousy of the child's position in the estimation of its mother, and with the desire of grown men to reduce their powerful (m)others as women to the "castrated body/sex," to deny their power, and to erase the memory of this embarrassing relation to the body of origin. All to avoid the fact that what really bothers Freud is the potential testimony of the (m)other/woman of the speaking/writing subject (male and female), himself included.

A testimony that appears to break through in the horrendous body/voice of the older/menopausal woman. A horror that Freud, when discussing the myth of the Medusa,[11] again transforms into a visual horror of her lacking organ, rather than noting the powerful similarity of the woman/mother's gaping mouth and deadly gaze with the sexual hole, where the subject originated. The severed Medusa's head was carried by Athena—the motherless daughter of Zeus—on her shield, the terrifying vision of which was supposed to "turn men into stone." Freud gives this again a positive phallic twist, by translating this as "producing an erection," that is, a confirmation of the presence of the male member. An erection under these circumstances might also amount to the emergence of sexual lust for this monster, but Freud's emphasis on the horror of her castration preempts such a connection, which only serves again to repress the generative/sexual power of Woman personi-fied in her open genital/mouth and to reinforce the power of the Phallus.

The importance of the Medusa head lies in the violent patriarchal severance of the seeing/speaking head from the maternal vaginal hole/womb-mouth. This separates the female body/sex from her mind/head, freezes the gaze, and silences the mouth, rendering her sex mute and petrified, open to phallic interpretation. In an uncanny insight, Freud spoke here of "decapitation as castration," though it was not, as he wants to imply, the sexual organ she was symbolically robbed of, but her voice. A capacity for "speaking in tongues," which refers to the female tongue as prophetic, the image of which has strong phallic allusions, is thus pre-vented from occurring. Moreover, literally "losing one's head" also can refer here to the state where the older woman comes face-to-face with a contradiction between her invisible, denigrated position of her body/sex in the culture and her feeling of renewed empowerment of body/mind in herself.

I am therefore arguing here that the myth of the Medusa's head actually rep-resents the murder of the specifically older mother/woman, who would be the only powerful figure in the culture capable of knowingly testifying in her speech to the history of a theft, that of the female body/sex's power for man's purpose. Perhaps his is why she is supposed to be suffering from a dreadful affliction of the brain due to a failing body/sex, her "menopause"! And mother can thus justi-fiably be certified as not being herself today.

Madelon Sprengnether, in her book *The Spectral Mother*[12]—like other femi-nists who are mothers—attempts to displace Freud's phallocentric emphasis on Oedipus (and its psychoanalytic feminist legacies) by including "the mother as an active figure in the process of enculteration." She argues that Freud, in his con-cept of the pre-oedipal mother, who appears to fascinate and repel him, gestures to her central function, but she remains a ghostlike figure because he can never really face her. Sprengnether shows convincingly that Freud repressed the figure of the mother, that linchpin of psychoanalysis, while in his own life the relation to his mother remained the most dominant. However, to reintroduce the (m)other/woman, as Sprengnether does, as this pre-oedipal figure of "enculter-ation," imprisons her again in the spectral service of the child/subject. She may live on as the essential ghost, but she does not come back with a narrative of her own and thus remains locked in a metaphysics of "the body of the (m)other as a carnal metaphor for the fundamental estrangement of Being."[13] Perhaps the older mother/woman's menopausal body carries then the real burden of repre-senting this impossible carnal metaphor in/for the culture as a sort of original sin, the betrayal by death and decay of a beautiful dream of youthful existence in blissful union with that imagined (M)Other.

What is it that makes it necessary to repress the existence of an older body/sex of the (m)other/woman in the history of the feminine in favor of this mythical figure of enculteration of the forever birthing, succoring body/sex of the Mother/Woman for the Subject? Are her speech and presence experienced as a revolt against "the predestined part she had to play" (as Freud called it) in the story of the subject? Is it that her decaying maternal femininity appears to escape our grasp on our eternity held in the comforting guarantee of the archaic spectral (M)Other, and presents us instead with a terrifying historicity of that fantasy we attributed to the child, but which may be our own fear of death?

Mother Death and the Maiden

It is conceivable (a useful pun here) that the idea of the "death of the womb" brings back for all subjects a memory of beginning in that sexed body of the (m)other/woman and introduces a horror of erasure, when this body appears to lose this specific symbolic purpose. In the patriarchal culture, which prefers to forget and no longer can symbolically deal with the fact that all human beings are born of woman, this painful contingency remains represented in the literary deployment of "the mother's body as womb and tomb" for the subject. An eternal return to the maternal body/sex, but, I suggest, dividing the body/sex of Woman in young/womb and old/tomb.

When Freud, always aware of the speaking subject's repression, but less so in himself, speaks of Mother Earth as the last aspect of the tripartite goddess in "The Theme of the Three Caskets,"[14] he evokes the "return" to the mother's body, no longer as birthing body but as disembodied sarcophagus, the entombment of the subject. In discussing the dying King Lear's lament about the loss of the mother and his desire to find solace for this loss in the loving arms of his daughter Cordelia, he remarks that man's relationships to Woman are threefold: she represents "the mother herself, the beloved one who is chosen after her pattern, and lastly the Mother Earth who receives him once more."[15] This threefold image attests to two curious repressions. First, Mother Earth stands in for the relationship to the real older (m)other/woman, to whom the man Freud cannot admit having any significant relation; she is simply excised. From mother/wife we move to the disembodied, symbolic Mother Earth/death. Second, the old man seeks the mother's arms/comfort in the arms of the daughter, who, in a typical incestuous pattern, stands in for the mother/wife of the aging man. In Freud's own familial history this pattern is strikingly evident: he himself admitted that the King Lear/Cordelia saga had personal resonances for him, mirroring his relationship to his second daughter Anna. But he avoided remarking that his mother and his wife, when no longer young, may also have played major, but repressed, parts in this story.

One would have to conclude that the symbolic meaning of woman's body/sex represents an oscillation between embodied youth and disembodied death for the subject. What is presumably too horrid to confront is the older (m)other/woman.

This may be because she is the only one whose power of knowledge is fearsome and who can no longer be trusted to hold her tongue.

The menopausal woman appears to represent the nasty reminder of this sensation for the subject in her very physical presence because of her body/sex, that locus of origin and death for the subject—and because of the knowledge she possesses and wields as a nasty power when she comes to be for herself. Thus, she literally revolts against her male-defined predestiny. Her physical state also revolts against this; she can no longer be assumed to be, not for herself either, as purely body/sex/(m)other. She stops being visible and useful when she arrives at her dreaded state of older woman, where she becomes ungraspable in her turning away from man's purpose. So, she is only allowed to return as a symbol of death and dust, Mother Earth.

The negative cultural image of the menopausal woman appears to be thus not a simple effect of "anophobia" (the term refers to phobia of old age) in the culture, but to have a specific relation to the unconscious meaning of (M)Other/ Woman, and thus there is a different psychical significance in the aging female body from that of older men.

Her symbolic construction as riddled with deteriorating essential functions derives obviously from the fear of the desiring subject, who speaks/writes/signifies Woman for her/himself, for the troubling presence of this female body/sex/mind, which is no longer amenable to maternality. Instead it becomes the harbinger of death, the death of the subject. In propping up her hormonal balance, what is perhaps created is then the unconscious illusion of an eternal virginal maternality (not simply a young sexually attractive body), which helps to stave off the fear of mortality in the subject. This is not an abjection such as Kristeva refers to, that of the unconscious memory of the maternal body for the child as threat to its separate subjecthood, of boundaries that are fuzzed. In Kristeva's theory, all abjection can be related back to the ambivalent attitude of the subject toward this maternal body of infancy.[16] The abject in this definition thus always manifests itself as displacement of the essentially unified unrepresentable pre-oedipal (m)other's body. There is no division in maternality, for which two persona of Mother/Woman stand as model, as I have been arguing for here. This takes no account of the peculiarly objectionable position of the older (m)other/woman, who appears to represent the abjectal *par excellence*, because her body/sex, whose "death" is announced in the "menopause," threatens to undo the certainty of the subject and to announce its finitude.

We find this split of the maternal feminine in the imaginary pre-oedipal (m)other, who functions as the subversive "alter ego" in/of the subject and repulsive older woman/mother, who is identified as abject obstacle to this transgressive desire in the so-called avant garde. In the work of Bataille, Artaud, Mallarme, Lautreamont, and Celine, the writers invoked as emblematic of the transgressive/abject by Kristeva, one can clearly distinguish between the function of the (pre-oedipal) subversive feminine as excess and the abjecting of the reality

encountered in the maternal relation: the former relates to the pleasure of perversity (absurd, scatological, cruel, shocking, etc.), and involves a playing with
the imagined (m)other's body/sex controlled by the subject; while the latter is
experienced as often graphic physical repulsion of the revengeful, dreaded, older
woman/mother, not seldom the writer's own (here Bataille and Artaud especially
come to mind). Equally the concept of "becoming woman" in a deconstructive
postmodern philosophy hinges on the pre-oedipal vivacious (m)other-for-the-
son fantasy, where "she" can bear no recognizable relation to the still living older
(m)other/woman, whose nonauthorized presence/utterance of menopausal
impunity intrudes vehemently in the currently fashionable dream of feminine
engenderment in/of the subject. The abject figure of the older/menopausal
woman relates to the terror in the adult subject of being-in-nothingness, of having no certainty of being, given that her maternality turns out to be of an
unwelcome concreteness and mortality rather than to present an eternal return
to the dream of eternal life of the subject and its (m)other.

Monster in the Mirror

Barbara Creed in her interesting study of the horror movie *The Monstrous
Feminine* argues that Freud obstinately insisted on the female body as castrated,
perhaps because of its actual power of life and death: men fear women's genitals
not because they appear castrated, but because women seem to have a castrating
power.[17] Creed situates this monstrous feminine, following Kristeva's reworking
of psychoanalysis, in the relation to the archaic mother, that dim, pre-oedipal
eternal young mother-of-the-child, who is supposed to threaten our self-certain-
ty. But does this figure not exist to avert our gaze from the really unthinkable
power of the older (m)other for the subject? Does the monstrous feminine of the
horror movie or the evil witch in the fairy tale not show what is at stake, to cover
our murderous tendencies toward the power/knowledge of that difficult and
objectionable older (m)other/woman? Her social status in the culture may no
longer have any credibility, but her recurring appearance as monstrous feminine
carries the mythical memory of her power to know and to exact the debt from
the subject.

    In many ways I agree with the trend of Creed's arguments about the function
of the terrifying female monster in horror movies, but her emphasis on the
"vagina dentata" and the many phallic implements (knives, vampire teeth) as the
manifestations of the castrating force of the monstrous feminine remains curi-
ously locked in a phallocentric reversal. The operation from castrated to
castrating assumes an easy identification with the maternal body for women's
self-perception. It is simply this "monstrous" power that women need to recognize in themselves, which sets them apart from men but in fact plays an equally
phallic role. This sets up an opposition between male fantasies of women's bod-

ies and women's identifications with the monstrous as a sort of archaic female power/knowledge to combat these fantasies. This cannot explain why young women in particular—as viewers of horror movies and murderous female-killer images—regularly opt to side with the slayer of these monsters, and generally express an even greater hatred and disgust for them than do men. To understand this we need to distinguish the maternal body as also (m)other/monster for women, and such a distinction is most pronounced in the relation to the older, menopausal mother, who is perceived as the obstacle for the young woman's self-generation and who has to be vehemently rejected as the Same.

The series of *Alien* films contain the recurring figure of Ripley, the forever ageless female savior who is typically caring; while not embodying maternality, she represents graphically this situation. The dreaded "maternal" monster/alien creature breeder could never be imagined as being the young (m)other/woman. "She" is the sci-fi variation of the evil witch, repulsive to look at and threatening to the young female protagonist and her brothers, who will combat her for mankind, even though in *Aliens 3* Ripley, invaded by the monster, pays the ultimate sacrifice in self-immolation.

Creed's interpretation leaves aside a perhaps more primal horror for both sexes: that of the monstrous (m)other/woman's body/sex as older female, when the subject has already installed itself as origin of its own body/sexuality and has managed to expel the relation to the maternal body. That site in which is combined the imaginary construction of a glorious but insecure event (the birth of the subject)—always already marred by the horrors of the bleeding female body (childbirth with all its blood, gore, shit, piss, etc.) and full of connotations of proximity between life/death, between excrement/birth, between being/nothingness—with that of a joyous excess of sexual pleasure (the "petit mort" of sexual bliss). All in the same body and in the same spot. And it is in the emergence of the older (m)other/woman that we experience the full impact of this monstrous feminine because she personifies this unthinkable combination of sex/life/death/decay in her knowing/speaking/revenging and particularly repulsive subjectivity. This figure directly confronts us as a force of destruction of our hard-won independent subjectivity as women and men, with no redeeming features of a self-sacrificing maternal femininity. If every woman is thus to be viewed as monstrous, it is because that repulsive old hole/mouth represents the unthinkable locus on/in the adult subject's mother's soon-to-be-barren or already barren body/sex. That body/sex is getting older and repulsive, with a frightening hold over the subject's imaginary self-engenderment in difference.

The monstrous older woman, the crazed avenger and destroyer, appears as a special case in Creed's book, with no special bearing on all the other apparitions of the monstrous feminine. Yet I maintain that she is the norm of abjection, of the Woman/Monster, the invader/destroyer of each female and male subject's integrity, who can appear to inhabit/invade a younger woman's (or man's) body as an outside force (cf. *The Exorcist* and *Aliens*). That she is the abjected older (m)other in all her different impersonations of other/woman is evident in our reactions to these figures in mainstream cinema. We experience young vampires as sexually excessive, over-the-top versions of the Sirens, and their murderous tendencies as "in the service of the evil (M)Other," but the monstrous older (m)other/woman in the horror-film (Kathy Bates in *Misery* comes to mind) is in the service of no one but herself, and her target is our sexuality, our very existence.

In the classic Hollywood cinema the evil bitches, murderous avengers, jealous mothers, and mean housekeepers were always played by stars who may have been young but who looked always middle-aged (Bette Davis, Joan Crawford, Barbara Stanwyck, Agnes Moorehead). They personified what we came to repel, that bitch who governed our lives, and she was not meant to be young and vivacious but bitter and twisted. In the modern film *Fatal Attraction*, which clearly has an antifeminist message, Glenn Close is perfectly cast as the destructive force. Close's face has a peculiarly skull-like form, tightly lipped, taut pale skinned, an always already aged and cold face. She seems born 44+, just as Davis and Crawford were. They make their monstrousness believable because they are perfect opposites to the imaginary virginal/innocent, maternal/feminine woman-for-man-and-children. The film *The Handmaid's Tale* presented this opposition between the beautiful Natasha Richardson as a sexual innocent/life-giving young woman and the cold, aging Faye Dunaway as the repulsive, fascist, virago/oppressor of men and women. The film operated also as sci-fi tale to warn against the future of a society ruled by older women (feminists?) as the cruel destroyers of love and life and the real power behind dictatorial order. These women were barren, incapable of giving or caring for life; they only spelled death. The film came closest to the general myth of evil old female power in fairy tales.

Wives' Tales

The legacy of the awesome confrontation with the older (m)other/woman as the knower of and witness to each and every subjectivity, who comes back to exact her price, is thus returning in all those proverbial monsters of the feminine: witches, evil stepmothers, "phallic mothers," and "castrating bitches" who support the fantasy of the feminine as evil force for the subject.

Something of this "monstrous feminine" can erupt in any grown woman: it emerges whenever she revolts against her allotted place and acts as if she is inhabited by an evil force, which turns her into the "biting, hysterical female"; but in those instances, what resonates in her for herself and for others is the older (m)other/woman, the archetype of destruction of our dreams of self-engendered existence, who confronts us with her rage and who has to remain the absolute other to our ego-ideal and to that ideal of "Woman as Man's Other" in the culture. Every woman knows the experience of recognizing "the monster in the mirror," and invariably this connects to the image of the older (m)other/ woman we have come to deny. This "woman" remains (m)other, even though she sometimes invades our own consciousness and seems temporarily to destabilize our difference, as long as we do not bodily and culturally come to occupy her place. That is, until we arrive at menopause ourselves.

The cultural significance of Woman as (M)Other to the Subject is thus divided psychically in an always already absent "real," good (m)other as fictive origin of the speaking/signifying subject and an old, abjectal (m)other who forms the obstacle in her/his path. This is most striking in fairy tales. "Good" mothers are young birthing mothers of innocence, mostly already dead, but generally powerless background figures. Not so the older (m)other/woman, the wicked witch, the evil stepmother, the dragon, the vulture, or the satanic force. She personifies for the young girl the frightful aspect of the power of the maternal as old ogre. Cinderella has an old wicked stepmother with a mean tongue plus two older disgusting stepsisters. She is the pliable, submissive, domesticated, never-talking-back virgin, who will please the prince (there are similarities here with Cordelia in King Lear) and marry him to keep house and to give him babies. The fairy godmother stands in for the lacking, loving mother. Snow White is threatened by a typical menopausal figure, the evil stepmother queen, who mourns her loss of youth and beauty. She is Snow White's rival, not her (good) birthing mother. She possesses the evil power to turn herself into a witch to offer the biblical poisonous apple. The story of Sleeping Beauty is another excellent example of the wrath of the older, (post)menopausal woman, in the figure of the noninvited evil godmother, who in her disguise as spinner brings about the girl's hundred-year sleep. Hansel and Gretel almost meet a sticky end in the hands—or rather mouth/body—of the evil witch.

In her book *From the Beast to the Blonde*, an extensive study of fairy tales, Marina Warner attributes the recurring figure of older gruesome woman, who is not the subject's birthing mother, to the fact that the mother-in-law often lived in and ruled the young mother/woman's household.[18] She argues that old women told fairy tales with "bad mother" figures to small children as a sort of "getting back" at the child's mother, an allegiance between grandmother and child against the power of the mother, which should be seen as an obstacle to the development and integrity of the subject. This sociological explanation of adult power relations as source for fairy tales may well be pertinent, because the tales seem to prefigure what will appear to be realized in the confrontation in the young adult's life with this ogre in the person of his/her menopausal (m)other/woman, who, just as in the fairy tale, prohibits the subject's free development with her mean behavior. My argument that it is the troubling presence of the older (m)other/woman that has to be averted by constructing fairy tales of the illegitimate, monstrous power of the female body/sex, including the fairy tale of psychoanalysis, seems to be supported here.

"Menopause": An Ending or a Beginning?

There is no doubt that these abjectal personae in horror films, fairy tales, Greek mythology, and psychoanalysis are to be thought as females of an older generation, and that they are characterized by possessing terrifying, destructive, and secretive knowledge/power. The old (m)other/woman speaks as the knowing subject bearing the truth of descent and affiliation in the sexed body of Woman. In the orally dependent culture, this amounted in all probability to a public and private authoritative power of the older mother/woman, which presumably was individually and collectively experienced as truly awesome, particularly by young women.

The processes and expressions of menopause, leading as they do to the status of old, nonreproductive, no longer "contaminated/contaminating" woman would in traditional orally organized cultures be connected to and received as a "coming to power" of a woman. Cessation of monthly bleeding, the end of the body as reproductive receptacle, coupled with changes in consciousness would then have distinctive psycho/sexual ramifications for the individual woman and for the social group. The reproductive center of the woman's body, as it were, moves from the genital region to the cerebral domain. In her body/sex are combined a mental maturity, that is, a profound experiential knowledge about life and death as a bodily and social experience (characterizing her domineering dealings with her sons and daughters) meshed with a psychological liberation from the recurring physiological ramifications (reproduction/sexual submission) of her body. This allows her, as a woman, to attain the sacred or the universal (to speak with Hegel), not by transcending the body but actually by uniting body/mind as transition, while holding in that unity as consciousness the secret of the continuation of the social group.

There is an interesting archaic representation of this in the Kerch figurines, gnarled, bald, and toothless, naked hags with heavily pregnant bellies, which Bahktin mentions as an example of the grotesque.[19] For Bahktin and others these figures are grotesque because of their sexual anomaly; their monstrousness consists in the abnormal, transgressive visual combination of old age and reproductive capacity.[20] Though they may have been images of what would nowadays be gynecological excesses (the uterus of old, postmenopausal women can sometimes develop benign growths, which in older days, when not removed, grew to giant proportions, producing an image of a very old woman with a pregnant belly), these freak occurrences seem to function as exceptional, mystical expressions of superior female magic and creativity. These statuettes carry a very evident reference to a continual life-spirit in the female body, which grows in and remains with the woman, possibly endowing her literally with sacred power, because her "spirit-child" never gets separated from its force, the woman's body. In this way they may have warded off the fear of the death of the female reproductive body for the subject, and combined in their anomalous presence a sacred coupling of life/death, reproduction/wisdom. Their function might thus be that adult subjects will continue to respect the old mothers/women as regenerative forces, who while no longer reproductive ensure the cohesive continuity for/in the social group through their spiritually "pregnant" bodies.

We have lost such a connection to the maternal feminine body of the older woman in the culture, but there is no doubt that the revolting body/sex of the menopausal woman keeps coming back to haunt us with the impossibility of her body/sex, which seems to indicate that there is life "beyond the phallus." Perhaps that is the meaning of the wide, toothless grin on my beloved Balinese Kerch figurine's face: the last laugh is from the older (m)other/woman.

Notes

1. G. Greer, *The Change: Women, Ageing and the Menopause* (London: Hamish Hamilton, 1991).

2. A. Rich, *Of Woman Born: Motherhood as Experience and Institution* (London: Virago, 1977), p. 284.

3. J. Kristeva, "Women's Time," in *The Kristeva Reader*, ed. Toril Moi (Oxford: Basil Blackwell, 1986), pp. 187–213.

4. Greer, *The Change*, p. 136.

5. S. Freud, *The Penguin Freud Library* (Middlesex: Penguin, 1990).

6. M. Whitford, ed., *The Irigaray Reader* (Oxford: Basil Blackwell, 1991); Toril Moi, ed., *Kristeva Reader*; N. Chodorow, *The Reproduction of Mothering* (Berkeley: University of California Press, 1978); J. Benjamin, *The Bonds of Love: Psychoanalysis, Feminism and The Problem of Domination* (New York: Pantheon Books, 1988).

7. S. Freud, "The Interpretation of Dreams," in *Penguin Freud*, no.4, pp. 363–66.

8. Though he mentions in *The Psychopathology of Everyday Life*, in passing, "the strange fact that the [Oedipus] legend finds nothing objectionable in Queen Jocasta's age." "The Psychopathology of Everyday Life," in *Penguin Freud*, no. 5, p. 232.

9. S. Freud, "Analysis of a Phobia in a Five-Year-Old Boy," in *Penguin Freud*, no. 8, pp. 169–305.

10. S. Freud, "Totem and Taboo," in *Penguin Freud*, no. 13, pp. 53–159.

11. S. Freud, "The Medusa's Head," in *Standard Edition of Complete Psychological Works of Sigmund Freud*, ed. J. Strachey (London: Hogarth Press, 1974), vol. 18, pp. 273–74.

12. M. Sprengnether, *The Spectral Mother: Freud, Feminism and Psychoanalysis* (Ithaca, NY: Cornell University Press, 1990), p. xi.

13. Ibid., p. 243.

14. S. Freud, "The Theme of the Three Caskets," in *Penguin Freud*, no. 14, pp. 233–47.

15. Ibid., p. 247.

16. J. Kristeva, *The Powers of Horror: An Essay on Abjection* (New York: Columbia University Press, 1982).

17. B. Creed, *The Monstrous Feminine: Film, Feminism, Psychoanalysis* (New York: Routledge, 1993).

18. M. Warner, *From the Beast to the Blonde: On Fairytales and their Tellers* (London: Chatto & Windus, 1994).

19. M. Bahktin, *Rabelais and his World* (Bloomington: Indiana University Press, 1984), pp. 25–26.

20. Bahktin uses the image of the Kerch for entirely metaphorical degendered purposes as model for the future body politic, repressing of course its corporeal and gendered signification for the sexes.

6

Resisting Pathologies of Age and Race

*Menopause and Cosmetic Surgery
in Films by Rainer and Tom*

E. Ann Kaplan

> *A man's as old as he feels
> A woman as old as she looks.*
> —Mortimer Collins (1812–1867)

> *What's a man's age? He must hurry more,
> that's all. Cram in a day what his youth
> took a year to hold.*
> —Robert Browning (1812–1889)

> *A man has every season while a woman
> only has the right to spring.
> That disgusts me.*
> —Jane Fonda, 1989

Introduction: Science, "Nation," and the Body

In the course of researching medical handbooks on cosmetic surgery and looking for information about such surgery in nonwhite patients, something unexpected emerged: Both the occidental eye and the aged eye were categorized as having the same "fault" in relation to the western Caucasian standard being used to judge eyes. Significantly, the eye appears as the crucial location for producing and maintaining both cultural/ethnic and young/old difference. For Richard J. Siegel, in his *Aesthetic Plastic Surgery: Principles and Techniques*, the "aging" and the Oriental are combined as the markers of "deformity" and "pathology" concerning the aesthetic of the eyelids. His description of what happens to the eyelid over the course of life strangely prefigures what he will say about the Oriental eye. Meanwhile, not incidentally it seems, Blair O. Rogers begins his brief "History of the Development of Aesthetic Surgery" with a quotation from *Henry IV* in which, he says, Shakespeare "described all too accurately for posterity those bodily changes that daily bring the suffering patient to the office of modern aesthetic surgeons." Summarizing the quotation, he notes that "Yellow cheeks, double chins, pendulous abdomens—the despised signs of ageing—form an unwelcome contrast to the smooth physiognomy of youth." But he continues, significantly, to say that these *"are easily removed by modern aesthetic operations"* (emphasis mine).[1] Rogers apparently accepts uncritically the use of the youthful Caucasian as the standard of aesthetic value, and measures all other positions from that one standard. Nonwhite and aged women both offend white culture because (for different reasons) they are not able to conform to the ideal standard for what counts as beautiful in dominant culture.

Implicit in the discourses just noted is the mythic "nation"-construct that Science so easily conjures from a white patriarchal position. I will shortly show that Hollywood, like Science, relies upon a similar mythic nation-construct that marginalizes women, the aging, and nonwhite peoples. The problematic relation of "woman" to "nation" is often overlooked in discussions of nationality and nationhood,[2] and urgently needs more research. Benedict Anderson's idea of "nation" as an imaginary construct[3] at least opens up a space for thinking about the relations between the categories "woman" and "nation"—categories with particular impact if one is an immigrant or a nonwhite woman. Anderson is one of the few theorists of nationalism who acknowledges the level of "the overwhelming burden of human suffering—disease, mutilation, grief, age, and death."[4] He points out that the questions people ask—"Why was I born blind? Why is my best friend paralyzed?"[5]—were answered by the great religions. Once these began to ebb, Anderson argues that another form of continuity was needed, and as part of that need the concept of nation began to develop.

However this may be, it is clear that while nation may begin to solve some men's needs for belonging and for recognition, the concept does little for women, on whom devolved the level of human suffering while (largely white) males (including scientists and Hollywood studio heads) were out making money[6] and expanding and defending their nation's resources and science discoveries.[7] It is important for what follows to note that implicit in formulations of science, nation, and Hollywood are ideas of the "normative" gendered body. Assumed "norms" for health (physical and mental) are in fact specifically western as I argue below.

In order to explore the impact of these parallel marginalizations (nonwhite/aged) on women, and the implications of their linked (but varied) *difference* from the dominant white/youth norms, I look at two films by independent women directors. In Pam Tom's *Two Lies*, I focus on the story of bodily self-fashioning by a Chinese woman to correct "hidden" eyelids (even this phrasing suggests the western eyelid as the norm); in Yvonne Rainer's *Privilege*, I focus on the words of black and white women interviewed in the film to tease out underlying conceptions of subjectivities struggling against prevailing norms of "age as decline" in the context of racism and class privilege. But before turning to Tom and Rainer, I review briefly differing constructs of aging for males and for females and Hollywood's marginalizing of aging females.

Hollywood and Contrasting Male and Female Constructs of "Aging"

In western cultures, menopause is often termed, colloquially, "a change of life." What it actually connotes is a change from being a reproductive to a *nonproductive* human. Males in western culture have constructed things so that they do not have an analogous so-called change of life, and they are seen to continue to be productive as they age. There is no specific marking of aging for them, no symbolic change from "useful" to "no-longer useful." Rather, some of the greatest epics and mature works by male artists (e.g., *King Lear*; Kurosawa's *Ran*) have featured the reluctance of aged males to relinquish their powers (see also Peter Yates's 1983 film *The Dresser*, based on the life of actor Donald Wolfit). The very concept of the "Lion in Winter" suggests virility, power, endurance into age for men, who basically continue to dominate until they die on the job.[8]

It is remarkable that concepts of menopausal women have somehow remained unchanged in the cultural unconscious despite the changes that feminism(s) have managed to produce regarding other kinds of female stereotypes. How is it that biological concepts regarding women's no longer menstruating at a certain point—concepts perhaps fitted to a much earlier phase of human society—are still active today? One has only to recall the horror at a British menopausal woman managing to conceive and give birth thanks to new birth technologies to glimpse the depth of stereotypes about woman and her "change of life."

An analogous sign of the cultural unconscious about menopausal women in the United States is the anathema of Hollywood (and of most popular culture) toward the subject. Commercial films about menopausal women? Inconceivable, almost. Like minorities, older women have traditionally been relegated to the fringes of classical narratives (viz. Lillian Gish's mother, imaged as white haired, chair-ridden, and beshawled in Griffith's *Way Down East*, even though her daughter is only sixteen years old or so!). If more active in the narrative than this mother, older women have traditionally only figured in Hollywood as "witches" in melodramas about mothers and daughters (e.g., Gladys Young in King Vidor's *Stella Dallas* [1937]; Bette Davis in *Little Foxes* [1946]).

Given that America's population is aging and creating a potential audience for films about old people, old age became a sentimental theme in a few commercial films in the 1980s and 1990s. The trend began with the success of *On Golden Pond*

(1983), continued with *Driving Miss Daisy* (1990), and focused on men in *Grumpy Old Men* (1993). The first two films were carried by the superb acting and long-standing fame of the female protagonists (Katharine Hepburn and Jessica Tandy), while *Grumpy Old Men*, starring two famous male actors (Jack Lemmon and Walter Matthau), develops into the story of how "old men" can indeed still be sexy. Jack Lemmon is rejuvenated by making love to Ann Margret (who wouldn't be?), herself looking not a day older than forty. As Jean Kozlowski points out, male stars' sexiness "can be stretched into a fantasy of ageless sexual potency,"[9] while women stars are summarily dismissed from sexy roles on the screen after menopause. In Kozlowski's words, "Movies tend to give us only an abrupt shove from cute ingenue to weird old crone."[10]

Popular culture, then, has no category for women in between sexy youth or young motherhood, on the one hand, and "old women," represented as tired, bitter, evil, or jealous, on the other.[11] The realities of menopause for women vary like anything else, but the cinema cries out not only for new images but also for making menopause visible in the first place and invisible in the second, as will be clear below.

Two recent mother-daughter films starring Shirley MacLaine, *Terms of Endearment* (1986) and *Postcards from the Edge* (1990), do begin at least to address

Walter Matthau and Jack Lemmon, sporting the phallic fish, prove their virility by carrying on a long-standing feud, that erupts daily over ordinary events. It gets earnest when they have to compete for Ann-Margret's sexual favors.

issues of aging women, even if they are unable to move beyond the binaries just noted. In her justified rage at the double standard for male and female stars, Kozlowski perhaps fails to recognize the limited advance that MacLaine's films represent. *Terms of Endearment* confronts the so-called empty-nest syndrome of menopausal women and the frequent overdependence of older mothers on their married daughters. But in portraying MacLaine as romantically involved with Jack Nicholson, the film provides images of older women being sexual, even if not entirely successfully.

Postcards from the Edge also addresses issues of aging, even if only within the terms of dominant discourses. The film assumes that older women *should* cede the ground to the younger in its story of competition between mother/daughter stars, loosely based on Carrie Fisher's struggles with her mother, Debbie Reynolds. Within this discourse, *Postcards* shows the difficulty for the narcissistic but, significantly, not evil mother (played by MacLaine) to recognize that she is aging, that she is losing her beauty, and that it is time to cede center stage to her daughter. The film is also about how the daughter (played by Meryl Streep) learns to empathize with her mother's aging difficulties and her need to be the center of attention. The scene in the hospital after MacLaine's accident captures Streep's growing ability to help her mother through this stage of life: Streep finds her mother looking weary and plain without her wig and make-up; Streep pulls out her cosmetics and gradually constructs MacLaine's image for her so that she can go out and face the reporters.

While the film does insist on father and lover figures to help Streep along and to provide the film's mandated heterosexual coupling at the end, Streep is also allowed to be a successful film star. In the concluding scene, her mother looks on with generative pleasure rather than with competitive jealousy.

These examples represent the standard Hollywood portrayal of "older" women. Most Hollywood films do not do more than allow women vicarious identification with some of the suffering that the male narrative of women's aging imposes. That is, these films offer images of women resisting aging and the required relinquishing of control over daughters; but they have to learn to "give up" gracefully. Neither film moves beyond the narrative that male culture has imposed on older women to move on to new goals and challenges.[12]

The rare films that seem to provide satisfying glimpses of menopausal women surviving aging without turning to men (viz. *Shirley Valentine* and *Fried Green Tomatoes*) only prove the hunger for such images. The first film traces the movement of the heroine from being an abused menopausal wife in a stifling British lower-middle-class environment to a woman who finds autonomy and refinds her youthful, somewhat rebellious self, by staying on a Greek island after her (already daring) vacation there with a woman friend. In *Fried Green Tomatoes* the heroine Evelyn befriends an eighty-year-old woman in a nursing home and learns how to deal with menopause, self-deprecation, and a sexless marriage through the inspiring story that the old woman tells her about a past event of

Shirley MacLaine as usual makes herself the center of attention when ostensibly helping her daughter (played by Meryl Streep) undergoing rehabilitation early in the film.

Menopausal Pauline Collins finally confronts her tyrannical husband (Bernard Hill) who is furious because she altered the weekly menu for their evening meal. This "last straw" episode confirms her decision to take off with a friend to a Greek island where she finds romance and a new life.

Jessica Tandy as Ninny Threadgood inspires menopausal Evelyn Couch (played by Kathy Bates) to struggle for autonomy from a domineering husband and to take care of herself.

two brave young women struggling for autonomy from abusive men. In one inspiring scene, after being beaten out of a parking space by two young flashy women, Amanda deliberately bangs into their spunky sports car and declares (seeing their horrified faces): "Face it girls. I'm older and I got more insurance." There is a need for films that actually confront in their narratives, as these do, the male discourse of women's aging as "decline" and uselessness.

Ethnicity/Aging, "Nation," and Bodily Self-fashioning

Analogous marginalizations and even worse stereotyping exist in dominant cinema's portrayal of U.S. minorities. Since such stereotypes have been extensively studied in general,[13] I need not elaborate here. Important for my purposes (and much less studied by film scholars) is that both aging and minority women may turn to bodily self-fashioning partly in order to avoid the marginalizing that being ethnically Other or an aging female may bring in American culture. Issues are exacerbated in the case of the diasporan female in the United States, who may have little sense of belonging to the *actual* national community within which she finds herself and yet who may have traveled to America in pursuit of the "American Dream." Such women travel with an imaginary, glamorous "America" in mind, which has to do with supposed economic and social opportunities, "freedom" (especially from oppressive patriarchal marital traditions), and pleasures of the kind American popular culture images. Realities of life in America often fail to live up to the imaginary, so that some internal negotiation has to take place.

As a result of not being included in the category "nation," women have traditionally worked these relations through the cultural sphere. Culturally "between nations," women are pushed and pulled by diverging sets of cultural/personal loyalties (viz. *The Joy Luck Club*). The intense needs of many women to please and to belong to various nation-groups make conflict inevitable. These needs, in turn, may render diasporan women especially vulnerable to the desire to normalize their appearances—a desire that also affects older white and black women.

In all cases, issues linked to those of "passing" (which normally refers to black women trying to "pass" as white) emerge: cosmetic surgery to "correct" eyelids or other parts of the face or body, or to "correct" wrinkles, lines and sagging skin, may be seen as trying to pass for a Caucasian woman or for a younger woman.[14] In the latter case, the effort is to restore something seen as lost through aging or to return to an earlier time. Similarly, "hormone replacement therapy" (HRT) seeks to return the menopausal woman to her premenopausal condition, complete with periods and a hormone cycle already biologically ended. One might view the search to replace what is lost or ended as a denial of the passage of time; a refusal to recognize the passage of time; a violation of the "natural" biological process. Alternatively, one could argue that the restoring, replacing, returning processes work in the service of resisting age as decline, disease, deterioration. One should not too readily adopt a moralizing stance toward restoring or normalizing efforts because such moralizing ends up essentializing the body as a biological entity that must "naturally" age.[15] The refusal of age as decline, as Friedan has argued, is in general admirable and essential.

However, the *commodification of a woman's desire to avoid age as decline* through commercial pressure, advertising, and debasement of the aging body *does* have to be taken into account. Given that American culture values youth over age, and that sight has priority over other senses, Woodward notes that "it should come as no surprise to us that representations of the ageing body are constructed primarily in terms of visual appearance."[16] Cosmetics and cosmetic surgery have long been promoted in popular women's journals and magazines as the panacea against aging—that is, against the "decline" and "deterioration" that the West characterizes as aging. But feminists have exposed the large profits accruing to the business and medical establishments through exploiting women's vulnerabilities.[17] Feminists have, in addition, dealt with the philosophical and political issues at stake.[18] I argue that taken in and of itself, bodily self-fashioning is neither good nor bad, although I also deplore the commodification of women's bodies by corporate interests: it comes down to *how* one goes about doing it, within what contexts, for what specific ends.

Interestingly, few Hollywood films have made stories explicitly about cosmetic surgery—except as it figures in crime genres when people (usually men) seek facial disguise (see *Dark Passage* [1947], *Let 'Em Have It* [1935], or *Dick Tracy* [1990]) or in stories about traumatic accidents.[19]

Yet in one sense every film is an advertisement for cosmetics and cosmetic surgery through the larger-than-life close-ups of flawless women's faces with perfect skin perfect features. These reinforce the imaginary ideal in every female spectator who longs to look like these celluloid women. Films dealing with cosmetic surgery and menopause realistically, from female perspectives, and taking in far more than just worries about the body's exterior[20] will not be financed by Hollywood and so must be made independently.

Bodily Self-fashioning in Pam Tom's *Two Lies*

"Authenticity" versus "Assimilation"

Pam Tom's *Two Lies* (1989), about a Chinese mother who opts for plastic surgery to "correct" her hidden eyelids, and Yvonne Rainer's *Privilege* (1990), about women's reactions to, and experiences of, menopause, address the pressures on minority and aging women to conform to the white youthful Hollywood ideal within complex narratives that also deal with racism and class.

Within the many complex issues in Pam Tom's *Two Lies*, I will here address just one, namely, the mother (Doris's) plastic eye-surgery and the issues of ethnic identity (linked to issues of nation)[21] it raises for Doris's daughter, Mei Lin, given her ambivalent relationship to Doris. I use Mei Lin's concern with Doris's eye-surgery to move out from the film to look more closely at the scientific discourse Mei Lin turns to in order to understand what is being done to her mother's body. The cosmetic surgery discourse assumes a politics of *assimilation* (i.e., the politics of diasporan groups wanting quickly to become Americanized) that in turn produces for Mei Lin its binary (opposing) discourse of *authenticity*. I'll argue that the film turns on this binary between assimilation and authenticity, which it arguably problematizes (through the mother/daughter tensions and the subtle shifts in position each woman undergoes), if it is unable to move beyond. I will argue that in the end the film shifts from Mei Lin's moralizing (and essentializing) view of self-fashioning as inauthentic to an understanding of the body as something available for change, not as something fixed, impermeable, rigid.

In the immigrant context of Tom's film, the politics of cosmetic eye-surgery (cutting the body) is approached through mother-daughter symbiosis or double identification. Mei at once overidentifies with her mother in relation to the surgery (viz. her obsession with the plastic surgery book) and rejects her mother for changing herself. The Lacanian cutting of the mother-daughter dyad, then, offers one level on which the literal cutting of the body reverberates: For the daughter to become a subject, she must reject her Mother, cut herself free, as it were, and enter the Symbolic—particularly since this mother, like many, tries to keep her child down with her in the Imaginary. Mei uses language, narration, precisely to release herself from the Imaginary Mother.

At appropriate moments during the film, Mei Lin and her sister, Esther, are seen preoccupied with their projects: Esther's is always that of building an Indian Pueblo (her current school assignment), Mei Lin's a book on plastic surgery in nonwhite patients. The two projects, constantly juxtaposed in the same image, suggest the two daughters' different ways of coping with being "different": Esther by identifying with another oppressed minority; Mei Lin by trying to learn what was done to her mother's eyes as a way of dealing with the uncertainty about her self image that her mother's surgery has produced.

That Mei Lin is working with a politics of authenticity is perhaps most explicit in the visit to the American Indian Pueblo. She is disgusted to discover the inauthenticity of the Pueblo (a house built by a man from Boston for his crazy wife) and takes further umbrage when she learns that the wife, Portia, used to dress in a kimono and coolie hat and became known downtown as "China Doll." The heady mixture of exotica without knowledge of origins outrages Mei, and here, as in the comments of the men Doris dates, Edward Said's *Orientalism*[22] may be seen enacted (and possibly deliberately referenced by the filmmaker).

Yet Mei herself seems very much part of a process of assimilation along with her mother. (How can it be otherwise, given that the family lives in the United States and the children attend American schools? This is a choice Doris had doubts about: "I should have kept you in Chinese school where you would have learned respect.") Yet for Mei, Doris's "two eyes" are "two lies," presumably because the change makes them not authentically Chinese anymore.

Mei has both fear and fascination regarding her mother's change; but the ideology of the assumed normative western face—and the plastic surgeons' assumptions about what beauty in a face is—must be clear to a woman who is reading a plastic surgery book. Mei Lin's repressed wish to have her eyes cut also, together with her fear of and fascination with her mother's mature sexuality, is obvious in the scene at a swimming pool in the motel that the family stop at on their way to the Indian Pueblo. In this scene, both Mei Lin and Esther are rejected because of their Chinese features: Mei Lin is passed over for another, a white woman; while Esther's eyes and language are ridiculed by the little girl who mimics her in a derogatory way. Mei Lin also has to hear her mother's flirting while not being able to attract anyone to herself.

It is following this episode, in the repetition in the motel of the scene in the family's flat, that some extended attention is paid to the plastic surgery book that Mei turns to, assuming that her mother is trying to assimilate or to get "the American look"—an idea that, as we've seen, Mei Lin has contradictory responses to.

As noted, scientific discourse is inserted in the film in the role of providing information for Mei Lin as she seeks to understand, and to relate to, her mother's operation. This is a common way that science is turned to when people have to undergo surgery or a loved one has such surgery. It is a way of gaining some

control over what is going on in the face of feeling powerless. It is a way of gaining some authority in a situation where one has very little or none. That is,
scientific discourse assumes the position of the "subject presumed to know," the
subject we can depend upon to clarify through diagrams, description, logic, and
order exactly what is going on. Such reasoned, apparently empirical, discourse
wards off fears of the unknown, of what one has never experienced. It lessens the
sense of the uncanny as one faces the unknown, where we have no fixed psychic
points to rely on,[23] so that one gladly accepts scientific authority.

Scientific Cosmetic Surgery Discourse

The authority of science is not commented upon in this text, as it will be in
Rainer's film, since the film's perspective remains close to Mei's consciousness,
and she is not in a position to take note of such issues. However, she does object
deeply to the surgery, as in her hostile comment to her mother, "Two eyes, two
lies," implying that Doris's operation is making her "inauthentic," that she
appears to be reneging on her Chinese heritage in order to get the American
look. I want to move away from the film briefly to look at plastic surgery discourse to explore how far that discourse does make assumptions about eye shape,
beauty, and an "American" look, and to explore the assumption of the desire of
nonwhite Americans to assimilate to the American bodily norm.

The film inserts discourses about surgery directly in repeated scenes where
the spectator is shown close-ups of pictures—in all their ugly details of the
required cuts—in the book on plastic surgery that Mei is reading, presumably so
as to know more about what has happened to her mother.[24] The book the film
features has a chapter on plastic surgery in nonwhite patients, but that's all we
know. I decided to see how far plastic surgery books, articles, or manuals paid
attention to cultural difference, and how far a white norm was assumed. I began
with a 1936 book on plastic surgery by Maxwell Maltz and found that it briefly
alludes to issues of race, although still in the patronizing, "colonialist," nineteenth-century manner. Indeed, Maltz's book shows his broad liberal learning,
since Maltz situates each kind of cosmetic surgery in its historical context.
History of cosmetic surgery is important, as it provides information about past
discourses as they influence and determine current ones as well as enables insight
into how current discourses depart from past ones for cultural/social reasons.[25] In
addition, Maltz is familiar with Adler's social theories about the results of undesirable pressures on people to conform (the "assimilation" discourse, again).

In the chapter on the mouth, instead of an historical prelude, Maltz turns to
anthropology and notes the cultural context of standards of beauty. "To
Americans," he says, "a protruding lip does not seem beautiful, but standards of
comeliness vary with geography. We, for instance, would consider the lips of the
tribesmen of remote Kyra Be, who live on the Bahr Keita River, in Bangassou,

Africa, quite heavy and pendulous. But the natives have quite a different standard of lip beauty." The text is accompanied by an extraordinary photo of women with these lips, with the caption "Lips of savages in remote Kyra Be (Africa)."[26] The photo, while pretending to be "factual," cannot help but evoke complex, even negative, responses in the exaggeration of the case that Maltz has chosen. In another part of the book, Maltz discusses the ways in which Mayan women press their babies' heads in boards so as to produce the elongated shape the Mayans consider beautiful.

This complicated nineteenth-century-style anthropological reflection upon different beauty standards is problematic. But contemporary books on cosmetic surgery and the medical handbooks often ignore issues of cultural difference altogether. In a recent handbook, for instance, the section on "Evaluation of Facial Skeletal Aesthetics and Surgical Planning" relies heavily on work done by L. G. Farkas, I. Munro, and J. Kolar on "The Validity of Neo-Classical Facial Proportion Canons."[27] Without rehearsing the arguments for the clinical plastic surgeons being addressed in the handbook, the authors proceed to "formulate a system of aesthetic facial form analysis," in which "recognition of what constitutes a 'normal face' is paramount."[28] They note that "the key to facial form analysis lies in the ability to analyze each region (upper face, mid-face, and lower face) separately with regard to both form and symmetry and to relate the sum of the parts to the whole,"[29] and a drawing of a Caucasian face with the ideal proportions accompanies the text. Throughout the article, the drawings are of white faces with blonde hair.[30]

Implicitly, such texts construct a discourse of assimilation—the other side of the politics of authenticity. This construction is made explicit in Francis Macgregor's 1984 book on *Transformation and Identity: The Face and Plastic Surgery*. He claims that a frequently stated motivation for surgery is to obtain the "American look," noting that:

> Reducing visibility by changing names or by altering physical appearance for the purpose of eliminating characteristics that set one apart from others is of particular interest . . . for insight these types of behavior may provide into . . . assimilation, stereotypes, identification and conformity. In the case of immigrant and minority groups in the USA both methods have been employed to aid assimilation and adjust to dominant culture. For example . . . Negroes have long used skin-whiteners and hair straighteners whereas American Indian and Asian women, by permanent waves, seek to correct straight hair. Steps are taken to reduce "differentness" by disguising traits that in an Anglo American society are familiar clues to group identity.[31]

Macgregor goes on to discuss cosmetic rhinoplasty to reshape noses that have symbolic significance. He attributes this to "the heavy pressure that society brings to bear on its members to conform to 'the American look.'"[32]

My research into plastic surgery discourses by western medical establishments showed that many of these construct such fears and desires of Asian women in order then to argue for catering to them. Nowhere in the materials does the reader find the voices of the women themselves, articulating their wishes and desires. The most obvious case is Richard J. Siegel's "Advanced Blepharoplasty"—this latter word meaning the removal of excess skin, muscle, and/or fat in order to produce a "fold" in the eyelid—in his *Aesthetic Plastic Surgery: Principles and Techniques.* As noted at the start of my discussion, for Siegel, the aging and the Oriental are combined as the markers of "deformity" and "pathology" concerning the aesthetic of the eyelids: he describes the Oriental eye in the same terms he uses for changes in the eyelid over the life course. The use of the youthful Caucasian as the standard of aesthetic value means that all other positions will be measured from that one standard.[33]

It is difficult to separate these discourses from early anthropological ones about the "races" of "mankind" (legacies of "research" of the 1920s and 1930s).[34] That is, as already indicated and as developed below, plastic surgeons use the white Caucasian race and its notion of renaissance (and Greek-derived) aesthetic form as the standard for what a "beautiful" face is, with an assumption that the white race is the "superior" one.

Given this remaining, if repressed, discourse, some immigrants may indeed be especially vulnerable to the symbolism of the perfect Caucasian body—a body touted in ads and the media as truly *American.* The film *Two Lies,* in its usual economic, understated manner, suggests the power of media images—as well as the example that ethnic media stars may exert on women from the same groups—viz. in the shots where we see behind the daughters a TV set with anchorwoman Connie Chung, whose eye surgery was much discussed by journalists as linked to assimilation and to her desire to be desirable in white terms.[35]

It is the absence of awareness of the cultural specificity of these "norms" in plastic surgery handbooks, and their obvious Eurocentrism (as in the Siegel volume discussed earlier) that troubles me, not the fact that for a given culture certain norms prevail for historical and other reasons. As a culture changes with new immigrants, however, so the norms should be opened out—something that seems to happen in the United States only with great difficulty.[36] Our research found that most Eurocentric authors characterize Asians seeking aesthetic eye surgery as pursuing "occidentalization" or "westernization." Patients' motivations are seen as a movement toward the West rather than as pursuing a conception of beauty specific to another culture. The case for the latter motivation we found only appeared in essays where authors were familiar with nonwestern thinking. Don Liu, for instance, urges surgeons to avoid "using terms such as 'correction, revision or Westernization' of Oriental eyelids," and notes that "in the Orient, an eyelid that has no crease is termed a *single eyelid,* and an eyelid with a crease, a *double eyelid.*"[37] In a rare volume devoted to *The Unfavorable Result in Plastic Surgery,* Yoshio Hiraga and Seiichi Ohmori suggest

The film suggests the power of media images through the example ethnic media stars may exert on women from the same groups. Here Mei Lin pores through plastic surgery volumes while Connie Chung's image is on the TV.

that a particular form of nonwestern beauty is being sought, namely "to fashion the double eyelids of the ideal oriental beauty."[38] The idea that women in the diaspora may well have their own reasons for undergoing plastic surgery is something mainstream western science is too arrogant to consider. Nevertheless, since the pressures on non-European women are heavy, women may rationalize as fitting their own cultural norms what are in fact western ideals.[39]

Menopause, Race, and Aging in Rainer's *Privilege*

Pressures on aging women to conform to the white youthful standard are also severe, and are also exploited by surgeons as seen in Rogers' earlier comment that signs of aging "are easily removed by modern aesthetic operations." Just as Tom's film begins to open up issues regarding cosmetic surgery in non-European women, so Yvonne Rainer's *Privilege* opens up the stereotypes of aging women and the pervasive paradigms about aging.

Rainer's film, much longer than Tom's, also takes up many complex issues, interweaving them with the main story about menopause to create a rich tapestry of interlinked perspectives and problems. My task here is to disentangle just the main thread relating to menopause, although the more I tried to do this, the more I found that this thread was so closely interwoven with others (that is Rainer's triumph, one might say) that it was nearly impossible to separate it out. For reasons of space and coherence, however, I will make an effort to show the film's contributions to discussions of menopause. I will focus especially on how Rainer exposes the disjuncture between prevailing cultural and medical menopause discourses and women's personal experiences, and also on how Rainer opens up the discussion of menopause to include black women.

Since Rainer made her film, Betty Friedan has summarized biases against menopausal women in popular journalism, advertising, and the media.[40] While Rainer's film, like Friedan's book, includes interviews with menopausal women about the experience itself, Rainer follows a less traditional narrative format: recitation is combined with re-enactment of subjects' remembered past events; documentary-style interviews mix with fictional modes; and bodies and voices are jumbled Brechtian style so as to provoke the spectator out of her would-be cinematic "spell" into the shock of recognition, or what has been called a kind of "catharsis." *Privilege* explores menopausal subjectivities from a variety of positions, deliberately displacing image/body and sound so as to refuse assigning any easy essentialism to menopausal women while at the same time invalidating dominating discourses. Sometimes, Rainer turns off the sound of an interviewee's voice, and inserts sounds from overlapping scenes; often, she intercuts within a sequence an image of Jenny as Jenny imagines herself, or she inserts a video image of another interview from one of her other films, disrupting and foregrounding the "documentary" interview through this sliding and slipping of subjects.

But the main way Rainer complicates and deepens her story about menopause is the strategy of a film-within-a-film. Rainer invents an Yvonne Washington (YW), a black filmmaker producing a documentary about menopause, who, as it were, takes over from the film persona, "Yvonne Rainer" (YR). This image of a menopausal black woman with agency, authority, and control reverses in one image prior Hollywood stereotypes of passive, invisible, infantilized black women, and of witchlike, evil, or "declining" menopausal women. It is YW's animated, teasing interview with Jenny that provides the main focus of the film. Within this "documentary," there is an extended and repeated flashback, which YW provokes in Jenny (who, to complicate further the relay of personas, "stands in" for Rainer and one version of some events in Rainer's past).[41]

Meanwhile, YW's film is framed by YR's "film," in which her cinematic persona also interviews women about menopause. Rainer intercuts citations of other women, like Helen Caldicott, talking about feminism in 1986, and there is also a prolonged monologue by film persona "Rainer" herself, which accompanies a close-up image of her on screen. In addition, Rainer (the subject putting the whole film together) inserts clips of Hollywood films, and alternates among the clear 16 mm color image, black-and-white film, and overcolored video. This mixture of kinds of footage reminds the spectator that she is watching a film, and prevents any "expensive illusionism," as Jenny scornfully calls it when questioned by YW about her image being the same in her "hot-flashback" as in her present-time interview.

Other "displacements" from the usual menopausal narrative include exploring menopause in white women and in black women, and juxtaposing the way race and aging are both marginalized in a society dominated by hysteria about youth and whiteness—as was clear in the cosmetic surgery discourse noted above, and as implied in Tom's film.

The women Rainer interviews regularly mention change in physical appearance as central to the experience of aging and something that, given prevailing cultural norms of the young white female as the standard for how *all* women should look, they have to struggle against or come to terms with. Jenny talks half-jokingly, half-seriously about her "luscious youthful self," whom she prefers to tell YW about, as against her present (unsatisfactory) menopausal self. She also talks of mourning for that young self, even if she's not sure which part exactly she mourns the most. Jenny describes her menopausal shock of realizing that being desired by men was "the linchpin of her identity," so that when men no longer desired her it felt traumatic.[42] A bit earlier, Jenny realizes how much she is dwelling on changes in her body. In order to dramatize the male perspective that is at stake, Rainer slows down Jenny's voice so that it sounds male. The good feminist in Jenny, we hear, "wags a finger at my belly-aching: 'Jenny, all you're doing is confirming what men already think, that our bodies are, by definition, defective and need changing.'" She concludes that "the medics try to fix us with hysterectomies and Hormone Replacement Therapy so we'll stay feminine forever." Rainer intercuts statistics confirming the increasing number of hysterectomies on the word-processor screen within the cinema screen (which reappears frequently with texts or to record a text a "character" has spoken). A bit later, accompanying found footage of a 1950s' teen movie, Jenny is heard declaring her inability to "get used to our screwed up morality that denies middle-aged women the right to be beautiful, loving, and idealized by men."[43]

Another menopausal woman, Minnette Lehmann, talks about still feeling sexual, still seeking "testosterone" (which the interviewer points out women also produce and do not lose with menopause), and liking to be in a room full of men and women where sex is everywhere. This woman betrays her fear of aging, her fear that naming her age will evoke negative preconceptions, when she refuses to tell the interviewer her age. All these comments show the real concern about continuing attractiveness and lapsing from the "ideal" (white) standard.

Some privileged career women are able to slough off regret for the ideal white young standard. One notes that after a period of memory of her girlhood and young womanhood, she began to savor her new freedom, and the fact the menopause meant that she was "off the hook" in many ways. Although she is not pushed to say more, one assumes she means in relation to attracting men; seeking sex, marriage, and children; and, in general, having to compete with other women about attractiveness, sexual desirability.

The authority of science discourse about menopause is deliberately featured in the film and is thoroughly critiqued through judicious editing. Rainer has assembled clips from 1960s' medical documentaries in which white male doctors (and an occasional male-identified female one) pronounce authoritatively on the symptoms, effects, and cures for menopause. Their discourse shows an unabashed male bias in the obvious concern for the husbands of menopausal women, omission of any mention of middle-aged men's sexual decline (as Jenny does not fail to point out), and inattention to menopausal women's desires, perspectives, agency. The doctors pronounce about menopausal women, but do not let them speak. Like the plastic surgeons quoted earlier, they do not try to find out what their female patients' desires might be, turning, instead, to talk with the husbands!

While feminists have begun to discuss male medical discourse recently, Rainer was ahead of her time in *Privilege*. The way in which Rainer exposes the largely (but not exclusively) male doctors is extremely effective, especially in the scene where she intercuts the white-haired, white-coated doctor's pronouncements about menopausal women, with Jenny telling her thoughts and feelings as she sought medical help for her menopausal symptoms. The entire sequence is prefaced by a series of more short declarations about menopausal women by different male doctors in clips from medical documentaries,[44] proceeds with the section of interview with Minnette noted above, and goes on to find Jenny finally willing to talk about her menopause with YW. Jenny describes different meetings with doctors, who prescribe first a hysterectomy and then estrogen replacement therapy. The doctors are barely civil, she notes, and she refuses their prescriptions. Intertitles, meanwhile, tell us that a woman's sexuality and desires were of great interest to friends and family as long as she was seeking a man, but become strangely of no interest once she was menopausal. Jenny continues her story of her meetings with doctors, as Rainer intercuts more clips of doctors pronouncing on menopausal women. Rainer ironically juxtaposes an image of one doctor saying how emotionally stressed menopausal women are with Jenny's voice-off account of how annoyed her doctors got at her questions! An African-American menopausal woman also reports the same lack of sympathy and patience from her doctors, who are not willing to answer her questions or to inform her about future impacts of drugs. She notes the importance of these male doctors not having gone through and thus not really caring about the menopausal experience. Both doctors and the women agree on symptoms of immediate menopause, but the women who have been through it describe a far more stable emotional life—something the doctors do not mention.

Fascinating in light of Tom's film is how Rainer links menopause and racism, just as Tom had linked racism and plastic surgery. In doing this, Rainer, like Tom, breaks new ground, since most books on menopause, like those on plastic surgery, do not deal with minority women to any great degree.[45] Why this story usually omits minority women is a good question: Is it that their marginalization is already so much a fact that the further marginalization of menopause cannot matter? Or is it that black women's marginalization is such that white women writing about menopause usually forget the specificity of minority women?[46]

Rainer's film provokes these important questions in its very title, *Privilege*, which reverberates throughout the film. For instance, in ironically following out an association between the "hot flashes" of menopause and the cinematic "flash-back" noted above, Rainer exposes the white/youthful privilege of her heroine, Jenny, in the 1960s, in contrast to her oppressed black and Latin American neighbors. Now menopausal, Jenny has lost her white privilege because of aging. As she tells her story—her "hot-flashback" (mixing menopausal hot flashes and the cinematic flashback)—it includes exposure of the racism her lower East Side friends endured in the early 1960s and her own complicity in unconscious racism in the rape story she recounts.

The main sequence that explores these difficult issues follows that noted above about the marginalization and humiliation of menopausal women, and the intercutting of Jenny's experience and agency with menopausal women's invisibility to male doctors. The climax of the ongoing, accompanying "race story" deals with the complicated sexual relations between black men and white women, but also between black men and specifically lesbian women. Filmed in black and white (as against the color menopause story) as film noir—with a deliberate pun, I'm sure, on the word "noir," which links blackness and the evil part of human nature that noir film brings to the surface—this section includes extended quotations from Franz Fanon and Eldridge Cleaver. It serves to highlight both parallels and differences between the oppressions and marginalizations of menopausal women, and those of minorities and gay/lesbians. The white menopausal women wanting still to be desired by men is problematized by the juxtaposed discourse of black-on-white rape. That is, Jenny seems to want a man almost at any cost. So desperate is she that she has an affair with an upper-class, conservative lawyer (himself clearly "slumming" in taking up with Jenny) who does not really share her values. Meanwhile, Cleaver's words about black men taking out their revenge on white men by raping white women—relayed through the bodies of Stuart, Carlos, and an unnamed white man—exposes the privilege (and triviality?) of Jenny's desire for a man at any cost.

The section continues with what is a ground-breaking sequence in which YW confronts Jenny's racism and critiques the story she now tells in which Brenda, Jenny's lesbian friend, makes an alliance with Carlos via the common enemy of the white man: "Our blackness, femaleness, shit, and blood dictate the moves of white men." YW resists Jenny's story being about the conditioning of white people in the West because it doesn't explain how it all started. YW provides political and economic reasons for racism, while Jenny is attracted to psychoanalytic theories because of their comfort of clarity, simplicity. For YW, "the psyche itself is the product of external forces, like history and economics." YW is further angered by how, as she puts it, "white women always manage to use their own victim status as a way of pleading innocent to the charge of racism."[47]

This important observation is exemplified in the following sequence where a new "class story," intermixed with the white woman's unconscious racism, is presented by Digna, Carlos's wife in Jenny's "hot-flashback" story. Digna shows her excellent understanding of Jenny's white liberal politics, which includes blindness to issues of race and class. Digna knows that Jenny is unable to *see* her—that she is simply invisible to Jenny because she's Puerto Rican. Rainer emphasizes this point by having Digna accompany Jenny on her dates with Robert (her new boyfriend, the attorney in the case against Carlos). Digna is visible to the film spectators but is not seen by the lovers.

In a splendid scene, Digna dresses as the Hollywood Carmen Miranda, foregrounding one of Hollywood's most outrageous Latin American stereotypes. Adorned in the garish Hollywood idea of Latin American dress, Digna sits in Robert's plush car, which Jenny soon enters, and comments on Jenny's inability to *see* her. Here Rainer marvelously literalizes Hollywood's elimination of women of color as subjects from the screen (until very recently). Women of color have always been mere objects at best (perhaps their figuring as the *abject* would be truer). Rainer now begins to reverse and to remedy this traditional absence by making Digna the subject talking directly to the spectator, but painfully reminding that spectator of how Hispanic women were ridiculed in Hollywood by speaking to us dressed in costume. From her oppressed position, Digna sees Jenny precisely for who and what she is and, reversing the normal subject-object positions, makes *Jenny her object*. Digna generously decides to look after Jenny and to try to educate her—and the spectator, too, in the process.

It is only toward the end of the film, after revisiting her 1960s' young womanhood, that Jenny begins to get a glimpse of the realities she lives within and to articulate her needs and losses: "So what do I do now that the men have stopped looking at me? I'm like a fish thrown back into the sea. . . . It's hard to admit that I still want them to look. . . . My biggest shock in reaching middle age was the realization that men's desire for me was the linchpin of my identity."[48]

Toward the end of the film, the dualities and ambiguities of privilege in relation to class, ethnicity, and aging become more clear. Following the film noir rape section, the spectator is given some "Quotidian Fragments" about race, although who is speaking is deliberately left unclear. Included here is a reflection about a woman's experience at a conference in El Paso, Mexico: the woman had earlier been disabused of her impression that a sexual liaison was starting with a man when he discussed the lure of younger women. Later, as she is being shown the sprawling shanties of Juarez, we read that: "In the gathering dusk, she realizes she is on two different sides of two frontiers: Economically, she is on the advantage side, overlooking a third-world country. And sexually, having passed the frontier of attractiveness to men, she is now on *the other side of privilege*." In these few lines, Rainer manages to suggest some of the main themes in the film, namely the paradoxes of the privilege whiteness confers and yet the varying oppressions of all women, including that of aging women.

The white heroine's unconscious racism is exposed by Digna, who accompanies Jenny and her boyfriend Robert on their trips, but is "invisible" to them. Here, Digna talks directly to the spectator.

Resisting Pathologies of Race and Aging

Tom's and Rainer's films both address in different ways the common "fault" that minority and aging women are seen to have in dominant western discourses— namely, that of deformity or pathology because they deviate from the Caucasian youthful ideal. Tom's film addresses issues from within a Chinese-American perspective, exploring conflicts about cosmetic eye surgery through a mother-daughter difference about such surgery. Oppressive white culture in this film is present in the white males' lascivious orientalism vis-à-vis Doris, in the white children ridiculing Esther, and in the benign but condescending music teacher. Doris's relatively privileged class position is not highlighted, but Mei Lin's resistance to the surgery that might alleviate her mother's alienation—her "fault" vis-à-vis dominant culture—exemplifies identity politics debates ongoing in many minority communities in the United States.

Rainer examines the parallel "fault" of aging black and white women, exploring the complexities of menopause and ongoing debates about it within dominant medical, feminist, and minority communities. However, the specificity of race within both the discourse and the experience of menopause is not highlighted: indeed, the individual experiences of black and white women appear very similar—possibly because all the women interviewed appear middle class. Yet the accompanying "race" story details the ethnic privilege of white women in comparison to less advantaged minorities. Perhaps Rainer intends the disjuncture between interviewees on the individual level, and the social analysis of the "race story" to reveal that class matters as much as race? Or that individual discourse blinds itself to the social power hierarchy, with white culture at the top?

Together, the films open up for spectators two main important perspectives on race and bodily self-fashioning: Rainer's film, more overtly political and polemical than Tom's, stresses the white and the male power hierarchies and the common pathologizing of race and aging. The film critiques the white male medical establishment and, through the women's words, allows us to see the self-doubt that aging creates through social pressures to be young. The privilege of whiteness is then contrasted with the double marginalization of black and Hispanic women as people of color and female. Tom's film suggests for future exploration the concept of a woman's body as something available for change for the woman's own ends, independent of the commodification surrounding her. The film casts doubt on the desire/possibility to return to some "pure" and "authentic" ethnicity, seen as essentializing and problematic, and offers a rich field for future debates.

Conclusion

Rainer's film lies somewhere in between documentary and fiction, and therein lies its power. Its mixed footage confronts us directly with the issue of genre, and the filmmaker YR within the film notes that she is seeking something "real" from her interviewees. The impact of the film is, indeed, to make spectators think about menopause in a new way, much as Brecht's techniques were intended to make spectators think in a new way about capitalism. *Privilege* certainly shocked me out of my denial that I was undergoing menopause. It was the first text I had seen that allowed me to lower my defenses against being interpellated as "menopausal." I had been trying to simply forget the whole thing and carry on as before, pretending that nothing had changed—one of the dangers that Friedan alerts us to.[49]

One of my fears was that losing attractiveness would mean losing the interest and attention of men—something that the movies had shown me was likely to happen. Young women are attracted to older men, and thus older wives have a genuine cause for concern. Men's imaginaries are locked into the white youthful ideal as a defense against their own aging, as Betty Friedan has convincingly argued. As the ones in the position of power, white males establish the positions they will occupy, but also those that others will occupy. White males are able, then, to construct positions for themselves and for others, such that they can defend themselves psychically from their own fears of aging and of losing control.

These fears of aging women are analogous to fears of some minority women regarding being acceptable to the dominant culture. Cosmetic surgery is an obvious temptation for aging persons and for minority women as a way to "correct" their "faults." None of Rainer's interviewees mention cosmetic surgery, although, as noted, some express concern about losing their attractiveness to men. I would like to know more about how menopausal women who have undergone cosmetic surgery later feel about it, in order to better understand psychic processes of aging in the United States.[50] Similarly, I would like to know more about what surgery achieves for minority women in regard to bringing about a sense of belonging to the U.S. national community, to U.S. national bodily norms. While I do not accept the pressures put on women to correct their faults, and while combatting such pressures is vital if we are to change prevailing gender constructs, it is important to attend to how individual women experience the oppressive norms and to understand the strategies they adopt to make their daily lives more bearable.

Both Rainer and Tom dwell particularly on the female body as it figures in the dominant white imaginary, and on the ideal white youthful feminine standard that male culture imposes and that all women have trouble disengaging from. Aside from western culture's pathologizing of both aging and a non-Caucasian eyelid, this same culture, as we've seen, seeks to reverse the "trouble" and delay the "decline" or the aesthetic disharmony: for aging, this restoring, which is also a return to youth and a replacement of how "the woman" is urged on women through "hormone replacement therapy." For the non-European woman, cosmetic eye surgery is also to provide a return to the Ideal, a replacement of what the woman has, and a restoring of the aesthetic deemed the norm. To accept that women can be *something* after being young and desirable to men, after childbearing and motherhood, is to suggest that women can be something in a role that does not *per se* depend upon men or seem to be interested in their voyeuristic gaze. It is in male interest to keep alive the myth that after menopause women have no particular function and therefore can be passed over for younger women who still depend on men. Much is at stake in menopause, therefore.

Rainer's film reminded me that being menopausal *had* produced change, but not the mythic kind of negative change western culture focuses on: I am freed from child care and the daily responsibility for the household, particularly for children's welfare. I am freed to be more, not less, sexual with no inhibiting children around. My intelligence flourishes in the space that opens up when thoughts do not have to turn on the hour to the child's next needs. If bodily signs of aging still distress, it may be that I am as yet unable to rethink the body as a surface available for change I might desire, as against change forced through commodification and pervasive youth images.

Could it be that this is what male culture fears? And that the fixation of the male imaginary on the youthful, unlined, firm young white body is a defense against acknowledging older women's superior skills and capacities, special energies and commitments, once their children are grown? For such capacities could bring women more political and economic power and independence, which may threaten men.

Could it be that the physical, cultural, and linguistic difference of minority women is also something that white culture fears for a complex mixture of psychic and economic reasons? That the pressure on minority women to assimilate to the U.S.'s bodily norms is precisely so as to erase a difference that threatens basic political and economic policies of U.S. capitalism, which relies on an unprivileged class?

These questions, stimulated by Tom's and Rainer's films, evidence the importance of independent women's films made outside of Hollywood constraints. We urgently need films in which female spectators can identify outside of the models white male hegemony provides for them, and thus begin the slow intertwined processes of changing consciousness and society.

Notes

1. Blair O. Rogers, "History of the Development of Aesthetic Surgery," in *Aesthetic Plastic Surgery: Principles and Techniques*, ed. Paul Regnault and Rollin K. Daniel (London and Toronto: Little, Brown, 1984), p. 3. In the passage in question, men are, I believe, the object of discussion. It seems that before the twentieth century, women were so far removed from the public sphere, so already "fallen" once child-rearing years were over, as not even to be pathologized in aging! It's as if the "disease" of aging that Shakespeare notes was conferred onto women as women began to move out of the home in the twentieth century. Meanwhile, partly because the pathology of aging had moved on to women, men were liberated from it at this time.

   Obviously, this is a complex comparative and historical problem that I cannot address here but that clearly warrants more attention in my future research.

2. See, for example, Chandra Mohanty, A. Russo, and L. Torres, eds., *Third World Women and the Politics of Feminism* (Bloomington: Indiana University Press, 1991); Lisa Lowe, "Heterogeneity, Hybridity, Multiplicity: Marking Asian American Differences," *Diaspora* (Spring 1991): 24–44; or Ann McClintock, *Imperial Leather* (New York: Routledge, 1995).

3. Benedict Anderson, *Imagined Communities: Reflections on the Origin and Spread of Nationalism* (London: Verso, 1983).

4. Ibid., p.10.

5. Ibid.

6. The link between the work of women (white or not) and "nation," however, cannot be taken for granted. It is something that has to be artificially forged by the State in times of crisis, like war, when states strive to incorporate women in a "national" sphere. In the case of emerging "nations" like the United States in the eighteenth and early nineteenth centuries, there was an effort to construct the "Republican Mother" as a fourth branch of government, so as to conceal the reality women face in their oblique relationship to the concept of "nation," produced through women's

global (material and symbolic) confinement to the domestic sphere. It is ironic that the very terms that exclude women—from the public sphere that "nation" demarcates—return back in the language of nation as "female" (Lady Liberty, Britannia); in the idea of nation as "home"; or in the appeal in wartime to the nation as "family" (as in Carol Reed's *This Happy Breed* [1939]).

7. On this matter, see Benedict Anderson's chapter on "Patriotism and Racism," in which he illuminates the oddity of people sacrificing themselves for their country, as always happens in wars. As he says, "Even in the case of colonized peoples, who have every reason to feel hatred for their imperialist rulers, it is astonishing how insignificant the element of hatred is in these expression [*sic*] of national feeling." (B. Anderson, *Imagined Communities*, p. 142) Further, Anderson notes: "Dying for one's country, which usually one does not choose, assumes a moral grandeur which dying for the Labour Party ... can not rival" (p. 144). Importantly, Anderson concludes that "from the start, the nation was conceived in language, not in blood, and that one could be 'invited into' the imagined community. . . . Seen as both a *historical* fatality and as a community imagined through language, the nation presents itself as simultaneously open and closed" (pp. 145–46). But of course, women do not have open to them this kind of connection to the imagined "nation," that dying for *It* produces.

8. This topic is obviously too large to develop here, but one only has to think of the number of extremely aged world leaders, not the least Deng in contemporary China, or, in America only recently, Ronald Reagan, none of whom are/were despised or ridiculed for being old at least in the mainstream press.

   It is interesting that Kathy Woodward, in a pioneering essay about aging, found detailed attention to aging in classical literature about male, not female, protagonists (e.g., *Death in Venice* [1911]), although she discusses a female aged heroine in a less well-known contemporary Australian novel (*The Eye of the Storm* [1973]). See K. Woodward, "Youthfulness as a Masquerade," in *Discourse* (Fall/Winter, 1988/1989): pp. 119–42.

9. Jean Kozlowski. "Women, Film, and the Midlife Sophie's Choice: Sink or Sousatzka?" in *Menopause: A Midlife Passage*, ed. Joan C. Callahan (Bloomington: Indiana University Press, 1993), p. 8.

10. Ibid., p. 6.

11. See Betty Friedan, *The Fountain of Age* (New York: Simon and Schuster, 1993) for more information on media marginalization of aging women in ads, soaps, and TV programming generally.

12. Even the satisfying Australian film about an aging mother who simply heads off into the bush, so irritated and fed up is she with her bourgeois-ifying family, does not *per se* question culture's attitudes toward menopausal women. We are given enjoyable images of this woman repairing her own car, traveling alone, camping in the bush, and resisting attempts of male gangs to steal from her and possibly rape her. The establishing of a mutually dependent relationship with a man her age is satisfying, but the film leaves it at that without actually foregrounding aging issues.

13. The bibliography for this topic is already enormous. For an overview of research that has taken place over the past twenty years, see Robert Stam and Ella Shohat, *Unthinking Eurocentrism* (London: Routledge, 1995).

14. As Ann Balsamo points out (A. Balsamo, "On the Cutting Edge: Cosmetic Surgery and the Technological Production of the Gendered Body," in *camera obscura* No. 28 [1993, pp. 207–36]), Kathryn Pauly Morgan sees cosmetic surgery as "one of the

deepest of original sins, the choice of the apparent over the real." While this seems an extreme point of view, it would also apply to passing, I would think. I do not, however, agree with the claim that there is a certain "real" that is chosen over an "apparent."

15. This important topic—namely, the pervasive stance toward bodily self-fashioning as somehow morally wrong or a violation of some sort—will be taken up in further research. Its premises need unpacking. For instance, isn't there an underlying naturalizing of the aging process as inherently biological and therefore to be submitted to? Isn't there a commitment to a developmental teleology in the objection to bodily self-fashioning? Isn't the phrasing of the function of cosmetic surgery and HRT *as* "return, replacement, restoring" itself an instance of commitment to the same teleology, only in reverse? Some of these issues are implicit in the drastic self-fashioning of the performance artist who deliberately has frequent cosmetic surgery to construct her face in the fashion of well-known models and figures in classical painting—carrying to a drastic extreme the kinds of masquerades and facial self-fashioning many of us carry out daily in the "make-up" we use.

16. Woodward, "Youthfulness": 121.

17. W. Chapkis, *Beauty Secrets: Women and the Politics of Appearance* (Boston: South End Press, 1986), pp. 37–52; Balsamo, "Cutting Edge": pp. 214–17; Friedan, *Fountain of Age*, pp. 37–46.

18. C. Spitzack, "The Confession Mirror: Plastic Images for Surgery," in *Canadian Journal of Political and Social Theory*, 12 (1–2) (1988): pp. 38–49; and Balsamo, "Cutting Edge."

19. I am currently researching titles of Hollywood and other films featuring cosmetic surgery for a larger project on imaging the face and changing the face. There are more films that refer to cosmetic surgery than I originally thought: e.g., *Seconds* (1966) by John Frankenheimer; Joan Crawford in *A Woman's Face, Looker*, etc.

20. Kathleen Woodward mentions, as other aspects of the body-in-age that are seldom explored, "the phenomenology and phantasies of motility, proprioception, and the interior of the body" (Woodward, "Youthfulness": p. 121).

21. I discuss Tom's *Two Lies* in the context of nation in my forthcoming book, *Looking for the Other: Feminism and the Imperial Gaze* (London and New York: Routledge).

22. E. Said, *Orientalism* (New York: Vintage, 1979).

23. T. Brennan, *History After Lacan* (London and New York: Routledge, 1993), pp. xii–xiii, 106–113.

24. I was unable to find a book with the title of the one in Tom's film, namely *Plastic Surgery for Black and White Patients*. However, the book seems to be from an earlier period, like that by Maxwell Maltz. The topic of plastic surgery in black and white patients is addressed by Maltz, and is sometimes referred to by other authors. However, in the main medical handbooks I found that attention to racial and ethnic issues was significantly lacking.

25. Several articles about cosmetic surgery focus on the matter of facial proportions from an historical perspective, going back certainly to Plato's "golden mean" but more often to Albrecht Durer's studies of proportion in 1528 (see C. K. Deutsch, "Disproportion in Psychiatric Syndromes," in *Anthropometric Facial Proportions in Medicine*, eds. L. G. Farkos and I. R. Munro [Springfield, Ill.: Thomas, 1987]). The 1984 edition of a medical handbook, *Aesthetic Plastic Surgery: Principles and Techniques*, ed. Paul Regnault and Rollin K. Daniel (Boston and Toronto: Little,

Brown) contains a brief overview of the historical development of aesthetic surgery by Blair O. Rogers (pp. 3–31). Rogers is careful to make the distinction between corrective (aesthetic) surgery and reconstructive plastic surgery, while recognizing that often the line between these two forms is hard to draw.

26. M. Malz, *New Faces, New Futures: Rebuilding Character with Plastic Surgery* (New York, 1936), p. 26.

27. L. G. Farkos, I. Munro, and J. Kolar, "The Validity of Neo-Classical Facial Proportion Canons," in *Anthropometric Facial Proportions in Medicine*, p. 57.

28. S. P. Bartlett, I. Wornom 3rd, and L. A. Whitaker, "Evaluation of Facial Skeletal Aesthetics and Surgical Planning," *Clinics in Plastic Surgery* 18 (1) (1991): 1–9.

29. Ibid., p. 2.

30. Anne Balsamo has also made this point looking at earlier medical plastic surgery volumes. I was surprised to find the same classical "rules" being advocated in the 1990s' books. It's important to note that the book publisher of the main medical handbook I looked at, *Textbook of Plastic, Maxillofacial and Reconstructive Surgery* (1993), is Williams and Williams with branches in Hong Kong, Sydney, Munich, and Tokyo, suggesting worldwide use of the volumes with their implicit western standards.

31. F. Macgregor and F. M. Cooke, *Transformation and Identity: The Face and Plastic Surgery* (Oak Brook, Ill.: Eteran), pp. 80–81.

32. Ibid., p. 81.

33. R. Siegel, "Advanced Blepharoplasty," in *Aesthetic Plastic Surgery: Principles and Techniques*, eds. P. Regnault and R. K. Daniel (Mass.: Little Brown, 1984). Ann Balsamo has also discussed this focus on the angles and proportions of the "ideal" face no matter what race the patient, in medical textbooks in her article "On the Cutting Edge." She also notes plastic surgeons' reluctance to operate on black patients because of supposed extra scar tissue. See also Carol Spitzack's interesting "confession" of a visit to a cosmetic surgeon (Spitzack, "The Confession Mirror").

34. See J. Deniker's *The Races of Man* (London and New York: Charles Scribner, 1901).

35. See also Wendy Chapkis, *Beauty Secrets*, pp. 37–52.

36. Things do seem to be slowly changing in regard to plastic surgeons' awareness of the manipulations of the media and of psychosocial impacts of plastic surgery. There was an article on "Plastic Surgery with Hispanic Burn Patients" that began to address the need to work with patients within cultural constructs familiar to them; and a conference on "Special Faces: Understanding Facial Disfigurement," held in New York in 1992, brought in cognitive psychologists as well as surgeons to address psychosocial issues.

37. See Don Liu, "Oriental Blepharoplasty," in *Oculoplastic Surgery*, ed. David T. Tse (Philadelphia: Lippincott, 1992), pp. 201–208.

38. Yoshio Hiraga and Seiichi Ohmori, "The Double Eyelid Operation," in *The Unfavorable Results in Plastic Surgery: Avoidance and Treatment*, ed. R. M. Goldwyn (Boston, Mass.: Little Brown, 1984).

39. When I was recently in Japan, I was shown special women's beauty parlors that advertise their expertise in creating the height of *Japanese* loveliness. But when you look at the procedures involved, many are indeed ones that mimic the western female body, such as enlarging breasts, changing eyelids, lightening hair. The preoccupation with a highly stereotypical white female and male body is most evident in the many "comic" books that overwhelm newsstands and to which entire book-

stores are devoted. The women drawn in these books are long-legged, with pert snub noses, and blonde long hair. The men are huge, with big muscles and again western (in this case Clint-Eastwood style) looks. All of this requires in-depth analysis to be understood properly. But again whiteness and youthfulness are viewed as the ideal standards.

40. Friedan, *Fountain of Age*, pp. 37–50.

41. Yvonne Rainer confirmed this connection in an as-yet-unpublished interview at the American Center in Paris, June 10, 1995.

42. S. MacDonald, ed., *Screen Writings: Scripts and Texts by Independent Filmmakers* (Berkeley, CA: University of California Press, 1995), p. 317.

43. Ibid., p. 300.

44. These include statements like: "It's not an easy matter to treat the menopausal patient, because she's undergoing certain physical changes" or "The way she faces up to these problems has an important bearing on what her menopause will be like." See MacDonald, *Screen Writings*, pp. 293–301.

45. Friedan's otherwise excellent volume has no index entries for "race," "ethnicity," "multiculturalism," or for specific ethnic groups, such as "African Americans," "Asians." There is one reference to a Mexican-American family and to a black grandmother in the discussion of different life courses for men and women.

46. In her book *The Silent Passage of Menopause* (New York: Random House, 1991), Gail Sheehy does have a brief section titled "Across Color, Class and Culture Lines," in which she very briefly surveys some anthropological studies of menopause in different cultures. Generally, she finds that women in Asian cultures and in African cultures, where older women are granted some respect and some specific roles, do not suffer the same kinds of physical symptoms as white women in the West, where youth and beauty figure so hugely. However, Rainer's film would seem to belie Sheehy's statement that African-American women reported few symptoms of menopause. Sheehy notes African-American women's statistical likelihood of having more hysterectomies because of fibroids. The entire issue of color, class, and culture in relation to menopause requires more study. Rainer's film stimulates many of the questions for researchers to pursue.

47. MacDonald, *Screen Writings*, p. 310.

48. Ibid., pp. 316–17.

49. See also B. D. Eddy, "The *Dangerous Age:* Karin Michaelis and the Politics of Menopause," in *Women's Studies* 21 (1992): pp. 491–504.

50. Some attention is given to aging women and cosmetic surgery in Friedan's book, especially in the section reviewing media images of aging (p. 36, then pp. 43–49), but elsewhere it only appears parenthetically. I am interested in learning more about the psychological impact on menopausal women of cosmetic surgery—if it makes women feel better and exactly why. Such information might expand our knowledge of the struggle to age without trauma in contemporary America.

7

Gynopathia Sexualis
Theories of Decline in Biology and Aesthetics

Robyn Gardner

> *The Classical is healthy, the Romantic is sick.*
> —Goethe

It is easy to forget that some of the disciplinary integrities between the natural and human sciences that we may now take for granted have a very recent history. Goethe's sharp relation of aesthetic categories to the "normal" and the "pathological" encapsulates widely pervasive associations consolidating toward the end of the eighteenth century and given dramatic expression in the nineteenth century. In addressing the subject of "the menopause," either in terms of biomedical definitions and their criticisms, or of more generally inculcated images, it is useful to return the invention of the "hormonal body" to a nineteenth-century European context. Here the biological sciences were marked by racial and evolutionary anxieties, concerns about disciplinary demarcation, and revisions in ways of seeing and saying determined by particular historical events as well as by the impact of new visualizing technologies.

The following overview attempts to relate the metaphorology of aging woman to nineteenth-century *fin de siècle* imaginings, and to a much older dialectic of the "textual" and the "visual." My emphasis is on underlying aesthetic imperatives in sociobiological theories or, more precisely, on the ways in which scientific theories invoke complexity in metaphors of the scriptural and hermeneutic while at the same time defining truth in terms of visual stasis—in the "real"-izing of a timeless moment. The dialogue is an ancient one, of *ekphrasis*, enacted famously in the nineteenth century in Keats's *Ode on a Grecian Urn*. The poet, faced with the tragedy of language (its temporality), yearns for the purity of stasis in the classical image, in his "unravished bride of quietness." That it is only the "reading" of timeless figures on the urn that brings them to vital life is part of the poem's much admired "well-wrought" irony.

The power of an increasingly sophisticated endocrine model lies partly in the ways in which it may accommodate and redefine the most persistent and persuasive narratives from older classical (Hellenic) and religious (Christian and Judaic) traditions. Images of "the hormonal body" articulate a sense of complexity and *mystery* (chaos, wilderness) while at the same time holding the promise of final revelation and the possibility of unimagined freedoms in "self-design." In the contemporary marketing of hormone technologies, the idea of an infinitely complex and opaque script of "inner nature" is persistently set over and against sophisticated processes of interpretation and the technical dream of the clean and clarifying visual image.

The endocrine model of physiology and behavior presents an increasingly powerful explanatory system, in that it promises to absorb alternative modes of understanding human behavior. For instance, the mass-marketed image of "chemical messengers" first formulated in 1905 is rapidly displacing (and accounting *for*) the psychoanalytical model of the emotions. At the same time, molecular biogenetic research at the cutting edge is profoundly complicating the interface of the genetic and the environmental, making inadequate the "nature and nurture" distinctions that still organize, implicitly and explicitly, many sociological and feminist critiques of medicine, as well as many existent medical practices. As we approach the end of the twentieth century, the models of the psychological and the hormonal, in conjunction, still determine the rhetorical field in which western women order their lives. The invention and development of the hormonal body is in many ways contemporaneous with the development of psychoanalysis. The histories are interrelated, demonstrating similar anxieties and preoccupations, and some important differences. Both systems are informed by images and structures derived from *fin de siècle* racial and biological anxieties. Both aestheticize complexity in terms of the "textual," although, as I will argue, it is in a greater capacity for mass commodification of visual "realizations" that the biochemical model will increasingly predominate. My beginning is therefore a backward glance at Freud's armchair journey into the "primitive" female mind. My intention is to define the ways in which social and political histories relate to traditions of technical imaging, which in turn determine contemporary representations of the menopausal body.

Into the "Dark Continent"

Writing in 1913 and attempting to apply the findings of an emergent psychoanalysis to what he called "unsolved problems of social psychology," Freud proposed his imaginative hypothesis of "the death of the primal father" as that originary event underwriting the social contract. In this first "oedipal scene," the sons in an incestuous, primal horde kill a jealous father who would keep all of the women for himself, and in their dawning realization that each individual's best chance of survival lies in such group action or *rapprochement*, they dismember and eat his body in (unholy) communion.[1] Thus the origin of totemic sacrifice; this shared meal is repeated ritualistically, as symbolic ratification of the wisdom of social contracts, repeated and elaborated upon until the original act is forgotten, returning only in dreams, in art, and in what Freud deemed pathological manifestations. The latter, which included such diseased behaviors as obsessions, compulsions, neuroses, and psychoses, are the tax that nature exacts upon culture, or the price of our civilization.

Like Levi-Strauss and later structural anthropology, Freud endorsed a vision in which the bonds of civilization are forged in an economic imperative, with women's bodies as base units of exchange. His imaginative reconstruction was explicitly presented as an attempt to reconcile Charles Darwin's theory of the evolution of species with the findings of contemporary anthropology—an attempt to "think the gap," as it were, between Darwin's image of the primal horde dominated by the physically fittest male, and the elaborate systems of kinship, ritual, and totemic practice then being documented in people as "primitive" as Australian aboriginals. For Freud, indigenous Australians were the most *un*cultured people on earth. It may be remembered that he also called female psychology "the dark continent" and asserted that studying the physiology and psychology of primitive peoples would reveal "a well-preserved picture" of our own development.[2] He imagined that the study of black Australians and the fervent anthropological activity then going on in Africa might well shed light on the psychosexual dysfunction of white Viennese women.

Freud's conflations were hardly novel. As classical scholars will testify, and feminists variously argue, rhetorical exchange between ideas of blackness, animality, femininity, and juvenility and senility is as old as recorded histories. Aristotle's views on the lesser natures of women are well known. In accordance with his homology of the four elements and concordant humors, he argued that male physiologies were "hot and dry" and female bodies "cold and wet." Because heat and dryness are essential to the forging of reason and the development of higher moral capacities, he deduced that the moistness of women (analogous to lower life forms) limits their human perfection. Women, in their reptilian dampness, are ruled constitutionally incapable of higher reason and therefore represent a lower order in a complex but static schemata of beings.[3] Galen, the most famous of the Greco-Roman medical writers (A.D. 131–201), modified Aristotle's views in light of his own medical observations and ruled that women represented "imperfect" or mutilated examples of an ideal (male) form. Females were therefore *de*formations caused by lack of heat at the moment of conception. Until the end of the sixteenth century, medical practitioners were still warmly debating the Aristotelian theory, offering recipes for "hotter" conceptions—with detailed instructions for sexual positioning, foods to be ingested before and after the act, and the best weather conditions for the creation of male children. The sixteenth century also produced a famous, anonymously authored treatise (attributed to Acidalius) titled *Mulieres homines non esse*, or "Women are not human beings," which dazzled wits and intellectuals with its metaphysical sleights and word play.

In the late eighteenth century, however, one may determine a shift from textual (or analogical) validation to a more emphatic belief in the "proof" of the visual, a movement consummated in the nineteenth century with the rise of "positivist" science and increasing sophistication in techniques of visual reproduction. There are also decided movements from description to the socially prescriptive. Social engineering, or the need to control "regressive" tendencies, to shape human history is more apparent and urgently argued. In 1884, with a lot of evolutionary theory under his belt, eminent German physiologist Paul Albrecht addressed an anthropological congress at Breslau with the more circumspectly worded and carefully researched proposition that the anatomy of the human female "showed" more pronounced animal traits than that of the human male.[4] His report was merely one among many. Women were not thereby eliminated from the category of the human but were increasingly identified as constituting a disturbingly "atavistic" difference within. Such scientific observations confirmed a consolidating awareness that women needed more refining (i.e., less taxing) educations, compassionate treatments, and more careful social controls. Albrecht's evidence was convincingly picturesque, appealing to the visual, to ideals of quantification and comparison, and the processes of colonial expansion and exploration were not irrelevant. By this time the European colonization of Africa was providing detailed and photographic data for some of the most significant treatises on the differences of and *in* female physiology in existence.

Reading "The Book of Nature"

Before turning in more detail to some of these racial, gynecological explorations, it is worth noting the fury and complexity of relevant debates in the realms of transcendental anatomy. Emerging ideas of evolution and devolution were rapidly incorporated into the spheres of physiology and anatomy in increasingly intricate flights of homologistic reason. If the German anatomist Ernest Haekel didn't actually formulate his triumphal slogan "Ontogeny recapitulates phylogeny" until late in the nineteenth century, the German *Naturphilosopher* Lorenz Oken had been fulsomely declaring even at the beginning of the century, "animals are the persistent foetal stage of man" and a human fetus is therefore "a whole animal kingdom."[5] Before Darwin's formulation of a mechanism for the evolution of species, European anatomists and embryologists were keenly determining the "vestiges" or recapitulative forms of progressively higher animals in

the developing human foetus. For instance, in 1828 French anatomists were seriously arguing with German counterparts about whether human embryos
recapitulated the *adult* forms of lower animals (gestating from mature fish shape
to mature bird shape and so on) or whether they repeated only the *embryonic*
physiologies of successively higher animals; this meant grappling with logical
paradoxes, not to mention rhetorical problems of adequately expressing the idea
of small structures that are at once prefigurations of an ideal plan as well as its
already complete inscription.[6]

Such preoccupations are partly explained by the fact that new scientific paradigms had origins in older religious doctrines and exegetic practices—in allegory
and *allegoresis* and hermeneutical traditions of reading the natural world as
"God's book."[7] Of course, developments in the natural sciences were not uniform. German *Naturphilosophie*, often referred to as Romantic biology, was
overwhelmingly preoccupied with the "grammar" of nature and the formulation
of rationally coherent systems in which all parts "integrated" the whole. (Indeed,
for some more extreme thinkers, the rules of grammar and rhetoric were natural
categories—homologous with particular life forms.) For many English "posi-
tivists," however, an ideology of direct observation and clarification was rapidly
predominating; English anatomists and embryologists therefore dismissed the
ratiocinative obsessions of German *Naturphilosophen* as "metaphorical mystifica-
tions" determined by an idealist obsession with "abysses" of language and the
unifying of radical alterities.[8] The self-reflexive preoccupations of German
Romantic science have been somewhat redeemed in the twentieth century with
the advent of quantum mechanics and the "linguistic" turn in contemporary philosophy. The meditations of Jacques Derrida and others on the subjects of the
repression of "writing" in European philosophy with reference to Judeo-
Christian traditions would seem relevant here. The differences between English
positivism (with its emphasis upon plain language and visible proofs) and the textual elaborations of *Naturphilosophie* might be explored with reference to
prescientific divergences between an inherently textual Judaic tradition with pro-
hibitions of graven images and Christian doctrines of revelation and iconic
reverence.[9] Such complex historical conjunctions determine that nineteenth-century biological sciences were heavily indebted to the metaphorics of difficult text
and clear picture—two kinds of revelation.

While the extent of Darwin's own acceptance of the mechanism of recapitula-
tion has been keenly debated, he does clearly preempt Freud's own recourse to
the idea of a preserved picture. Both thinkers conjure revelation in a "caught"
moment, in which the secret and inner text of the human body (which is a
palimpsest of *all* evolutionary history) is graphically realized.

> Thus the [human] embryo comes to be left as a sort of picture, preserved by
> nature, of the ancient and less modified condition of each animal.[10]

If transcendental anatomy implied a predetermined movement toward more complex life forms, later evolutionary theories were complicit with ideals of "healthy competition," espousing survival of the fittest and the perfectability of species. But *therein* lay the dark side: a new and profoundly biological anxiety about the integrity of the human. Transcendental anatomy presented epiphanic moments or "preserved pictures" (vestiges, or recapitulations) of more primitive life forms already *in* the human, while Darwinian evolutionary theory added a frightening dimension of temporality, chance, and instability—in the idea of regression determined by environment, as well as "throw-back" atavism.

Anthropological activities in the outposts of empires variously "proved" such thinking. The integrity of empires and the development of western civilizations seemed to be threatened not only by the existence of "savages" elsewhere but also by atavistic "traits" being identified within—not only in fetuses but also in large sections of adult populations. In the last decades of the nineteenth century, the Italian criminologist Lombroso was exhaustively documenting the visible stigmata of "criminal degeneracy" in the skulls and facial characteristics of vast numbers of Europeans, calculating ethnic diversity as one variable.[11] Such science has been well documented in terms of eugenic culpabilities, but is worth reviewing in reference to traditions of technical imaging and a rhetorically structuring dialectic of obscure text and clear picture. With the aid of copious statistics, wax works, drawings, and photographs, Lombroso sought to "freeze" the processes of evolution, to thereby catch the individual characteristics of a "backward movement" increasingly apparent in the advances of western cultures. In his studies of cretinism he distinguished between "absolute cretins," born irretrievably subhuman, and a variety of associated "traits" or stigmata of cretinism in the normal population, signifying a widespread degeneration caused by inbreeding and environmental factors. Building on Bénédict Morel's earlier studies, Lombroso thus presented "cretinism" as an absolute pathology that defined the limits of the normal. The normal was now a severely "compromised" category—a matter of gradations and vulnerable to contingency, to a *movement* of degenerative changes.

While implying the decadence and pace of modern life as a factor in physiological degeneration (compounding the problem of biological atavism), Lombroso's particular interest in the "primitive" state of southern Italy looked toward Africa.[12] Indeed, it was a common wisdom of the period that Calabrians were Africans; "the Dark Continent" was often conjured as beginning anywhere between Florence, Rome, or Naples, and might even include all of Italy, depending upon the birthplace of the speaker. A similar geographical exorcism was apparent in common constructions of homosexuality as either a "decadent" effeminacy or a biological degeneracy. Homosexual practice was designated as either "the French disease," "the Italian habit," "the Greek way," or "the Arab abomination," according to one's own latitude.

Different Bodies and Degenerate Texts

Lombroso's criminal science was given a most famous (or notorious) social extrapolation in Max Nordau's *Degeneration* in 1892. Urban crime, disease, prostitution, madness, poverty, the lower classes, the social disruption threatened in female emancipation (and the putative weaker physiologies and lesser intellectual capacities of women)—along with the "primitive" derangements of modern art—were here defined and conflated in terms of a "massive flaw" in the progress of civilization. Nordau's vision of the degeneration of modern life was implicitly and often explicitly feminized as a general "hysteria" derived from Charcot's examinations of (mostly) female hysterics, and postulated in terms of an increasing sterility and decline across whole populations. Offering detailed physiological explanations (of agitated brain cells, nerves, and decomposing tissues), he related such cerebral disintegration causally to the massive "disorders" he found in *fin de siècle* art. The metaphorical excesses and plot disintegrations of writers such as Emile Zola, and the anamorphoses of all Modernist painters (those "impressionists," "mosaists," "pappilloteurs," "quiverers," and "roaring colorists"), were the results of brain disease. It is the sense of agitation captured by such artists that preoccupies Nordau, and he rules such works as intelligible in light of Charcot's demonstrations of visual derangements in hysterics and Lombroso's proofs of congenital criminality.[13]

Nordau's often brilliant (deliberately hyperbolic and polemical) association of biology and art, hysteria and primitivity is commonly thought to have found its grim apotheosis in the Nazi exhibition of "Degenerate Art" in Munich in 1937, in which Africa, primitivism, expressionism, insanity, hysteria, anarchism, Judaism, and Bolshevism were presented as evidence of biological retardation and racial degeneracy threatening the purity of German race and culture.[14] As Daniel Pick argues in his comparative study of the concept of degeneration, it is difficult now to read such writings except in terms of this teleology, as (in George Mosse's words) moving inexorably "Towards the Final Solution."[15] With this hindsight, we too often reject the logic of some of Nordau's connections and ignore the ways in which such theories and rhetorical habits still structure our contemporary understandings. Whatever we may think of the racism, misogyny, and absurd causalities of his tirade, a simple but crucial revaluation, an overturning, makes such connections the commonplace emphasis of poststructural and postcolonial scholarship. The designations of "modern art" being formulated toward the end of the nineteenth century are affirmed in critical relation to European exploration and conquest of other places; Expressionism, Impressionism, Decadence, Symbolism, Fauvism, Dadaism, Primitivism, and Naive Art record the modern as very much an *ethnographien*—an anxious projection of the civilized, rational, and fully integrated self of the West through the expression and exorcism of what is "other."

Nineteenth-century popular fictions made the same association of figures of blackness, femininity, and primitivity with disease and decline—often very consciously. The images in which R. L. Stevenson's Dr. Jekyll regresses into the amoral Mr. Hyde are overtly apelike, and his "recessivity" is structurally enacted in the text in a narrative movement from the street, to the interior of his house, to his laboratory, and then to a "cabinet" *within* the laboratory, before his violent eruption into the streets again. Similarly, the text of Bram Stoker's *Dracula* invokes the facial features of Jewishness presented in numerous racist caricatures—a theme often overlooked in contemporary versions. That the vampire's bloodsucking intentions in the original text are often explicitly homoerotic reinforced such resonances, for racial biology of the period dwelt increasingly on the "effeminate" nature of Jews and their greater susceptibility to typical female disorders such as hysteria and neurasthenia. The vampire's bloodsucking interest in acquiring English property and seducing English women, entering and replicating himself, is conveyed in the tropes of parasitology, of insemination and dissemination, common to popular anti-Semitism. Virgins (and certain young men) swoon to the vampire's "foreign" charms, thereby conjuring an external threat compounded by weakness within. Jews were often blamed for the spread of syphilis and were represented *like* syphilis (in their supposed infection of English virgins, and economic infiltrations); through this one might read the "black beast" of the vampire as a brilliant aggregate of English anxieties about boundaries, about the integrity of categories of color, race and nation.

The idea that "savages" reflected the physiological and intellectual infancy of the human race, and that the animal aspects of female reproduction similarly clouded the picture of mankind's civilized progress, pervaded Europe in all disciplinary spheres. The opening up of "uncivilized" places to European inspection kept pace with an eager penetration of the darkest recesses of different female anatomies. Animal, Negro, and female physiologies were persistently equated and minutely compared in terms of deviation (excess or diminution) from an ideal white (male or female virginal) body that was derived implicitly, but often very explicitly and without reservation, from classical Greek aesthetics.

The eighteenth-century love affair with an Hellenic ideal and its visual compendia is well documented. In 1738 the Idealist Lord Shaftsbury thought that "matter" (before the synthetic and aesthetic operation of higher Reason) resembled "the savage" and the "idiot."[16] J. J. Winckelmann defined the end of an ideal Hellenic period in terms of a "stain" and corruption from Asiatic "foreign ways" and defined Rococo artistry and interdisciplinary hybrids as "unnatural" and "deformed." Similarly Goethe, largely in ignorance of the fact that time had erased the earthy colors from Greek statues, was influential in disseminating equations of whiteness with timelessness, order, and conceptual purity. His lifelong obsession with disproving Bacon's prismatic theory of the color spectrum, which he called "that muddy spectre," was grounded in an ideal and originary "pure white light" that opposes darkness; color gradations were thus degradations in an ideal harmony. Both Shaftsbury and Winckelmann seemed to feel that the Ideal also manifested in the mental and physical harmony of "lovely children," a sensibility that Goethe demonstrated in his personal relationships.[17]

It is important to recognize that those now disparaged nineteenth-century passions for phrenology and craniometry grew out of the eighteenth-century "art" of physiognomics, technical practices in which aesthetics and biology were far less concerned about their disciplinary distinction. As early as 1791, a Dutch surgeon, anatomical drawer, and university professor named Petrus Camper (1722–1799) set the model, or technique, for the geometrical "sorting" of anatomical differences. In his *Dissertation physique*, he sorted ape and human cranial differences via a complicated instrument for measuring facial lines; the standard for his developmental series (from lowest ape to highest human) was a facial angle (of one hundred degrees) thought not to exist in reality but "given" by the ideal forms of Greek statues—or, more particularly, by the bust of the *Apollo Belevedere*.[18] The utmost deviation permitted any European was ten degrees behind or before the perpendicular line H1, while Negroes might demonstrate deviation of sixty-five degrees, close to the profiles of dogs or snipe. Camper's informing idea was to capture, through the rules of art and geometry, the hidden regularities in the seemingly chaotic text of nature. While invoking a similar ideal of clarification in the static image, Johann Caspar Lavater's silhouettes and famous *Essays on Physiognomy* (1792) sought an opposite value; his "profiles" of types, traits, and particular individuals were imagined as lie detectors that reveal inner corruption. Only in the static image might an "inner truth" be realized. Elaborating upon Etienne Silhouette's invention of shadow painting, Lavater asserted his stylized series and use of *camera obscura* over and against the limitations of language; the stasis of the visual image renders "sensible" signs, expressions, and shades that cannot be described in words. In fact, Lavater's clearest revelation is deathly:

> Death puts an end to the agitations to which the body is a perpetual prey. . . . It stops and fixes what was before vague and undecided. Everything rises and sinks to its level; all the features return to their true relation.[19]

Lavater preempts by several centuries some of Roland Barthes' meditations on death and photography in *Camera Lucida*. The inordinately "textual" Barthes found, near the end of his life, that photographs hold a "realization" beyond the power of words. For him, such revelation is of what is irretrievably lost, rather than of timeless orders to which all life forms revert. His modernity perhaps lies in this nostalgia.

Anamorphia: From Greek Statues to Black Women

Nineteenth-century photography, infused with aesthetic values given by painting and earlier visual techniques, became an important adjunct in reinforcing the more "objective" status of scientific disciplines. In the dark races of Africa and in the Orient, a fall from an ideal, putatively white and Hellenic physiology was "realized" in photographs. Photographic technology meant unlimited replication of images for an expanding mass market as well as circulation in scientific and pedagogic contexts. Images might be infinitely circulated, wrenched from "original" contexts. The intertwining of discourses of racial biology with aesthetic traditions of technical imaging—this conjunction of *arte* and *techne*—has been significant in the development of modern gynecology. The instance of Ploss and Bartels's mammoth *Das Weib* is vividly instructive. At the time of its English translation in 1935, *Das Weib* had already been a standard German textbook for half a century. Originally subtitled *The Natural History of Woman*, it had eleven editions and a series of editors who deleted and added according to their own medical and ethnographical interests. The work exists as a palimpsest text of competing male voices, an agonistic and territorial exercise. Its three thick volumes, finally subtitled *An Historical, Gynecological and Anthropological Compendium*, presented information and images solicited from all corners of the globe, implying its ideal reader in a preface that said: "Every better educated man will find pieces of information . . . that will broaden his horizons with respect to the field of physiology of the female sex."[20]

Das Weib's production is exactly contemporaneous with Krafft-Ebing's *Psychopathia Sexualis* (managing almost as many editions) and presents an interesting visual comparison.[21] In Krafft-Ebing's lexicon of mental derangement, the conceptual integrity of the mind is threatened by a vast array of precisely designated deviations (agorophobia, claustrophobia, thastophobia, dipsomania, aboulia, algophobia, algophilia, satyriasis, nymphomania, necrophilia, onomatomania, coprolalia, arithmomania, pyromania, exhibitionism, etc.) that define the pathological as a matter of intensity and of variation. In *Das Weib* one finds a *gynopathic* and racial equivalent, a definition of "normal" female physiologies, in its exploration of differences. It is significant that in the geographical space of Africa a rhetorical emphasis on "richness" and variation slides into explicit constructions of deviance from an ideal, white form. The English edition carried thirty-five photographs demonstrating variations (racially correlated) in breast shape alone, and an entire chapter is devoted to the "hypertrophic" genital configurations of African women. An Hellenic ideal is conveyed in the photographs of German women (posed romantically on mountain tops or dancing by streams) in relation to stark and full-frontal images of African women presenting variation in skeletal structure, adipose tissue, breast and genital shape, or hair distribution. The "excess" and "atrophy" defined in healthy African physiologies is implicitly (and often overtly) equated with what would be malformity, degeneracy, and a glandular pathology in white European bodies. While the pages of *Das Weib* overtly eroticize "exotic" variation, certain limit cases are established. The supposed "paedomorphosis" of native Bushmen is pathologized as atavism and/or environmentally restricted development (thus presenting an interesting contradiction to the paedophilic idealism of Winckelmann and Goethe). Similarly, the steatopygia of some black physiologies is explicated with reference to analogous characteristics in animals.[22]

Sander Gilman, with characteristic erudition and exhaustive scholarship, has explored the commonplace nineteenth-century representation of the Hottentot's body as "the black female *in nuce*" in ways that are relevant here. He demonstrates, with convincing evidence, that the generous physiology of Cuvier's Black Venus was persistently invested in European painting and literature with amorality and "excessive" animal appetites, characteristics that were then attributed to *all* black women but related to "errors" in white female gynecology and to deviant behaviors such as prostitution and lesbianism.[23] Such equations were not merely commonplace in art and pornography but were the stuff of scholarship. Gilman notes the obvious case of Havelock Ellis; in *Studies in the Psychology of Sex* (1905), Ellis meditated on the significance of such primitive "disproportions" in terms of a vertical principle. Like many others, he believed in an absolute scale of beauty that is objective and that

Austrian girl with lozenge of Michaelis. From Ploss, Bartels, and Bartels, vol. 1, p. 285.

ranges from the European to the black. Men in lower races admire European women more than their own, and women in lower races "naturally" aspire upward; this, Ellis suggests, is why they attempt to "whiten" themselves with face powder.[24] Such spatial investments underwrite the most objective imaging strategies; the popular nineteenth-century human evolutionary series depicting the march from "lowest ape to upright human" conveys early Christian connotatations of a journey and difficult progress. This widely circulated model at once preserves the integrity of the categories (the distinction between animal and human), *articulating* these differences through analogy. Static spatial figures move (motivate, emote) a moral continuum, and pure geometry is always and already a narrative—the etymological relation of *parabola* and parable is not unimportant. In myriad nineteenth-century medical works defining the normal and pathological, classical aesthetics is reinvest-

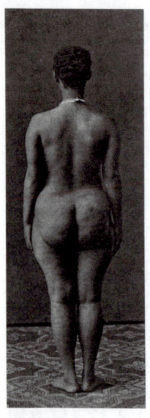

Hottentot woman of 22 years with steatopygia and crural obesity. From Ploss, Bartels, and Bartels, vol. 1, p. 304.

ed with Christian value. Scientific measurements confirm common-sense perceptions: the bodies of adult blacks are "like" the bodies of children and old people; old people often look and act like children; blacks act like children; and women demonstrate, in their lighter and slighter physiologies (or their excess fat) and in their intuitive and emotional thought processes, more childlike and/or primitive mental and physical capacities. Indeed, for some theorists of degeneration, women manifest less true biological atavism and demonstrate fewer degenerative stigmata simply because they *are* lower down the evolutionary scale. Being *generally* less highly evolved (like blacks and animals), their sex logically shows fewer instances of dramatic "throwback." Of course, this theorizing did not invalidate assiduous correlating of female moral degeneracy and behavioral disorder with particular body shapes. In a host of studies, including one by Lombroso, the physiologies of prostitutes revealed a kind of abnormal fat distribution that was explicitly compared to the steatopygia of Cuvier's Black Venus.[25] Prostitutes were also like cretins in that they evidenced low fecundity—their "cases" therefore construed as part of the threat of a degenerative drift toward sterility in the larger population.

It should be emphasized here that each and every one of these racist biological conclusions was vociferously contested in its time; such theories were the sites of methodological argument and ethical debate, and it would be mistaken to imagine any simple consensus of opinion in matters of racial difference. However, this being said, it would be difficult to overstate the pervasiveness of such equations and the acceptance of ideas of degeneration in all disciplines and aspects of European culture. We tend to relegate such interests and anxieties to the sphere of "illegitimate" science, the province of a few brooding eccentrics such as Lombroso, whose compassionate and ground-breaking research into the effects of syphilis and the demography of thyroid deficiency tends to be overshadowed by recollection of his visual documents. His "portraits" of criminal faces, or parts of faces, have become the signifier of a "degenerate science" almost as efficiently as the image of Van Gogh's bandaged ear "stands for" not only his own madness but also the eccentricity of artists. Such containment and exorcism of degeneration was common after World War II, especially in the United States, where revelations of Nazi genocide resulted in anxious disassociation—determined partly by America's own very fervent prewar interest in eugenics. Theories of degeneration crossed all disciplinary boundaries, from physics to the philosophy of history and to economics. This process was often subliminal and determined by the practicalities of technical reproduction. Such works as *Das Weib* were not simply purveyed within interested academic spheres; medical and anthropological works were regularly pirated and "extracted," photos and passages repackaged as erotica, *curiosa*, or for gentlemen's editions. Techniques of medical and anthropological imaging thereby played a part in wider cultural appreciations. Images of hygiene and disease intricately structure twentieth-century erotic perceptions and have political consequences. Of course, the borrowing process is not unidirectional. The photographs in medical and ethnographic texts such as *Das Weib* were sometimes "readymades," and were determined by the kinds of people *already* amenable to being photographed naked: German *Wandervogelers*, artist's models and performers, prostitutes, mental patients, the poor, the imprisoned, the sick and the dying, as well as coerced indigenous peoples.

Declining Figures, Menopausal History

Toward the end of the eighteenth century, other very clear lines of thought were devolving on the aging female body as a site in which the true stigmata of "hidden" biological degeneracy inexorably appears.

Freud's image of woman as the "dark continent" was at least a consciously heuristic expression of far more exacting equations. In 1864 (forty years before Freud's formulation), the celebrated German anatomist Carl Vogt had written with more precision and "factual" confidence:

> By its rounded apex and less developed posterior lobe the Negro's brain resembles that of our children, and by the protuberance of the parietal lobe, that of our females. . . . The grown-up Negro partakes as regards his intellectual faculties of the nature of the child, the female and the senile white.[26]

For many comparative anatomists and physiologists, such equations of blackness, infantilism, and senility with the "feminine" were entirely valid, as they were determined by direct observation and precise measurements. In the context of such analogistic reasoning, the body of the aging woman provided a compelling model for larger processes of historical decline. In 1879 Gustave le Bon, author of a highly respected study of crowd behavior, extrapolated the figure of a female degeneracy into the movement of history. Endorsing Vogt's equation of Negro and female skull shapes (and noting the sameness of both to gorillas), he defined female atavism as the cause of historical decline.[27] In his theorizing of "mass" behavior, of crowds and revolutions, women are not only active agents of atavistic behavior; history (figured in terms of revolutions) is cyclical and increasingly hysterical, finally degenerating into a state of sterility.

This strikingly menstrual and menopausal image had been variously conjured in the wake of the French Revolution. All revolutions were perceived as a return to "barbarism," and socialism was often presented as a regression to a past age. For le Bon, Taine, and other social historians, the crowd was not merely an aggregate of people in a geographical space. Rather it was an entity, literally "demonstrating" the connection between past and present, between the individual and a vast array of ancestors. The events of the French Revolution, with its bouts of "bloodletting" and hysteria and the supposed extra-animalistic behavior of women, presented an array of associations that demarcated the movement of history as a female pathology.[28] Oswald Spengler's later vision of western decline is similarly *gynopathic;* albeit with a more poetic and tragic sense, he conjures an "endless uniform wave-train of the generations" as the natural rhythm of the species and presents western history as climacteric.[29] Like a woman's body, western civilization has advanced through ages of cyclic revolution and bloodshed and now degenerates into a state of sterility.

In a trajectory from Bénédict Morel's theories of *dégénérescence* in the 1850s to Spengler's *Decline of the West* in 1918, infertility or sterility marks the dividing line between the normal and pathological. Morel, like Lombroso, had found the infertile bodies of "absolute cretins" to be frightening limit cases, signifying the direction and end result of larger processes of historical degeneration; he also roped the lower fecundity of prostitutes into this equation. Unlike male bodies, women's bodies must "naturally" become infertile, must traverse this space between the normal and pathological. A feminized pathological is thus incorporated into the normal as a *temporal* ruination of an ideal stasis.

If, in the eighteenth century, the static image "captured" inner truths (of natural or moral order), the nineteenth century often found frightening revelations in the process of ageing. J. J. Winkelmann, so influential in disseminating a classical aestheticism, had presented the bodies of "beautiful youths" as a synthesis of moral and physical ideals, and this theme is later confused with evolutionary anxieties. In the nineteenth century, the youthful body is often presented with intense nostalgia—an ideal, but also (and by the same token) a duplicitous, "cover" that must fall away, perhaps revealing a frightening "undertext" of degenerate transmissions. This erotic investment of a young body with Hellenic idealism and "monstrous" racial biological imagining has dramatic literary condensation in the writings of Edgar Allan Poe. Poe's confusion of classical idealism, aging, and themes of degenerative transmission is explicit in the short story "Ligeia." Ligeia's premature death through a ravaging disease is prefaced by a meditation on her "exquisite" beauty, which is "not classic" but haunted by "some strangeness of proportion," a dark and foreign asymmetry that is "of the Hebrews." After her death the narrator affirms her "purity"; she is the "august, the beautiful, the entombed." However, her disease is transmitted to the narrator's second child-wife, the very fair, English, and proper Lady Rowena, who hideously withers and dies and is "revived" in the narrator's fevered imagining as Ligeia—with "dark, wild eyes" and dishevelled hair *"blacker than the raven wings of mid-night."*[30] In Poe's dreamscape, disease *is* accelerated aging, and death while still young and perfectly "intact" is an aesthetic ideal—a formulation he attempts to justify in "The Philosophy of Composition" with its famous assertion about "the death of a beautiful woman" being "the most poetic topic in the world."

In this context one may speculate on the allegorical significance of the body of Joan of Arc; her youth, purported virginity, and *lack* of menstruation are invoked in the midst of intensely gynecological (menopausal) images of revolution and decline. Her chastity and purity make her quite literally "the statue" of several revolutions. This desire for stasis, enacted in the death of a young and very white female body, was the staple of numerous lurid fictions in the wake of the French Revolution. The pivotal scene of the Gothic novel (which has no pretensions to fine art but caters to popular tastes) is the seduction and penetration of a swooned girl-child by a daemonic figure—usually in a crypt. In many cases she is dead before the act of penetration, and her body (always very white and cold as a statue) is the site of intense eroticization. In such works as Mathew Lewis's *The Monk*, the rape and death of the maiden is helped or hindered by a *grotesquerie* of older women: fat and garrulous duenne; incidental crones and harridans; incestuous and sexually rapacious stepmothers; and such archaic apparitions as a "Bleeding Nun" who, like Poe's prematurely aged women, refuses to be peacefully buried.[31]

Contemporary readings of such works might emphasize allegories of anxious transition from older "patriarchal" religious structures to secular and "paternal" institutions of power, such as law, medicine, and the nuclear family; demonic figures (often a corrupt priest) represent an archaic institution, and "encrypted" maidens the Catholic Church's anxious control of female sexuality. This fantasy of stasis and "containment" inflicted upon young female bodies is replayed in the aforementioned *Dracula*, in the fact that an archaic and foreign power is warded off by a secular brotherhood of the professions. In the transfusion scene the doctor, the professor, the lawyer, and the American businessman stand in a tableau of paternal protection around the dying Lucy (deathly white and drained of blood), at once rhapsodic over her translucent body and bent upon "infusing" her with their mingled lifeblood. The scene (overtly playing with insemination) is staged as a "blood-bonding" of the professions, a forging of middle-class mercantile power against an older and corrupt aristocracy, which has too many "foreign" links and origins. This benevolent caretaking of the sexuality of British womanhood not only conjures the bloodletting of Freud's primal scene (a societal bonding grounded in the sharing of women) but also Foucault's narrative of an institutionalized power of the gaze replacing other forms of social containment. It is the birth of the clinic, no less, in which Bentham's panopticon provides the emblematic image of a decentralized (authorless) and intricately commodified system of repressions.

Difficult Texts and Clear Pictures

If one accepts that human thinking is always analogistic, synthetic, and ratiocinative, then it is hardly surprising that the dark places of the human psyche, the "primitive" past of human history, and the so-called savage places of the earth should become confused or mutually informing. Practices generate metaphors, and the metaphors "engender" other practices. Age-old oppositions of light and dark, of good and evil, became implicated in ideas of reason and unreason, purity and impurity, evolution and devolution. The development of increasingly sophisticated technologies of microscopy, magnification, radiography in conjuncton with photography meant that the "dark places" of bodies were poetically, as well as literally, opened to the light of reason. Michel Foucault argues in *The Order of Things* that a "vitalized" science of the body did not exist before the nineteenth century, that eighteenth-century discourses of the body primarily presented mechanized models and static categories. There is an Enlightenment preoccupation with genera, phyla, and taxonomical definitions rather than with fluid and vital articulations. The invention of the X-ray not only allowed a literal image of inner recesses but also brought with it more complicating "negative" associations, with *Doppelgängern* and older figures of inversion given new rhetorical investments. The "vitality" and various incandescences of Percy Bysshe Shelley's poetry, for instance, had more than a little to do with his fascination with the new technology of electricity—with his passion for "galvanizing" himself with a homemade apparatus, and his interest in the possibility of "revivifying" inanimate bodies. One need not wait upon the heirophant of discourse theory for an awareness of such epistemological shifts. It is almost a disciplinary cliché for historians of science to think of a "galvanization" of the static body of the "Elizabethan world picture." As some critics of the cleanness of Foucault's "epistemological breaks" have argued, the edges are *more* messy—both between "eras" and *in* the writings of particular writers.[32]

Whatever the quibbles about periodization, it seems entirely valid to conjure a period of time in which technical developments in the biological sciences determined a new "fluidity" and "vitality." Metaphors of cathexis (expression and repression) abounded, and studies of the permeability of tissues and of circulatory mechanisms enriched a tropology of infiltration and dissemination, as well as provided new resonances in an existent poetics of illumination and penetration. Electrical models were giving way to even more dynamic and complex visions of "invisible" secretions, and such models were subtly imbricated with images of racial and genetic contamination. For instance, in an early essay on the psychical mechanism of hysteria (1892), Freud suggested that "the psychical trauma—or more precisely the memory of the trauma—acts *like a foreign body* which long after its entry must continue to be regarded as an agent that is still at work."[33] Some recent commentaries emphasize this point as "the birthplace" of psychoanalysis. Here Freud wrests his thinking away from his teacher Charcot and from a model of electrical excitation then dominant in mental pathology. His inseminating "alien" metaphor (common in an age grappling with the legacies of syphilis and anti-Semitism) is represented as *integral* in the formulation of a new linguistic model, for now the hysteric's symptoms are not simply "cathected" charges but coded messages, full of substitutions, displacements, and duplicitous (*double* agent) representations.[34] However, such readings often overstate the idea of a "paradigm switch," ignoring catachresis and tropological returns. Freud's new paradigm of decipherment was in many senses already established in French psychiatric practice, his image of the *alienated* mind already an *idée fixe*. At the Saltpétrière, Pinel (1745–1826), famous for his mythical, revolutionary act of "unchaining the insane," had established an influential working methodology of directly observing the surface manifestations of illness in severely insane patients. His elaborations were "textual" in the sense of an hermeneutic model of reading a coded logic in madness. Widely regarded in other disciplines, Pinel's writings on insanity made illness the site for defining the limits of the "normal." While endorsing theories of electrical excitation, it is significant that he read widely in anthropology and ethnography and was predisposed to construct the behavior of his patients as "like a foreign language," an uncivilized utterance (of tics, jerks, grimacing, and gibbering) that would reveal a hidden order not beyond the penetrative capacities of reason.

Charcot (Max Nordau's inspiration) extended Pinel's decipherment model into the realm of the gaze with his attention to the visual, surface manifestations of disorder in the "body language" of hysterics. If his public and professional "demonstrations" of female patients secularized a methodology with origins in religious exorcism, his valuable photographic records of internal disorder (often with "painterly" captions) looked toward the future and new technologies of "visual" proof that, in their amenability to mass production and replication in other and *other* contexts, would revolutionize not only the domain of public understanding but also rationalize scientific teaching practices. It is in this capacity for replicable, schematic imaging that Charcot's representations of insanity may be deemed more "modern" (technologically adapted to mass commodification) than Freud's talking cure. The latter's "science of the mind" has regularly been denied scientific status because it can never be refuted, or is not provable in terms of the positivist credo of direct observation. Whatever the wonderful homologies wrought by a Freudian analyst, and no matter what "cures" apparent, no one can ever really *see* an Oedipus complex—and a rapidly packaged *approximation* (simulation) of one is difficult to imagine. It is in this sense that psychoanalysis remains textual, determined by the ancient order of allegory and *allegoresis*, of priestly initiate illuminating veiled meanings, bringing curative "enlightenment" to common people. Such dispensations are less effective in a global context in which the logic of the simulacra, or *"la société du spectacle,"*[35] increasingly prevails.

It is at this point, then, that Freudian psychoanalysis parts company with a more modern "biochemical" science of the body (embracing "mind"), which so very successfully "embodies" two kinds of revelation: those of complex script and clear picture. While successfully transposing an old model of difficult text, Freud's science doesn't answer the need for graven images, for revelation in the *public* sense—of miracles. The rise of psychoanalysis, particularly in the United States, has had something to do with its emphasis upon "nurture" and the fact that previously fervid interests in "nature" were less acceptable after World War II. As the events of the Holocaust recede or are rapidly recast as entertainment (the *phantasmagoria* of public expression and exorcism), an infinitely more sophisticated biogenetic determinism is asserted. While many of the conclusions and implications are the same as those that fascinated prewar eugenics, the research is depersonalized at the "distant" level of biochemical exchange and genetic coding, and yet made more visually accessible; computer-enhanced images, PET (positron emission tomography) and MRI (magnetic resonance imaging) play upon codes established by painting, photography, and almost a century of moving pictures.

Designing Bodies, an Expanding Aesthetic

It is within this larger field of computer-enhanced molecular biogenetic mapping that the medical model of "the menopause" will be refined. (Alzheimer's is a testing case for PET technology.) Refinements in available hormone treatments have resulted in a marketing expansion of the domain of the pathological, proposing the problems of aging (fleshly excess and atrophy, diminution of "feminine" hormones) to a younger market in increasingly aesthetic terms. Synthetic estrogens ensure future protection against the insidious "hidden" processes of osteoporosis, now visually demonstrable at an early age through Dexa scans and comparative tables; the conceptual "space" of old age is thus expanded. Girls take the pill not only for prevention of pregnancy but also for regulation of their hormonal bodies—for "imbalances" that affect appearance and *thereby* physical "well-being." The last ten years have also witnessed the advent of more popular "medical" publications, a mass-media dissemination of research information that depends, for accessibility, on visual compendia as simply schematic and didactic as anything invented by eighteenth-century physiognomists.[36] Template representations (simple drawings) of "normal" female body types as either android, gynoid, lymphatic, or pituitary (reminiscent of Galenic humors) articulate, through a rhetoric of "imbalances," an implicit ideal mien as slim and symmetrical as anything dreamed by Winckelmann. Just as for comparative anatomists in nineteenth-century Africa, frightening pathologies articulate the more or less "normal" distribution curve(s) of woman. This modern *gynopathia*, reproduced in countless magazine articles, finds its limit cases in polycystic ovarian syndrome, Cushing's syndrome, and acromegaly as conditions that provide dramatic evidence of "the hidden power of hormones" to scribble their "messages" in visible stigmata. The cognates of such disease and more minor imbalance (skin discoloration, excess adipose tissue, atrophy, distorted bones, hairiness, male-pattern baldness, mental degeneration, and sterility) are of course coincident with common (but distressing and now preventable) signs of aging. And it is not merely coincidental that the signs of metabolic disorder and "imbalance" replicate very closely the visible stigmata of criminal degeneracy identified by Lombroso. Modern biochemical research has redeemed many of his observations: occult "secretions" do shape bodies, and profoundly effect human behavior. Molecular biogenetic profiles (PET) play an increasing role in the American criminal justice system and determine social welfare policy as well as general public appreciation.

In the instance of Australian doctor Sandra Cabot, the gynopathic compendium is also utilized in performances. She does television and public demonstrations in which, much like a phrenologist reading skulls, she assesses body shapes, relegating women to one or another "natural" category, prescribing the proper balancing diet or the appropriate "natural" *or* artifical hormones—depending on the extent of an imbalance. With television, the theater of presentation becomes global, subverting the boundaries between "information"/"entertainment" (between educated middle classes and others) in ways that Charcot with his public lectures might only dream of. While appealing to "the natural" (dietary advice, exercise, homeopathy, and vitamin therapy for each body shape), the schemata of "natural" female body types relies heavily upon the new and lucrative *redesignation* of such drugs as spironolactone and cyproterone acetate as "anti-androgens." This agonistic rhetoric, newly emergent in the public sphere, also has historical resonances. Like the visual table (or *tabula rasa*) of body shape, it depends upon earlier "medical" models and vocabularies. For example, historians of medicine trace the "history of hormones" from an early dualistic vision proposing strict differentiation of male and female "natures" determined by sex-specific structures and their secretions.[37] This differential or complementary model was variously challenged by "sex antagonism" theories until the 1930s, a time that often overtly reiterated the primitivity/femininity equations I have traced above. The recently popularized language of the anti-androgenic thus reaches back to a "Middle Ages" in the development of a hormonal body, for recent research models eschew simple binary formulation for a more complex construction of endocrine feedback systems that involve *all* bodily tissues in ways that invalidate a hydraulic model of "blocking" grounded in such sex-specific antagonisms.

At the level of biochemistry, therefore, there are conceptual problems that bemused Aristotle as well as Goethe: should sex differentiation be articulated in

THE FOUR BODY TYPES

As an exercise, envision yourself as one of the following four types of physique. You can practise fitting your friends and family members into one of these categories.

The Gynaeoid Type

In the gynaeoid type of woman, the sex glands (ovaries) and their secreted female hormones have the most influence on body shape and fat distribution. Excessive weight is distributed in feminine areas such as buttocks, pelvis, hips, thighs and breasts. It is unfortunate that this type of fatty tissue may become uneven and lumpy resulting in cellulite.

The typical gynaeoid woman craves fatty foods and spices which stimulate her ovaries to produce even more oestrogen to exaggerate her body shape.

To correct the metabolic imbalance in the gynaeoid woman, it is necessary to establish a diet that does not stimulate the ovaries, but instead stimulates the thyroid and adrenal glands. (See Table 7 on Page 114).

The gynaeoid type of woman may be worried that if she loses her excessive pounds, her sexuality may diminish, but this is not true; the increased energy and wellbeing of a normal body weight can only enhance sexuality.

Gynaeoid women need to stay with their ideal diet for life as of all types of fat, lower body fat is hardest to lose.

The Thyroid Type

The thyroid type resembles the thoroughbred racehorse with long, fine-boned limbs and a slender neck and can be described as lean and rangy. They lack the enduring stamina of the android types and crave stimulants such as caffeine, sugar and cigarettes for a burst of energy.

Because their thyroid gland is the dominant gland, they have a high metabolic rate and generally burn up calories quickly which explains why they need frequent snacks of sugar and caffeine to keep them going.

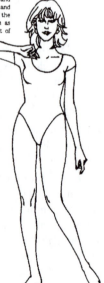

Thyroid types can be excessive in their habits and may become addicted to sugar, caffeine or diet pills. If they continue with these poor eating and lifestyle patterns, they may cause the thyroid gland to become exhausted and from this point on they start to gain weight. Typically, the weight gain is rapid and fat is deposited upon the abdomen and thighs while the limbs remain relatively slim.

An overweight thyroid type needs to rebalance her metabolism by avoiding sugar, soft drinks, sweets, refined carbohydrates and caffeine. (See Table 9.)

From Sandra Cabot, *Don't Let Hormones Ruin Your Life* (Sydney,

The Android Type

The classical android woman is square-shaped with a solid, thick big-boned frame and she is athletic and powerful in appearance. Obesity tends to give her a more masculine appearance. Excessive fat accumulates on the trunk, neck and abdomen causing the stomach to protrude and the waistline to disappear

If you are an android woman, you will usually be energetic and strong with good staying power when others about you need a coffee break. You have a tendency to overproduce male hormones and may be told you take after your dad

Android types are definitely not sugarholics or "sweet tooths", but instead crave foods high in cholesterol and salt that stimulate their adrenal glands to pump out more steroid hormones. These steroid hormones increase the appetite and unfortunately promote further accumulation of fat and muscle and more masculine features

To restore metabolic balance in android types, it is necessary to avoid high cholesterol and salty foods. (See Table 8.)

Dr Caterson suggests that in android types weight loss can be easier and more effective if the excess of male hormones is corrected first. This can be done with hormone therapy. (See Page 101). As the android type loses weight, her production of male hormones will diminish and she will regain a more feminine physique.

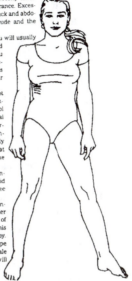

The Pituitary Type

The pituitary type is the epitome of the cuddly baby doll type who has never lost her baby fat. She is round all over with a round shaped face and may have a relatively large head. Her limbs, hands and feet are chubby and she has a layer of fat over her chest, although the breasts may not be unduly large.

The typical pituitary type of woman craves dairy products such as cheeses, yoghurt, cream, ice cream, butter and milk. Dr Abravanel's theory, although unproven, is that dairy products are stimulants to the pituitary gland because they contain the hormone prolactin. To find the ideal diet to restore metabolic balance and promote weight loss in the pituitary type, see Table 10.

Women's Health Advisory Service, 1991), pp. 110–113.

terms of a profoundly determining opposition, a spectrum, or complementarity and harmony? The rhetorical slip *between* such constructions in what we may regard as a unified field of practice—such as the biomedical—is instructive. In this instance, the imperative of mass commodification of an easily graspable construction (one that already meshes with general cultural desires/fears) determines reinvestment in agonistic language. One may speculate on the kinds of affirmation afforded. However, at the level of practical application in the medical marketplace, such "target specific" drugs as the newly designated anti-androgens present a significant advance in women's health care, providing individuals with more precise and immediate control over distressing conditions—which were previously designated trivial, emotional, or natural (i.e., destiny). Such popularizing of biomedical language (however inadequate at research levels) thus participates in a discourse of feminist and social criticism against still-established medical practices and understandings, while *at the same time* neutralizing some of the tenets of earlier feminist criticism grounded in naive conceptions of the "natural" body.

Such instances serve to elucidate temporal disjunctions that confound those criticisms grounded in integrity of "the biomedical" (over and against the "aesthetic" or the popular cultural), not to mention any assumption of unilinear development in the history of medicine. Popular publishings that condense "medical information" for a wider market and the "women's health" genre may therefore perform the same critical function—in relation to traditional or preexisting domains of medical science—that the category of "popular culture" has played in the postmodern denegration of the idea of any *essential* value in high culture, fine art, and the literary canon.

Entrepreneurial medical practices and the mass-media disseminations of scientific information not only erode existing critical oppositions but may also modify rhetorical and practical structures *within* that space we may still wish to preserve as more strictly "biomedical." The popularizing of anti-androgens unsettles previously established medical norms of good health, such as longevity, in favor of more instantly gratifiable and more obviously aesthetic definitions of affectivity. An established ideal of the *preservation* of life is thereby contested by a complicating emphasis on the *quality* of life—a value supported by a much wider discursive field, not merely in debates about euthanasia but also in the new politics of "life style." However, this desire for *quality assurance* must be returned to free-market contexts: socialist and feminist criticisms that might otherwise oppose "rampant commercialism" must (humanely) affirm a consumerist idealism in which, as Roland Barthes noted so long ago, a persistent renegotiation of the natural/cultural intricately articulates class distinction. For example, *quality* of products and levels of personal "refinement" or one's "culture" (income, taste) may be asserted, paradoxically, by appeals to the natural: "raw" silk; "pure" linen; "real" leather; "natural" fibers; "virgin" cooking oil. No substitutes. After all, emphasis upon *quality* of life is the privilege of those who take a principle of *maintenance* for granted.

Paul Rabinow's ironic speculations about the unifying effects in sites of apparent contestation (specialization) do service here. The convergence of transnational interests in biotechnologies with social welfare values means that in the future

> groups may form around the chromosome 17, locus 16,256, site 654,375 allele variable with guanine substitution. They will have their separate culture, of medical specialists, laboratories, narratives and traditions and a heavy panopoly of pastoral keepers to help them experience, share, intervene in and "understand" their fate.[38]

Whatever the critical efficacies afforded by the rapidly growing domain of "women's health" (and its amalgamation of "natural" practices with high-tech drug manipulations), its own sphere too is necessarily riven by contradictions determined by the general assertion of a new aesthetic value as well as particular and conflicting "interests." For instance, the paradox implicit in the advocacy of corticosteroid drugs (known to contribute to bone density loss) in the treatment of "excess" hair, in practices simultaneously asserting osteoporosis prevention, may be explained in terms of contesting interests (ethical, commercial, technological, specialist) within a rhetorically unified field of "women's health." The patient's complaint is targeted now (just as advertising *targets* a particular audience) rather than treatment being modulated through a paternalizing medical vision of the overall well-being of a patient—of which the patient was clearly deemed to be not the best judge. This specializing process conceptually fragments the body while at the same time affirming an ideal of the "whole" self, just as in wider cultural contexts young people may say "Do you mean workwise, relationshipwise, healthwise?"—so dividing their time in order to achieve a "well-rounded" and "balanced" life, a life *styled.* The general "interest" unifying such paradoxes (of corticosteroid use/osteoporosis screening) is found in reference to an endless renegotiation of the aesthetic and the pathological—the process Georges Canguilhem defines, with reference to scientific practice, as not incidentally "norm" indexing but as *normativity.*[39] The cosmetic investment in smooth skin and no "excess" hair is obvious, but technically "distant" imaging depends upon, as well as subliminally activates, older models, given desires and fears. It is not entirely coincidental that the little old osteoporotic lady declining in increments, so popular in calcium-supplement advertisements, seems to be walking backward through evolutionary history—from upright human to the shape of lowest ape.

Seeing the Last Word: The Code of Codes

Between the too simple demonizing of medical sciences perpetuated by much feminist and sociological critique, and historically ignorant medical interests, it is difficult to formulate the terms of a criticism conscious of aesthetic ideologies without being part. The writings of Michel Foucault have to date proved immensely valuable for the interrogation of biomedical histories, yet his legacy is divided—especially in this context. His late turn to an aesthetics of self-care enacts its own kind of purifying idealization of Greek culture. For some, this constitutes a disappearance up the garden path of "self-cultivation." At the very least, his loose appropriation of Heidegger's care (*Sorge*) settles for a late-capitalist "supermarket" rhetoric of "free-choice" and self-design—just as Heidegger's own meditations fell in with National Socialism. Foucault's rejection of a "relentless theorizing of the 'text' (meaning Derrida) pointedly turns away from those lines of criticism that do interrogate such ascesis in the lived political.

Barbara Maria Stafford, in her mammoth and wonderful *Body Criticism*, also pits herself against the too "textual" valorizing of much poststructuralist theory and argues for a need to return to the primacy of the visual. She argues that a global and increasingly mass-visual culture requires the art historian's training to reveal the ways in which we still labor in the shadows of Enlightenment thought, undergoing a paradigm shift of overwhelming proportions from the textual to the visual.[40] Her formulations ignore the complex considerations of this very problematic in the writings of Derrida and others. If a textual paradigm yearns for revelatory pictures, by the same token we seem unable to articulate an image without reverting to metaphors of text. It is also the case that very "elite" systems of knowledge production depend upon a binary, differential system given by language.[41] And if the "informational" model is integral to data processing, biogenetic science in its most intricate understandings leans heavily on the idea of the text. The Human Genome project is articulated in terms of the Code of Codes—the Last Word. This is not merely a poetic glossing for mass consumption, for a *scriptural* understanding operates at the most refined and technical levels.[42] And while visualizing technologies do determine new directions, they also tend to "realize" the shapes in which we *already* think.

> The pictures that are particularly attractive that you have seen in general are *doctored*, in the sense of making them more attractive than they are at first. Removing things.[43]

With the downgrading of the American space program and the subsequent multibillion dollar allocation for the Human Genome Project (as the new "big science" in the United States), and the rapidly consolidating transnational interests in patenting and copyright, there is an increasingly general investment in the idea of an "inner nature" and a rhetoric of return to primal "origins"—to the very "blueprint of our human nature." Just as in Darwin's schema, the most rigorous biogenetic determinations do not preclude chance and random conjugations—*ineffability*. As in the Christian worldview, the idea of omnipotent creation will not preclude free will. Added to older conceptual models of reading and clarifying is the late twentieth-century conceit of "reprogramming," which displaces culpable racial "hygiene" and clumsy social "engineering." Just as the female psyche was a darker "continent," it is not unreasonable to assume that female biochemistry will remain a more difficult and mysterious text; or that such implications will be mapped back into the larger circuits. Already, as the first euphoria of DNA sequencing wanes, some researchers are discerning a certain *recalcitrance* at the molecular level.[44]

In transnational corporate capitalism, biology both is and isn't destiny. If Cuvier's Venus appeared today it is unlikely that she would win a supermodeling contract. If she did, the sanctions imposed on her appearance on the catwalk would not only be "uneducated" ones; they would be severely academic, concerned with matters of exploitation, with protection of vulnerable minorities from "degrading" representation, and dealing therefore in vague intimations of obscenity, of the burlesque, intimations that hover around the depiction of bodies not *already* culturally invested as admirable. Whatever the prohibitive, protective, or "correct" motivation, the result would be the same. Silencing— and thereby reinvestment of what is already "obscene," in the most literal sense of the word—as that which should not be *seen:*[45] Excess is much easier in theory, in the text. And whatever the promises of self-design afforded by new hormone technologies, it is very unlikely that many women will choose to reconstruct themselves "in the manner of" the Willendorf Venus. The ideal model, the still-point in the restless *pathognomia* of self-style, cannot be *exactly* the same as that dreamed by a lot of classically educated eighteenth-century gentlemen: slim, smooth, and symmetrical. In late capitalism's profoundly new convergence of *arte* and *techne* biology will return, shamelessly (or should I say with *prodigality*), to beginnings in aesthetic ideology.

Notes

1. Sigmund Freud, *Totem and Taboo*, trans. James Strachey (London: Routledge and Kegan Paul, 1950), pp. 125–26.

2. Freud's reference to Australian aboriginals and a "well-preserved picture" is in *Totem and Taboo*, p.1; for his reference to female sexuality as a "dark continent," see *The Standard Edition of the Complete Psychological Works of Sigmund Freud*, ed. and trans. James Strachey, 24 vols. (London: Hogarth Press, 1953–74), 20: p. 212.

3. Aristotle, in *De generatione animalium*, trans. Arthur Platt (Oxford: Clarendon Press, 1910), and *Historia animalium*, trans. D'arcy W. Thompson (Oxford: Clarendon Press, 1910).

4. Paul Albrecht, referenced in "Status," in Hermann Heinrich Ploss, Max Bartel, and Paul Bartel, *Woman: An Historical Gynaecological and Anthropological Compendium*, ed. Eric John Dingwall (London: William Heinemann Medical Books, 1935), chapter 1.

5. Lorenz Oken, *Elements of Physiophilosophy* (London: The Ray Society, 1847), pp. 491–92.

6. Cf. Evelleen Richards in "'Metaphorical Mysticisms': The Romantic gestation of nature in British biology," in *Romanticism and the Sciences*, ed. Andrew Cunningham and Nicholas Jardine, 130–43 (Cambridge: Cambridge University Press, 1990).

7. Cf. Jesse M. Gellrich, *The Idea of the Book in the Middle Ages* (Ithaca: Cornell University Press, 1985).

8. The English critique of German *Naturphilosophie* was wide-ranging and multifaceted but is commonly thought to have had its apotheosis in T. H. Huxley's debates with Richard Owen. Huxley and the Darwinians took pride in their "plain, prosaic inquiry" into "objective truth" over and against Owen's "taint" of German analogizing. See T. H. Huxley, "Owen's Position in the History of Anatomical Science," in *The Life of Richard Owen*, 2 vols., ed. R. Owen (London, 1894), pp. 273–332.

9. Cf. Gillian Rose, *Judaism and Modernity* (Oxford: Blackwell, 1993). While not addressing the biological sciences, Rose's philosophical essays demonstrate the history and significance of a Judaic "textual" tradition for poststructuralist philosophy. Derrida's play with Greek, Judaic, and Christian differences repeatedly. See also Harold Bloom's *Kabbalah and Criticism* (New York: Seabury, 1975), which relates Kabbalah to literary criticism.

10. Charles Darwin, *On the Origin of Species* (London: Murray, 1859), p. 447.

11. Cesare Lombroso, *L'homme criminel*, 2d ed., 2 vols (Paris: 1895), and *Crime: Its Causes and Remedies*, trans. H. P. Horton (Boston: Modern Criminal Science, 1911).

12. Cesare Lombroso, *In Calabria* (Reggio Calabria: Studi Meridionali, 1973), pp. 146–52. This work collects essays from 1862–1898. Cf. Daniel Pick, *Faces of Degeneration* (Cambridge: Cambridge University Press, 1989), chapter 5.

13. Max Nordau, *Degeneration* (London: University of Nebraska Press, 1993), pp. 17, 27–32. Originally published in Germany in 1892; first English edition published in New York by D. Appleton & Co., 1895.

14. Cf. George L. Mosse, "Beauty without Sensuality/The Exhibition *Entartete Kunst*," in *"Degenerate Art": The Fate of the Avant-Garde in Nazi Germany*, ed. Stephanie Barron (New York: Los Angeles County Museum of Art & Harry N. Abrams, Inc., 1991), pp. 25–33.

15. Daniel Pick, *Faces*, p. 27.

16. Anthony Ashley Cooper, Earl of Shaftsbury. *Characteristics* (London: n.p., 1738), pp. 402–405, 411–12.

17. J. J. Winckelmann, *Versuch einer Allegorie, besonders fur die Kunst* (Dresden: In der Walterischen Hof-Buchhandlung, 1766), p. 121. See also Barbara Maria Stafford's convincing relation of Winckelmann's aesthetic to preformationist ideas of *embôitment*, in *Body Criticism* (Cambridge: MIT Press, 1993), p. 251.

18. Petrus Camper, "From Ape to Apollo Belvedere," in *Dissertation physique*, 1791 (Bethesda, MD: National Library of Medicine), p 1. 3.

19. Johann Caspar Lavater, *Essays on Physiognomy* (1792), p. 177.

20. Hermann Heinrich Ploss, Max Bartels, and Paul Bartels, *Woman: An Historical Gynaecological and Anthropological Compendium* (London: William Heinemann Medical Books, 1935), vol.1. On breasts see chapter 3, steatopygia, pp. 327–36. See also Paula Weideger's own feminist revisionary "selection" from *Das Weib*, and her critical overview, in introduction, of this editorial history, in *History's Mistress* (Middlesex: Penguin Books, 1985). Weideger explicitly sets "nurture" against Ploss and Bartel's misogynistic "nature."

21. Richard Von Krafft-Ebing, *Psychopathia Sexualis*, trans. from the 12th German ed. by Franklin S. Klaf (New York: Stein and Day Publishers, 1965).

22. Ploss, Bartels, and Bartels, *Woman*, pp. 300–308.

23. Sander L. Gilman, "Black Bodies, White Bodies: Toward an Iconography of Female Sexuality in Late Nineteenth Century Art, Medicine and Literature," in *"Race," Writing and Difference*, ed. H. L. Gates Jr. (Chicago: Chicago University Press, 1986), pp. 223–62. Gilman references Billroth's *Handbuch der Frauenkrankheiten*, which links prostitution with lesbianism.

24. Sander L. Gilman, "Black Bodies," p. 237.

25. Cesare Lombroso and Guillaume Ferrero, *La donna deliquente: La prostituta e la donna normale* (Turin: 1893), pp. 349–50, 361. Cf. Lombroso, *The Female Offender*, trans. W. Douglas Morrison (New York: Philiphil Press, 1985).

26. Carl Vogt, *Lectures on Man* (London: Longman, Green, Longman and Roberts, 1864), p. 192.

27. Gustave le Bon, *The Crowd: A Study of the Popular Mind* (London: 1917), pp. 35–36, 118–19. See also Robert Nye's study of the importance of a medical model in ideas of national decline in the Third Republic in *Crime, Madness and Politics in Modern France: The Medical Concept of National Decline* (Princeton: Princeton University Press, 1984).

28. Cf. Daniel Pick, *Faces*, pp. 92–96.

29. Oswald Spengler, *The Decline of the West* (New York: A. A. Knopf, 1918), p. 106.

30. Edgar Allen Poe, "Ligeia," in *Edgar Allen Poe: Selected Tales*, ed. Julian Symons (Oxford: Oxford University Press, 1980), pp. 39–40, 51–52; Poe's italics; and "The Philosophy of Composition" (1846) in *Essays and Reviews* (New York: Literary Classics of the United States, 1984), p. 19.

31. Matthew Gregory Lewis, *The Monk: A Romance* (1795), in ed. Howard Anderson (Oxford: Oxford University Press, 1973).

32. Cf. Daniel Pick, *Faces*. Pick argues that Foucault's power/knowledge model underplays "internal textual struggles" and underestimates the "work of representation," p. 43. See also Robert Nye's detailed critique, "Love and Reproductive Biology in *Fin de Siècle* France," in *Foucault and the Writing of History*, ed. Jan Goldstein (Oxford: Basil Blackwell Ltd, 1994), pp. 150–65.

33. Sigmund Freud, "On the Psychical Mechanism of Hysterical Phenomena: Preliminary Communication," in *The Standard Edition of the Complete Works of Sigmund Freud in 24 Volumes*, ed. James Strachey (London: Hogarth Press, 1956–66), pp. 11, 6.

34. Cf. Jan B. Gordon, "Freud's 'Secret Agent' and the Fin du corps," in *Fin de Siècle/Fin du Globe*, ed. John Stoke, pp. 117–38 (London: Macmillan, 1992).

35. My references here are to Baudrillard's use of simulacra and Guy de Bord's *La société du spectacle* (France: Buchet Chastel, 1967).

36. Sandra Cabot, *Don't Let Hormones Rule Your Life* (New South Wales: Women's Health Advisory Service, 1991).

37. Cf. Nelly Oudshoorn, *Beyond the Natural Body: An Archeology of Sex Hormones* (London: Routledge, 1994), pp. 20–41.

38. Paul Rabinow, "Artificiality and Enlightenment: From Sociobiology to Biosociality," in *Incorporations*, ed. J. Crary and S. Winter (New York: Zone, 1992), pp. 234–53.

39. Georges Canguilhem, *Le normal et le pathologique* (France: Presses Universitaires de France, 1966).

40. Barbara Maria Stafford, *Body Criticism: Imaging the Unseen in Enlightenment Art and Medicine* (Cambridge: MIT Press, 1993), pp. 471–77.

41. Cf. Martin Jay, *Downcast Eyes: The Denigration of Vision in Twentieth-Century French Thought* (Los Angeles: University of California Press, 1994).

42. The technical language of *messengers, transcription,* and *translation* was consolidated in the 1950s. See Francis Jacob and Jacques Monod, "Genetic Regulatory Mechanisms in the Synthesis of Proteins," *Journal of Molecular Biology* 3 (1961); pp. 318–56. The term "Code of Codes" is used along with "the Search for the Grail" in a variety of overviewing histories. See Horace Freeland Judson, *The Eighth Day of Creation: Makers of the Revolution in Biology* (New York: Simon and Schuster, 1979).

43. Michael Ter-Poggosian in interview, Joseph Dumit "Twenty-first-Century PET: Looking for Mind and Morality through the Eye of Technology," in *Technoscientific Imaginaries: Conversations, Profiles and Memoirs,* ed. George E. Marcus (Chicago: University of Chicago Press, 1995), pp. 87–128, 997; my italics. Ter-Poggosian is the "father" of PET.

44. Cf. Horace Freeland Judson, "A History of the Science and Technology Behind Gene Mapping and Sequencing," in Daniel J. Kerles and Leroy Hood, eds., *The Code of Codes* (Cambridge, Massachusetts: Harvard University Press, 1992), pp. 37–83, on the difficulties of "the mapping."

45. Sandar Gilman's representation of racial hygiene photographs and images of black women from nineteenth-century texts to illustrate his essays on such culpable histories may occasion feminist reservation. He risks academic fetishization and "repeating the crime" of degrading representation of vulnerable minorities. I find such reservations extremely problematical. Political "correction" may be ethically necessary in so many contexts, yet it participates in forgetting, erasing culpable histories. This dilemma is being exhaustively explored with reference to "Holocaust representation"—the need to document (*anamnesis*) and the awareness of the dangers of reinvestment in a sadomasochistic, racist, and sexist imaginary. Thus the "deconstructive" Geoffrey Hartman, while endorsing "play" with linear histories and definitions of truth in literary theoretical contexts, asserts another imperative of *visual* documentation in his work for the Yale Holocaust Archive; the visual "testimony" of particular and individual stories is necessary in the face of "revisionist" histories, *posthistoire* movements in Germany, and Hollywood's relentless *Schlubladendenken.* My own work on *Das Weib* has confronted such sanctions, such as an editor's selection of a highly romanticized and beautiful picture of a Maori "mother and child" to illustrate an essay addressing the pathologizing of black women's bodies, because he felt that the more appropriate photos were sadomasochistic (cf. *Rosemarie Trockel,* ed. Gregory Burke [Wellington: Goethe Institute/City Gallery, 1993].) While understanding the ethical imperative, such romanticizing and paternalizing gestures need to be returned to their own culpable histories, in Romantic sentimentality and "noble savage" mystification and Christian paternalizing, which would "cover the bodies" and erase the narratives of primitive peoples—in the name of "corrective" education. What erasures of guilt, in such repetitions? I think I agree, finally, with Roland Barthes, that a photograph indexes something beyond words—*especially* of what is lost. Its replication, through time, can *never* mean exactly the same thing, whether that thing is Nazism in its early twentieth-century meanings or racist and sexist scholarship in its nineteenth-century

significances. *Other* culpabilities may emerge in representation of visual images (their meanings are not containable), but locking them up in the archives (as the Vatican did with the penises of Greek sculptures) is a suspect *hygiene*-ascesis. I've attempted to address these issues otherwise, with reference to the visual and textual and deconstruction (cf. "Antigone's Shadow: Theory after the Holocaust," *Meridian*, 13.2 [October 1994]: pp. 107–125).

DISCURSIVE STRATEGIES

8

Facing Change
Women Speaking about Midlife

Jeanne Daly

The sound of silence breaking makes us understand what we could not hear before. But the fact that we could not hear does not prove that no pain existed. The revolutionary must listen very carefully to the language of silence. This is particularly important for women because we come from such a long silence.
—Sheila Rowbotham[1]

In 1990 the Australian National Health and Medical Research Council announced menopause as the subject for a round of special initiative grants. The Australian Consumers Health Forum approached a number of researchers, encouraging us to submit proposals that would focus on the experience of women as consumers, in part to offset the expected medical focus of proposals submitted under this initiative. The proposal that won through the selection process sought to analyze the social construction of menopause, especially the way in which women in their midlife years see "menopause." It was to be based on the accounts of women who saw themselves as "menopausal," aiming in part to identify the criteria that led them to this perception.

The full study was to have a number of arms. One of these involved interviews with women: it is this that I am reporting here.[2] What follows is an account of the conduct of this study, including the way in which it was conceptualized, its results, and its implications for women's health policy.

Women Talking: Beyond the Stereotypes?

My commitment in the study was to conduct a feminist sociological analysis of women's experience, taking careful account of the dynamics of the interview process,[3] and to contribute to women's collective interests. One hundred fifty women who saw themselves as menopausal were interviewed in an unstructured focus group format. Study participants were selected from a range of backgrounds that could be expected to have an effect on the ways in which midlife was experienced, including middle-class and working-class women, women from migrant backgrounds, and women living in isolated rural settings. Women attending a tertiary referral menopause clinic were included to strengthen the understanding of women's experience of the medical treatment of menopause. When in the first two interviews the use of hormone therapy emerged as a contentious issue, it was decided to approach one woman from a particular background and to ask her to invite as participants a group of like-minded friends who would feel comfortable discussing potentially contentious areas of midlife with each other and with us. This had the additional advantage that women who became distressed in the interview had a circle of friends to support them in the interview and afterward. Indeed, one result of the interviews was that a number of self-help groups were established, especially in the rural areas. Women who felt uncomfortable with the group format were interviewed individually.

Menopause is a "blood mystery" faced in silence, argues Gail Sheehy,[4] but in our interviews the silence broke. It is this breaking of the silence that placed a responsibility on us as researchers to report the interviews in a way that would serve our collective interests as midlife women. From the first interview it was clear that this was going to be a troublesome task. The experiences the women attributed to menopause were so varying as to appear idiosyncratic. The range of physical problems recounted was as long as that in any medical text. Women could experience the full range of problems at one time; or the problems might fluctuate or come in cycles, with one specific problem being more troublesome all the time or for some of the time. Women also saw as relevant to the experience of menopause the full range of their life experiences from childhood, including their relationships with mothers, their experience of marriage, childbirth, mothering and careers; and the anticipation of their own and their partners' transitions to older age. Interactively, these contributed to attitudes to midlife (as a time) and menopause (as an experience) that ranged from the positive to the extremely negative.

Faced with such complexity, it was tempting to follow in the footsteps of the large prospective cohort studies of women in midlife by defining menopause in terms of menstrual cessation and assessing "symptoms" as those changes, measured by validated survey instruments, that accompany menstrual cessation[5] or correspond with shifts in blood hormone levels.[6] This approach is useful in being able to tell us how many women experience particular "symptoms" (and this is useful information), but it fails to give credence to women's own accounts of what menopause means to them. Patricia Kaufert argued that women did not define menopause in this medical manner but used a "self-anchoring" definition in which they saw themselves as menopausal when there was a change in their accustomed patterns of menstruation. Relying on the experience of changes in their bodies made menopause not a single event "but a complex and long drawn-out process of physiological change."[7]

Physiological changes certainly occur in midlife, but the women in our study did not always separate out the effects of physiological change and other changes in their everyday lives. The changes the women themselves associated with menopause (often referred to as "symptoms") varied in intensity and frequency, but women had various degrees of resilience or vulnerability in meeting these changes depending on their health in general, their social circumstances including families and friends, resources (financial and educational), and the degree of negative stereotyping in the social group to which they belonged. At one extreme were women entering midlife with happy confidence while, at the other, there were women already living miserable, disrupted lives. Not surprisingly then, some negotiated their situation with ease and took in their stride those problems that did present, but this was not true of all.

The women who experienced difficulties faced a range of problems. To describe their experience with some degree of generality, we drew on the description most often used, a description that rings true to the audiences to whom we have presented this material. Whatever their individual problems, women spoke in terms of a loss of their accustomed capacity to cope with change (however high or low that might have been): they spoke of a loss of balance, of feeling "out of kilter." Some women related the loss of balance in their lives to changes in menstrual patterns, in which case it was commonly identified as hormonal; while others felt "thrown" by the combined effect of "everything going wrong all at once" as their menstrual patterns became irregular. While these problems could start well before menstruation ceased, unsettling episodes of instability could persist for years after cessation.

In reporting these experiences, the words behind the silence, we had two primary audiences. The first audience comprised women themselves, especially midlife women, who wanted to know how other women had fared in midlife. The second audience, however, was that set of experts who aim to "cure" menopausal complaints. Their methods are reductionist in the sense that they separately categorize menopausal "symptoms," referring each such "symptom" to an appropriate expert for treatment. From medical texts it was clear that the medical process of categorization and referral led to an overwhelming emphasis on hormones and endocrine dysfunction in explaining the experience of menopause. Women's more complex accounts make no sense in this discourse. Silencing is achieved by focusing on bits of women (their hormones) rather than on women as people. Any complaints seen as nonhormonal (since they are resistant to hormone treatment) may then be regarded as having some other (social or psychological) cause that requires resolution by the woman herself, perhaps with pharmacological or psychiatric help.

The medical profession is not alone in offering reductionist theories based on a stereotyped view of women in midlife. The literature on midlife transition commonly ignores the role of biology, emphasizing instead the importance of changing family roles (including the "empty nest syndrome") and economic status.[8] "Symptom formation" in midlife has been attributed to "socio-cultural factors,"[9] and women's negative experience of menopause has been seen as "a Western cultural behavioral disorder."[10] Psychological distress has been seen as attending an early or late menopause rather than as menopause itself.[11] Thus menopause is seen as a normal life event that troubles few women, except in the short term or where there are pre-existing problems.[12] Importantly, depression in midlife has been attributed not to hormonal deficiencies but to social events and to circumstances in midlife. This emphasis has set the scene for what McCrea described as a "stigma contest," with feminists arguing that menopause is a normal life event, and the medical profession seeing it as being either "all in the head" or symptomatic of a deficiency disease.[13] Alternative therapists offer their own remedies, including diet and herbal treatments.[14] Midlife women writing about their own experiences have prescribed the invocation of the Goddess[15] or taking on the role of hag or virago.[16] A limited, narrow focus can therefore be a feature of both medical and feminist prescriptions.[17]

Within this debate, reporting the confusing complexities of women's midlives carries the risk of increasing the negative stereotype of the complaining middle-aged woman who does not know how to take control of her life. Alternatively, increasing our knowledge of the complexity of the experience might increase the tendency to focus on a single cause for menopausal ills, since the full complexity is too difficult to analyze except by reduction to simpler constituent problems. In displaying sensitive areas of concern (such as changes in sexuality), we might also be seen as inviting further reductionist prescriptions. The obvious solution for our study seemed to be that women's public silence about menopause should be maintained by reporting our results only to groups of midlife women. This was our first strategy.

Ignoring the public audience dominated by medicine, could, however, be counterproductive. Many women felt themselves in need of medical treatment but saw current forms of treatment as unsatisfactory. Especially in the menopause clinic where some women were interviewed, midlife women and women clinicians did have a common goal, that of helping women negotiate problems in midlife. Since the menopause clinic was a specialist service, many of the women had been referred there when their problems could not be resolved in general practice settings. Clinicians had a limited range of prescriptions they could use, largely relying on hormone treatment. They were concerned about the lack of evidence of effectiveness of hormone therapies and were keenly aware of every medical review that raised questions about benefits or risks. They resolved their difficulties by explaining to women what the risks and benefits were and then offering women a "choice." Some women saw this as unhelpful:

they had gone to the clinic for advice on issues that lay outside their realm of technical expertise and felt that the offer of a "choice" was merely placing responsibility for the decision on their own technically inexpert shoulders.

The problem remains that menopause is a terrain where various "experts" peddle their wares while women in general remain silent. Ignoring the experts would not make them leave the arena, and the systematic exclusion of women's voices from the analysis of menopause makes it easier, rather than harder, to trivialize the complex variety of women's lives. My aim, however, is not simply to argue for the inclusion of women's various experiences, making medical science more responsive to women's needs. This might do no more than to provide better data for reductionist analyses, in the process strengthening the belief that women's problems in midlife are to be resolved by experts through technically rational means not accessible to public debate.[18] In this context, giving women a "choice" between different forms of technical resolution of their problems does little to resolve the problems associated with medical domination of the process by which some women are diagnosed as having a disease and some women are seen as not having a medically legitimate complaint. Rather, we need to focus on the way in which "disease" itself is socially constructed.

Karl Figlio argues that defining a disease is one of the ways of dealing socially with distress.[19] When the latter is expressed as a set of complaints, commonly in the context of social change, the medical profession provides a social resolution for both distress and complaints by diagnosing a disease to be treated in a defined manner. What is created is a fluid social space within which distress is resolved by technically rational means. In some contexts, technical medical interventions do indeed save lives and resolve distress; however, the ideology of technocratic rationality claims for the whole what is true only for part of the enterprise. In the case of menopause, claims of technically effective means of resolving women's problems lead to the subjugation of women's own accounts of the social nature of their problems in midlife and a foreclosing of their struggles for change. The problem for us as feminist researchers is therefore to argue for a differently defined social space in which women's accounts are presented free from medical interpretation, and in which the stereotypic "menopausal" woman gives way to multivariate, multidimensional creatures with knowledge and specific demands. Only when it is a precondition of this feminist-defined social space that the choir of women's voices has absolute legitimacy can we acknowledge the additional voices of those experts whose aim is to help women in midlife.

Donna Haraway's interpretation of Sandra Harding's "successor science" points to possible directions for achieving this new social space. Haraway argues that we can draw on a tradition of feminist critical empiricism in order to "translate knowledges among very different—and power-differentiated—communities."[20] On the one hand, we can therefore engage in critical analysis of dominant viewpoints, including an acknowledgment of the role, within limits, of technical treatment of disease. On the other hand, we can emphasize "situated knowledges" in which "subjugated" standpoints, translated here into women's telling of their experiences in midlife, are given full weight. Instead of one form of knowledge we therefore have partial, locatable, critical knowledges. Such an analysis, Haraway argues, sustains "the possibility of webs of connexions."

My task in this paper is not one of critically analyzing medical claims to success in the management of women's midlife problems; this is the focus of other papers in this collection. Rather, my aim is to show the very many different ways in which women experience, and make sense of, midlife. Emphasizing variety, however, carries the danger that the phenomenon itself can slip through our fingers. As a result we can leave individual women talking about their individual experience in voices that are feeble in competition with the organized discourse of prescriptive "experts." Nor is this necessary. When women talk about midlife, what emerges from their stories are differences in their experiences ranging from the extremely troublesome, with the result that women need access to help, to the positive, which allows women better to realize the potential of midlife. These negative and positive experiences are the two ends of a spectrum, with most women having experiences that fit somewhere in between. It is important to note here that women cannot be located within one or the other of these experiences in any static way, since their experiences can change radically over a relatively short period of time. The danger of not recognizing these differences is that the women most in need of help, those with the most negative experiences, can all too readily have their problems overlooked, with possible serious consequences.

I start this description of women's experiences of midlife with the accounts of those women who are sorely troubled by the combined effect of their problems. As far as possible, I draw on the way in which the women themselves described their experiences. I then give an account of women who manage to negotiate their problems with some degree of success, finally emphasizing the positive experiences of midlife and the potential this holds for more constructive strategies for negotiating midlife.

The Experience of Being Besieged by Problems

Based on their own accounts, we classified 20 women of the 150 participants as having an extremely negative experience.[21] In contrast to the studies that show no increase in depression associated with menopause, twelve of the women identified their major problem as a high level of depression, starting with increased premenstrual stress that steadily worsened as their periods became more irregular. The remainder described a range of other problems interacting with depression.[22] The majority of the women who had a negative experience had considered suicide or actually attempted it; the others suffered severe disruption to their lives.[23]

Sheila is one of the women who attempted suicide. She recognized the contribution made to her state of mind by the demands of a multigenerational family and an unemployed husband, and she acknowledged that she sets high standards for herself but was convinced that her periodic and overwhelming sense of *angst* derived from hormonal shifts, what she called the "internal maelstrom of menopause." The feeling of having been "cut adrift from her life" started in her early forties, but the intensity increased when her periods became irregular, reaching an almost unbearable level by her late forties. Her general practitioner saw her problems as psychosomatic; he advised her to restructure her life and prescribed tranquilizers to help her in this task but ignored her complaint of a dry vagina which ended up being so dry that it was cracked and bleeding. Later, when she was prescribed hormones at a menopause clinic, she took the treatment only until her vaginal wounds healed. This helped her gain an acceptable degree of control over her life.

Marianne sees health as a "well-integrated articulation of mind and body." Increasingly, premenstrual stress destroyed this equilibrium, bringing on periodic bouts of suicidal depression that led her to identify herself as menopausal. She became intolerant and was afraid that her family would classify her as "a common or garden nag or a menopausal semipsychotic." She is a successful author of children's books and was able to restructure her life to be away from home before her periods. Curled up in a hotel bed, she would lie down and cry. When increasingly irregular periods made it difficult to predict depressed times, which finally persisted for as long as a fortnight, she found it more difficult to hide her problems from an unsympathetic husband. Her gynecologist diagnosed the "empty nest syndrome," prescribed vitamin tablets, and suggested she get a part-time job. Instead, she gave up writing and for seven years committed herself to a quiet life while she waited for her body to metamorphose. Her fear was that it would leave her "a black-clad old lady with a scarf over her head who is in her element only at family funerals."

Anne is an older woman who dismissed menopause as "nothing at all." Her niece, who had suggested that we interview her, reminded her that she had prepared for death on her fiftieth birthday. She had tidied her life, including her linen cupboard, tying sheets and towels with blue ribbon so that her husband's next wife would think well of her as a housewife. Reminded of this, Anne shrugged and spoke of a day when her husband came home to lunch and she calmly asked him for his handgun because she thought she should shoot herself. Her husband was a doctor. He hid the gun and left the house to return an hour later with a colleague, the superintendent of the local "lunatic asylum." She was tranquilized, admitted, and spent the next six months there. At that stage they told her that she would have electroconvulsive therapy unless she "pulled herself together." She did, returned home, gradually recovered, and is now a hale and hearty seventy-six year old. The worst part of her experience, she says, was her isolation: "We weren't supposed to talk about our problems." She believes that the feminist movement has made such gains in putting women's issues on the political agenda that no woman should again have to suffer in isolation as she did.

Sheila, Marianne, and Anne are articulate women with considerable education and other social privileges. Sharon is not. Her problems are more clearly related to a combination of various debilitating problems in which depression played a contributory role. At the age of thirty-six years, she identified herself as menopausal because of hot flashes, heavy periods, and excruciating migraines, all of which she remembered seeing her mother suffer at menopause. She struggled to get to her doctor on public transport and he prescribed tranquilizers that knocked her out. She felt unable to go back to him, because she believed he intended to have her "locked away." Her alcoholic husband and her children started avoiding her. Despite these difficulties, she gave birth to two more children when in her forties. Her husband died soon after the last (sixth) child was born. Their relationship had been so difficult that she saw this as a relief; however, it was financially devastating. The intensification of the various menopausal problems led to her taking too much sick leave and she was fired from her factory job. Finally, she became severely depressed and alcoholic so that the younger children were removed from her care for two years. With the end of her periods she slowly regained control over her life. It took the next fifteen years for her to find a sense of peace and to enter into community activities with other older women.

Only three of the 20 women had full-time employment. While their problems made it extremely difficult to remain employed, they felt unable to cite menopause as a reason for extended sick leave; it was simply not an option. Jean was encouraged to take an early retirement on the grounds of "arthritis," although she suspected that there was additional concern about "homicidal rages" which made her lock herself into her office while she fought to control her feelings. Other women felt such a sense of general malaise that they became convinced that they had terminal cancer. When these problems persisted year after year, some women became desperate and felt that their lives were no longer worth living. Other women had one or more episodes of deep depression when they contemplated taking their own lives, driving a car into a tree, or attaching a hose to the car exhaust. In talking about this dark experience, they emphasized the terror of not knowing what was going on. Being able to attach the label of menopause to explain at least some aspect of what they were feeling was a relief in itself: it held the promise that the problems would pass. For Jean of the "homicidal rages," the realization came only after she had lost her job.

Every one of these women took her problems to a medical practitioner, some of them so often with such a diverse set of complaints that they perceived their doctors as groaning when they entered the office. The women saw their ills as hormonally induced, but saw their doctors as unconvinced, all too readily dispensing tranquilizers or fatuous social advice. Their doctors, the women said, failed to hear them and failed to give them credit for understanding their own bodies. This was no simple omission but an active denial: they were told to "pull themselves together." With their lives stretched to the limit, these women were manifestly unable to do so.

The Experience of Battling through Problems

The largest group, 105 women out of 150, were managing with some degree of success to keep a balance in their lives despite problems. Some women experienced one set of problems, some women another. Hot flashes were common, as was increased premenstrual tension. Some women talked of memory problems like developing "holes in the head that ideas fall into" and of not being able to remember telephone numbers, a very disturbing problem for women in a professional situation. Some women were plagued by pains in the joints or insomnia, waking up at 2 A.M. with eyes wide open, worried about how they would perform at work the next day—especially if the day had to be faced with hot flashes and memory loss. Common "symptoms" like menstrual flooding may sound relatively innocuous but could be sorely trying and disruptive:

> But life was hell while I had all that flooding. Oh, it was a scream! If I went shopping up at [the supermarket], I'd go in and it didn't matter whether you had one, two, or three pads on, it was useless, absolutely useless! And, I'd go in and I'd do my shopping and I think, "OK, I'm going to be fine today!" I'd end up, I'd have to leave the store, and I'd walk out with a plastic bag hanging in front of me of groceries and plastic bag behind to hide myself, and that was one of the more embarrassing things. (Jenny)

Helena had a hysterectomy because of her embarrassment at work when sudden flooding left her with blood running into her shoes before she could reach the toilet. In contrast, Joy dreaded losing her periods and described graphically her pleasure at menstruating, including the smell of her own blood. Some women mourned the loss of their reproductive powers, especially if they had valued their mothering role very highly and if they felt that their menopause was premature. For Catholic women who had relied on the rhythm method for contraception, irregular periods raised the specter of a midlife baby younger than their grandchildren. The cessation of menstruation meant freedom from this fear of pregnancy for the first time in their lives. For many women, the end of their periods was keenly anticipated as signaling the start of the end of the midlife torture of cycles of depression and fragility and the start of a return to equilibrium.

The family lives of the women interviewed were extremely varied. Some lived in families, some were single. Some were "childfree," some had grandchildren, some still had primary school children, and some were facing pain due to their childlessness. They were often not reluctant to have grown-up children leave home. For women who had spent many years in childrearing, midlife was a time when they could spread their wings. Jeanette, married to a wealthy businessman in a country town, bought herself a second house in the city so that she could complete a Ph.D. in women's studies, see her children, and immerse herself in art and music. Such plans could, however, be frustrated:

> You know, you manage to sort of hold this juggling act together with little kids, job, never having enough time, and just getting to the stage where there is a sense that . . . you've got maybe the time to do what you wanted, your career, or to do things that you've always wanted to do, and never had time to do. And then suddenly your system starts fouling up again. So, that's the anger I think that a lot of women feel. (Bea)

Some women who had successfully juggled family commitments for many years lost their sense of accomplishment when they tried to enter the work force. They found that their skills were out of date and family finances precluded tuition in new skills like word processing. When employers preferred younger women as receptionists, they felt that, instead of being able to spread their wings, they were "on the scrap heap." At home there could be a concatenation of problems. Joyce was unable to find work after twenty years at home raising children. Her husband was unemployed, as were her two adult sons. While they watched daytime television, she was "going up the wall" in the kitchen. The men's alcohol intake led to rising levels of violence in the home. Joyce is religious with high moral principles; she felt that her life was being violated by their behavior, but she had no means of escape. Hot flashes that left her wrung out and panting seemed unendurable.

Particularly when women have intense symptoms, they seek medical help but hormone treatment is not a simple matter. Priscilla's problems arose very abruptly after a hysterectomy and the loss of one ovary and she was dramatically cured with hormone therapy, but it took time to get the therapy right:

> And I just think that womanhood's a tale of hormones, depending on the mixes, who you are. And, also depending on the mix that they give you is what you feel, you just have to experiment, try and find someone who'll take you through the reins to find your balance.

Apart from getting the right balance and the time this takes, hormone therapy brings its own complications. Sandra, the mother of a toddler, attributed her problems to a tubal ligation after the child was born, so she felt that "I got menopause without asking for it."

> It is really, really rotten having your interest in life reduced when you are only forty-one. . . . I'm faced with dreadful PMT, erratic periods coming every

three weeks, mood swings, and no sex life. I don't want to spend the next twenty years like this.

Hormone therapy brought some relief of her hot flashes, premenstrual stress, and loss of sexual interest but the downside was the financial cost. With only one wage and young children, the cost of hormone therapy or the alternative of natural therapy put a dent in a tight family budget. She faced the choice of being "selfish" or of facing years of distress.

In addition, therapy could alleviate one problem but precipitate another. Susan found immediate relief as a result of hormone therapy: "I just felt so *good*. My headaches went, my depression went, I was able to sleep, my bone aches and pains went. . . . I felt *fantastic.*" Like a number of other women she then found that the hormones had "side effects"—in her case, intense gastric pain—and she discontinued the treatment. Other women spoke of problems like sore breasts, weight gain, and increased depression that led them to flush the pills down the toilet. Some then felt guilty, aware that they would be seen by their doctors as "noncompliers."

There were few women who saw hormone therapy as uncomplicated. Some women put the prescription in their handbags but left it there. Angela asked her woman pharmacist what she thought about HRT. The pharmacist explained that a lower dose pill was available in other countries but that only the higher dose pill was available in Australia. Together they decided that Angela should cut the pills in half. For safe measure, Angela painstakingly cut all the pills into quarters—but she then decided that she would not take them after all. She still had vivid memories of years spent dependent on the contraceptive pill. Freda, in the same situation, weighed up the risks and the benefits as follows:

> I started on the pill at seventeen, on a very heavy dose, and because I didn't catch up with a woman doctor until about twenty years, I saw male doctors for twenty years, they renewed the fucking prescription and they never checked it. And although minipills had come onto the market, they never revised it, and so I was onto the heavy dose for twenty years. . . . Fortunately, I don't have flooding problems or anything as bad as you, but I mean for me it would have to get very bad before I considered HRT because I've had so much estrogen already. So there's, you know, all these kinds of balancing things that most women would want to consider and put it in weighing scales and sort of say, "Okay, there's this and this and this, there's these, there's the uncertainty factor." And yet, you know, if I'm suffering badly, well, stuff it, you know I'll get some!

As in Freda's case, resistance was strengthened if women did not trust their doctors:

> *Jill:* I suppose that is what bothers me. I actually just don't trust doctors.
> *Chorus:* No, neither do I!
> *A voice:* Just one!
> *Another:* I wouldn't trust *any* doctors!

The perception that doctors were not listening to their problems made the problem worse:

> *Fay:* Well, I mean, that was my experience of going along to the doctor, feeling stressed by the things that one's entitled to be stressed about, I'll put it that way. And the immediate answer was, "Oh yes, well, we'll put you on hormone replacement therapy," and I thought . . . that's saying, "Go home, dear, this is your fault, you're menopausal, just go home and pop the little pills and then everything in the family will be okay." I felt that was terribly wrong.
> *Bridget:* She obviously didn't investigate. She didn't really want to hear about what the real problem was, so she just superficially treated you and got you out the door.

The strongest resistance, however, was called forth by the medical perception that sexual interests were to be manipulated hormonally:

> My biggest thing is I've lost my sex drive. I used to feel as if I needed a fix . . . I used to get all uptight and be angry, it was really strange. My husband would say, "Well, I think it's time!" I did enjoy it a lot. I saw the doctor about it a few weeks ago. He said, "That's actually the male hormone side of it," and he said, "You, perhaps, had a little more than normal, because women don't, but men get more uptight if they don't get it." That is what he was telling me! And he said to go and talk to the gynecologist, who suggested I have testosterone implants.

Horrified at this, Jane described her real problem as not feeling "nice" about herself. For help with problems expressed in this more general way, there was no substitute for the comfort of sharing problems with other women:

> I mean, bit by bit we are working our way through these things, and we can say one to the other, "Look, I really empathize with you, I truly understand how you are feeling but just hold on, it will go, it will go!" (Sandra)

Gliding through Midlife

Twenty-five of the women in the study were "gliding" their way through menopause. Carol described herself as one of the lucky ones:

> We were going to America and I went off with my case packed with all the necessary bits and pieces and so on. It was only when I came back and unpacked, I thought, "My goodness, I've missed." . . . But I didn't have a twinge, headache or anything. I think I might have had a hot flash occasionally. I don't even quite remember that. But my main thing was I had wasted all that good space in my suitcase!

Women in this group experienced some problems, but these problems failed to distress them. Some were only aware of a "quite astonishing" feeling of well-being when their periods ceased. Emily said that she felt as though a weight had been lifted off her:

> I recall a neighbor of mine saying to me about her mother, once she got through menopause, she did Scottish dancing and she could dance any man under the table, she felt so great.

These women are better able to realize the positive potential of menopause:

> Your first third of your life, I found that I did everything to please my family. Went all out. It was expected of me. I was happy to do it. I was a very good daughter. Then I spent the next third of my life pleasing my family. And I said to my husband, "If I can't get out of life what *I* want now, I'm going to go it alone!" (Meg)

Angela first took hormone therapy because her glasses steamed up during hot flashes. She had taken the pills for so long that she did not know whether her happy state was related to the pills or to the other strategies she used, including remarriage and going for a swim and a coffee before work every morning. She described herself as storing up credits for her old age: "I just want to be a healthy old lady." Paradoxically, this group of well women was often encouraged to take hormones for their preventive effects, but if the hormones then produced "side effects," the long-term benefits seemed a long way away. Judy became increasingly skeptical about taking hormones when they nauseated her. Other skeptical women also looked around and found that a healthy old age was not necessarily dependent on medication.

> And I know somebody who is absolutely a fantastic woman. She must be about seventy-five. I said to her, "Eileen, do you take any of these newfangled things, tablets or anything?" And she said, "Nothing!" And she is magnificent, she really is. She is very active and she has got a good mind. She said, "I don't think I could tolerate them, anyway." I said, "I've been made to try them and I can't tolerate them so I'm retiring too."

The perception that doctors were "pushing" hormones added to the resistance of women who did not like to "muck around" with their bodies. Erin described her internal debate as follows:

> I also have friends and clients with their patches on, you know, and I'm thinking, "Do I want this?" And I'm thinking, "No, I don't want this!" [laughs] And I think to myself, "What did women do twenty years ago and before when there was no hormone replacement?"

Even for women gliding their way through midlife, however, there were negative stereotypes to overcome. More resilient, these women poked fun at the
medical use of language, the talk of "drying up, drooping down, and dropping
off," and they poked fun at themselves instead of suffering in shamed silence:

> *Pippa:* Well, my middle age spread is thickening on the tummy . . .
> *Bridget:* [Interrupts] Just a personal landslide, things going down!
> *Pippa:* When you sit in the bath and everything meets everything else!

Women in midlife are aware that their bodies are aging, but aging is not a
process that starts or ends with menopause nor is it a problem confined to
women. Most women were reconciled to these changes, with one woman saying
wryly: "I never have looked like Julia Roberts." "Menopausal" changes like facial
hair growth, potentially distressing, can be the source of laughter. Pippa told her
friends: "If I'm on a desert island in a few years, friends, I'm going to be beard-
ed!" They then made a pact to visit each other if they ever ended up in intensive
care to pluck out the offending hairs so that they could look good as corpses.
Buoyed by their sense of camaraderie, these women who had known each other
for a long time spent a lot of time together and took their holidays together, but
some of them felt that they would have to wait for their husbands to die before
they could fully realize their sense of fun. Other women talked of calmly taking
over the family's financial planning, dealing with stockbrokers and banks as their
aging husbands "lost the plot."

Changes in sexual activity can be new and distressing. One woman came for
an interview but then denied that menopause was a reality for her. She was
actively seeking new relationships with younger men in singles clubs. Another
woman who had a discreet but very exciting extramarital affair felt that age was a
distinct advantage: "If two people whose combined age comes to more than 100
years can't have a good sexual relationship, who can!" Some women reported an
increase in sexual interest and complained about their partner's lack of response.
One woman commented that she did not have a dry vagina when she masturbat-
ed but only with her husband, who had lost any interest in foreplay. Some
women left the "marriage bed" because of their own disturbed sleep, some
because of their husband's incessant snoring, and some left for a more sympathetic lesbian relationship. Other women described the joy of putting sexual
urges behind them in order to concentrate on a life of the mind.

From Deficiency Disease to Well Woman Clinic

The public social space within which menopause is constructed is dominated
by a static stereotype of the "menopausal woman" that denies the range of
experience of the women interviewed in this study. From within any narrow per-

spective on menopause, the range and nature of women's complaints, or lack thereof, seem hopelessly confused, unlikely to repond to "treatment." As a result, women's complaints are separated out and given legitimacy only if seen as responding to a prescription. While women in the study clearly saw benefit in medical prescription, this benefit was assessed critically. Women with the worst experience, those most in need of help, could face a devastating, complex range of problems but they were often denied access to treatment. In contrast, women with a positive experience, those least in need of medical intervention, could be encouraged to see themselves as susceptible to the ills of older age and prescribed hormones to delay the onset of fragility. This failure to identify women's various needs for help must count as the single most telling criticism of medical intervention in midlife.

Medical treatment was the subject of considerable additional criticism and resistance, pointing to the gulf that exists between women and those clinicians who aim to help them. Since women experience their problems as a complex interweaving of physiological change and social experience, any one simple solution is unlikely to be of overall benefit. This is especially true when pills, implants, or patches are presented as the solution for problems requiring social action: in particular, access to employment and improved family relations. What was clear from the interviews was that women were in the process of trying to renegotiate their social roles as much as they were coming to terms with physiological changes. We know little about the private striving of midlife women in the past, but it is quite feasible that the rise of feminism has set up an expectation that women like Anne will not need to suffer in silence, that they have a right to support in their struggles for personal change.

To improve the health of midlife women, a range of strategies is necessary. Women who see their lives as unbalanced by hormonal instabilities—and who are we to contradict the experience of women who have felt their bodies respond with the waxing and waning of 500 or more menstrual cycles?—need medical credibility. Clinicians who wish to engage in a new science, a science with less bold claims and more limited aims, will need a new humility and caution in their assumptions about what women know and understand. They will also need to listen to women telling them where there is a need for help and whether it meets, or fails to meet, this need. More important, they will need to heed the skepticism with which women view the intrusion of medical "solutions" where women do not experience problems. This caution applies also to those other forms of prescription whose stereotypes do not fit with the experience of women themselves. To have menopause described as normal and not involving more than shortterm problems is a stereotype not made acceptable even if it comes from a woman researcher imbued with feminist principles.

Women in midlife are resistant to prescription, albeit in their private discourse, and are practiced in the art of critical analysis. As Rowbotham argues,[24] women's lives are "rich in the most bizarre of complexities and combinations." It is our knowledge of this complexity that is essential to the debate if we are, on the one hand, to relieve those suffering the worst ills of midlife and, on the other, to avoid the stereotype that sees all women in midlife as being in need of treatment. We must, she says, "translate these strange phenomena of female life as we now live it into the language of theory"—but into a new theory, based on the new connections and communications. Some form of medical prescription has a role to play, but the emphasis women place on drawing comfort from the experiences of other women offers an antidote to the medicalization of midlife.

What emerges clearly from the accounts of the women interviewed is their need to come to an understanding of their own experience in relation to that of other women living similar lives. They wanted to know how other women accommodate the variety of their experiences in the process of their everyday coping; wanted to gauge their own experience against that of women with whom they could identify in their roles as mothers, daughters, career women, in sickness, and in health. For women with a lack of social resources, this may mean a return to the Well Woman Clinic that proved of great benefit to some of these same women in their childbearing years. Such a setting could provide both access to a range of treatment selected by women themselves, but it could also encourage women who are silent and silenced to talk where they are safe.

Notes

1. S. Rowbotham, "Through the Looking Glass," in *An Anthology of Western Marxism: from Lukacs and Gramsci to Socialist-Feminism*, ed. R. S. Gottlieb (Oxford: Oxford University Press, 1989), pp. 279–95, 282–83.

2. Funding for the project entitled The Social Construction of the Menopause was awarded to Jeanne Daly and Lyn Richards by the National Health and Medical Research Council and the Victorian Health Promotion Foundation. The analysis reported here is my own but I am indebted to Lyn Richards, whose interest in feminist research methods helped structure the study. Gail Roberts and Di Palmer participated in arranging, conducting, and analyzing the interviews. The study benefited from thoughtful comment from Renate Klein and from debate with the members of the Women's Health and Feminist Theory collective, especially Julia Shelley, Priscilla Pyett, Anni Dugdale, and Marylis Guillemin.

3. P. Cotterill, "Interviewing Women: Issues of Friendship, Vulnerability, and Power," *Women's Studies International Forum*, 15 (5/6) (1992): pp. 593–606.

4. G. Sheehy, "The Silent Passage: Menopause," *Vanity Fair* (October 1991): pp. 118–57.

5. J. B. McKinlay, S. M. McKinlay, and D. Brambilla, "The Relative Contributions of Endocrine Changes and Social Circumstances to Depression in Mid-Aged Women," *Journal of Health and Social Behavior*, 28 (4) (1987): pp. 345–63.

6. L. Dennerstein, A.M.A. Smith, C. A. Morse, H. Burger, A. Green, J. L. Hopper, and M. Ryan, "Menopausal Symptomatology: the Experience of Australian Women," *Medical Journal of Australia*, 159 (4) (1993): pp. 232–36.

7. P. Kaufert, "Menopause as Process or Event: The Creation of Definitions in

Biomedicine," in *Biomedicine Examined*, ed. M. Lock and D. R. Gordon (New York: Kluwer, 1988), pp. 331–49, p. 333.

8. K. R. Smith and P. Moen, "Passage through Midlife: Women's Changing Family Roles and Economic Well-being," *The Sociological Quarterly*, 29 (4) (1988): pp. 503–524.

9. P. A. van Keep and J. Kellerhals, "The Impact of Socio-cultural Factors on Symptom Formation," *Psychother Psychosom* 23 (1974): pp. 251–63.

10. J. Wilbush, "Climacteric Expression and Social Context," *Maturitas* (4) (1982): pp. 195–205.

11. M. C. Lennon, "The Psychological Consequences of Menopause: The Importance of Timing of a Life Stage Event," *Journal of Health and Social Behavior* 23 (1982): pp. 353–66.

12. M. Lock, "Introduction," *Culture, Medicine and Psychiatry* 10 (1986): pp. 1–5.

13. F. B. McCrea, "The Politics of Menopause: The 'Discovery' of a Deficiency Disease," *Social Problems* 31 (1) (1983): pp. 111–23.

14. J. Lyttleton, "Management of Menopause," *Australian Journal of Acupuncture*, 12 (1990): pp. 5–10.

15. C. Downing, *Journey through Menopause: A Personal Rite of Passage* (New York: Crossroad, 1987).

16. G. Greer, *The Change: Women, Ageing and the Menopause* (London: Hamish Hamilton, 1991).

17. J. Posner, "It's All in Your Head: Feminist and Medical Models of Menopause (strange bedfellows)," *Sex Roles* 5 (2) (1979): pp. 179–90.

18. J. Habermas, *Toward a Rational Society* (Boston: Beacon Press, 1971), p. 82.

19. K. Figlio, "How Does Illness Mediate Social Relations? Workmen's Compensation Practices and Medico-legal Practices, 1890–1940," in *The Problem of Medical Knowledge: Examining the Social Construction of Medicine*, ed. P. Wright and A. Treacher (Edinburgh: Edinburgh University Press, 1982), pp. 174–224.

20. D. J. Haraway, *Simians, Cyborgs and Women: The Reinvention of Nature* (London: Free Association Books, 1991), pp. 187–91.

21. Since these women had been selected for interview, these numbers cannot be taken as an indication of how common the problem is in the general community. What is important is that this group exists.

22. J. Daly, "Caught in the Web: The Social Construction of Menopause as Disease," *The Journal of Reproductive and Infant Psychology* 13 (2) (1995), pp. 115–126.

23. It is important to note that when these women described themselves as depressed, we accepted this account without attempting to test or to verify it.

24. Rowbotham, "Through the Looking Glass," p. 294.

9

Menopause as Magic Marker

Discursive Consolidation in the United States and Strategies for Cultural Combat

Margaret Morganroth Gullette

In the United States 1992–1993 was the year of the horrific menopause anecdote. Women were inundated with menopause discourse: all the loss, misery, humiliation, and despair supposedly in store for us unless we took the pharmaceutical exit from female midlife aging. Daily press stories, women's magazine articles, talk-show discussions, major magazine essays, two books for popular consumption by well-known women writers (both achieved best-seller status, for a while simultaneously), obligatory reviews of the best-sellers, a menopause anthology. Merging and overlapping and reinforcing at the overlaps, the discourses made menopause as public as fame can, leading (since men overhear everything) around back again into private life. The circulation/dissemination was remarkably thorough, in a mainstream culture based on repetition passing for the new. (Readers feel they are getting important new news, without being able to say what distinguishes it from the old news.) As the menoboom tails off, it will already have done its job on the relevant generation of women. Within our age/sex system it will have produced for "menopause" a *cultural consolidation*, a discursive phenomenon of popular culture in which for a space of time—which can last decades—a set of beliefs and issues and verbal formulas and tropes and binaries become fixed as the only terms in which talk on a particular subject makes sense to the speakers.

There was next to no "news" about menopause in 1992–1993, certainly nothing that kicked off this particular discursive exfoliation. What happened in fact constitutes a *re*consolidation of an older age-graded discourse about women's lives, the most inclusive and effective in the twentieth century.[1] This discourse is

176

really a life-course decline narrative, which requires an event as its pivot, its critical moment. The event crudely divides all women's lives into two parts, the better Before and the worse After, with menopause as the magic marker of decline. "What, *this* menopause again?" was my reaction when the first article in what was to be the menoboom appeared.[2] Whatever else it did, the current reconsolidation did reestablish menopause as a major life event. One effect has been to crowd out all midlife women's other diverse contexts, by writing MENOPAUSE across the social text in large, thick, quasi-indelible strokes.

The American menoboom provides a case of culture impinging on gender and age at the midlife—a clear case of women *being aged by culture*. Why are our mainstream media producing this *now?* How do midlife men fit in? Do women endure the consolidation without resistance? If we can propose answers to these questions, we might yet be able to intervene to ameliorate the cultural situation of the midlife woman—the situation for which the word "menopause" now more often reductively stands.

In the Year of the Midlife Woman

Why now? The stock answer makes this a feminist epistemological issue: The Baby Boomers want to know! "Sexual enlightenment has gone so far that it's time to tackle the last taboo subject." This view presents menopause discourse as a triumph of feminism, like making sexual harassment public or shaming TV talk shows into finding more experts in economics and international politics who are women. Silence implies taboo, feminism breaks silences; ergo, women need to "speak menopause." Let me break into this artifact of a syllogism at every point.

Women in general, and Baby Boomers in particular, are always at risk of being told what they "want to know." How can it be a taboo subject when the word appears everywhere you look? How can it be taboo when women are signing the articles? When there are more items for a bibliography than a scholar can easily keep up with? Women can be told by a woman writer that other women are talking about "it" at dinner parties. (The implied taunt of "Do *you* dare?" keeps alive the implication that speech about menopause has been cruelly repressed.) Far from being taboo, however, it's in real danger of becoming obligatory. And what it obliges us to do is "prepare" ourselves early for the marker event as a disaster foretold.

The timing of the menoboom was determined by demography, marketing considerations, and the need for a backlash. Historically, backlash occurs when a subordinated group has made enough progress to be viewed as a threat. Menopause discourse flourishes at a moment when (some) women are seen to be powerful, rich, and attractive. (Some) men start worrying that women are getting too much of the good things of life: some think men must be losing out; others know it. These worries center on midlife women, because now—in the nineties—it's in their middle years, if ever, that women show their power; some are getting the broadest array of cultural goods that midlife women have ever gotten. The historical basis for this once preposterous sentence is that Americans (along with women in other countries) are twenty-plus years into the ongoing feminist revolution. One vast branch of American feminism from the beginning supported and produced women's desire for education, ambition, upward mobility, and political power, and it and they keep cracking open the ceilings.

Publicity follows success the way a dog follows a bone that's being dragged away. At such historical moments of progress, we note the textual emergence of "wonderful women of forty."[3] It happened in the first wave of Anglo-American feminism, between 1900 and World War I, and it's happening now in the United States, except more so. Nowadays the wonderful women can be fifty or sixty or more, and the goods are more plentiful and widespread—and more of an encroachment on male power. The presidential election year 1992 was nicknamed in the press "The Year of the Woman," although there was no woman at the top of any of the major-party tickets, the Senate's gender composition could change only very slightly, etc. There's a direct connection and a thousand indirect ones between the menoboom and the subcultures that kept reproducing that wistful, hypocritical, or envious label.

Mainstream politics in this country must now take account of the voting strength of women (54 percent of actual voters in 1992), and this includes the political anger and the potential activism of millions of women over the treatment of Anita Hill, the weakening of Roe v. Wade, the pauperization of women and children, the neglect of women's health, and the misdiagnosis of women's heart ailments. A few women did get big titles: Senator, Congresswoman, Attorney General, Secretary, and the power and influence that go with them. Behind Senators Braun and Feinstein and Boxer stand mayors, prosecutors, CEOs. In the glamour classes, midlife women are seen to get money, prestige, fame, and the related perks: gorgeous clothes, fit bodies, handsome postures, undistracted eyes, and sexual partners. The public and visual representatives of these wonderful women include, nowadays, not just actresses and government officials but also filmmakers, businesswomen, etc. About the other classes, we have midlife "progress novels"—about wonderful women who grow as they narratively age in ways that often do not rely on class and money, who overcome bad fate, survive with courage, find a *modus vivendi*, or actually move on in some wished-for direction. The narratives are about spiritual triumphs and moral developments potentially accessible to all.[4] From Zora Neale Hurston's *Their Eyes Were Watching God* back in 1938 to Margaret Drabble's *The Realms of Gold* in 1975, and since then to Doris Lessing's *Diary of a Good Neighbor*, Anne Tyler's *Breathing Lessons*, Toni Morrison's *Beloved*, and May Sarton's *The Education of Harriet Hatfield* (among many others), enough older and freer heroines have come out to convince many readers that the midlife of women can be a time of growth and accomplishment.[5] Most striking of all, at all levels of society, midlife women have become verbally more assertive, economically more ambitious, and psychologically more self-reliant than they were when they were young. Many have made it their business to unlearn the silly, flirty, self-defeating mannerisms that they were taught in youth. In short, they have produced themselves and can be represented in midlife as competent, energetic, nurturing, tireless. "Ageless." Continuing education depends on such women. There's a magazine and book industry devoted to this theme of stage-graded progress, gone upscale. This re-representation has historically subversive salience: the midlife cohorts of women are aging in such a way that the *age* of the women in question need not be the major fact to know about them.

In everyday life, in an era marked by feminist advances, at every class level there will be female heroes out there for the men of that class and below to envy. All midlife men know some women like this. If they haven't divorced them earlier, they're likely to be married to one. Their sisters have changed before their eyes: once negligible fluff, now with real weight at the family table, heads of households, survivors of unemployment, or, it may be, makers of breathtaking deals in seven figures. Some women have real money and power, and more have psychological power—but it's never been the reality that counted. Unless they are invested in equality, men imagine more power transferred to women than women ever feel they possess.

What woman, sniffing the stale sweat of male alarm, can't anticipate the backlash? Gender backlash by definition targets women, but as far as age is concerned, it's different strokes for different folks. Younger women get hit in the canonical ways, with sexual harassment and rape, abortion limits, pornography, battering, and murder; and, at the level of representation, images of themselves being tortured and murdered on TV and film. These techniques have been amply documented and their mechanism seen for what it is: cultural control over women's inner lives. Where they can't control the reality, entirely, they can still try to control the imagery. And—back to us now—midlife women get hit with ageism in the form of widespread public menopause discourse, male science that assumes we've all got a deficiency disease, and male commerce that sells us the supposed remedies. The imagery and "information" and language fueling the backlash are published by men who would deny their envy or alarm or even their interest in control, and written by women who would not do it if they understood their complicity and their vulnerability.

"Only Women Age"

Before I describe how the current consolidation of menopause discourse (when unresisted) age-grades women, diminishing them and producing "aging" as a decline, we need to hear in a minimalist sentence what menopause means as a biological universal, on the order of menstruation.[6] It's the end of menstruation.[7] As such, it's an absence, the end of a gender marker. Making an invisible absence into huge social graffiti and keeping the ink fresh in the public view requires an immense textualizing apparatus.

Everything else women are told is not universal, and cannot be an attribute or (as the media and gynecologists and now women unreflectively say, using the language of disease) a "symptom." This is true even of the perspiration that has been given a special signifier, because it's midlife women who are perspiring. Nota bene: some midlife women, not all. "We do not know why only some women flush after the menopause."[8] Likewise, any other condition, even if it could be highly correlated statistically with the end of menstruation in a convincing way, is not a necessary concomitant. Women should be wary of the statistics produced in the menopause discourse—except, of course those like mine, which come I hope sufficiently "unmasked" as part of my explicit project of disrupting the consolidation. Mary Poovey comments, "As a discourse that *claims* a transparent relation to the objects it represents, statistical representation masks the meanings it does produce at the same time that it puts these meanings into play."[9] For example, medicosociological sampling sometimes asserts what percentage of sampled women have "flushes" or "flashes." But the production of such statistics (or, for the ordinary woman, being made to care about percentages at all) itself has a negative effect by making skin-temperature change seem important, even dominant, in the lives of women of a certain age. Yet skin-temperature changes turn out to be trivial (for most women); or, when they are severe, of limited duration. What is being created is a common emotion: fear of flushing—of being *seen* to be a midlife woman in a sweat. That fear, along with a host of other interrelated, age-graded, inextricable emotions, was part of the consolidation.

In fact, for most women who have stopped menstruating, it's probably safe to say that the incident doesn't loom large in their whole-life story. (The vast majority of women finish having children long before menopause; not menopause but birth-control ended their reproductive period.[10]) So much else is going on in the years between forty and sixty nowadays. Before this current consolidation, postmenstrual women were unlikely to want to spend much time in the beauty parlor, their women's group, or other female spaces talking about it. Women often rely on their mothers to provide prophecies about the life course; thus some women in my cohort have blamed mothers for not telling them enough about menstruation and intercourse. Now they read their mothers' silences about menopause as prudishness. My mother never told me anything about hers until I asked her, but then she said there wasn't anything to remember. Moreover, since what doctors said about menopause included "frigidity" and "involutional" insanity, what our mothers chose not to repeat may have represented tactical silence. But all the alternative meanings of maternal silence are obliterated by the theory of the "taboo."

If so, perhaps women today should be cautious about whatever they are repeating to their daughters, since it too comes from an antifemale consolidation. And perhaps, despite the enormous cultural pressure to tell and to magnify and to make this an *event*, the marker that divides a younger woman from herself growing older and divides midlife men from same-age women, real cultural power might consist in *refusing* to join the public discourse. Unfortunately, silence is now nearly useless as a resistance. Once mainstream discourse forces a public consolidation on an age/sex group, its members lose powerful weapons: privacy and private interpretation of bodily experience, the luck never to run across stereotypes. Yet there are always pockets of culture that a consolidation never reaches, and individuals who for different reasons can ignore it as it is occurring. And conscious resistance, to which I will return.

Feminism's response can only be to start up mainstream discourse about menopause again by interrogating the menoboom's negative effects on the social construction of midlife women and, then, to try to control the discourse more effectively. The strategy I favor is to keep representations of menopause proportional to its place in a whole-life story, or better yet, since women need to be reinscribed as indelibly diverse, in many different whole-life stories. What we convey thereby is our sense of the *continuities* in our lives, or the discontinuities unrelated to menopause. Thus we discursively override both the biologism and the pessimism of the menoboom. Before the end of this essay I hope to have made it clear why we need to override both at once. Feminist movements that attack only the pessimism—from Eliza Farnham in the antebellum period to the crone movement of today[11]—fail to disrupt the cultural situation of midlife/"older" women. The "after-is-better" rhetoric may elevate women who can identify with it. But the before/after binary only reinforces the marker event, so the next wave of pessimism rides in on it yet again.

Our discourse should *use* that hopeful, promising, speaking "silence" as a truth that—biologically and even psychologically speaking—on the whole nothing happens. Or that even if something does happen, our adult competence manages it handily. A recent anthology of menopause-accounts was prefaced by writer and activist Grace Paley, who said she had no story: "I seem to have forgotten those years or maybe that year."[12] But the rest of the book was inevitably eventfulness, since that's the only story that sounds like a story. "Nothing happened that I couldn't cope with" has to become more public—as well as becoming a bigger part of woman-to-woman conversations. One woman who had very hot flashes for years, and vehemently refused "hormone replacement therapy" (HRT), wanted to tell me her successful strategies for coping. She didn't tell a horrifying anecdote. She didn't represent herself as a menopause "survivor."

Cultural critics are not ignoring individual pain by querying how female suffering gets used discursively. In the mainstream, while women were being encouraged to tell all in the name of sisterhood, a selection of the worst anecdotes was plucked like plums and reheated in the mainstream press in a stew of statistics. However poorly written, a dreadful anecdote will become memorable. Indeed, in badly written articles, only dreadful anecdotes will be remembered.

An Associated Press reporter who interviewed me about menopause asked me what my "menopause status" was. I explained that I preferred that this not be public (in the context she was providing) so that readers would be unable to reduce my life and work to my "status." Anecdotes imply: "Menopause is hush-hush because it's too awful to talk about." And like statistics, such anecdotes also imply that "menopause dominates your life," that it's "cataclysmic," that, in another canonical term reintroduced by the menoboom, it's "*the* change."[13] As has been the case since the 1890s, when "sex" hormones were discovered and their source immediately called the "puberty gland," menopause-as-magic-marker has instantly led to rejuvenation-drug-as-magic-eraser.[14] This is where marketing joined the backlash of the year of the woman. To construct endocrinology as the way out, the marker event must be biologized for all it is worth, its terrors must be magnified, and women's readiness to take pills must be deftly aligned with "other" midlife progress stories.

Hormone replacement "therapy" is the regimen of estrogen and progesterone currently being "offered," discursively speaking, not only to all postmenopausal women but to all the Baby Boomers for up to thirty or more years of life. One implication of the reconsolidation is that "you" have to take it; another, that "everyone" already does. In fact, one statistic might for a while remain important, rhetorically, for resistance: the indeterminate but rather small percentage of American women without hysterectomies who take HRT. "Only 20% of women report symptoms [*sic*] severe enough to seek medical attention," says the U.S. Department of Health and Human Services; even if gynecologists convinced half this number to go on HRT, that would make a ratio of 10 percent vs. 90 percent. One study cited "recent physician surveys indicating 75–95% of gynecologists would prescribe estrogen therapy to most of their patients."[15] But even a 9:1 ratio of users—the future currently being prepared for us—could still be meaningless to a woman bent on cultural resistance, since another woman's "severe enough" isn't mine, and there's no way I'm going to start speaking as if menopause were my disease. HRT discourse, as we'll see, circulates the ideas that midlife women without drugs are sick, aging, old. Tirelessly, feminism needs to expose its tactics and effects.

If feminism had a broad, effective, menoboom-resistant strain of writers, we could be hearing other voices talking out loud in public about the longed-for freedoms of being postmenstrual. Leaving behind menstrual cramps, fibroids, tampons, shields. Wearing a white suit any time you want (unless you're on HRT, which re-produces monthly bleeding in most women). Having better sex without pregnancy fears. Journalists could write articles as long as they like about "Better Sex after Menopause," and "Carefree After Fifty." It's doubtful that they could publish them now in the mainstream unless they promoted HRT (in the sly, offhand way that suggests it's noncontroversial). And if they could, the weakness of such articles tactically would still be that, despite being positive, they make "postmenopausal" a narrow synonym for what might be the most original unscripted years of our lives. Is it in our interest to talk about every quality of older womanhood in such terms? Witness the maddening overuse of "post-menopausal zest" in this consolidation: the dot of "reassurance" that asserts how fundamental menopause *must* be, however broad our lives; the stain of biologism that reduces the powers of later life to an automatic mechanism. Is being post-menstrual what made Eleanor Roosevelt a great woman? We are asked to accept a kind of condescending praise as the explanation of the fact that most women (miraculously) do not succumb to midlife decline and depression.

"I have a vast life elsewhere" could be the most effective recontextualizion. It makes sense for our splendid new comprehensive genre, the midlife woman's progress novel, to deal with menopause this way. How much attention would Celie and Shug have paid to menopause in *The Color Purple?* How would a Fay Weldon heroine react to a gynecologist prescribing HRT? The wise psychiatrist in Lisa Alther's *Other Women* flushes intermittently without losing her place in her life. In appropriate circumstances and genres, women writers might include a sentence or a paragraph about what becoming postmenstrual was like for them, or interviews with public figures might include their modes of interpretation and contextualizion. In short, feminist resistance begins by breaking the medicocultural grip of the anecdote (hypostatizing female dread of "symptoms") and of the master narrative (hypostatizing the female aging "event").

Finally, women who want to control the discourse need to talk in print as big as they can find about the gendering effects of having their supposed female-hormone deficiency diseases made so public. I've said the bad news was brought to us because of male envy, male medicine, male commerce in aging, and the complicity of some women in the process. The discourse is willed into print in indirect ways by men who until recently have had no movement of their own to buoy their self-confidence. Midlife men benefit passively from the double standard of aging, insofar as they can still take advantage of their culturally constructed differences from same-age women.[16]

That's the other half of the backlash story. The fact is that, even as a commerce in male aging grows, until recently men have managed to keep their own midlife problems and their own fears of aging relatively secret.

We can now see *how* they did it. Within the mainstream, silence is an achievement managed by a dominant age/sex class. The reconsolidation made female menopause the code word for midlife aging. Thus, in an ageist, prosex society that fears old age and notes its despised signs even in thirty, forty, and fifty year olds, discursively speaking *only women* age.

Thus, the more there is in print about the female menopause, the more it reinforces—or, in "The Year of the Midlife Woman," reinstates—a weird illusion of disparity.[17] Men who have no part in producing menopause discourse and get no income from the commerce, even men who worry about their prostate or wonder whether getting testosterone shots might be an asset, are led to think "poor dears" and to thank their chromosome that their plumbing is different. "A man" is that half of the human race that doesn't need to know the word "osteo-porosis."[18] If living with a man who believes that his biology is superior is repulsive for a woman, it can also be dangerous—for him, and for both of them. "For a man who cannot come to terms with his own fears of inadequacy, aging, separation, and death, connection to the menopausal partner may be emotionally untenable."[19] Heterosexual women are more at risk from a discourse that makes them out to be the "menopausal partner" than from menopause itself.

That men age is a truly taboo subject. There's a silence that needs to be broken.

Collapsing the Later Life Course

Many women believe that it is menopause (rather than menopause *discourse*) that ages women; they accept the culture's conclusion that it's a biological marker of decline. But how is this accomplished discursively, as a cultural power play—par-ticularly when all the public evidence about wonderful women implicitly denies it?

A surprising amount of so-called menopause discourse is actually not about what supposedly happens around ages forty-five to fifty, but about biological bad news that may or may not occur, to both men and women, at much older ages. The articles of consolidation tend to have a common structure. In the guise of telling readers not to worry, most medical and popular presentations tell women what there is to worry about, so that women are effectively briefed and prepped as medicalized subjects. I call these articles and books the "Reassurance, but . . ." texts. They din into our ears a monstrous muddled list that includes but is not limited to alleged losses of beauty, an asymptomatic condition (osteoporosis), sexual discomfort or pain (this too has its special name), accidents (bone frac-tures), costs (we're always told how expensive hip fractures are), diseases (heart disease), and even death.[20] HRT is slipped in as a remedy. The manual that used to be given out by my managed-care medical-and-insurance plan baldly asserts, "Women who do not use 'estrogen replacement therapy' (ERT) may lose 5–8 inches in overall height in the postmenopausal years."[21] "News" about osteo-porosis almost always implies what I call the quick-step bone-mass sequence: osteoporosis leads to falls, fall to fractures, fractures to expense and death. It implies that the HRT saves me all eight inches.

Counterfacts or counterattitudes that might disrupt the horror of the inevitability of the items in the list, or their scientific basis (or the claims for HRT), get effaced in mainstream discourse. None of the items is a quick-step from the next. Some are about processes that are not midlife events at all. They take twenty, thirty, or more years to occur—if they ever do. The image of female old age they construct is preposterously decrepit, particularly since some of these processes have little to do with age *per se*. Some progressive medical researchers believe that reduction of bone mass needs to be clearly distinguished from its possible sequelae; and that the latter are determined by factors other than hormones or age, such as weight, diet, smoking, drinking, exercise, poverty. Some of the quick-step problems we hear about in an irrational disproportion to their likelihood of occurring, like dying of a fall. "Less than 2% of falls in the aging population result in fracture," one study reports.[22] Such a statistic can be used to break the inevitability of the mystic bone-mass sequence. As earlier writers have pointed out, the institutionalized elderly have the highest incidence of fractures and the worst prognosis; studying their risk factors and preventing falls for them is important.[23] "Reducing the number of risk factors might reduce the number of fractures more directly than estrogen."[24] These are social issues that we should concern ourselves with; they should not be used to terrorize midlife women, even if old women—mostly by dint of living longer, outliving same-age (male) caretakers, and being worse off economically than men—are more likely to be among the vulnerable.

Some researchers now believe that dietary supplements of Vitamin D and calcium can not only prevent or reduce the loss of bone density but can also reduce the incidence of fractures in women as young as 69 and as old as 106.[25] In fact, this research discovery (untainted by commercial tie-ins) had the only title to being called the hot "news" in the menopause field. If played up appropriately it could have done something to counter the consolidation. What men suffer from over this period, and die of, and how much younger, and what it costs, is also kept mum. What else women die of is usually mum. This discourse is carefully framed to be narrow, deterministic, demeaning, and terrifying.

Via this uneasy agglomeration, the other scares I have mentioned, and the complementary silence about men, the culture has managed to make women fearful that midlife marks the fall into aging, and menopause means you wake up overnight an alarmingly diminished person. Menopause resonates for women as a *sudden* loss of bodily integrity, a loss that must involve an enormous "change" in self-concept. (This fear about discontinuing to be oneself is represented as though it afflicted only women.) *When* the fear begins to seem relevant to a woman is another effect of culture. The relevant cohort is the market now ubiquitously styled as "aging Baby-Boomers." A woman may begin to feel that this is an obligatory topic for her long before she nears the likely age—as early as thirty-five or forty. Menopause is on its way to becoming a *psychosomatic* disease for the age-class of women who haven't had it yet.[26] And the whole cultural endeavor makes women this young hyperconscious of the ailments of old-old age and of "female" causes of death. Our whole last half of adulthood is collapsed into itself, mercilessly shortened. This is a form of cultural terrorism.

No other cohort, male or female, at any age, gets told a future-health-risk story like this. We do not tell girls of eleven, for example, that the childbirth that they will soon be physiologically ready for can involve miscarriage, edema, episiotomy, and loss of sexual pleasure, cesarean sections, malformed or diseased children; magazines do not tell young women all the things that can go wrong in pregnancy. Although men are told they can suffer at midlife from sexual decline and impotence,[27] there is less equivalent discourse striving to make men of forty-plus as anxious about their aging and self-concept—although their midlife aging may include similar losses of self-esteem, and they are more vulnerable earlier to at least one of the items on the list (heart disease). If a man breaks a bone at forty, people say, "Bad luck"; if a woman does, they tut-tut "Osteoporosis." The culture fits *her* bone into a premature decline story.

By making women's problems so medical, so visible, so traumatic, and so tied up with "aging," the culture achieves mysterious and implausible effects. It's not only that it treats women as if they alone aged, bad as that would be in itself. It treats longevity, because it's female, as if it were solely a disaster. (Perhaps men should congratulate themselves on dying younger!) It treats the problems of illness in old age as if they modeled normal old age, relying on our ignorance of normal old age. Women of all ages have been made to feel anxious and defensive and exposed. Once they have internalized these feelings, they are taught to buy the products that are sold to relieve anxiety and exposure. Because the press dwells on women's disease, defects, decline, and their "vanity" (a culturally constructed emotion if ever there was one), men have been imaged as exempt from anxiety about aging, heedless of vanity—and they become invisible as anxious agers and consumers of remedies. They don't let themselves be pressured into humbling disclosures. They manage to manage the news about themselves. When something leaks out, it's rarely something embarrassing; it's framed as an existential crisis, something for which manliness is needed and ready.

In the middle years, then, the vast cultural imbalance between men and women (a specific form of age-graded sexism) is to great extent produced by what is included and what is left out of menopause discourse. That's why women should be cautious about how they break their personal silence. We even need to consider a tactical talk-rule: never mention anything alleged to be a "symptom" except in an unrecorded conversation with another woman or a man who loves you reciprocally. If a woman thinks she has a symptom, she need not share it around the water cooler. When her lover tells her that he *thinks* he's a trifle slower than he used to be, *then* she can tell him (her choice): "Women experience no clitoral changes however old they get," or, "I am too. But let's not begrudge the time." Even women with high control over their personal circumstances will want to take the menoboom's effects seriously, however.

Unequal Power in the Discursive War

Although my ruling metaphor has been that of consolidation, which might imply hegemony, there is actually a skirmish on, potentially a war, about representing menopause. Almost all the big guns are on the other side: the pharmaceutical industry (especially Wyeth-Ayerst, the company that produces the second most frequently prescribed drug in America, Premarin, as well as menopause "information" that many clinicians rely on and repeat or reprint for their clientele),[28] gynecologists, the producers of beauty products, the media that shill for the companies through "infomercials," and of course the menopause mediators, especially the women chosen to write on the subject, who almost to a woman write as if they have no standing to counter hormone theory, and lack the feminist skepticism or indignation to query it. The target of all these are women readers in their middle years, a multimillion-dollar market.

On our side there is a small but increasing number of critically trained women and some men, teaching us how to think better about all this and pressuring the medical establishment to break out of its gender and age biases. Plenty of feminist material is available in books, feminist journals, and specialized publications (and there may be private experiences, a subculture of resistant lore provided by mothers, older women, friends). The problem is that the antagonists are not (yet) getting read widely enough. Some are feminists and some are medical researchers and epidemiologists; some have a conscious anti-ageist agenda, and others work to the same end without knowing it. They teach concepts like "deficiency disease" that everyone should learn.[29] They remind us that "the health system has been forced to search for previously untapped markets of healthy people."[30] They have done skeptical research on the history of the medicalization of women's bodies and the suffering that it has entailed. They have attacked specific deficiencies in assumptions and in research, based mainly on heterosexual white women of some means.[31]

A feminist and anti-ageist agenda must be ambitious. By the millennium (and I can't say that I expect it by the year 2000) every woman (and not just feminists who read the fine print and know how urgent it is to deconstruct our sexist and ageist culture) and every man should know that "midlife aging" like aging in general is a unisex dilemma with a powerful component of cultural construction. If midlife women form groups, they won't be narrowly focused on "menopause"—they'll meet to teach one another cultural resistance and to work out in detail theories about the sources of ageism and women's victimization by (and then collaboration in) the process.

We'll know more facts about men, and put them into critical relation with facts we know about women. Men can have hot flashes, and when they do they are urged to take hormone "therapies" whose long-term effects are unknown. Men have sexual dysfunctions, physical losses, and pains that they are encouraged to connect with age. They too suffer from the sort of culturally cultivated anxieties inflicted on women—so far they have had them privately, without shame, but that's changing.[32] Men can also lose bone mass as they age; it is estimated that 17–20 percent of those known to have osteoporosis are men. Boys between the ages of fifteen and twenty have more fracture sites than any cohort of women below age seventy.[33] "Flushes in both sexes may relate to the absence of some (unidentified) substance secreted by both ovary and testis," conjectures one researcher who has overcome gendered thinking to this extent.[34] The "discovery" of a *gene* for osteoporosis, recently announced, could further weaken the reliance on a gendered hormone theory.

Differences between groups of women, now largely neglected, will have to be explained. There's research arguing that most women lose bone mass normally—at about 1 percent a year in later life—while a much smaller group are "fast losers."[35] Some quite young (premenopausal) women get osteoporosis. Together these anomalies hint that factors other than gender or age determine a disease now tied to menopause. Everyone with an interest in women's health knows how poorly researched other matters of intense importance to women are. Why don't we know more about arthritis or lupus (predominantly women's diseases, but ones that do not get connected with menopause)?

The one thing that the muddled list of women's "postmenopausal" conditions and diseases appear to have in common (that separates them from, say, arthritis) is that they can now allegedly be prevented to some degree (the claims seem to be getting smaller) by HRT. Perhaps even nonscientists can be suspicious of a process that isolates and groups an array of medical problems that affect diverse populations and calls them female and menopausal. As a historian of hormone discourse, I can't help but wonder to what degree medicine's hundred-year-old reliance on hormones to explain so much (female) alleged ill health and asexuality may have distracted researchers and clinicians from more diverse and fruitful paths.

HRT has to become inflamed as an issue. Even if it were not a controversial drug, its marketing would maintain the aging discourses that have such harmful effects. But it is extremely controversial. Every popular article should mention that the FDA requires the estrogen-producing companies to include a package insert with the medication listing its risks. Many women learn them that way, not from their gynecologists or from the media.[36] HRT should be seen not as a standard prescription for our disease (*de rigueur* in the "medical model" of aging) but as a site of possible resistance to the medical model, and to sexism and ageism in general, and to the unnecessary anxieties and psychological distress and confusion that they cause. According to Sonja McKinlay, a statistician and expert on menopause, letting it be known that you're on HRT may become a requirement for women in upper levels of management and government to prove that they're "in control" of possible symptoms and not declining. Margaret Thatcher made it known that she was a user. In the current panicky climate about rising health-care costs, insurance companies may pressure doctors to pressure women to go on HRT, or employers may do so directly, on the premise that this will reduce illness and keep costs down.[37] If this occurs, women on HRT should then keep quiet about it, so women's competence doesn't get confused with their medications. And all concerned should protest.

The entire issue of "risk" needs to be problematized. Midlife women who are not a high risk for anything—and those who are—may take HRT primarily because they want to look "young," although no estrogen product now dares to claim that effect. The market's widely circulated imagery of juvenation has made taking HRT a covert choice over whether to grow old or not—part of the endless cultural coercion on women to "pass"—although, as Cynthia Rich reminds us, "Passing—except as a consciously political tactic for carefully limited purposes—is one of the most serious threats to selfhood."[38] Women choose to take HRT (as one interview study reports) specifically to avoid the "symptom" whose antifemale name is "vaginal atrophy" and "loss of libido."[39] These conditions were invented in the early twentieth century, by (I am convinced) older heterosexual men angry that they were supposed to be learning the new art-of-love, impatient with foreplay, proud of rapid ejaculation if they could still manage it, and careless about the feelings and sexual pleasures of midlife women.[40] Because some men still feel the same way, and because menopause discourse links sex problems at midlife to women[41] and not to their male partners, some heterosexual women may fear vaginal atrophy more than osteoporosis or heart disease. One sentence in an article about it may do more to sweep them into internalization of age-related body blaming than any other rhetorical feature of the "Reassurance, but . . ." texts. Yet current testimony from sexually active older women outside of clinical samples suggests that few experience symptoms, and that symptoms can be relieved by noninvasive means (such as topical lubrication) without hormones. Other studies usefully report "little or no change in [women's] *subjective* sexual arousal."[42] One or more of these lines of rebuttal might dissipate the fears that lead women to elevate their sense of being "at risk" if they *don't* take HRT.

Risk assessment seems quite primitive at the present time. My own gynecologist didn't try to discover whether I'm at high risk for osteoporosis (even to the extent of taking a family history) before she announced that I ought to start HRT as soon as I stopped menstruating. She didn't mention calcium or other alternatives, like calcitonin and exercise.[43] Since she hasn't done a baseline bone-mass test, she has no idea how much bone mass (if any) I've lost already, or whether I'm a fast loser. She sees her HRT patients every six months (to her caseload without financial advantage) when some doctors see theirs only once a year, so she's not entirely at ease about risk. Some researchers doubt that any of the existing markers enable clinicians to decide who is most at risk. Although HRT is given to women with family histories of heart disease, even pro-HRT writers like Sitruk-Ware and Utian admit the possibility that "cardiovascular risk will be increased [*sic*], as some progestins would reverse partly the beneficial effects of estrogens."[44] The greatest risk of HRT is now breast cancer, epidemic among American women: "There is more consistent evidence to suggest that the risk of breast cancer increases with longer durations of therapy," say Hunt and Vessey.[45] It's amazing to me that writers who can notice such evidence can use the word "therapy" without quotation marks in such a sentence. Although Sitruk-Ware and Utian somehow find their way in the face of all this adverse evidence to see a "clear advantage for benefits" of HRT, they conclude by conceding honestly that prescribing it over the long term for women rests on "a balance of risks and benefits, dependent on a number of unanswered questions."[46]

The recent failures of the medicalization of women's bodies ought to give women pause: the overuse of hysterectomies, the Dalkon shield, DES, silicone-breast implants, and, most relevant of all, the reluctant response of the profession to the discovery that unopposed estrogen (ERT), the form taken by women in the 1970s, was linked to endometrial cancer. One response was that it was an easy cancer to cure.[47] Add the possibility of more iatrogenic illness to internalized middle-ageism, and add to that patriarchy's history of updating the bad-news-about-menopause list as items (like "involutional melancholia") drop out. Shouldn't that make women skeptical about any discourse that argues them into taking expensive and inadequately tested chemicals for the last half of their lives? Even after a woman has been told she specifically has a higher risk of something, skepticism should embolden her to get another opinion or to plunge into the specialized monographs—particularly those that query reliance on estrogen as a cure-all. After so much malpractice and denial, why should we trust the pharmaceutical companies and researchers who are selling us HRT? One current National Institute of Health study will be released in a few years; health-care feminists believe it will shed more unbiased light on terrible questions of risk.

If women take HRT in such unscientific conditions, there cannot even be a gain in knowledge from the vast unlabeled "experiment" that midlife women are being subjected to. One useful strategy would be to lobby the Food and Drug Administration to label HRT as "experimental" as it did in April 1992 for silicone implants. Practically speaking, this would force gynecologists now recommending it to strengthen their warnings about its risks (if only because of the possibility of malpractice suits if HRT turns out to cause cancers).[48] The effort would also bring medical ethicists into menopause discourse. Up until now, only some feminists have seen menopause treatment as a set of ethical problems. Rhetorically, it would be useful to call the issues around menopause "ethical" and "cultural" as well as "feminist" and "anti-ageist."

Toward Cultural Combat

Discourse is not just "talk," it's never just talk. That women feel forced to attend to a particular discourse, and what they are then exposed to reading, over and over again; what editors permit into print or prevent from appearing—all this affects our self-image, our human relations, our cultural identity, our mental health and quality of life, our attitude toward aging, and our understanding of old age and death. The average midlife woman relying on mainstream publications has little or no access to resistant discourses and an enormous amount to lose from listening to scare (pain/embarrassment) anecdotes and the master narrative of "Change" disguised as "information"; and from feeling she has no choice but to take them to heart, repeat them as truth, and rush off to get her steroid prescription. Even when well-educated and curious, women may not be adequately trained to see how the discourse operates or may be too constrained by respect for current sexual science to see that women have a right and reasons to be dubious and to resist. We're all more vulnerable because of the way the consolidation of 1991–1993 framed menopause discourse—young women, midlife women, and old women. Middle-ageism in general constructs self-centeredness in the bad sense, distracting women from our dense, multilayered, interesting lives, draining energy and confidence and subverting midlife power that could go into politics—ending war, hunger, poverty, sexism, and ageism itself.

At this moment, we don't in fact know much about the specific, differential effects of the consolidation on women's anticipations of menopause or their descriptions of their choices. In a set of 1994 interviews of twenty Radcliffe College alumnae, five out of seven women (aged 46–57) using HRT had started since 1991, and four others said they would like to take it but their doctors forbade it.[49] The HRT takers in Harris's California sample were not only whiter but thinner, did more aerobic exercise, and had fewer children.[50] The most likely users of HRT are well-educated, higher-income women, according to Sonja McKinlay.[51] Olesen comments that "the social stratification system which denies lower- and working-class women this therapy also enables them to avoid its risks."[52] Higher socioeconomic status may put women more at risk: money makes expensive bodily interventions like HRT feasible; education opens them to the ideology of "information." Feminist education carries with it training in ideas of "entitlement" and "empowerment" and "control." Indeed, women who feel good about themselves—who fit the model of the "wonderful woman" of the nineties (and this definition certainly can include feminists)—may be quite vulnerable to menopause rhetoric about "taking control of their aging."[53] Instead of using HRT for a short term, as most women have done, such women, living in the consolidation period, may decide never to stop.

In the current situation, as expected, we don't find sufficient cultural space in which resistance or "mixed experiences" could get textualized. Cushman's interviews uncovered women (not using HRT) happy with "feminist valorization" of menopause, who use language of "naturalness" and consider medicine an unnecessary or dangerous intervention. But such important information about how women resist the prescribed in a culturally defined moment is relatively inaccessible.

In conversation, and possibly in their own inner colloquoys, women I know appear not to know that they may be ordering their beliefs and preparing to make their "choice" on the basis of information tainted by gender and age biases and marketing imperatives. Even feminists fall into ways of speaking that augment the consolidation. A theorist leading a mixed-gender meeting, reporting that she is having a hot flash, adds wryly, "For the next twenty years." This is a scenario so clinically exceptional that I had never before seen or heard it mentioned. A professor tells me blithely that she will need HRT because she is "small boned," and another that she is on HRT because of a family heart history. The latter's gynecologist hadn't mentioned the research that has casts doubts even in the minds of its advocates on the efficacy of HRT in preventing heart disease.

And what of the gynecologists who have pervasive doubts about HRT? One of them tells me that some women who come in to consult her are "wrecks." She feels an ethical obligation to present the anti-HRT argument in the strongest terms. But is she in a good position, professionally or psychologically or cultural-ly, to inquire to what degree a "symptom" is exacerbated by our culture? And what will she do confronted by a woman without symptoms who asks for med-ication (which is now a frequent occurrence as a result of advertising campaigns in magazines and the unpaid forms of propaganda for HRT that I have been considering all along)? The consolidation has made this doctor's situation much more difficult. Even if she tried to persuade women not to use the drug, or to use it for a short term, her rhetoric might fall on ears deafened by the menoboom.

Even more depressing, I meet women I consider feminists, who are aware of the ubiquitous presence of cultural mediation, who are skeptical of "informa-tion," who respond to the phenomenon of menopause as if they were personally helpless. They're looking in the mirror asking if the catastrophic "signs" have (yet) appeared on their faces or bodies that will identify them to an imagined gaze, or their own, as "postmenopausal." The form passivity takes is this: howev-er ably this or that woman might feel herself to be living at midlife (performing important work, loving and being loved, healthy and asymptomatic), as a body in the world she is vulnerable to ageism. Whatever her private truth or her profes-sional power, she feels that she cannot convince others (men?) of her true worth. One way out is for her to will herself to believe in HRT's anti-aging effects. At her most self-disliking, she wishes for a face lift, she punishes her body in subtle ways, she "trusts" her gynecologist, and, asymptomatic, she takes HRT. I say this on the basis of intimate conversations with a small sample representative only of highly educated, mostly academic, straight white women aged from about forty-five to fifty-five. Most starkly put, menopause is close to being lived—even by relatively demystified women—as a descent into aging that is *only* apparent, but feels no less real. This is a difficult state of double consciousness.

Some of these women are angry at me, I gather, for talking about menopause as a socially constructed experience. Not that they're naive about other internal-izations, like those of gender difference; many have fought successfully against their own erstwhile young-adult belief that men were intellectually superior to women, for example. But age-related difference works on a different, intrasub-jective binary: it makes a woman less than her*self,* inferior to her (apparently biological) self at an earlier phase. By pitting her against her younger self, decline appears free of construction, as if there were not a hostile ageist world outside manipulating the comparison. (It's as if "wrinkles" were exempt from rules of signification.) This decline, she believes, she herself can *see,* in the signs that "others" see. And she may whipsaw, or drift, in and out: now seeing herself through a critical age-graded gaze, now seeing herself in an ungraded, private, continuous, or progressive way—as (perhaps) one of the wonderful women.

This double consciousness is not necessarily a fixed feeling, even though many women may now be living it as such. "There is frequent tension between the received interpretations and practical experience. . . . But the tension is as often an unease, a stress, a displacement, a latency: the moment of conscious comparison not yet come, often not even coming," as Raymond Williams has sensibly pointed out, in a passage about "fixed forms" of "feeling" and what might disrupt them.[54] What could disrupt it? The disruptive potential has to be latent in the woman herself, and once she feels it, it needs to be welcomed—reflected and reinforced—by women's networks and then by the culture beyond. What may make women willing to try to transcend the state of double consciousness, I suspect, is that they find it to be both intellectually suspect (too contradictory) and deeply fatiguing, distressing, and incapacitating. Out of this moment of psychological dilemma and apparent impasse, women might derive anger and resistance and find the momentum for a new phase of feminism much more conscious of age issues and much more active around age-related issues that surface in the media. High time too. At some point feminists should want to ask themselves why feminism was not—I won't say better prepared for a menopause consolidation, but more resistant in the face of it.

Might the current menopause consolidation liquefy by itself? I'm not sanguine about this, but I can name some areas of potential meltdown. As a society, the United States has been moving away from the mystique of pronatalism, as do modernizing societies that need the work of women and a reduced birth rate. If these needs continue, in a gradual but more retarded way the cultural values connected with pronatalism should weaken—not disappear but become firmly subcultural. The claims that HRT can make may wither; and losing this marketing pressure on the culture might result in fewer descriptions of menopause as a disease state and short conduit to old age. The situation of men may exert pressure on the consolidation also. Midlife men are becoming more vulnerable in their own aging: the same medical/commercial forces that have been bringing women their public menopause are on the verge of bringing same-age men their public climacteric or their midlife "crisis." Men too will be told their biology is their disease; they'll be pressured to become anxious, to buy cosmetic surgery and rejuvenation drugs and other prepackaged remedies. Some of this is already happening.[55] Driven by their own misery, encouraged by feminist theory and age theory, men might discover that they have their own reasons for rejecting "the change of life," aside from solidarity with same-age women.

What might happen when both genders learn that ageism internalized is a stressor, a depressant—what I want to call a psychocultural illness? Feeling demoralized when you look in the mirror, assuming that no one will take a sexual interest in you henceforth, believing that your future ended yesterday—all are symptoms of middle-ageism, not aging. What might happen when they share the

Too Late Syndrome and want to discard it? Men and women both need to acknowledge that it's not their looks or their climacteric "status" or anything else objective about them that produces the syndrome. "Midlife crisis" is a culturally constructed disease. Learning all this could change male-female relations in the middle years for the better, lessening cross-gender competition, teaching interdependence, and leading to age-connected activism. This would be the right decade for men to join up with feminists to learn how to fight the mutual enemies; then together we could invent the new talk strategies against the next reconsolidation. This future, if it were to come about, would leave intact only all the *other* sources of ageism in our culture.

Whatever the future brings, women have to decide that this cause is theirs. We know we'll all age by nature. Should we let ourselves be aged by culture too?

Notes

I dedicate this essay to Alix Kates Shulman, who always resists. The essay is exerpted from *Cultural Combat. The Politics of the Midlife* (1997). A shorter version, titled "What, Menopause *Again?*" appeared in *Ms.* Magazine, Summer 1993; and, in a somewhat different form, in *Discourse* 17 (1) (Fall 1994). My thanks to Jeanne Daly and two anonymous reviewers for astute theoretical editing.

1. I know of no single history of the menopause in the twentieth century. But we know enough about the construction of the menopause in the 1920s and '30s to say with assurance that reconsolidations after feminist disruptions have occurred. The basic narrative of Woman's life as told from a pronatalist view is of course much older. But a history of twentieth-century menopause could point out distinctly new features that continue to characterize it at the end of the century: specifically, a reliance on hormone theory. For a brief overview, see Lois W. Banner, *In Full Flower. Aging Women, Power, and Sexuality. A History* (New York: Knopf, 1992), pp. 273–310. For the premodern era, see Ruth Formanek, "Continuity and Change and 'The Change of Life.' Premodern Views of the Menopause," in *The Meanings of Menopause. Historical, Medical, and Clinical Perspectives*, ed. Ruth Formanek (Hillsdale, NJ: The Analytic Press, 1990), pp. 3–41. Other periodizations can also be useful: post– *Feminine Forever* (another reconsolidation), post-ERT (moment when ERT is linked to endometrial cancer, a moment of potential disruption).

2. *Vanity Fair* published an article by Gail Sheehy in October of 1991; because of its location and prominence, I take it to be the first item in the new consolidation.

3. See Gullette, "Brief Golden Summer of the Woman of Forty; or, the Post-Sexual Woman," in progress.

4. See Gullette, *Safe at Last in the Middle Years* (Berkeley: University of California Press, 1988); also "Midlife Heroines, 'Older and Freer,'" *Kenyon Review* Vol. XVIII (2) (Spring 1996): pp. 10–31.

5. In the spring of 1993, I gave a course at the Radcliffe Seminars that centered on twelve such narratives and referred to many others. Participants also kept notebooks of clippings taken from the popular press that represented midlife women.

6. A moment of consolidation frequently tries to link puberty and menopause, "menopause, puberty's dark twin," in the words of Tony Cappasso, "For Him. What the Passing of Fertility Means to Women," *Seasons* 2 (3) (1992): p. 17. *Seasons* is published by Wyeth-Ayerst Laboratories, which produces the hormone most often prescribed for postmenopausal women. The company thus has a stake in the discourse that reproduces pronatalism and related younger women/older women differences by emphasizing "the passing of fertility."

7. "Menopause is natural and takes place smoothly for most women. The only sign of menopause for many women is the end of menstrual periods." U.S. Department of Health and Human Services, *The Menopause Time of Life* (Washington, DC; n.d.), p. 5.

8. Jean Ginsburg and Paul Hardiman, "What Do We Know about the Pathogenesis of the Menopausal Hot Flush?" in *The Menopause and Hormone Replacement Therapy. Facts and Controversies*, ed. Regine Sitruk-Ware and Wulf H. Utian (New York: Marcel Dekker, 1991), p. 41. The collection (henceforth Sitruk-Ware) exemplifies the medical model: it's so tied to considering menopause a deficiency disease that one chapter can actually say that "cessation of estrogen can be considered a medical oophorectomy" (60). I use it often because the hesitations and admissions in its own discourse make it useful. It would not be a good starter book.

9. Mary Poovey, "Figures of Arithmetic, Figures of Speech. The Discourse of Statistics in the 1830s," *Critical Inquiry* 19 (2) (Winter 1993): p. 275.

10. Postmenstrual women who wanted children but had infertility problems sometimes feel that the social-constructionist approach to menopause overstates its case.

11. See Margaret Morganroth Gullette, "Eliza Farnham. Brief Life of a Visionary Woman," *Harvard Magazine* (November–December 1991): p. 44. The crone branch of feminism advises women to welcome aging at fifty with a ceremony of positive feelings. This is an attractive and plausible formulation. Yet in its eagerness to help women appreciate aging, the crone movement ages us too quickly. Like mainstream discourse, and inadvertently reaffirming mainstream discourse, the crone movement treats menopause explicitly and implicitly as a great Change. I believe, from teaching recent popular midlife novels about women, that many women prefer the alternative narratives of the life course that emphasize either continuities or self-chosen discontinuities. But a woman can enjoy the ceremony and also agree that it's better to downplay change.

12. Grace Paley, "Introduction," in *Women of the 14th Moon: Writings on Menopause*, ed. Dena Taylor and Amber C. Sumrall (Freedom, CA: Crossing Press, 1991).

13. The full-length book by Germaine Greer uses this as its title.

14. Eugen Steinach was the major inventor of rejuvenation-through-hormones. He is well discussed in the context of old age by Thomas Cole in *The Journey of Life. A Cultural History of Aging in America* (Cambridge: Cambridge University Press, 1991), p. 180. I am writing a history of the invention of the middle years of life, which includes a section on the terrible procedures women submitted to when rejuvenation first became operational in the 1920s.

15. In one California study of mostly white affluent women, 40.6 percent of women ages 50–54 were taking hormones, as compared to only 23.1 percent of women aged 60–65. "Younger women reached menopause at a time physicians were increasing their postmenopausal hormone prescribing." Robin B. Harris, et al. "Are Women Using Postmenopausal Estrogens? A Community Survey," *American Journal of*

Public Health 80 (10) (October 1990): p. 1267. Press accounts may also be a factor in women's decision making. The postmenoboom percentages could rise drastically across the country.

16. See Susan Sontag, "The Double Standard of Aging," in *Psychology of Women. Selected Readings*, ed. Juanita H. Williams (New York: Norton, 1979), pp. 462–78. This is the classic description, dating from the early seventies. My own view is that much has changed in twenty years. See Margaret Morganroth Gullette, "All Together Now. The New Sexual Politics of Midlife Bodies," *Michigan Quarterly Review* 32 (4) (Fall 1993): pp. 669–95.

17. Actually, even when articles about midlife men are paired with articles about midlife women, the disparities are glaring. See Natalie Angier, "A Male Menopause? Jury is Still Out," *New York Times* (May 20, 1992), p. C14; versus, on the same page, Jane Brody, "Personal Health." Angier carefully keeps reminding readers about how "gradual" the slump in testosterone is. Brody assumes from the outset that every woman not on hormones will be anxious to learn all other possible ways to counter what she calls "health effects [meaning illness effects] of the menopausal decline in estrogen."

18. A man writes about his discovery at age seventy-two that he has lost height. He tells his wife. The following dialogue ensues:

"A touch of osteoporosis, I'd say," she offered helpfully.
"Osteo-what?"

"Humor: The Incredulous Shrinking Man," *Modern Maturity* (October–November 1992): p. 92. Nevertheless, this article (in the major magazine for the over-fifties) is the first time I'd seen any mention, not to mention a first-person account, of male bone loss in a mainstream publication.

19. Suzanne B. Phillips, "Reflections of Self and Other. Men's Views of Menopausal Women," in Formanek, p. 290.

20. "Even 'asymptomatic menopause' may initiate silent, progressive, and ultimately lethal sequelae"—Wulf Utian, the High Priest of HRT (Callahan, Joan, ed. *Menopause. A Midlife Passage.* Bloomington: Indiana University Press, 1993, p. 32). Greer links menopause and "death" in emphatic ways several times in her opening pages.

21. Waye, "Menopause." A *Boston Globe* article (April 5, 1993: p. 32 ff.) ended with an anecdote about a woman who had lost *nine* inches.

22. Robert Lindsay and Felicia Cosman, "The Risk of Osteoporosis in Aging Women," in Sitruk-Ware, p. 54.

23. *Ibid.*

24. Andrea Boroff Eagen, "Reconsidering Hormone Replacement Therapy," *Network News* 14 (3) (May–June 1989): p. 5 (citing a study by Dr. Mary Tinetti of Yale).

25. The study, produced by Lyonnais researchers at INSERM, was published in the *New England Journal of Medicine*, December 3, 1992. I first saw information about the conclusions in Richard Saltus's weekly column in the *Boston Globe*, called "Medical Notebook," of the same day, where it received only four column inches. Saltus pointed out that while previous studies had shown that dietary supplements could prevent the loss of bone mass, this one showed an effect: fewer fractures in the treated population. The dosage was 800 milligrams of calcium daily.

26. I discuss an "age-class" and its differences from a cohort in "Cultural Combat."

27. I am working on a book to be called *The Invention of Male Midlife Sexual Decline*, which occurred between 1900 and about 1930 in England and America.

28. Premarin has 80 percent of a $750-million market. "Aging Baby Boomers Take Fresh Look at a Milestone," *New York Times*, May 17, 1992, p. 30. Ciba-Geigy produces Estraderm, a patch; it recently put a full-page ad in my local paper, the *Boston Globe*; on the reverse was a quarter-page of tiny type conveying the warnings.

29. MacPherson; see also McCrea. Two older edited collections I value are *The Meanings of Menopause*, edited by Formanek; and *Changing Perspectives on Menopause*, edited by Voda, Dinnerstein, and O'Donnell (Austin: University of Texas Press, 1982). Voda, MacPherson, and others can be found in the new anthology, *Menopause*, ed. Callahan. See also Betty Friedan's chapter on menopause in *The Fountain of Age* (New York: Simon & Schuster, 1993). In all the popular writing, only one brief article seemed to me sufficiently debunking: Katha Pollitt, "Hot Flash." Pollitt also reviewed Germaine Greer's book for the *New Yorker*.

30. Nancy Worcester and Mariamne H. Whatley, "The Selling of HRT: Playing on the Fear Factor," *Feminist Review*, No. 41 (Summer 1992): p. 2.

31. "The major biases in published menopause research are that samples are generally drawn from clinical populations, and that there is a virtual across-the-board assumption that all respondents are heterosexual." Ellen Cole and Esther Rothblum, "Commentary on 'Sexuality and the Midlife Woman,'" *Psychology of Women Quarterly* 14 (4) (December 1990): p. 510.

32. See Gullette, "All Together Now, The New Sexual Politics of Midlife Aging," in *The Male Body*, ed. Laurence Goldstein (Ann Arbor: Michigan University Press, 1994), pp. 221–47.

33. According to one study, cited by Robert Lindsay and Felicia Cosman, "The Risk of Osteoposis in Aging Women," in Sitruk-Ware, p. 56.

34. Jean Ginsburg and Paul Hardiman, "What Do We Know about the Pathogenesis of the Menopausal Hot Flush?" in Sitruk-Ware, p. 41.

35. Egon Diczfalusy, "Demographic Aspects: The Menopause in the Next Century," in Sitruk-Ware, p. 8.

36. One study of "all the articles on this topic in the magazines most regularly read by US women" between 1985 and 1988 found that "three-quarters were clearly pro-hormones: fully half . . . did not mention any risks with oestrogen use." Nancy Pearson, testimony before the FDA, cited in Worcester and Whatley, p. 7.

37. Norma Swenson's warning, cited in Betsy Lehman, "Cultural Anthropologist Says Menopause Can Be Seen as 2nd Adulthood," *Boston Globe*, April 29, 1993, p. 29.

38. Cynthia Rich, "Aging, Ageism, and Feminist Avoidance," in *Look Me in the Eye: Old Women, Aging, and Ageism* (San Francisco, Spinsters Ink, 1983), p. 55. Worrying about what constitutes "passing" is another psychological problem exacerbated by the menoboom.

39. In the interviews, "a surprisingly large number of [Radcliffe College] alumnae" mentioned vaginal dryness or sex problems they assumed were related to menopause, and some were angry at feminist discourse for not addressing this need. Phoebe Cushman, "The Hormone Replacement Therapy Decision: Women at the Crossroads of Women's Health," B. A. thesis, Harvard University, 1994 [1995], p. 79.

40. See Gullette, "The Brief Golden Summer of the Woman of Forty; or, the

Postsexual Woman" in *Midlife Fictions. The Invention of the Middle Years of Life
1900–1935* (in progress).

41. "Vaginal lubrication . . . may take 10–30 seconds in the younger woman, it can take
from 1 to 3 minutes in women over 60." Norma McCoy. "The Menopause and
Sexuality," in Sitruk-Ware, pp. 73–100. The author of this article labels this a case
of diminution "to an obvious degree" (p. 78). This is a painful example of a woman
taking on a hostile male subject position.

42. S. R. Leiblum, "Sexuality and the Midlife Woman," *Psychology of Women Quarterly*
14 (4) (December 1990): p. 498. Alice Rossi's forthcoming edited collection on the
menopause will confirm this.

43. Exercise is the only remedy that can increase bone mass (Linda Gannon, "The
Potential Role of Exercise in the Alleviation of Menopausal Disorders and
Menopausal Symptoms: A Theoretical Synthesis of Recent Research," *Women and
Health* 14 (2) (Summer 1988): p. 118). On calcitonin, see Lindsay and Cosman, p.
62. Diet, exercise, and life-style changes are quite well-known in some circles.
Although these make sense at any age, for older women alone they are sometimes
named "alternative therapies"—which suggests how medicalization in general and
HR "Therapy" in particular have taken powerful hold of midlife women.

44. Sitruk-Ware, p. 287.

45. *Ibid.*, p. 151.

46. *Ibid.*, p. 287. If women taking estrogen have lower mortality rates than women not
on estrogen, is this (in part? what part?) because women given estrogen are richer,
more used to getting medical care, able to get better care in general, and for these
reasons healthier than the control group? This is the kind of question that should be
asked.

47. Linda Gannon, "The Endocrinology of Menopause," in Formanek, p. 222.

48. "In a climate of malpractice suits, it was becoming wiser to have a patient actively
involved in the treatment decision when there was a risk of iatrogenesis." Patricia A.
Kaufert and Sonja M. McKinlay, "Estrogen Replacement Therapy: The Production
of Medical Knowledge and the Emergence of Policy," in *Women's Health and
Healing: Toward a New Perspective*, ed. E. Lewin and V. Olesen (New York:
Tavistock, 1985), p. 132.

49. Cushman, pp. 92, 64–65.

50. "McKinlay, McKinlay and Brambilla found that menopause status per se was less
associated with physical complaints than was a prior health history marked by a tendency to utilize health services" (Cole and Rothblum, p. 497, citing a study that
appeared in the *American Journal of Epidemiology*). One feminist gynecologist I spoke
to thought that the automatic taking of birth-control pills had prepared the current
midlife cohort to think of medication as the answer to all "reproductive problems."

51. Private communication.

52. Virginia Olesen, "Sociological Observations on Ethical Issues Implicated in
Estrogen Replacement Therapy at Menopause," in Voda, p. 356.

53. See *The Selling of Contraception: The Dalkon Shield Case, Sexuality, and Women's
Autonomy*, by Nicole J. Grant (Columbus, Ohio: Ohio State University Press, 1992).
Rickie Solinger, reviewing it, says that Grant wanted to discover "why these women
used the IUD despite the lack of consensus within the medical community about its
safety," and "she found that these women had faith in the concept of 'choice,'

believed in the 'value of information and education as insurance against injury,' and trusted in the rectitude of the experts, a set of attitudes that may have deepened their risk" (p. 19). Here too, these were attributes of economically richer and better educated women.

54. Raymond Williams, *Marxism and Literature* (Oxford: Oxford University Press, 1977), p. 130.

55. Margaret Morganroth Gullette, "The New Gender Politics of Midlife Bodies," *Cultural Combat* (forthcoming).

10

Situating Menopause within the Strategies of Power

A Genealogy

Roe Sybylla

Prologue—A Video Script: "Understanding Menopause"[1]

Scene: A doctor's consulting room, in a large public hospital. Behind a large desk sits the doctor—not any doctor, but a gynecologist, and not any gynecologist but a professor, a man of great authority, a spokesman on matters of menopause, often called on by the media when expert knowledge on this currently topical subject is needed. Before him sit the patient—a pretty, timid, small-voiced, woman—and her husband. Both appear in awe of the doctor, their remarks uncertain by comparison to his succinct assurance, but the two men nevertheless enjoy some rapport. Together, they subject the woman to their gaze. It is she who is being examined.

Wife (explaining how menopause affected her): I was terribly self-indulgent; I was too introspective altogether; I thought about death and dying a lot.

Doctor: Your husband has a miserable time?

Wife: I didn't make a very good [sexual] partner; I got moody and er . . . *(smiles contritely at husband)* . . . bitchy.

Husband: I was very relieved. *(There is nothing wrong with him!)* "Those little brown tablets . . . I don't know what's in them but they've got a kick. *(He is not concerned about any side-effects upon his wife of taking this miraculous medication.)*

Wife: Bob was still blazing away. I felt left behind. *(It is clear from the submissive and appealing looks she gives her husband that HRT has saved the marriage.)*

Doctor: *(confirms that the patient has been restored to normal)* Mood swings and lack of confidence show a similar improvement and a normal lifestyle can be

200

resumed. *(Sounds like a robot, his voice flat, lacking inflection, consistent with his impersonal style of language.)*

The Audience: *(Is it clapping and cheering at the happy ending, thrilled that the wife has been successfully normalized and disciplined into her proper role? Yes, mostly. But among them there may be more than one woman looking a little taken aback.)*

Introduction

What underlies the unease produced by the scenario I've just outlined? On the one hand, we have the woman confessing the misdeeds and failings of her menopausal self.[2] On the other hand we have the two men who hold her in their gaze, both in agreement that it is she who needs rectification, that this can mean nothing but restoring her to normal, to what she was before menopause, and that medication is the appropriate means of achieving this. Between the doctor and his aide-de-camp there is an alliance. The relationship between the two men and the woman is not reciprocal: there is no questioning of their normality. The power of knowledge and truth flows in one direction; the normal interrogates the pathological. Yet the woman is complicit in all of this. All three agree in their certainty; for them the facts and the appropriate remedy are self-evident. For all three, truth is uncomplicated and, once established, certain, constant for all time.

The problem is that the woman is subjected by these ways of knowing: she has become the kind of being that looks into herself and lo! discovers that she is what the experts say she is. The events in that consulting room can be described as a disciplining or shaping of the woman to suit masculine and medical professional requirements. For her part, through no fault of her own, the woman lacks the knowledge that would enable her to become more autonomous in relation to herself. By this I mean that she would relate to herself as a possibility for self-creation, an activity of conscious choice, rather than as a set of truths that are to be accepted, not transformed.

In his later works, Michel Foucault suggests that in modern western cultures, we have been subjected to particular beliefs, ideas, and practices that cause us to look within ourselves for explanations and to follow the advice of the experts. Rather than looking outward and acting to transform ourselves and the world, we confess the truth of our selves. For the woman in the video, there is an unchanging truth of menopause, a knowledge the doctor possesses. She looks within and confesses her failings to the all-knowing doctor, who attributes them all to menopause. How clever! What a conjurer he is![3]

What is at stake here is the woman's subjectivity in relation to the masculine, that is, her particular form of sexuality, her femininity. In medical hands, menopause turns out to be an occasion for the reinforcement of the form of sexuality that she has, perhaps unreflectively, adopted. For her it may be that there is no alternative, not least because she thinks of her self as a true self that cannot be changed, only conformed to or perilously shattered. An understanding that her sexuality is a particular construction, created within the power games of our times, would, I believe, free her from imprisonment in ideas that she has not chosen. On this basis she could move toward taking a more active, and less reactive, part in her own creation.

My object in this chapter is to demonstrate that the truths of menopause are contingent. By this I mean that our truths are relative to our time and culture, just as the truths of the past were relative to the times in which they were established. In terms of power, we are dangerously deceived if we are led to believe that the people of the past were ignorant while only we, through our "progress," have access to the truth. In order to show that the knowledge and practices concerning menopause have much to do with historical circumstance, and much less to do with progress, I examine the changing relationship between menopause, the feminine, and various social groups and forces at particular points in time in some western cultures. Thus, my aim is not to show the historical improvement of ideas and knowledge concerning menopause. Rather, it is to show how the ideas and knowledge concerning it have changed in keeping with wider changes in the coalitions and oppositions in the complex network of power relations between institutions, businesses, diverse groups, and individuals.[4]

For Foucault there can be no outside to power relations; we are all present on various fronts of the "battlefield" of power, and it is necessarily within the field of power that we live and construct ourselves. A relation of power is "a mode of action upon actions": "That is to say," says Foucault, "power relations are rooted deep in the social nexus, not reconstituted 'above' society as a supplementary structure whose radical effacement one could perhaps dream of."[5] Thus power, for him, is productive: it is what constitutes society, as well as the forms of subjectivity of individuals. Power can produce "good" or "bad" outcomes, for it is a force, a means for getting things done, or "power to." But it is primarily what power does, rather than what it is, that interests Foucault.

In speaking of power, I am not claiming that there has been a conscious plot to gain tactical advantage over women. Rather, there have been effects of certain practices and discourses, as though these had been conscious strategies. For Foucault, power is deployed in what can be understood as "games" or contests that can have very serious and far-reaching outcomes. As in all games, it is not the intentions of players that count, but the effects of their actions. Hence my discussion is not concerned with moral condemnation but with showing the results of certain practices, often quite unintentional or well-meaning. Since power is part of life, we cannot object to its existence or its use. It is unequal power relations that are objectionable, above all when domination occurs, when "the relations of power, instead of being variable and allowing different partners a strategy which alters them, find themselves firmly set and congealed."[6]

The existence of domination does not mean that acts of opposition do not occur, or that the situation is irreversible, but that while the situation of domination persists, acts of resistance cannot alter the asymmetry of forces. My examination of historical change in this chapter shows that it is at those times when forces realign and regroup that resistance can become effective and domination can be overthrown.

As far as medical practice and discourse themselves are concerned, domination occurs when the profession (or more often, a subgroup of it) captures the field of knowledge, creating truths for its own purposes. In this situation, the relation of power is asymmetrical between profession and public. While the profession actively creates knowledge, naturally from its own point of view, the patients and public tend to accept passively that knowledge as transhistorical truth.

The Remarkable Discrepancies of the Discourse

Striking changes have occurred in the discourse on menopause over the last two centuries. I have chosen three examples of such shifts in order to demonstrate that the quest for truth alone does not explain the beliefs held in any era, and that other forces are at work in their formulation. At the present time, changes in knowledge are often explained in terms of truth and error. It is considered that earlier generations had faulty access to truth and that ours is far superior, which explains why the knowledge they developed was dubious and ours, once established, can be trusted. Our concern with truth and falsehood obscures more relevant concerns. The pertinent question is why particular aspects of knowledge are searched for in the first place, and promulgated in the second. This use of Foucault's "genealogical method" seeks to contribute to an account of the creation of today's women—that is their historical form of subjectivity—while constantly keeping in mind that it is power that creates.[7]

In the mid-nineteenth century, menopausal women were warned that they should avoid sexual arousal and that intercourse was harmful. For example, the French gynecologist Columbat thought that

> the generative organs . . . should henceforth be left, as far as possible, in a state of inaction. . . . Under such circumstances, it is the dictate of prudence to avoid all such circumstances as might tend to awaken any erotic thoughts in the mind and reanimate a sentiment that ought rather to become extinct.[8]

The English gynecologist, Edward Tilt, thought that sexual desire in a menopausal woman was a sign of "morbid irritation" or "uterine disease" needing medical treatment.[9] Both Columbat and Tilt were highly respected writers of widely used medical texts, and their views were accepted truths.[10]

Thus, during the nineteenth century, sexual arousal after menopause was to be considered highly undesirable, causing or exacerbating disease, and its absence was to be considered a blessing. By contrast, in the mid-twentieth century the major reason given for the promotion of hormone replacement therapy

(HRT) was the *restoration* of sexual powers. HRT insured against the loss of interest in sex, which, according to gynecologist Robert Wilson, was that "vastly enriching element that is the key to wholly new dimensions in the development of the human personality."[11] Although Wilson has been discredited in more recent years, the view that sex was the absolute core of marital and personal fulfillment was a very widely held truth.

Now, at the end of the twentieth century, from having been an absolutely vital necessity in the earlier period, sex has become a matter of personal choice. Loss of libido is merely mentioned in a long list of lesser problems of menopause, whereas the main preoccupation is with health and disease. Doctor Barry Wren, who not so long ago believed that "every effort should be made to encourage continued activity and enjoyment [of sex],"[12] now says much less forcefully: "Lower levels of sex hormones may well reduce libido. Some women will be very distressed at the loss of their ability to respond."[13]

The second striking historical difference in menopause is that in Victorian times a postmenopausal woman was thought to gain masculine qualities, which were seen as an improvement over her former femininity. Finding herself (after the severe crises of the perimenopause) "safely anchored in this sure haven . . . from the tranquillity she has attained . . . [she will say] 'formerly, when I was a woman'," says Tilt.[14] After menopause "her mental facilities assume a masculine character"[15] and her "greatest mental vigor" is reached at the age of 56.[16] Doctor Hicks agrees: "losing sexuality and its various impulses, she becomes more capable of rendering herself useful."[17] Thus, according to the medical discourse, the Victorian woman could with equanimity face the loss of femininity, something that became unthinkable a hundred years later.

By the mid-twentieth century, the prospect of women developing masculine characteristics would be viewed with horror. Femininity had come to be seen as absolutely essential to a woman's personhood and sense of worth. There was a belief that what makes life worth living for a woman lies intrinsically in her ability to attract a man. Without this she was nothing; as Robert Wilson expressed it: "A woman's awareness of her own femininity completely suffuses her character and . . . the tragedy of menopause often destroys her character."[18] In other words, the absolute importance of femininity became a patent truth in the twentieth century. In the nineteenth century, it was an obvious truth that other characteristics, such as being useful, were at least of equal value to femininity.

It is notable that in the mid-1990s this totalizing emphasis upon femininity in the discourse has lessened. HRT is commended for its youth-giving properties and for the more gentle moods it promotes, but this expresses the desire for youth, health, vitality, and success in relationships—not just femininity. We are told, for example, that it will keep the skin and breasts looking young, enhances "well-being" and mental activity, and prevents the stridency of (haglike) mood changes.[19]

The third historical difference, already indicated above to some extent, concerns health. Not only did Victorian doctors believe that a woman's character and mental abilities improved with menopause, they also saw an improvement in her physical health.[20] Tilt, for example, finds some 500 diseases of menopause, but these generally refer to the perimenopause, not to postmenopause, when he says that, provided women take medical advice and follow a strict regimen during the "critical period," "they have only blessings to expect."[21] Today, the absolute opposite obtains: menopause is very far from being seen as a cause of improvement in health, personality, or mental faculties. Instead, numerous health problems are attributed to it. In popular works, gynecologists tell women that menopause increases the likelihood of bone fractures, heart attacks, strokes, cancers, hypertension, endocrine disorders, bladder problems, failed memory, and psychological problems.[22] Dr. Sandra Cabot, advocating long-term HRT, says that a "total shrinkage of the mind . . . could occur without the presence of the sex hormones."[23]

In the course of two centuries or so, "truth" has changed dramatically. In summary, in the nineteenth century sexual activity was bad for a menopausal woman, to be less feminine could be good, and menopause brought improved mental and physical health. In the mid-twentieth century, sexual activity was imperative for a menopausal woman, and to be less feminine was highly unfortunate. By the end of the twentieth century, menopause brings serious deterioration in fitness and health, and for some reason that previously crucial factor, femininity, is hardly mentioned in the medical discourse. How did medical practitioners come to such astonishingly contrary conclusions in the name of truth?

Situating Menopause within the Emerging Power Relations of the Nineteenth Century

The Victorian medical discourse saw women as victims of their reproductive organs. Earlier in the nineteenth century, the *uterus* was the cause of female weakness:

> It will be readily conceived that any derangement of this organ, or defect in its regular functions, must influence . . . the growth and healthy development of the female. . . . So remarkable a control does it exercise over the mind and its reasoning powers, that the greater frequency of insanity . . . has been referred to the mode and regularity with which menstruation is performed.[24]

Later, the *ovaries* were the cause:

> The ovarian nisus [impulse] seems to . . . so influence the brain that woman, no longer the mistress of her own actions, is literally "fuddled with animal spirits." . . . The same ovarian nisus . . . breaks out, spending its energy in hysterical convulsions, which may be followed by temporary paralysis. . . . Finally, when the ovarian nisus is at the highest, if it be suddenly disturbed by intense mental

emotion, . . . [its] whole energy is thrown on the central ganglia [nerve cells],
and reacts on the brain with such intensity, that in a few hours death ensues.[25]

Women of reproductive age were vulnerable, unstable, and were to be kept
passive and dependent for their own good. To avoid the possibility of irregular
menstruation or other injurious disturbance of their organs and consequent illness (mental or physical), they must obediently follow the doctor's prescribed
regimen: "avoidance of everything that excites the general sensibility," including
reading of romances, intellectual pursuits, balls, the theater, too much or too little sexual activity. A woman needed "a strong guiding influence," preferably of
"some judicious medical man," whose directions she should "implicitly obey."[26]
Independence and assertiveness in a woman were "against nature," dangerous,
and needed strong treatment, even to the extent of clitoridectomy[27] or, more
commonly, ovariotomy. Ovariotomy was widely practiced,[28] but the point here is
that it enhanced the power of the medical profession over women in general for,
as Ehrenreich and English say, "the very threat of surgery was probably enough
to bring many women into line."[29]

This endowing of women with a particular kind of body constituted a very
strong effort to dominate them, to produce them as beings who behaved in the
required manner. The gynecologists had a professional interest in setting themselves up as exclusive experts in matters of women's health and in having the
women "implicitly obey" them, for the profession was then striving to constitute
itself as the true source of knowledge against myriad "ignorant women."[30]
Women did not obey simply out of fear of ill-health, however; as noted above,
power acts not simply oppressively but creatively. Within this network of struggle, the feminine was being created as a particular embodied character or ethos.
The terms within which women constructed themselves were set within a struggle of several players, including women themselves, but medicine had command
of the most telling techniques. As Foucault says, "Nothing is more material,
physical, corporal than the exercise of power,"[31] and medicine had unequaled
access to the body and thus the opportunity to probe and to characterize it.

Working with the poor in the hospitals, having power over life and death and
knowledge of the human body, the leading medical men could pronounce with
authority upon the proper conduct and government of human life, of the nature
of "man," and of the universalized "woman." Through his knowledge of
woman's body and consequent authority in defining and determining its nature,
the medical expert was well placed to speak on behalf of several of the forces, or
players, with common interests in defining woman, as a strategic move in a larger game of power. The leading medical men had close contact with those other
forces—that is, with leading members of the middle class, of parliament, and of
the bureaucracy, through their membership of the hospital boards.[32]

To understand the orchestration of power relations, "one needs to study what
kind of body the current society needs."[33] Although Foucault thinks that power is

exercised over the body largely to produce the appropriate form of labor power for the economic system,[34] he recognizes that it is not only the bodies directly required that need to be reshaped for this purpose.[35] Thus he thinks that the emphasis upon decency, order, and health (both public and private) of the nineteenth century operated upon the bodies of men, women, and children to provide the rising industrial and trading classes with justification for their rule (contrasting nicely with the dissipation of the supplanted aristocracy), with legitimate and loyal sons for lines of inheritance, with a means of establishing order among the lower classes, and with docile bodies suitable for insertion into the production process.[36]

In this account, woman's body was reshaped mainly to enhance its reproductive qualities, as an indirect strategy for producing the body that was directly required in the general population and in the work force:

> The hysterization of women, which involved a thorough medicalization of their bodies and their sex, was carried out in the name of the responsibility they owed to the health of their children, the solidity of the family institution, and the safeguarding of society.[37]

The "hysterization" of middle-class women—their identification with their wombs and thus with motherhood—and the extreme degree of fragility that was attributed to their health status[38] thus confined them to the home and to domestic duties. But this also suited another player in this game of power, and that was the middle-class man. As Simone de Beauvoir has explained, man constructs himself as essential through comparison with, and in opposition to, woman as inessential Other, and this process is not reciprocal.[39] This unequal process is a strategy of power that is not incompatible with Foucault's general understanding of power.

In the nineteenth century, the dominant and ideal figure of "man" had come to be the bourgeois entrepreneur of industry and trade. These people had to be strong and powerful, able to grapple with the unknown—with developing new large-scale capitalist enterprises and, in particular, with implementing new forms of control over others necessary for large-scale production. In this colonialist period, capitalism was nation based. Imports flowed into the center, exports flowed out, all under the aegis of the entrepreneur who, far more directly than today, exploited and controlled factory workers and colonial subjects. The entrepreneur's body had to be extremely forceful, independent, powerful, and dominating, bestriding the world, in charge of the welfare of home and country, hard and rational. The feminine body required as Other, against which this powerful controlling figure could construct itself, had to be extremely weak, unable to survive without guidance and direction (needing the control of the dominant other), attached to home, in fact unable to survive outside of it, soft and emotional, a child in relation to him.

A further significant suggestion concerning the body of nineteenth-century woman has been made by Londa Schiebinger, who thinks it likely that the search for bodily sex differences begun in the 1750s was inspired by the fear that women would take up the rhetoric of the Enlightenment to demand equality, an appeal for natural rights that could be countered by the discovery of a natural inequality.[40] Thus a group of men also participated in the network of forces with an interest in woman's weakness.

Now to explain the nature of Victorian menopausal woman: The belief that woman's weakness originates in the functioning of her reproductive organs does lead logically to the conclusion that she must improve when these organs have ceased activity. However, this conclusion could easily have been avoided by finding some other problem in the bodies of menopausal women, had this been a necessary strategy in a game of power.[41] It was not necessary, and this is because menopausal woman was not of importance. Her value had never been primarily as a sexual object, either for her husband, the state, or the economic forces, but as a reproductive one. In Foucault's terms, the power of the state and of the middle class took two main forms in the nineteenth century. The first, "bio-power," was directed toward "life"—that is, toward producing suitable, healthy populations and docile bodies: "an indispensable element in the development of capitalism."[42] In this game menopausal woman, no longer reproductive, was not a player. The second form of power, "pastoral power," was directed at the individual self. It "proceeded through examination and insistent observation" and "a technology of health and pathology."[43] Through these technologies, sexuality became "a mode of specification of individuals."[44] Naturally, the "aim" was to specify the individual at an early, rather than at a late, stage of life. Each form of power intertwined and influenced the other, but in each the focus was upon younger, reproductive women.

Under these influences (and probably the man's own preference for youthful bodies), menopausal woman was not the Other against whom man created himself, and he had no need to construct her as weak in mind or in body for this purpose. Now unsuitable to support the structure of identity and difference, she could even be somewhat like him. As a grandmother, she had invested her life in the family institution and had an interest in its maintenance. She could be trusted—although the warning against sexual intercourse can be interpreted as a strategy to guard against climacteric sexual rebellion, which would subvert the bourgeois image of decency and order.

The Network of Power in the Mid-Twentieth Century and Its Construction of Menopause

Turning now to the conditions of the mid-twentieth century, when medical advice and symptoms of menopause were in diametrical opposition to those of the nineteenth century, it is notable that a much broader array of woman was now invested within the scope of the discourse. The middle class had grown considerably, and although the ideal "woman" remained middle class, even some working-class women now had the time and opportunity to read and to be influenced by magazines, newspapers, and books that provided "expert" advice on all matters related to woman and her role.

This was the time of the domestic and human sciences, when a multitude of experts, creating for themselves an ascendant position in the field of power, subjected the housewife, the home, and the family to intensive scrutiny and appraisal.[45] Under this new regime of scientific nutrition, childrearing, health, hygiene, and sexual relations, the home, and especially the child, took on a new importance. The housewife's and, above all, the mother's work became a grave responsibility for which she was accountable to expert opinion. The result was a change in relations between the sexes. According to Ehrenreich and English, the experts had stepped between husband and wife, subjecting her to other authorities; and although her proper role continued to lie in serving others, it was now primarily the child that she served.[46] However, as I show below, the relationship of power among husband, wife, and the socioeconomic system was more complex than this suggests.

At this time the home also became the locus of the increasing drive of industry toward higher consumption. Experts employed by industry directly collaborated in escalating the needs of the exemplary modern, efficient housewife. The husband, according to Ehrenreich and English, became the mere provider of income until rescued by the experts, who found a role for him in providing therapeutic sex for his wife and a manly model for his children.[47] The purpose of the therapy was not, as might be thought, the wife's sexual release, but in giving her a "sense of her own worth."[48] The woman's sexuality remained essentially passive, and her satisfaction came from her attractiveness, which rendered her a worthy human being.[49] It was sex that held the marriage together, stimulating pleasure in her "womanly role" in the wife, while the husband could satisfy his urgent animal desire in her. The wife provided home comforts and a warm, receptive acceptance of his sexual needs, much like the image of the breastfeeding mother.

Concentrating on the strategies of the experts alone does not provide a complete picture of the operations of power occurring at that time. What kind of male body was required by economic forces, and what was the role, if any, of woman as man's Other? The answer to the former question is that in this age of increasing mechanization and emphasis on efficient use of resources, industry required a highly docile body that was unquestioningly obedient to the "laws" of the "science of management." Except for a tiny elite of "thinkers," an attitude that brought reliability, dependability, and attentiveness to the task, rather than creativity, was required at all levels.[50] Whereas economic and political conditions during World War II had provided a temporary "honeymoon" between employers and labor,[51] the return of the fighting men threatened disruption and a return to the militancy of prewar unions. In such conditions, it was a strategic move that men and women be divided, rather than uniting in one work force, and that both groups be disciplined to become the required kind of body. The woman at home was now available to satisfy the other need of industry brought on by the increases in productive output for an unquestioning consuming force. If woman was to leave her work in industry and return to her "proper place" in the home, following the experts' advice to efficiently serve men and children,[52] the proper role of man was to obey the laws of efficient management, to disregard unions, and to provide the necessary income for his wife's expenditure. Thus, I argue that both women and men were dominated by industry, their powers and capacities having been "captured" and put to the use of this other force. Women, however, were subject to additional layers of domination.

In the twentieth century, under these influences, there was an important change in the relation between husband and wife. In many respects, the Victorian husband had been like a patriarchal father to his childlike wife. Now the wife was more like a nurturing mother to her childlike husband. Her main role continued to be to reproduce the bodies directly required by industry and by the state, but she was now more directly under the authority of the experts of state and industry, and, correspondingly, less under her husband's. Nevertheless, hers remained a body that gained its value from servicing other bodies.

In her role as man's Other, her body was desired to be yielding, soft and passive against the returned serviceman's own closed hardness. The war had bought the triumph of science and technology, setting up a new ideal of masculine attainment. Man's task now was the building of a new problem-free world, a modern technological paradise, a world of plenty. Hardheaded, ultrarational, efficient, scientific technoman needed an Other who was soft, emotional, "dumb," passive, and sexually appealing. Compared to his patriarchal Victorian counterpart, the man of the 1950s and '60s was a boy, playing with his technical toys and perhaps not a little awed by the weapon he had created. He needed a modern wife who coped with home and children without his supervision or assistance, but, as she well knew, she also had to play the inferior Other who was in awe of his superior knowledge and who gladly satisfied his compelling sexual desires.

The final player in this game was gynecology, which now had to share its preeminence in knowledge of woman with a great variety of experts, much more so than in the nineteenth century. Women too had begun to challenge medical and other expert opinion. Betty Friedan's *The Feminine Mystique* appeared in 1963, generating great public debate. Viewed from the point of view of power, Robert Wilson's *Feminine Forever*, appearing in 1966, was a strategic move toward defending gynecology's position in defining woman, as well as speaking for those wider social forces that saw a strategic advantage in keeping women in the home serving men and children. An important element here was the state, which, in its perennial concern with the stability, health, and control of populations, had provided experts to encourage and to supervise the housewife's role.

For Wilson, the loss of estrogen at menopause brought the end of femininity, which basically translates as sexual appeal.[53] But it goes deeper than this, for it is sexual appeal that preserves personality and character and bestows personhood.[54] Wilson publicized the notion that menopause was a "deficiency disease," like diabetes.[55] However, unlike diabetes, menopause occurs only in women and to all women. In pointing out this universal defect in women's bodies, Wilson was keeping up the tradition of the nineteenth century, when women's bodies were problematized for a variety of strategic purposes.[56] Now, however, the problem was reversed in time, manifesting itself during the postreproductive years of a woman's life, whereas previously it had occurred during her reproductive phase. Wilson agreed with other opinion that menopause was a time when women are likely to take stock of their lives and to consider leaving their marriages.[57] Strategies were necessary to keep them in place, for by 1966 the divorce rate in America was rising dramatically and the peak age after marriage at which women had paid work was 45–54 years, when some 50 percent were employed and thus financially independent.[58] If, according to Wilson, the loss of sexuality was a tragedy for the menopausal woman, it was also a tragedy for the aging man, for he continued to need his nurturing mother/wife.

In a seeming paradox, the Victorian wife was the mother of her husband's children and less a sex object for him; the wife of the 1950s and '60s was sex object and mother to her husband. Thus, the Victorian husband had less need of his wife after her childbearing years were over, whereas the usefulness of the modern wife did not diminish. Her loss of reproductive ability need not mean that she could not continue to nurture her husband, but her ability to attract must be maintained. So, the mission of HRT was to maintain the well-being of husband, state, economy and herself.

Accounting for Menopause Today

In the late twentieth century, the medical discourse on menopause has taken on an air of equality, advising rather than directing, professing to offer women facts upon which to make up their own minds about how to deal with their menopause. While it is tempting to believe that this is a response to feminist criticism, offering a more symmetrical power relation, or even that this particular game of power has been almost won, I suggest that this very rhetoric of truth and choice operates as a strategy of power.[59]

Like all people, women are involved in power relations and can and do act strategically. Although it is thus erroneous to see them as simply the passive objects or victims of the strategies of others, the efforts of individuals acting singly are almost invariably ineffective against the power of assemblages sharing common aims and strategies. Acts of resistance carried out by individual women unsupported by others expose them to the forms of discipline that have been devised by a united opposition. These can be severe, as in the case of clitoridecto-my and ovariotomy, mentioned earlier. The most efficient form of control, however, is not discipline after the event but a strategy of "pacification" or "tam-ing," where the object is the creation of a being who is actually docile in the first place. Success in this involves using subtle methods so that the object is lulled into accepting the truths of the other. Thus, for example, many women in the 1950s did believe that their proper role consisted of serving children and hus-band. It is only when women unite and make positive discourses of their own that their combined power can have a real effect in the network of power relations.

As I have already pointed out, women were confronted by a different, more extensive network of power by the mid-twentieth century, when industry, experts, and state were addressing them directly. In the 1970s, women began to make strategic moves of their own, in large numbers. Not only did married women increasingly enter the work force, but single women began to take their work more seriously, seeing it as a lifetime career rather than as a mere interim measure prior to marriage.[60] Rather than remaining dependent, many women began to adopt an ideal of realizing their lives and selves as independently viable, rather than as essentially needing a husband to complete them. For the single woman, this involved a strategy of setting up her own domicile, complete with the consumer items that had previously been required only upon marriage. Most of these women did not cease to desire heterosexual relationships, but there was a decided change in what they wanted from them. Their ideal became a relation-ship between equals and a reciprocal fulfillment of needs. For example, many women began to expect sexual satisfaction for themselves rather than vicarious satisfaction through the other.

Although it will exploit sexual difference, capitalism is not primarily con-cerned with the biological sex of the body it utilizes. It has profited by operating a broad strategy of reinforcement of sexual difference, both to divide possible opposition and to keep women and men in line as docile subjects amenable to continued exploitation, but a body of either/any sex will suffice provided it has the characteristics necessary to the economic circumstances of the time. As we have seen, particular tactics are chosen to suit the changing circumstances. Thus the change in young women's aspirations and living arrangements, far from being seen as detrimental or threatening to economic forces, was grasped as an opportunity for increasing and diversifying consumption.[61] With the new ethos, men too could be drawn into forms of consumption that had been preponderant-ly the province of women, men's toiletries and fashion wear being obvious examples.

Capitalism, however, is concerned not only with marketing but also with the creation of a suitable work force. In the late twentieth century, its needs changed dramatically as the methods of high-volume production, which had ensured prosperity in the industrialized nations for decades, were adopted by newly industrializing nations with greater success. Profit rates, productivity, standards of living, and real incomes declined while unemployment soared in the industrialized countries. Many workers, already highly individualized under capitalism and not realizing their strategic position in the game of power, tended to accept the arguments of employers and state that the problem was to be explained in terms of individual merit and blame. This tendency was augmented by the capitalist response to the falling rate of profit. One move was to become more "clever"—to invest in highly skilled processes, such as precision engineering, custom production tailored to highly specific requirements of individual customers, and advanced, rapidly changing technologies. The body required for this was decidedly different from before—mobile, active, innovative, resourceful, creative, flexible, risk taking, and highly individualistic. There also emerged a new-fashioned form of profit making, involving sophisticated market manipulation of shares, futures, and entire companies, which Reich calls "paper entrepreneurialism."[62] The attitudes of paper entrepreneurialism—that assets and workers can be rearranged for short-term profits—have also resulted in increasing movement in the labor market, with consequent insecurity, competition, and "economic individualism." Today's form of capitalism assumes, even more strongly than previously, that "those privileged, clever, or ruthless enough to have acquired productive assets are entitled to use them as they see fit, to their own anticipated advantage."[63] The strategies of power have become more explicit and intense, with righteousness on the side of the winners, while losers are objects of blame.

Under these conditions, in a strategic move to ally itself with other powerful players, the state has adopted a similar logic, applying the policies of "economic rationalism" in which individuals are increasingly expected to provide for their personal survival. Funds for the care of the sick, aged, and unemployed are seen as being in short supply, and there has been a corresponding emphasis upon bodily health and fitness, which have also become questions of virtue and blame. I am not arguing here that health and fitness are not to be desired, but rather that discourses about them are immersed in power relations. Strategically, they have the effect of warding off criticism of state and capitalist practices through the creation of a quiescent population that sees social problems exclusively in terms of individual responsibility.

Seemingly in response to feminist criticism, the medical discourse on menopause has changed: where in the past it contained many normative assumptions concerning woman, these are now, apparently, carefully avoided by most practitioners. But in the wider context described above, the success of women's criticism upon the discourse cannot be taken for granted. While women have united to make strong critiques of the medical discourse and to build counter-knowledges (and these have had their own effects on women), the other reasons I am suggesting for the change in the discourse are compelling. The key word in the discourse now is "choice"—it is said to be up to the woman herself, fully informed by her medical advisers of the facts concerning HRT and her individual health status, to decide whether or not to take HRT. This may look like a big improvement over being told that we exist to serve men or to have healthy babies, but the discourse is actually promoting the very kind of working and consuming individuals required by economic forces, and the very kind of "independent," "fit," body required by today's state.

The belief that you have only yourself and your lack of effort to blame if you suffer reverses in your life has produced the converse belief that, if you try hard enough, you can do anything. Not only can you make more money and get a better job, you can remake yourself. As industry, company structures, and the bodies of workers can be rearranged in space and time, so can the body of the individual. A person can have a new body, a new self, a new face, a longer life, fitness, good health, a technologically produced pregnancy—it's a matter of effort, the choice is there. Again, the problem I am pointing to is not these beliefs and practices as such,[64] but that they are enmeshed in power relations in such a way as to promote the normalizing and individualizing notion that since you can do anything, be anything you want, if you allow yourself to become unfit or decrepit this is moral failure. In this strategy of power, the perpetrators of these "crimes," preoccupied with their guilt, tend to be silenced, and their needs can be disregarded.

Once again, it is noticeable that the body is the target in this creation of a docile population. There is a strategic "purpose" in focusing upon the faults in bodies and in setting up an ideal for its reconstruction, for body and self are not separable. Power produces particular bodily qualities with particular personal characteristics: the active, youthful body required by industry, the other bodies that have failed, and the bodies that understand themselves to be self-sufficient and thus see no need for criticism of social, industrial, and medical practices.

The medical discourse on menopause in the 1990s is consistent with these notions of individualism and freedom of choice and with the ideal personal characteristics of the era. Through HRT, menopausal women are offered the fit, active, flexible body required by economic forces. If they want to be sexy as well, the technical expert will add a dash of testosterone, and if they want a baby, that can be done too. As the Californian woman who bore a child after menopause, Jonie Mosby Mitchell, says in reply to concerns about her age when the child goes to college, "So I'm just going to work harder. I'm going to stay younger. I'm going to stay healthier. . . . You can do anything you want. Obviously, I did."[65] Sandra Cabot thinks similarly: "I believe that as women we can become what we visualise ourselves to be."[66] The problem here is that what we visualize has all too often been strategically introduced by forces interested in exploiting us for their own purposes.

Consistent with this, Barry Wren's book is entitled *Your Choice*, but his choice is between carrot and stick:

> BE ABSOLUTELY CLEAR ON THIS POINT: Women do not "get over" the menopause. Once the ovaries stop producing oestrogen and other hor-

mones, the body will usually be in a state of oestrogen deficiency. This deficiency is characterised by hot flushes, sweats, vaginal and bladder discomfort,
mood swings, and a whole range of other symptoms. . . . Therefore all women
who reach the menopause should consider the advantages and disadvantages of
taking HRT.[67] (Emphasis in original.)

Estrogen, he says, will prevent osteoporosis and cardiovascular disease; maintain youthful skin, breasts, and vagina; improve the sense of well-being and
mental functioning; give four years longer life; and reduce by at least 50 percent
the risk of various cancers, stroke, hypertension, heart attack, and bone fracture.
There is, he says, the choice of "the nursing home alternative," with its "loss of
independence, loss of privacy, loss of control over food selection and preparation, inability to continue previous lifestyle, boredom, loss of rights generally."[68]
Finally, Wren calls on the normalizing rhetoric of virtue and blame by reminding readers of the huge cost to the state of refusal of HRT in the maintenance of
countless thousands of osteoporotic women.[69]

That many of the gynecologists speaking or writing for the general public on
menopause make claims that are exaggerated, inadequately researched, or based
on selectively chosen research findings indicates far more than simply their personal interest in promoting HRT.[70] In promoting the fit, independent,
menopausal body, medicine speaks once more for state and broad economic
interests. Medicine remains in a prime position for targeting the body to create
the required self-sufficient and quiescent population.

Medicine also continues to need its Other, a flawed body from which to create
itself as the unquestioned and unquestionable knowing One. Although so far the
female body continues to be medicine's Other, there is, for the reasons I have
given, a particular focus upon the older woman's body today. In this, medicine
again speaks on behalf of other forces, as well as for itself. While the fit, healthy,
young body is, to us today, an obvious ideal of medicine, it is also the ideal of
industry, of men, of worker, and of state, to all of whom the aged, infirm female
body has become a useless and burdensome Other. Thus Otherness is not an
uncomplicated dichotomy referring simply to man/woman.[71] For example, as
Lock points out, medicine sets up the menopausal woman as Other to the young
woman, in its practice of using as a standard the "normal" body of a young
woman to assess the "pathology" of the bodies of older women.[72] This, of course,
has the effect of a strategy of power, dividing women, and enticing young women
to identify more readily with men than with other women.

As for man, what is his part in today's strategies? The new man, of course an
object of power relations himself, needs a playmate, a fellow consumer, and necessarily a fellow earner of income, a woman who can appreciate and actively
participate in his life style. Aged woman is the Other of both man and his playmate. However, such men are now in direct competition with women in their
work. The menopause discourse, in problematizing the female middle-aged

body, strikes a blow at women at the height of their careers and enables their male competitors to set themselves up as problem free against this flawed Other.

Conclusion

Menopause is an aspect of female life that is particularly heavy with possibilities of meaning for the feminine. It seems likely, therefore, that the truths of this event will continue to be contested. It is important that women see that it has relevance not only to a short span of women's lives but to the defining of what it is to be a woman. Unless women recognize these power games for what they are and participate actively in them, formulating their own strategies, the games will continue to be one-sided. Women will continue to be baffled and effectively to concede that they are the weaker, the imperfect, sex, and to be targets of the various objectives of other powerful forces. For Foucault, autonomy comes only through struggle and through actively creating our selves.

In the field of power/knowledge, the medical profession has been at the forefront of a campaign that has been exceedingly influential in the creation of the modern form of feminine subjectivity. Facts have been irrelevant to the production of the female body and of women themselves as ailing and weak. But the problem is not so much that these forces say we are weak as that we tend to accept this as true and incorporate this truth into our selves. My aim has been to show that such truths are creations, and to encourage the idea that if one group can produce truth, so can another.

Foucault thinks that there is something much deeper at stake than winning or losing in particular games of power. He believes that in the modern age we have been subjected by a particular relation to the self, a looking within that leaves us unfree, unable to choose how to act ethically. Taking our social construction seriously, Foucault thinks that we must try to understand how we have become what we are. In his thought, we must find out what we are so that we can become something different, something consciously chosen. This is to be opposed to the modern way of looking within to discover what we are, as an end in itself.

As Foucault says:

> Thought is not what inhabits a certain conduct and gives it meaning; rather, it is what allows one to step back from this way of acting or reacting, to present it to oneself as an object of thought and question it as to its meaning, its conditions, and its goals. Thought is freedom in relation to what one does, the motion by which one detaches oneself from it, establishes it as an object, and reflects upon it as a problem.[73]

Once we have understood our genealogy, how we have become what we are, then, instead of being blindly operated upon by exterior forces to develop a "nature" suited to their needs, we can make conscious decisions about fashioning ourselves. Rather than being constructed and ruled by these exterior forces, we can choose to govern ourselves and to construct our own actions.

> The problem is not of trying to dissolve [relations of power] in the utopia of perfectly transparent communication, but to give one's self the rules of law, the techniques of management, and *also the ethics, the ethos, the practice of self*, which would allow these games of power to be played with a minimum of domination.[74]

Notes

1. The following text describes parts of a video made by a major Australian women's teaching hospital: Queen Victoria Hospital, *Understanding the Menopause: How Can Hormone Therapy Help Me? Recommended Viewing For All Women between 30 and 50 Years of Age* (Adelaide, South Australia, 1988), sponsored by Upjohn Pty Ltd.

2. I am taking this woman as a a generalized example, not as a specific person who may have various personal motives and desires, none of which are open to individual criticism. The same applies to her husband and the doctor.

3. I do not dispute that biological facts of menopause exist. But there are many ways of dealing with facts, all of them necessarily choices and thus acts of power. Facts may be used, or selected, in constructing truths, but the truths we take for granted are not all fact.

4. In this short study, I can do no more than draw a rough outline of the forces involved. The network of power relations is far more diverse and complex than my sketch depicts.

5. Michel Foucault, "Afterword: The Subject and Power" in *Michel Foucault: Beyond Structuralism and Hermeneutics*, ed. H. Dreyfus and P. Rabinow (Sussex: Harvester Press, 1986), p. 222.

6. Michel Foucault, "The Ethic of Care for the Self as a Practice of Freedom," in *The Final Foucault*, ed. James Bernauer and David Rasmussen (Cambridge: MIT Press, 1988), p. 3.

7. On genealogy see Foucault, "What is enlightenment," in *The Foucault Reader*, ed. Paul Rabinow (Harmondsworth: Penguin, 1984), pp. 45–46.

8. de L'Isere Columbat, *Female Diseases* (USA: Meigs, 1850), p. 551.

9. E. J. Tilt, *The Change of Life in Health and Disease* (London: John Churchill, 1870), p. 241.

10. As with the truths of our time, this is not to say that they were invariably followed, or that everyone accepted them. In other words, my focus is upon the truths of that time, not upon whether people actually had sex or not.

11. Robert A. Wilson, *Feminine Forever* (New York: M. Evans and Co., 1966), p. 28.

12. Barry Wren, "Health Needs of Climacteric Women," paper presented at 4th International Congress on the Menopause, Lancaster, UK, 1986, p. 55.

13. Barry Wren, *Your Choice* (Sydney: Centre for the Management of the Menopause, 1994), p. 26.

14. Tilt, *The Change*, p. 68.

15. Ibid., p. 67.

16. Ibid., p. 27.

17. J. Braxton Hicks, "The Croonian Lectures on the Difference Between the Sexes," *British Medical Journal*, April 21, 1877: pp. 475–76.
    As late as 1949, Simone de Beauvoir held a rather similar belief: "And in truth, while they are not males, they are no longer females. Often, indeed, this release from female physiology is expressed in . . . a balance . . . that they lacked before." Simone de Beauvoir, *The Second Sex*, trans. H. M. Parshley (Harmondsworth: Penguin, 1953), p. 63. De Beauvoir gave a different cause for this but, I would argue, she did believe, in the final analysis, that the masculine was superior to the feminine.

18. Wilson, *Feminine Forever*, p. 21.

19. See Dr. Sandra Cabot, M.D., *Hormone Replacement Therapy and Its Natural Alternatives* (Werombi, NSW: Women's Health Advisory Service, 1993), pp. 15, 22, 24; Dr. John F. Kemp, *The Menopause: Make It a Change for the Better* (Sydney: G.B. Wallace and Associates, 1989), p. 5; and Wren, *Your Choice*, pp. 21, 22.

20. Again, de Beauvoir echoes this: "Her vitality is unimpaired," she has "health" and "vigor" that she did not have before (*Second Sex*, p. 63).

21. Tilt, *The Change*, p. 110.

22. See, for example Wren, *Your Choice*, p. 36.

23. Cabot, *Hormone Replacement Therapy*, p. 15.

24. Samuel Mason, *The Philosophy of Female Health* (1845), as quoted in Pat Jalland, and Hooper, John, *Women from Birth to Death: The Female Life Cycle in Britain 1830–1914* (Brighton: Harvester Press, 1986), pp. 1–3.

25. Tilt, *The Change*, p. 203.

26. Ibid., p. 188.

27. See E. Showalter, *The Female Malady: Women, Madness and English Culture, 1830–1980* (New York: Pantheon Books, 1985), for an account of this "efficient . . . form of reprogramming."

28. "In 1906 a leading gynecological surgeon estimated that there were 150,000 women in the United States who had lost their ovaries to the knife." (B. Ehrenreich and D. English, *For Her Own Good: 150 Years of the Expert's Advice to Women* (London: Pluto Press, 1979), p. 111.

29. B. Ehrenreich and D. English, "The Sick Women of the Upper Classes," in *The Cultural Crisis of Modern Medicine*, ed. John Ehrenreich (New York: Monthly Review Press, 1976), p. 138.

30. There have been several accounts of the struggle of medical men to replace mid-wives as experts in the area of women's health. See, for example, for the United States, Barbara Ehrenreich and Dierdre English, *Complaints and Disorders: The Sexual Politics of Sickness* (London: Readers and Writers Publ. Coop., 1973); for England, J. Donnison, *Midwives and Medicine Men: A History of Interprofessional Rivalries and Women's Rights* (London: Heineman, 1977); and for Australia, Evan Willis, *Medical Dominance* (Sydney: Allen and Unwin, 1983).

31. Michel Foucault, "Body/power," in *Power/Knowledge*, ed. Colin Gordon (Great Britain: Harvester Press, 1980), p. 57–58.

32. See I. Waddington, "General Practitioners in Early Nineteenth Century England: The Sociology of an Intra-Professional Conflict," in *Health Care and Popular Medicine in the Nineteenth Century*, ed. J. Woodward and D. Richards (London: Croom Helm, 1977), pp. 164–88 ; and F. B. Smith, *The People's Health 1830–1910* (London: Croom Helm, 1979), pp. 31–32.

33. Foucault, "Body/power," pp. 57–58.

34. Michel Foucault, *Discipline and Punish* (Harmondsworth: Penguin, 1982), p. 26.

35. Foucault is not suggesting a crude economic determinism in saying that power is exercised over the body largely to produce the appropriate form of labor power for the economic system. He sees power as operating in a very complex network. However, the necessities of the economic system are highly influential in determining what is possible, what is needed, and what is desired.

36. Michel Foucault, *The History of Sexuality*, vol. 1 (Harmondsworth: Penguin, 1981), pp. 139–47; see also J. Weeks, *Sex, Politics and Society: The Regulation of Sexuality Since 1800* (London: Longman, 1981), p. 29. Thus it is clear that the nineteenth-century discourse on menopause applied directly only to a narrow group—to women of the upper classes. Lower-class women were in no position to accede to bodily weakness at that time. For reasons of space, I am unable to deal adequately with the very complex question of class difference in this chapter. I think it is fair to say that in both centuries, it has been middle-class standards and beliefs that have been promoted, and quite widely accepted, as general human truths. This does not mean that there has not also been dissent, or that there have not been important differences between classes. It should be noted also that in terms of the spread of ideas and beliefs, the boundaries of class are more permeable today than they were in the nineteenth century.

37. Foucault, *History of Sexuality*, pp. 146–47.

38. Of course women in childbirth were at far greater risk than today, but this does not explain the intense preoccupation with female disease centered on the reproductive organs. Menstruation was fraught with dangers, and young girls were seen as virtual invalids the closer they came to puberty. For a fuller discussion, including women's own resistance to being categorized as invalids, Ehrenreich and English, *For Her Own Good*, pp. 99–104.

39. Beauvoir, *Second Sex*, pp. 17–18.

40. Londa Schiebinger, "Skeletons in the Closet: The First Illustrations of the Female Skeleton in Eighteenth-Century Anatomy," *Representations* 14 (1986): pp. 42–43.

41. That older women past the years of childbirth probably *were* healthier is not the point. In the game of power relations, facts are relevant only for strategic purposes.

42. Foucault, *The History of Sexuality*, pp. 140–41.

43. Ibid., p. 44.

44. Ibid., p. 47.

45. In the section on the nineteenth century, I used examples mainly from Britain and Europe, because these were then centers of great influence. The hegemony of the United States in the twentieth century means that it is now the better example.

46. Ehrenreich and English, *For Her Own Good*, pp. 165–89, 214–17. See also Julie A. Matthaei, *An Economic History of Women in America* (New York: Schocken Books, 1982), pp. 268–70.

47. Ehrenreich and English, *For Her Own Good*, pp. 216–24.

48. Wilson, *Feminine Forever*, p. 21.

49. Ibid., p. 15.

50. For a description of the principles of "scientific management" or "Taylorism," which dominated industry during the period 1920 to 1970, see Robert B. Reich, *The Next American Frontier* (New York: Times Books, 1983), pp. 64–69. This system sharply separated a very small elite group of "thinkers" from the large body of "doers," including managers, who were "programmed" or trained to carry out the thinkers' decisions without question.

51. Douglas Dowd, *Capitalist Development Since 1776: Of, by, and for Which People?* (New York: M. E. Sharpe, 1993), p. 166.

52. The actual labor-force participation rate of women increased between 1940 and 1950, and again by 1960. However, the rate of participation by women aged 25–34 years did not rise in these years. It is clear that young married women did give up their jobs, the participation rate dropping from a high at age 19 to a low between ages 25 and 34 during the entire period 1940–1960 (see Matthaei, *An Economic History*, p. 280, Table 12–1). Matthaei's figures do not indicate participation rates during World War II, but, in any case, my argument concerns the prevalent ideal for women rather than what actually occurred.

53. Wilson, *Feminine Forever*, pp. 17–18.

54. Ibid., pp. 21, 34, 62.

55. Ibid., p. 19.

56. Ironically, Wilson acknowledges that "a woman's body is the key to her fate" while finding it universally defective (ibid., p. 60).

57. Ibid., p. 87.

58. Matthaei, *An Economic History*, pp. 280, 311.

59. In Foucault's thought, of course, games of power can never be eliminated, and I argue that the truth of menopause will very probably always be contested.

60. By 1980 a large rise in work-force participation of women in general had occurred, and there was only a small fall during the usual childbearing years of 25–34 (Matthaei, *An Economic History*, p. 280).

61. Ehrenreich and English, *For Her Own Good*, p. 262.

62. Robert B. Reich, *The Next American Frontier* (New York: Times Books, 1983), p. 141.

63. Dowd, *Capitalist Development*, pp. 4–5.

64. Many experts do take very serious and unnecessary risks with the bodies they operate upon. However, I am not attempting to address that here.

65. BBC Enterprises Ltd., *Cheating Time*, videorecording (*Horizon:* London, 1993).

66. Cabot, *Hormone Replacement Therapy*, p. 45.

67. Wren, *Your Choice*, p. 38.

68. Ibid., p. 39.

69. Ibid., pp. 34–35.

70. Wren's claims are of this kind, as are Sandra Cabot's, who repeats the long-discredited belief in "involutional melancholia" and threatens "total shrinkage of mind and

body" (Cabot, *Hormone Replacement Therapy*, p. 15), turning into "a wizened up old prune" (p. 22), and "devastating" effects upon a woman's sexuality (p. 24). John Studd, of Kings College Hospital, remarks that HRT keeps women "out of the orthopaedic wards, the divorce courts and the madhouse" (quoted in ibid., p. 15) and believes that "men are far better designed when it comes to fertility and hormones" (quoted in *Cheating Time*). A more reasonable style is used by Wulf Utian, who says, "It is paradoxical that the decision whether to prescribe long-term hormone replacement therapy for all women after menopause rests on a balance of risks and benefits which in turn is dependent upon a number of unanswered questions." Despite these admissions, Utian advocates HRT. Wulf Utian, "Menopause in Perspective," in Marsha Flint et al., *Multidisciplinary Perspectives on Menopause: A 3-day Symposium under the Auspices of New York Academy of Sciences and the North American Menopause Society*, ed. Marsha Flint, et al. (New York: New York Academy of Sciences, 1990), p. 5.

71. Of course, old men, too, are Other, to young people, for example.

72. Margaret Lock, "The Politics of Mid-life and Menopause," in *Knowledge, Power and Practice: The Anthropology of Medicine and Everyday Life*, ed. Shirley Lindenbaum and Margaret Lock (Berkeley: University of California Press, 1993), pp. 336.

73. Foucault, *The Foucault Reader*, p. 388

74. Foucault, *The Final Foucault*, p. 18; emphasis added.

METAPHORS AND MUTATIONS

11

Sources of Abjection in
Western Responses to Menopause

Wendy Rogers

A barrage of advertising, information, and promotional material crossed my desk in 1993. There were seminars, dinner meetings, video launches, free samples, and patient leaflets galore, all focusing on menopause, its symptoms and sequelae, and the way(s) to avoid it. This was an interesting phenomenon; a blaze of publicity about a hitherto ignored event in women's lives now making news, and now "treatable," thanks to hormone replacement therapy. Yet despite all the publicity, all the apparent openness, I felt uneasy; the lists of symptoms in the leaflets were disembodied, sanitized, impersonal. The smiling faces of the women on so-called "hormone replacement therapy" (HRT) advertisements told nothing of the experience of menopause and did not tally with the low numbers of women taking HRT long term. I felt targeted as a medical practitioner; it was my responsibility to ensure compliance with medical treatment. If not my patients faced a life of broken bones, hot flashes, depression, dry vaginas, and poor bladder control, not to mention increased risk of cardiovascular disease and the enormous cost to public health of treating all these preventable complications.

Was it simply the case that menopause is the start of a lifelong hormone deficiency disease, or was this advertising, bordering on hysteria, a demand for more control over the lives of women, or a revenue-raising venture on the part of pharmaceutical companies? What of the experience itself? Does menopause represent such a dramatic and fearful end to reproductive life or does it herald a different way of being, in no way inferior to that of the premenopause? There was a lot of ambiguity and hysteria in the air. Menopause was presented as a dreadful border, patrolled by ever-vigilant patients and doctors armed with lists of symptoms and statistics, ready to pounce with HRT at the first hot flash. Typical of genre is the patient information leaflet produced by Upjohn called *A*

225

Balanced Approach to the Menopause, in which the menopausal state is presented as a morass of hot flashes; sweats; muscular aches and pains; more frequent urination; loss of lubrication and elasticity of the vagina; infections; irregular and unpredictable bleeding; emotional symptoms such as confusion, loss of memory, mild depression, and general irritability; not to mention osteoporosis and heart disease. Fortunately for the reader, "Your doctor may prescribe hormone replacement therapy to help restore your body's natural hormone balance," thus overcoming the short-term symptoms and reducing the long-term risks.[1]

If menopause is a border, *the change of life*, in the way suggested by this type of information, what does it divide? Why is such a common event the object of such powerful medical rituals? Are we as doctors merely trying to do the best by our patients and society by practicing preventive medicine, or is treatment of menopause an expression of our horror at the inevitable aging and decay faced by all humans?

In reflecting upon these matters I have found Kristeva's concept of abjection to be of use.[2] In brief, abjection is a way of explaining the repressed, unacknowledged, and feared parts of both personal identity and of societies, a way of understanding both our horror and the ways in which we deal with it. Abjection is characterized by ambiguity, by that which "disturbs identity, system, order."[3] The ways in which we deal with the abject help to define it; we repress, control, exclude, and ritualize that which we fear. Here was menopause, previously ignored and excluded from social and medical attention, suddenly achieving a rare prominence, yet in a way that disturbed me. Why should this common occurrence incur such strong responses, virtually threatening women with all kinds of physical and mental ills if they did not repress the very event of menopause with treatment?

In what follows I shall explore the links between abjection and menopause to try to determine what makes our reaction to menopause one of fear, control, and regulation. The current social and medical response to menopause is consistent with understanding menopause as an abject event. I will then ask why should this be so, and whether this social response accurately mirrors the individual lived experience of menopause. A general discussion of the salient features of abjection will be followed by a detailed exploration of the links between abjection and menopause.

Abjection: The Powers of Horror

What is abjection? In general terms I understand the abject to be a depository for that which is threatening, fearful, incomprehensible, or vile. It is that against which order is defined, both at the level of the subject and of the society. At times the abject is characterized by a visceral response of loathing and fear, at times it is the invisible unstated premise underlying some of our most powerful social practices. Kristeva's account of abjection, which in large part I accept as a way of understanding both the individual's and society's responses to various phenomena, embraces both the abject in the formation of the subject and as the "other facet of religious, moral, and ideological codes on which rest the sleep of individuals and the breathing spells of societies."[4] I shall explore both of these facets in the belief that examining and analyzing that which is abject leads to a better understanding of both the individual and the social mores that influence our lives.

In Kristeva's account, for the individual the abject is the object of primal repression. It is formative of the "I" in that it is only through the definition of the individual's boundaries that one may acquire a sexual and psychological identity and hence enter the symbolic order as a social being. This identity is achieved at the cost of expelling and rejecting that which threatens the borders of the self. But that which must be rejected is also part of the self (an unacknowledgeable pleasure in defecation; a physical desire for the body of the mother), leaving a tension between the attractive and yet repulsive powers of the jettisoned horrors and the stable identity achieved via this expulsion.

Abjection itself is "a reaction to the recognition of the impossible but necessary transcendence of the subject's corporeality, and the impure, defiling elements of its uncontrollable materiality."[5] Abjection is concerned with the processes of the body and the borders of the body; ambiguous zones that are the interface between the inside and the outside of the body. What is inside is part of the subject, but once past the border of the body it becomes an object for the subject. The abject is simultaneously a necessary condition of the subject and what must be rejected in order to achieve an identity.

The categories of the abject that interest me are those concerned with corporeal waste and the signs of sexual difference; menstruation is a process that embodies these two categories simultaneously, the loss of which is the sign par excellence of menopause. Menopause is also a sign of aging; the symptoms to be warded off by treatment are those associated with age-related decay of the body. Perhaps these are reasons for our current abject responses to menopause, reasons I shall later explore further.

Clean and proper boundaries are a prerequisite for the formation of the sexual and psychological identity of the individual, and hence entry into the Kristeva's symbolic order—that is, the social and political life of societies, characterized by language, rituals, and roles. This concern with cleanliness gives rise to the abject category of bodily waste. It is the body's waste products that show me what I discard to live: "These body fluids, this defilement, this shit are what life withstands, hardly and with difficulty, on the part of death. There, I am at the border of my condition as a living being. My body extricates itself, as being alive, from that border. Such wastes drop so that I might live, until, from loss to loss, nothing remains in me and my entire body falls beyond the limit—cadere, cadaver."[6]

Among the waste products of the body, feces and menstrual blood are particularly abject. Why is it that these forms of corporeal waste (but not tears or semen) represent the objective frailty of societies? Kristeva argues that excrement symbolizes the danger threatening the individual's identity from without—the ego threatened by the nonego, life threatened by death. It is certainly true that the rituals surrounding defecation are deep and strong and learned at an early age. The baby innocently enjoying her own excretory functions is soon replaced by the toddler who may take pride only in excreting in a socially approved fashion, rather than in the act itself.

Menstrual blood is a more complicated case. The rituals surrounding the management of menstruation ("feminine hygiene products") are not a prerequisite for entry into the linguistic order in the way that control of defecation is. Kristeva argues that menstrual blood symbolizes the danger issuing from within the identity, threatening the relationship between the sexes within society and the identity of each sex in the face of sexual difference.[7] I do not entirely agree here, for girls are socialized as girls long before the onset of menstruation; it is not enough to label menstruation *per se* as the sign of sexual difference. Menstruation may be accepted by girls as confirmation of their sexual identity, or even celebrated as a sign of maturity and fertility as well as being seen as the onset of forty years of monthly abjection. What is certainly abject about menstruation are the social responses, the obsession with concealment, control, and cleanliness, the imperative not to disturb, to keep the event invisible and "sanitary."

On another level menstruation is seen to be the sign of the mother, potential or actual. Gross writes: "Horror of menstrual blood is a refusal to acknowledge the subject's corporeal link to the mother. It is a border separating one existence, the mother's body, from another, the foetus, which both is and is not distinct from it. It marks the site of an unspeakable and unpayable debt of life, of existence, that the subject (and culture) owe to the maternal body."[8] Again I am reluctant to collapse the sexual signs of the mother into the single sign of menstruation. Both male and female children have internalized the notion of mother before any awareness of menstruation, thus reactions to menstruation are not at such a fundamental level as reactions to excretion. Menstruation may well serve as an unwelcome reminder of the subject's mortal links to the maternal body, but it is not alone in that function.

There are other reasons why the maternal body may be seen as abject. Mapping the boundaries of the body, teaching the child what is clean and proper and what is not, is the role of the mother in western society. As the child grows, she must separate from and reject the mother in order to take her place in the symbolic order. The mother becomes abject, that which must be rejected as a reminder of boundaries, as it is she who has cleaned up the shit and taught the child to wipe her bottom and thus serves as a constant reminder of the individual's frailty. I think it is this rejection of the mother, this leaving her behind in the realms of bodily waste, that contributes as significantly to the abjection of the adult female body as does the association with menstruation.

Social Dimensions of Abjection: Ritual and Custom

These categories of the abject, horror of corporeal waste and of sexual difference, are represented by rituals and customs within society. This is the second aspect of abjection I wish to explore briefly prior to relating this material to menopause. The cultural taboos surrounding corporeal waste are understood by Kristeva to define the border that separates the body from the signifying chain. Kristeva describes the defilement from which rituals protect us as neither sign nor matter but as "the trans-linguistic spoor of the most archaic boundaries of the self's clean and proper body."[9] Here we have a kind of split between the territory of the body that vomits and shits un-self-consciously, traditionally the domain of nature and the mother, and the world of socially signifying performances complete with embarrassment and guilt, the symbolic order.

Social rituals warding off the abjection of menstruation and the signs of sexual difference are widespread throughout many cultures. Kristeva takes one of her examples from the pure/impure distinction codified in Leviticus 12. Here it is written that the parturient woman is unclean. If she gives birth to a daughter, she is unclean for two weeks and must follow purification rituals for three-score and six days. If the child is a boy, she is unclean for only one week until the time of his circumcision, which ends her uncleanliness and shortens the purification period to thirty-three days. Kristeva understands this to be an insistence that the identification of the speaking being with his God is based upon the (violent) separation of the son from the mother.[10] No such separation is possible for daughters, thus leaving the female children trapped in the abject domain of the mother.

Other cultures have other rituals based on isolating and controlling menstruating women. Among the Bemba, a menstruating woman who touches a fire will become sick if she eats food cooked upon that fire.[11] (My grandfather prohibited menstruating females of the household from participating in butchering pigs.) Societies in which patrilinear control is precarious have more pollution rituals, perhaps in an attempt to subdue and to control the generative power of women.[12]

Given abjection, what are the ways in which individuals and societies deal with it? Repression is the first way, denying its existence, papering over the cracks that appear as we deny aspects of our corporeality. Societies also repress that which is abject; defecation is an invisible process, alluded to only by advertisements featuring cats and toilet paper. Menstruation is similarly invisible, an event through which women may continue to play tennis or even to swim, according to current advertising.

Religion is seen by Kristeva as a second possible response to abjection. A society must distance itself from and control the abject to avoid defilement; this distancing occurs through the powerful taboos and rituals of organized religion. Religion is a systematic wresting away of the subject from abjection, displacing abjection with rites and rituals that void those abject acts and objects from discourse. Abjection is the other facet of religious codes upon which rest the "sleep of individuals and the breathing spells of societies."[13] Rituals seek to control and to limit the powers of horror. In secular western societies medicine fulfills many of the functions of religion. Medicine prescribes and proscribes, lays down rules for bodily parameters and still shrouds many of its acts in incomprehensible rituals, reducing the horror of bodily decay to changes on an X-ray or specimens in the pathology lab. The sign of menopause, absence of menstruation, is "cured" by HRT. This reinstates monthly bleeding, not the irregular and unpredictable bleeding of menopause but well controlled and regulated losses unaccompanied by hormonal fluctuations. Accepting the treatment also regulates other aspects of the physical body, keeping the bones at an acceptable density, warding off heart disease, meeting the prescribed parameters for health.

What are the points that I wish to take from this account? First, the abject is that against which the identity is defined. It is the hidden, other repressed part that cannot be acknowledged in the symbolic order; that which is discarded in order to show the society what it is not. The abject is essentially corporeal and hence aligned with the feminine, the procreative, the maternal. Much of the power of abjection stems from a fear of the unknown, and a fascination with the possibilities inherent in ambiguity.

Second, abjection lies at the root of much social control—it underlies codes and traditions and is made articulate by the rituals erected to ward off its powers. In the Judeo-Christian tradition, the female body, especially the menstruating body, is associated with impurity and with polluting powers. The medicalization of western society has perpetuated this, particularly in the demands made of women to be endlessly screened and smeared; demands that implicitly create a version of the female body as needing surveillance and control in order to remain proper, disease free.

The abject requires some method of control, exclusion, or distancing to keep it at a safe, nonpolluting distance from the symbolic order. Yet despite displacement, repression, and sublimation, the abject does not go away. It remains, endlessly testing the limits, reminding us of that which we would rather forget, threatening us with disintegration; a perpetual reminder of frailty.

In summary, abjection is created by exclusion and fear, by the very rituals that seek to control it. These are the threads I shall follow with my account of menopause.

Menopause

Is menopause essentially abject? To answer that question we need to understand exactly what is meant by the term "menopause" and to spell out the differences between the actual menopause and our responses to it. Let me explore some definitions of menopause in order to clarify the point.

Most scientific/medical authors agree that menopause is a permanent cessation of menstruation due to lack of ovarian follicular activity, usually retrospectively diagnosed after twelve months of amenorrhea. This cessation of menstruation is a universal experience for all women who have menstruated. More than this bare fact of cessation of menses cannot be assumed. The interpretation placed on this event varies enormously: "The menopause may be regarded as either a 'life-cycle transition' or as an 'estrogen deficiency disorder'. The two views lead to differing perspectives on management."[14]

The age of menopause varies between the early forties and the early fifties. The reasons for this variation are not known.[15] The symptomatology of menopause varies even more. Avis, et al. have found that Japanese women aged 45–55 years experience hot flashes at the same rate as the general population.[16] This is despite the widely held view that hot flashes are strongly linked to variations in estrogen concentrations that occur at the time of menopause. This finding throws into doubt the notion of a universal menopausal experience and severely questions the accuracy of leaflets such as the one quoted previously. The same study found that in two North American populations of menopausal women the prevalence of hot flashes and sweats was not particularly significant—only 31 percent and 34.8 percent. These symptoms were experienced by these women at rates comparable to those for headaches, aches and stiffness in joints, and lack of energy—which are not symptoms usually attributed to menopause. The authors' conclusion was that the impact of menopause is not great, and far from being a universal experience with significant symptomatology, menopause is uneventful for a large proportion of women.

Other authors have found that menopause is eagerly anticipated and free from unpleasant symptoms in cultures in which women gain higher social status following menopause.[17] My point is that there is no discrete entity, disease or otherwise, that may be labeled as "the menopause." Is there something abject about this? If abjection is characterized by disorder and ambiguity, then our current definitions of menopause are certainly abject. The symptoms for which hormone replacement therapy offers respite are not unique to or solely attributable to the cessation of menstruation. It is as if menopause has been built up into a fearful event just so that it can be controlled and regulated—a medical ritual to ward off that which we fear.

The diagnosis of menopause is equally evasive, apart from its retrospective nature. New terms are introduced, such as perimenopause, which is "the time prior to menopause (when hormonal and clinical signs of approaching menopause occur) and at least the first year after the final menstrual period."[18] The duration of the perimenopause may be as long as three to four years prior to the last menstruation. During this time there is a decrease in follicle number, fluctuating and elevated levels of the hormones FSH and LH, combined with declining levels of estradiol and progesterone. However none of these changes are diagnostic in themselves, and even with clinical features of amenorrhea and elevated FSH and LH levels, it is not possible to determine menopause with absolute certainty.[19]

What is the significance of these points? It seems that despite the involvement of the scientific community, menopause remains somewhat elusive. The last menstrual period is the sign par excellence, but this passes unknown at the time. Symptoms that have been linked to documented hormonal changes vary culturally, suggesting a weaker link than initially assumed. Other symptoms such as depression, loss of libido, tiredness, irritability, and joint pains do not have any independent correlation with menopause.

Both the definition and diagnosis of menopause can be understood as abject in terms of ambiguity and temporal elusiveness. There is no single time at which one can say "this is the menopause"; no physical event to pinpoint the event. The notion of a border is applicable here, an in-between region of change. Yet for an event to be slippery in this way does not necessarily entail abjection. Abjection is created by the responses of the individual and the society, by the acts of distancing and rejection and the adoption of rituals. In the next section I wish to look at responses to menopause, at the individual experience and the social/medical construction in terms of abjection.

Abject Menopause

Menopause is a time of change. The changes are quite variable, from culture to culture and between individuals within the same culture, yet behind the difficulty in defining and documenting exactly what does happen, there is a change. There is a border crossed by the menopausal woman. This border is vague and ambiguous, characterized by three to five years of "perimenopause." For the menopausal woman it may be impossible to say, "Yes, that is what is happening to me," for it is easier to recognize in others or in retrospect those gradual and variable changes characteristic of this stage of life. The symptoms she may feel can be attributed to hormone changes or may be part of the fabric of everyday life. Even in retrospect the relationship between physiology, psychology, and environment will be unclear. Menopause is an obvious milestone in the cycles of a woman's life, yet it is not something clear that she can catch hold of at the time, not something that her medical advisers can confidently diagnose.

Menstruation is the sign of fertility, abject in itself yet at the same time a sign that is recognized in the symbolic order. A child serves as a token of authenticity in our society, in which the maternal role is recognized if not valued. Following the growth of the child, menstruation continues as a reminder of that fertility. With the loss of that sign, a woman may lose the status and identity that followed from being fertile. Here the woman is in an unenviable position.

Menstruation is abject, a ritual to be controlled with defined behaviors, referred to only obliquely by advertisements featuring sporting activities. Yet not to menstruate is even more abject. There are no references in culture to menopausal women, no rituals to dispose of the last unneeded feminine hygiene products. Germaine Greer has noted the absence of menopausal women in literature, the absolute silence surrounding this transition into a space peopled by crones and witches.[20] How can a woman mourn or even acknowledge the passage of her fertility when menstruation has always been a repressed process?

The perimenopause may be accompanied by physical turmoil. The menstrual cycle at this time may be variable, with a mixture of ovulatory and anovulatory cycles of between twenty and sixty days.[21] Instead of the periods that a woman is used to, she may not bleed for weeks, think "This is it, the menopause," and then find herself again menstruating when she least expects it. The clean and proper body may be in revolt, with unpredictable bleeding and hot flashes. Hot flashes are reminiscent of adolescence, that other period of physical turmoil in which the body is struggling to find its equilibrium. Yet the physical embarrassments of adolescence are acknowledged and tolerated far more openly and with more understanding than those of the climacteric. These changes within the body, the fabric of the woman, are experienced by her but remain invisible to the world at large. How can she reestablish her control, bring her chaotic being back into some semblance of order? These events must take place at the periphery of her being. She is already a mother, a wife, a professional; roles that have no patience with her losing her grasp on her physical self. To deny and repress may be the obvious solution, maintaining her clean and proper demeanor at the cost of denying the transitions that are taking place. Conversely, menopause may pass quietly, with periods gradually becoming infrequent and stopping without drama. This quiet crossing of the border may be problematic in its own way, causing the disquiet felt when an important experience passes unnoticed at the time.

In terms of borders, changes in identity, and the unknown, it is certainly possible for menopause to be an abject individual experience. The endless horror of a hot flash during an important meeting, the dread of unpredictable bleeding, the exhaustion following night sweats—all threaten the integrity and function of the social being, making menopause an experience to be feared. The loss of menstruation signals impending old age, the loss of fertility, perhaps the loss of sexuality. On this understanding, menopause is abject, but in accepting this understanding I have subscribed to the myth rather than speaking with certainty about women's experiences. I have implied that menstruation is an important part of a woman's identity; so are children, yet their departure from the family home may be greeted with as much relief as sorrow. I have assumed that the power to bear children is an important part of female identity, an assumption made questionable by the numbers of women who choose not to have children. It is easy to impose abjection upon the menopausal woman, but the individual experience is only abject in that it is feared, found abhorrent, excluded, and ritualized. I must now look at society's response to menopause for sources of abjection.

A society may deal with the abject in one of three ways; by repression, by sublimation, or by ritualization. All three of these methods are apparent in western cultural approaches to menopause. Repression is perhaps the most longstanding and widespread approach. Greer has explored the lack of menopausal heroines in literature in detail, having searched the biographies and memoirs of women writers in vain for even oblique references to menopausal experiences. Part of this invisibility may be explained circumstantially in that many of these writers died before reaching the age of menopause. A further factor is the general absence of female bodily functions in literature. Yet despite this, "the utter invisibility of middle aged women in English literary culture is baffling."[22]

The absence of middle-aged women from western cultural representations of necessity entails the invisibility of menopause. Perhaps one could argue that this has more to do with our culture's obsession with youth than with our horror of menopause, yet the two are not unrelated. The stereotype of the aging women's body is precisely that which is associated with the postmenopausal state; a drab body that is no longer fertile, prone to fractures, and only one step removed from the ultimately abject state of death. In a culture with a horror of corpses and death, it is easier to repress menopause than to acknowledge it as a universal sign of the inevitable passage of time. The aging process in men is not marked by any event as universal or final as the cessation of menses; hair grays gradually, the prostate enlarges slowly and silently at a time when men are often at the peak of their powers in the work place. There is no physiological tap on the shoulder to remind them of the approach of old age. It is women who are forced to notice the changes of menopause and then to hide them lest they remind society at large of the frailty of the human body. I do not know whether there is a large body of rejected material in which the lives of menopausal heroines unfold upon the page, yet I suspect not. Despite the assaults upon the traditional canon, some topics remain "unfit" as subjects for literature. This repression also carries overtones of "shooting the messenger." If the menopausal woman is a chilly reminder of mortality, she must be banished from our consciousness.

Similarly, the women who feature in films are not menopausal, at least not overtly so. The paucity of roles for actresses over the age of forty is well known. There are some roles for much older women, but here we enter the realms of sublimation. This is not Kristeva's literary sublimation, in which the horror can be heard bubbling beneath the text, evoking apocalyptic laughter, but rather a kind of sanitation. If the older woman must be seen, she is the grandmother of margarine advertisements, safely identified with a role of feeding and nurturing, with carefully coiffed gray hair and a tribe of grandchildren. A woman like this cannot pose the threat of impending death or be seen as a member of the alternative role available to old women, that of the witch. Our literature contains many images of powerful witches that have now been trivialized into that of the endearing and slightly dotty octogenarians of recent films. (Any appearance of older women in films may be welcomed, yet their treatment often lacks the respect accorded to similarly aged men. Jodie Foster may have made it as an FBI agent, but we have no female equivalent of Clint Eastwood as an older yet still potent agent.)

Ritualization is the final way in which a society may grapple with the abject. For Kristeva, religion is the dominant cultural mechanism laying down rites and rituals to protect society from the abject. In our more secular society, medicine has assumed some of these roles. Medicine prescribes ideal weights and cholesterol levels, defines who may or may not occupy the sick role, and what may be recognized as ill health. Opinion as to what constitutes a disease changes over time, reflecting not only "advances" in medical knowledge but also changes in societal norms.[23] Defining menopause as an estrogen-deficiency disease with extensive symptomatology and serious long-term sequelae requiring treatment is a very powerful ritual, the obverse side of which is necessarily abject.

There are two points here that relate to abjection. First, medical practice may be both reflecting and reinforcing society's horror of menopause. Taking over a universal physiological experience, defining it as a disease, and prescribing the treatment is an effective way of controlling the phenomenon. Menopause is no longer an inevitable and normal part of a woman's life, but the onset of a lifelong deficiency state requiring constant treatment. The whole experience of menopause may be aborted and avoided, and with it the associations of aging and mortality. Kristeva has noted that pollution rituals proliferate in societies where patrilinear power is poorly secured, as if these rituals sought a support against excessive matrilinear power.[24] Is it possible to understand the medical response to menopause as a pollution ritual aimed at warding off the power of post-menopausal women? They are the very group of women finally free from the work of child rearing and, as Greer argues, free from the tasks of appearing sexually attractive to men: "Only when a woman ceases the fretful struggle to be beautiful can she turn her gaze outward, find the beautiful and feed upon it. She can at last transcend the body that was what other people principally valued her for, and be set free both from their expectations and her own capitulations to them."[25] In western societies with increasingly aging populations in which women live longer than men, postmenopausal women are potentially a powerful force. By defining them as diseased, as deficient, society has a ritual with which to control and to intimidate this group, which is paradoxically polluted by a lack of menstruation rather than by its presence. The ritual of hormone replacement therapy wards off aging and death while simultaneously transforming the recipients into deficient beings who can only function properly (i.e., by youthfully menstruating) with the permission and help of medical practice.

The other aspect of abjection pertaining to the medical rituals of menopause concerns corruption. Kristeva writes that "the abject is related to perversion . . .

it curbs the other's suffering for its own profit. . . . Corruption is its most common, most obvious appearance."[26] There is certainly something perverse if not perverted in defining and treating a universal state as a disease state. Obviously there are huge profits to be made by encouraging all postmenopausal women to take hormone replacement therapy. The distinction between information and "therapy" is blurred by the common practice of sponsorship of clinical meetings by pharmaceutical companies. There is nothing so crass as any direct financial inducement for individual practitioners to prescribe, but the complex obligations created by the giving and receiving of gifts have unknown repercussions for the treatment of patients.

In this climate in which the majority of "free information" issues from the manufacturers of the promoted treatment, finding an unbiased account or advice is problematic. Information for women is widely available in the form of leaflets, often produced and supplied by the pharmaceutical companies involved. As I have mentioned, the promotions to medical practitioners are more complex, with appeals to the interests of society as a whole as well as the treatment of the individual women. Postmenopausal women are presented as an excessive financial burden upon society. It is claimed that by prescribing HRT the medical practitioner may ward off osteoporosis and cardiovascular disease, lowering the death rates for these women by some 40 percent and saving millions of dollars.[27] Thus it becomes morally incumbent upon the medical practitioner to promote HRT, simultaneously saving lives and money.

The Varieties of Menopausal Experience

The purpose of this paper has been to use Kristeva's notion of abjection as a focus for discussing menopause. Fear of the unknown, exclusion, and horror are the foundation of much that is abject.

How does this apply to menopause? First, there is no one menopause that is either abject or not. As some researchers have suggested, the menopausal experience differs enormously both at an intersubjective as well as at an intercultural level.[28] To construct "the menopause" as a symptom/disease complex is already part of a ritual designating abjection on the part of those defined by that very ritual. Ambiguity is inherently part of the cessation of menses; the common strands between women sharing the experience may well be outnumbered by the differences. But this ambiguity is not of necessity abject; the abject aspects are linked to women's perceptions of their bodies and the relationship between aging, menopause, and self-worth. These are all factors that are changeable if not changing: menstruation is less "shameful" than it used to be; the equation of female with mother no longer balances; and those years between fifty and seventy are the very ones in which women may find the time and energy to make a place for themselves in the social arena. Ambiguity may be as much cause for celebration as abjection; just as the bodily changes of pregnancy may be a source of wonder and enjoyment, the final hormonal outpourings may be a uniquely pleasurable experience.

The gap in our knowledge about women's lived experiences of menopause creates a vacuum that has been filled by abject social and medical rituals. The promotional leaflets list symptoms of bodily decay (mental, physical, sexual) that do not tally with the paucity of women who actually take HRT. Of the women who start HRT, less than 50 percent remain on it after one year, for reasons that are not clear. Stumpf and Trolice address the question of compliance (!) problems with HRT, citing lack of education and bothersome side-effects as the main patient problems, but this is not documented in any detail.[29] Does it feel "wrong" to be menstruating past the fifth decade, creating a conflict between the age one feels and the activities of the body? Do the women who continue HRT long term do so for their own benefit, for that of their partners, or to please their medical advisers?

The social portrayals of menopause are abject in the repression that leaves this part of the population invisible and in the rituals used to regulate the experience. This creation of a disease stigmatized by "deficiency," this lumping together of the physical manifestations of being alive as "symptoms," this universalization of what is a uniquely individual experience for reasons that include profit, control, and regulation, are the manifestations of society's abject response to menopause. By exposing and questioning these practices and their underlying assumptions it is possible to destroy the foundations of abjection, leaving menopause to be approached on an individual basis; to be lived openly by women armed with accurate information who may then choose to accept or to reject that which medicine has to offer.

Notes

I would like to thank Philipa Rothfield, the reviewers for this chapter, and others who offered helpful comments on earlier drafts of this paper. I would also like to thank Jill Need for her interest in and support of my work in this area.

1. Leaflet entitled *A Balanced Approach to the Menopause*, produced by Upjohn Pty. Ltd, Rydalmere, NSW.

2. J. Kristeva, *Powers of Horror: An Essay on Abjection*, trans. L. Roudiez (New York: Columbia University Press, 1982).

3. Ibid., p. 4.

4. Ibid., p. 209.

5. E. Gross, "The Body of Signification," in *Abjection, Melancholia, and Love: The Work of Julia Kristeva*, ed. J. Fletcher and A. Benjamin (London: Routledge, 1990), pp. 87–88.

6. Kristeva, *Powers of Horror*, p. 3.

7. Ibid., p. 71.

8. Gross, "The Body," p. 92.

9. Kristeva, *Powers of Horror*, p. 73.

10. Ibid., p. 100.

11. Ibid., p. 78.

12. Ibid., p. 77. See also J. Lechte, *Julia Kristeva* (London: Routledge, 1990), p. 164.

13. Kristeva, *Powers of Horror*, p. 209.

14. A. Gilbert, E. Hurley, and J. McNeece, *DATIS: Hormone Therapy* (Adelaide: Cathryn Charnock Corporate Publishing, 1993), p. 15.

15. M. Flint, "Menopause—The Global Aspect," in *The Modern Management of the Menopause: A Perspective for the 21st Century*, ed. G. Berg and M. Hammar (New York: The Parthenon Publishing Group, 1994), p. 17.

16. N. E. Avis, P. A. Kaufert, M. Lock, S. M. McKinlay, K. Vass, "The Evolution of Menopausal Symptoms," *Balliere's Clinical Endocrinology and Metabolism*, 7 (1) (1993): p. 30.

17. This point is discussed by P. A. van Keep, "Psychosomatic Aspects of the Menopause," in *Handbook of Psychosomatic Obstetrics and Gynaecology*, ed. L. Dennerstein and G. D. Burrows (Amsterdam: Elsevier Biomedical Press, 1983), p. 484, in which he cites the work of J. Maoz, "The Perception of Menopause in Five Ethnic Groups in Israel" (thesis, Leiden, 1973) and that of M. Flint, "The Menopause—Reward or Punishment," *Psychosomatics* 16 (1975): p. 161.

18. Gilbert, et al., *DATIS*, p. 1.

19. Ibid., p. 27.

20. G. Greer, *The Change: Women, Aging and the Menopause* (London: Hamish Hamilton, 1991).

21. Gilbert, et al., *DATIS*, p. 26.

22. Greer, *The Change*, p. 21.

23. Cosmetic surgery and treatment for infertility are two examples of the medicalization of circumstances previously considered to lie outside of the realm of medicine.

24. Kristeva, *Powers of Horror*, p. 77.

25. Greer, *The Change*, p. 430.

26. Kristeva, *Powers of Horror*, pp. 15–16.

27. Comments made by a contributor at a clinical meeting in Adelaide, in 1993.

28. Avis, et al, *Balliere's*.

29. P. G. Stumpf and M. P. Trolice, "Compliance Problems with Hormone Replacement Therapy," *Obstetrics and Gynecology Clinics of North America: Primary Care of the Mature Woman* 21 (2) (1994): pp. 219–30.

12

The Woman in the Menopausal Body

Emily Martin

Among the most pervasive images used in western medicine to conceptualize men's and women's bodies metaphorically are the body as a factory producing goods and the body as a system processing information. In this paper I explore the profound implications of these images for medical accounts of women's bodies, in particular those bodies in the processes of menstruation and menopause. Then I consider, as a thought experiment, the possibility of another image—a complex system based on nonlinear dynamics—as a model for female physiology. Let us begin by looking at ways the body has been constructed as a factory.

The Body as Factory

The metaphor of the factory producing substances is applied to the smallest parts of the body. At the cellular level, DNA communicates with RNA, all for the purpose of the cell's production of proteins. In a similar way, the system of communication involving female reproduction is thought to be geared toward production of various things: the ovaries produce estrogen, the pituitary produces follicle-stimulating hormone and luteinizing hormone, and so on. Follicles also produce eggs in a sense, although this is usually described as "maturing" them, since the entire set of eggs a woman has for her lifetime is known to be present at birth.

Beyond all this the system is seen as organized for a single preeminent purpose: "transport" of the egg along its journey from the ovary to the uterus[1] (and preparation of an appropriate place for the egg to grow if it is fertilized). In a chapter titled "Prepregnancy Reproductive Functions of the Female, and the Female Hormones," A. C. Guyton puts it all together: "Female reproductive functions can be divided into two major phases: first, preparation of the female

239

body for conception and gestation, and second, the period of gestation itself."[2] This view may seem commonsensical and entirely justified by the evolutionary development of the species with its need for reproduction to ensure survival.

Yet assuming this view of the purpose for the process slants our description and understanding of the female cycle in particular ways. Let us look at how medical textbooks describe menstruation. They see the action of progesterone and estrogen on the lining of the uterus as "ideally suited to provide a hospitable environment for implantation and survival of the embryo"[3] or as intended to lead to "the monthly renewal of the tissue that will cradle [the ovum]."[4] "The whole purpose of all these endometrial changes is to produce a highly secretory endometrium containing large amounts of stored nutrients that can provide appropriate conditions for implantation of a fertilized ovum during the latter half of the monthly cycle."[5] Given this teleological interpretation of the purpose of the increased amount of endometrial tissue, it should be no surprise that when a fertilized egg does not implant, these texts describe the next event in very negative terms. The fall in blood progesterone and estrogen "deprives" the "highly developed endometrial lining of its hormonal support," "constriction" of blood vessels leads to a "diminished" supply of oxygen and nutrients, and finally "disintegration starts, the entire lining begins to slough, and the menstrual flow begins." Blood vessels in the endometrium "hemorrhage" and the menstrual flow "consists of this blood mixed with endometrial debris."[6] The "loss" of hormonal stimulation causes "necrosis" (death of tissue).[7]

The construction of these events in terms of a purpose that has failed is beautifully captured in a standard text for medical students (a text otherwise noteworthy for its extremely objective, factual descriptions) in which a discussion of the events covered in the last paragraph (sloughing, hemorrhaging) ends with the statement, "When fertilization fails to occur, the endometrium is shed, and a new cycle starts. This is why it used to be taught that 'menstruation is the uterus crying for lack of a baby'."[8]

It has been argued that a particular horror for people living in late capitalist society is the lack of production: the disused factory, the failed business, the idle machine. Winner terms the stopping and breakdown of technological systems in modern society "apraxia" and describes it as "the ultimate horror, a condition to be avoided at all costs."[9] Perhaps one reason the negative image of failed production is attached to menstruation is precisely that women are in some sinister sense out of control when they menstruate. They are not reproducing, not continuing the species, not preparing to stay at home with the baby, not providing a safe, warm womb to nurture the offspring of a man's sperm. I think it is plain that the negative power behind the image of failure to produce can be considerable when applied metaphorically to women's bodies. Vern Bullough comments optimistically that "no reputable scientist today would regard menstruation as pathological,"[10] but this paragraph from a recent college text belies his hope:

If fertilization and pregnancy do not occur, the corpus luteum degenerates and the levels of estrogens and progesterone decline. As the levels of these hormones decrease and their stimulatory effects are withdrawn, blood vessels of the endometrium undergo prolonged spasms (contractions) that reduce the blood flow to the area of the endometrium supplied by the vessels. The resulting lack of blood causes the tissues of the affected region to degenerate. After some time, the vessels relax, which allows blood to flow through them again. However, capillaries in the area have become so weakened that blood leaks through them. This blood and the deteriorating endometrial tissue are discharged from the uterus as the menstrual flow. As a new ovarian cycle begins and the level of estrogens rises, the functional layer of the endometrium undergoes repair and once again begins to proliferate.[11]

In rapid succession the reader is confronted with "degenerate," "decline," "withdrawn," "spasms," "degenerate," "weakened," "leak," "deteriorate," "discharge," and, after all that, "repair."

In another standard text, we read:

The sudden lack of these two hormones [estrogen and progesterone] causes the blood vessels of the endometrium to become spastic so that blood flow to the surface layers of the endometrium almost ceases. As a result, much of the endometrial tissue dies and sloughs into the uterine cavity. Then, small amounts of blood ooze from the denuded endometrial wall, causing a blood loss of about 50 ml during the next few days. The sloughed endometrial tissue plus the blood and much serous exudate from the denuded uterine surface, all together called the menstrum, is gradually expelled by intermittent contractions of the uterine muscle for about 3 to 5 days. This process is called *menstruation.*[12]

The illustration that accompanies this text captures very well the imagery of catastrophic disintegration: "ceasing," "dying," "losing," "denuding," and "expelling."

These are not neutral terms; rather, they convey failure and dissolution. Of course, not all texts contain such a plethora of negative terms in their descriptions of menstruation, but unacknowledged cultural attitudes can seep into scientific writing through evaluative words. Coming at this point from a slightly different angle, consider this extract from a text that describes male reproductive physiology. "The mechanisms which guide the remarkable cellular transformation from spermatid to mature sperm remain uncertain. . . . Perhaps the most amazing characteristic of spermatogenesis is its *sheer magnitude:* the normal human male may manufacture several hundred million sperm per day."[13] As we will see, this text has no parallel appreciation of female processes such as menstruation or ovulation, and it is surely no accident that this "remarkable" process involves precisely what menstruation does not in the medical view: production of something deemed valuable. Although this text sees such massive sperm production as unabashedly positive, in fact, only about one out of every 100 billion sperm ever makes it to fertilize an egg: from the very same point of view that sees menstruation as a waste product, surely here is something really worth crying about!

What applies to menstruation once a month applies to menopause once in every lifetime. In the early 1960s, new research on the role of estrogens in heart disease led to arguments that failure of female reproductive organs to produce much estrogen after menopause was debilitating to women's health.

This change is marked unmistakably in the successive editions of a major gynecology text. In the 1940s and 1950s, menopause was described as usually not entailing "any very profound alteration of the woman's life current."[14] By the 1965 edition, dramatic changes had occurred: "In the past few years there has been a radical change in viewpoint and some would regard menopause as a possible pathological state rather than a physiological one and discuss therapeutic prevention rather than the amelioration of symptoms."[15]

In many current accounts, menopause is described as a state in which ovaries fail to produce estrogen. The 1981 World Health Organization report defines menopause as an estrogen deficiency disease.[16] Failure to produce estrogen is the leitmotif of another current account:

> This period during which the cycles cease and the female sex hormones diminish rapidly to almost none at all is called *menopause*. The cause of menopause is the "burning out" of the ovaries. . . . Estrogens are produced in subcritical quantities for a short time after menopause, but over a few years, as the final remaining primordial follicles become atretic, the production of estrogens by the ovaries falls almost to zero.[17]

Loss of ability to produce estrogen is seen as central to a woman's life: "At the time of the menopause a woman must readjust her life from one that has been physiologically stimulated by estrogen and progesterone production to one devoid of those hormones."[18]

Of course, I am not implying that the ovaries do not indeed produce much less estrogen than before. I am pointing to the choice of these textbook authors to emphasize above all else the negative aspects of ovaries failing to produce female hormones. By contrast, one current text shows us a positive view of the decline in estrogen production:

> It would seem that although menopausal women do have an estrogen milieu which is lower than that necessary for reproductive function, it is not negligible or absent but it is perhaps satisfactory for *maintenance of support tissues*. Menopause could then be regarded as a physiological phenomenon which is protective in nature—protective from undesirable reproduction and the associated growth stimuli.[19]

The Body as Information Processing System

Development of new molecular biology brought additional metaphors based on information science, management, and control. In this model, flow of information between deoxyribonucleic acid (DNA) and ribonucleic acid (RNA) leads to the production of protein. Molecular biologists conceive of the cell as "an assembly line factory in which the DNA blueprints are interpreted and raw materials fabricated to produce the protein end products in response to a series of regulated requirements."[20] The cell is still seen as a factory, but, compared to Gates's description, there is enormous elaboration of the flow of information from one "department" of the body to another and exaggeration of the amount of control exerted by the center. For example, from a college physiology text:

> The systems of the body, if they are to function effectively, must be subjected to some form of control. . . . The precise control of body function is brought about by means of the operation of the nervous system and of the hormonal or endocrine system. . . . The most important thing to note about any control system is that before it can control anything it must be supplied with information. . . . Therefore the first essential in any control system is an adequate system of collecting information about the state of the body. . . . Once the CNS [central nervous system] knows what is happening, it must then have a means for rectifying the situation if something is going wrong. There are two available methods for doing this, by using nerve fibres and by using hormones. The motor nerve fibres . . . carry instructions from the CNS to the muscles and glands throughout the body. . . . As far as hormones are concerned the brain acts via the pituitary gland . . . the pituitary secretes a large number of hormones . . . the rate of secretion of each one of these is under the direct control of the brain.[21]

Although there is increasing attention to describing physiological processes as positive and negative feedback loops, so that like a thermostat system, no single element has preeminent control over any other, most descriptions of specific processes give preeminent control to the brain, as we will see below.

In overall descriptions of female reproduction, the dominant image is that of a signaling system. Lein, in a textbook designed for junior colleges, spells it out in detail.

> Hormones are chemical signals to which distant tissues or organs are able to respond. Whereas the nervous system has characteristics in common with a telephone network, the endocrine glands perform in a manner somewhat analogous to radio transmission. A radio transmitter may blanket an entire region with its signal, but a response occurs only if a radio receiver is turned on and tuned to the proper frequency. . . . [T]he radio receiver in biological systems is

a tissue whose cells possess active receptor sites for a particular hormone or hormones.[22]

The signal-response metaphor is found almost universally in current texts for premedical and medical students:

> The hypothalamus *receives signals* from almost all possible sources in the nervous system.[23]

> The endometrium *responds directly* to stimulation or withdrawal of estrogen and progesterone. In turn, regulation of the secretion of these steroids involves a well integrated, highly structured series of activities by the hypothalamus and the anterior lobe of the pituitary. Although the ovaries do not function autonomously, they *influence*, through *feedback* mechanisms, the level of performance *programmed* by the hypothalamic-pituitary axis.[24]

> As a result of strong stimulation of FSH [follicle stimulating hormone], a number of follicles *respond* with growth.[25]

And the same idea is found, more obviously, in popular health books:

> Each month from menarche on, [the hypothalamus] acts as elegant interpreter of the body's rhythms, *transmitting messages* to the pituitary gland that set the menstrual cycle in motion.[26]

> Each month, *in response to a message* from the pituitary gland, one of the unripe egg cells develops inside a tiny microscopic ring of cells, which gradually increases to form a little balloon or cyst called the Graafian follicle.[27]

Although most accounts stress signals or stimuli traveling in a "loop" from hypothalamus to pituitary to ovary and back again, carrying positive or negative feedback, one element in the loop, the hypothalamus, part of the brain, is often seen as predominant. Just as in the general model of the central nervous system, the female brain-hormone-ovary system is usually described not as a feedback loop like a thermostat system, but as a hierarchy, in which the "directions" or "orders" of one element dominate: "Both positive and negative feedback control must be invoked, together with *superimposition* of control by the CNS through neurotransmitters released into the hypophyseal portal circulation."[28]

> Almost all secretion by the pituitary is *controlled* by either hormonal or nervous signals from the hypothalamus. . . . The hypothalamus is a collecting center for information concerned with the internal well-being of the body, and in turn much of this information is used to *control* secretions of the many globally important pituitary hormones.[29]

As Lein puts it into ordinary language:

The cerebrum, that part of the brain that provokes awareness and mood, can play a significant role in the control of the menstrual cycle. As explained before, it seems evident that these higher regions of the brain exert their influence by modifying the actions of the hypothalamus. So even though the hypothalamus is a kind of master gland dominating the anterior pituitary, and through it the ovaries also, it does not act with complete independence or without influence from outside itself. . . . [T]here are also pathways of control from the higher centers of the brain.[30]

So this is a communication system organized hierarchically, not a committee reaching decisions by mutual influence. The hierarchical nature of the organization is reflected in some popular literature meant to explain the nature of menstruation simply: "From first menstrual cycle to menopause, the hypothalamus acts as the conductor of a highly trained orchestra. Once its baton signals the downbeat to the pituitary, the hypothalamus-pituitary-ovarian axis is united in purpose and begins to play its symphonic message, preparing a woman's body for conception and childbearing."[31] Carrying the metaphor further, the follicles vie with each other for the role of producing an egg like violinists trying for the position of concertmaster; a burst of estrogen is emitted from the follicle like a "clap of tympani."[32]

The basic images chosen here—an information-transmitting system with a hierarchical structure—have an obvious relation to a very common form of organization in contemporary societies. What I want to show is how this set of metaphors, once chosen as the basis for the description of physiological events, has profound implications for the way in which a change in the basic organization of the system will be perceived. In terms of female reproduction, this basis change is of course menopause. Many criticisms have been made of the medical propensity to see menopause as a pathological state.[33] I would like to suggest that the tenacity of this view comes not only from the negative stereotypes associated with aging women in our society, but also as a logical outgrowth of seeing the body as a hierarchical system held rigidly in order by its central control system in the first place.

What is the language in which menopause is described? In menopause, according to a college text, the ovaries become "unresponsive" to stimulation from the gonadotropins, to which they used to respond. As a result the ovaries "regress." On the other end of the cycle, the hypothalamus has gotten estrogen "addiction" from all those years of menstruating. As a result of the "withdrawal" of estrogen at menopause, the hypothalamus begins to give "inappropriate orders."[34] In a more popular account, "the pituitary gland during the change of life becomes disturbed when the ovaries fail to respond to its secretions, which tends to affect its control over other glands. This results in a temporary imbalance existing among all the endocrine glands of the body, which could very well lead to disturbances that may involve a person's nervous system."[35]

In both medical texts and popular books, what is being described is the break-down of a system of authority. The cause of ovarian "decline" is the "decreasing ability of the aging ovaries to respond to pituitary gonadotropin."[36] At every point in this system, functions "fail" and falter. Follicles "fail to muster the strength" to reach ovulation.[37] As functions fail, so do the members of the system decline; "breasts and genital organs gradually atrophy,"[38] "wither,"[39] and become "senile."[40] Diminished, atrophied relics of their former vigorous, functioning selves, the "senile ovaries" are an example of the vivid imagery brought to this process. An anatomical text whose detailed illustrations make it a primary resource for medical students despite its early date describes the ovaries this way:

> The senile ovary is a shrunken and puckered organ, containing few if any folli-cles and made up for the most part of old corpora albincantia and corpora atretica, the bleached and functionless remainders of corpora lutia and follicles embedded in a dense connective tissue stroma.[41]

In more recent accounts, it is commonly said that ovaries cease to respond and fail to produce. Everywhere there is regression, decline, atrophy, shrinkage, and disturbance. The key to the problem connoted by these descriptions is function-less. Susan Sontag has written of our obsessive fear of cancer, a disease that we see as entailing a nightmare of excessive growth and rampant production. These images frighten us in part because in our stage of advanced capitalism, they are close to a reality we find difficult to see clearly: broken-down hierarchy and organization members who no longer play their designated parts represent nightmare images for us. One woman I talked to said her doctor gave her two choices for treatment of her menopause: she could take estrogen and get cancer or she could not take it and have her bones dissolve.

Like this woman, our imagery of the body as a hierarchical organization gives us no good choice when the basis of the organization seems to us to have changed drastically. We are left with breakdown, decay, and atrophy. Bad as they are, these might be preferable to continued activity, which because it is not prop-erly hierarchically controlled, leads to disorder, unmanaged growth, and disaster.

Revising the Metaphors

I have presented the underlying metaphors contained in medical descriptions of menopause and menstruation to show that these ways of describing events are but one way of fitting an interpretation to the facts. Yet seeing that female organs are imagined to function within a hierarchical order whose members sig-nal each other to produce various substances, all for the purpose of transporting eggs to a place where they can be fertilized and then grown, may not provide us with enough of a jolt to begin to see the contingent nature of these descriptions.

Even seeing that the metaphors we choose fit very well with traditional roles assigned to women may still not be enough to make us question whether there might be another way. Here I suggest some ways that the imagery applied to menstruation and menopause could be modified.

First, consider the teleological nature of the system, its assumed goal of implanting a fertilized egg. What if a woman has done everything in her power to avoid having an egg implant in her uterus, such as by using birth control or abstaining from heterosexual sex? Is it still appropriate to speak of the single purpose of her menstrual cycle as dedicated to implantation? From the woman's vantage point, it might capture the sense of events better to say the purpose of the cycle is the production of menstrual flow. Think for a moment how that might change the description in medical texts: "A drop in the formerly high levels of progesterone and estrogen creates the perfect environment for reducing the excess layers of endometrial tissue. Constriction of capillary blood vessels causes a lower level of oxygen and nutrients and paves the way for a vigorous production of menstrual fluids. As a part of the renewal of the remaining endometrium, the capillaries begin to reopen, contributing some blood and serous fluid to the volume of endometrial material already beginning to flow." I can see no reason why the menstrual blood itself could not be seen as the desired "product" of the female cycle, except when the woman intends to become pregnant. After all, normal shedding elsewhere in the body (skin, hair, stomach lining) is valued as part of a process of renewal and replenishment.

Would it be similarly possible to change the nature of the relationships assumed among the members of the organization—the hypothalamus, pituitary, ovaries, and so on? Why not, instead of an organization with a controller, depict a team playing a game? When a woman wants to get pregnant, it would be appropriate to describe her pituitary, ovaries, and so on as combining together, communicating with each other, to get the ball, so to speak, into the basket. The image of hierarchical control could give way to specialized function, the way a basketball team needs a center as well as a defense. When she did not want to become pregnant, the purpose of this activity could be considered the production of menstrual flow.

Eliminating the hierarchical organization and the idea of a single purpose to the menstrual cycle also greatly enlarges the ways we could think of menopause. A team that in its youth played vigorous soccer might, in advancing years, decide to enjoy a quieter "new game" where players still interact with each other in satisfying ways but where gentle interaction itself is the point of the game, not getting the ball into the basket or the flow into the vagina.

Forging New Metaphors

A set of metaphors with implications quite different from the body as machine or the body as centralized processing system is currently exercising a significant amount of influence in some medical specialties. These metaphors derive from chaos theory, also known as nonlinear dynamics or complexity theory. Under their impact, cardiologists, for example, are coming to see the heart not as the quintessential mechanical body part, a clocklike pump, but as a self-organizing and responsive system that only beats with a clocklike regularity when the body is near death and the heart can no longer respond to all the changes going on around it. Then and only then does the heart settle into a metronomic mode with little variation or "chaos."

> Until recently, it was widely held that sudden cardiac death represented an abrupt change from the apparently periodic state of the normal heartbeat to one in which chaotic arrhythmias occur. Work from several sources has suggested that under *normal* conditions the heart has chaotic dynamics and that fatal disturbances of the cardiac rhythm are often preceded by a *decrease* in the degree of physiological chaos. This represents a reversal in the conventional usage of the term "chaos" when applied to the injured heart.[42]

This shift in imagery brings about a revolution in what is considered "normal" behavior for the heart, with consequent direct applications to therapy.

> With pacemakers, for example, chaos theory suggests that rather than stimulating the heart at regular intervals as the devices do now, they should be designed to "mimic one of the low-dimensional chaotic patterns that exist in [healthy] hearts."[43]

Flexible, effective "control" in a complex system necessarily yields chaotic output—not chaos as in random disarray, but behavior that is bounded, patterned, intrinsic chaos, intrinsic irregularity.

In addition to cardiology, explorations are underway in applying a chaos model to numerous other physiological systems: HIV infection, epilepsy, cancer, genetic development.[44] Beyond the body altogether, many researchers are trying to understand the behavior of complex systems such as the economy, the weather, earthquakes and avalanches, ecosystems, and traffic in terms of a chaos model.[45] Particularly intense efforts are underway to understand the behavior of successful business firms in the present era as following many of the principles of a chaotic system.[46]

A Thought Experiment on Menopause

What would happen if we thought about describing menopause in terms of a chaos model, leaving aside both the body as mechanical factory and the body as centralized information processing system?

First consider two fundamental characteristics of chaos:

1. It is both deterministic and aperiodic. Although if the underlying conditions and underlying system of mathematical equations are known, the behavior of the system can be predicted, "chaotic behavior never repeats itself exactly. There are no identifiable cycles that recur at regular intervals."[47]

2. Chaotic systems have sensitive dependence on initial conditions. In other words, very tiny differences in initial conditions will result in very large differences later on.

    The so-called baker's transformation provides a material metaphor of sensitive dependence. Take a piece of dough and sprinkle it with raisins, taking note of their initial positions. Stretch and fold the mixture repeatedly. Now compare the final positions of the raisins to the initial positions. Even a small change in the initial position of a particular raisin will result in a very different final position if one does enough stretching and folding.[48]

Both these features go to make similarly structured systems vary greatly over time and one from another. In spite of the great amount of change they undergo, these systems are not without order.

Chaotic behavior is constrained to a relatively narrow range. Although it appears random, the behavior of the system is *bounded*, and does not wander off to infinity. In the baker's transformation, for example, the raisins always remain embedded in the dough no matter how long or how vigorously we knead it. The behavior tends to wander because of the stretching, but always returns to a small region because it is folded back on itself. . . . Not only is the behavior constrained, but there is a particular pattern to the behavior. Common examples are the swirls seen as cream is mixed in coffee, the pattern of cigarette smoke as it rises in a calm room, and the pattern observed as a running stream of water is transformed into a rapid.[49]

Our thought experiment might pose the question: Have the *regularities* of the female hormonal and bleeding cycles between puberty and menopause been overemphasized just as the regularities of the heartbeat have been? In the current medical model of the female cycle, regular periodicity between narrow limits is taken as the norm. Estrogen, progesterone, and other hormones are produced (if all is normal) with machinelike regularity; menstruation occurs (if all is normal) with the periodicity of a metronome. Disease produces irregularity, and shifts between stages of maturation (puberty and early menopause) produce irregularity. Regularity is normal, good, and valued; irregularity is abnormal and negatively valued.

Menstrual irregularity is often regarded medically as a pathology related to some organic dysfunction. The dysfunction can be variously attributed to a "presumed" malfunction of the ovaries,[50] ovarian mitochondrial DNA deletion,[51] hyperandrogenism,[52] diabetes,[53] premenstrual syndrome (PMS),[54] or anorexia nervosa.[55] I do not mean to suggest that these correlations are spurious. Rather I want to call attention to the unexamined assumptions that "normal" entails being periodically regular. There is a sharp contrast set up in the typology of the normal and regular versus the abnormal and irregular. To begin to move toward a different view, one might ask, exactly how regular are most women?

I know of no ethnographic study of the topic, but it seems very likely that women experiencing what they take to be "irregularity" in their periods in puberty or during early menopause will be disturbed and anxious about the irregularity itself. If the body is a machine, then a faltering or erratic pattern of behavior seems to portend its imminent failure, the onset of pathology. Women who are deemed irregular may be given medication to produce regular periods. (Epidemiologically, "correction" of irregularity is deemed a short-term benefit of oral contraception.[56]) Women who are uncomfortable with a menstrual pattern they perceive as irregular may demand relief.

In the machine model, regularity is a sign of health, irregularity a sign of disease or impending death. In the chaos model, it is just the opposite.

> The conventional wisdom in medicine holds that disease and aging arise from stress on an otherwise orderly and machine-like system—that the stress decreases order by provoking erratic responses or by upsetting the body's normal periodic rhythms. In the past five years or so we and our colleagues have discovered that the heart and other physiological systems may behave most erratically when they are young and healthy. Counterintuitively, increasingly regular behavior sometimes accompanies aging and disease. Irregularity and unpredictability are the important features of health.[57]

This new picture overturns the earlier notion of the heart as part of a homeostatic physiological system, in which the goal was to reduce variability and "to maintain a constancy of internal function. According to [the homeostatic] theory . . . any physiological variable, including heart rate, should return to its 'normal' steady state after it has been perturbed. The principle of homeostasis suggests that variations of the heart rate are merely transient responses to a fluctuating environment."[58] In contrast, the new findings suggest that "the mechanism that controls heart rate may be intrinsically chaotic. In other words, the heart rate may fluctuate considerably even in the absence of fluctuating external stimuli rather than relaxing to a homeostatic, steady state."[59]

The reason chaotic organization might be an advantage to the heart is that "chaotic systems operate under a wide range of conditions and are therefore adaptable and flexible. This plasticity allows systems to cope with the exigencies of an unpredictable and changing environment."[60]

In an era when flexibility, adaptability, and the ability to change rapidly in response to an ever-changing environment with agility and grace is becoming an ideal characteristic of the person, the work organization, the government, and the educational institution,[61] it should not be surprising to find the virtues of this stance recognizable inside the body. The question is how to recognize these traits in the female reproductive system?

The following are a few suggestions toward that end:

1. Describe "irregularity" as an adaptive response to the internal and external environment. The young woman whose menstrual cycle is affected by exercise, by stress, or by puberty could then think what a good job her endocrine system is doing in adjusting flexibly to her life, rather than worry unduly about a pathological "irregularity." Epidemiological studies that have shown greater menstrual irregularity in women who work at night[62] and women who are vegetarians[63] could be taken to reveal the responsiveness of these women's female physiological systems to their particular environment, rather than a pathological deviation from a putative norm of periodicity. The older woman whose menstrual cycle is affected by approaching menopause or other aspects of her life could do the same.

2. The change women undergo during menopause itself could be described as a phase change, of the sort complex systems often undergo. "Complex systems sometimes behave discontinuously. Systems simply change states. In models of complex systems, a controlling loop may reach a threshold state and transfer control to another loop altogether. The system appears to have experienced a discontinuous jump from one set of apparent relationships dominating the action to another."[64] For a woman undergoing menopause, thinking of it as a state change from reproductivity to maintenance of non-reproductivity would constitute a far more positive view of her body than thinking of it as breakdown of centralized control.

The thought experiment of imagining female physiology as a complex, nonlinear system opens many doors. We would no longer be faced with the impossible choice of the woman whose doctor told her she could take estrogen and get cancer or not take it and have her bones dissolve. Instead of posing only two alternatives—between a form of order controlled by a central authority and total disorder and collapse—we could consider the possibility of a "nonlinear, predictable order without periodic repetition."[65] "Chaos" in this sense, is constrained, is bounded, and is formed in a definite way.[66] But its form is nonlinear and the system as a whole is capable of abrupt state changes. Imagining the female body this way would give women a flexible, adaptable, responsive physical self, one that participates in ideal notions of the kind of self—agile, quick, graceful, in constant change, nimbly responsive to alterations in the environment—now widely thought necessary to survive in the contemporary world.

For these shifts in imagery to occur, women would have to be open to more active, positive self-images at the same time as medical practitioners would have to be willing to help women construct them. Menstrual "irregularity" or

menopausal "symptoms" might still be treated medically in some cases to alleviate intractable discomfort or other serious problems. But if women themselves
saw the phase changes of menstruation and menopause as a result of their bodies'
remarkable adaptability, then perhaps women would experience them as less
problematic. This in turn might allow doctors, in a synergistic way, to rely less
on hormonal treatments to create a mechanical regularity to either menstruation
or to menopause.

Notes

1. A. J. Vander, *Human Physiology*, 4th ed. (New York: McGraw Hill, 1985), p. 580.

2. A. C. Guyton, *Physiology of the Human Body*, 6th ed. (Philadelphia: Saunders College Publishing, 1984), p. 968.

3. Vander, *Human Physiology*, p. 576.

4. A. Lein, *The Cycling Female: Her Menstrual Rhythm* (San Francisco: W. H. Freeman, 1979), p. 43.

5. Guyton, *Physiology*, p. 976.

6. Vander, *Human Physiology*, p. 577.

7. Guyton, *Physiology*, p. 976.

8. W. F. Ganong, *Review of Medical Physiology*, 11th ed. (Los Altos, CA: Lange Medical Publishers, 1983), p. 63.

9. L. Winner, *Autonomous Technology: Technics-Out-of-Control As a Theme in Political Thought* (Cambridge: MIT Press, 1977).

10. V. L. Bullough, "Sex and the Medical Model," *Journal of Sex Research*, Vol. 11 (1975): p. 291.

11. B. Mason, *Human Physiology* (Menlo Park, CA: Benjamin Cummings, 1983), p. 525.

12. Guyton, *Physiology*, p. 624.

13. Vander, *Human Physiology*, pp. 483–84; emphasis added.

14. E. Novak, *Textbook of Gynecology*, 2d ed. (Baltimore: Williams and Wilkins, 1944).

15. E. Novak, et al. *Novak's Textbook of Gynecology*, 7th ed. (Baltimore: Williams and Wilkins, 1965).

16. P. A. and G. P. Kaufert, "Women, Menopause, and Medicalization," *Cult. Med. Psychiatry*, Vol. 10 (1986): p. 7.

17. Guyton, *Physiology*, p. 979.

18. Ibid., p. 979.

19. H. W. and G. S. Jones, *Novak's Textbook of Gynecology*, 10th ed. (Baltimore: Williams and Wilkins, 1981), p. 799.

20. R. C. Lewontin, S. Rose, and L. J. Kamin. *Not in Our Genes: Biology, Ideology, and Human Nature* (New York: Pantheon, 1984), p. 59.

21. D. F. Horrobin, *Introduction to Human Physiology* (Philadelphia: F. A. Davies, 1973), pp. 7–8.

22. Lein, *Cycling Female*, p. 14.

23. A. C. Guyton, *Textbook of Medical Physiology*, 7th ed. (Philadelphia, PA: W. B. Saunders, 1986), p. 885.

24. R. C. Benson, *Current Obstetric and Gynecologic Diagnosis and Treatment* (Los Altos, CA: Lange Medical Publishers, 1982), p. 129.

25. F. H. Netter, *A Compilation of Paintings on the Normal and Pathologic Anatomy of the Reproductive System. The Ciba Collection of Medical Illustrations*, Vol. 2 (Summit, NJ: Ciba, 1965), p. 115; emphasis added.

26. R. V. Norris, *PMS: Premenstrual Syndrome* (New York: Berkeley Books, 1984), p. 6.

27. K. Dalton and R. Greene, "The Premenstrual Syndrome," *British Medical Journal*, Vol. 1016 (1953): p. 6; emphasis added.

28. V. B. Mountcastle, *Medical Physiology*, 14th ed., Vol. 2 (St. Louis: C. V. Mosby Co., 1980), p. 1615.

29. Guyton (1986) *Textbook of Medical Physiology*, p. 885; emphasis added.

30. Lein, *Cycling Female*, p. 84.

31. Norris, *PMS*, p. 6.

32. Netter (1965), p. 6.

33. F. B. McCrea, "The Politics of Menopause: The 'Discovery' of a Deficiency Disease," *Social Problems*, 31 (1) (1983): p. 111.

34. Lein, *Cycling Female*, pp. 79, 97.

35. D. J. O'Neill, *Menopause and Its Effect on the Family* (Washington, DC: University Press of America, 1982), p. 11.

36. Vander, *Human Physiology*, p. 597.

37. Norris, *PMS*, p. 181.

38. Vander, *Human Physiology*, p. 598.

39. Norris, *PMS*, p. 181.

40. Netter (1965), p. 121.

41. Ibid., p. 116.

42. J. E. Skinner, "Neurocardiology: Brain Mechanisms Underlying Fatal Cardiac Arrhythmias," *Neurologic Clinics* 11 (2) (1990): p. 1019. See also T. A. Denton, G. A. Diamond, R. H. Helfant, S. Khan, and H. Karagueuzian, "Fascinating Rhythm: A Primer on Chaos Theory and Its Application to Cardiology," *American Heart Journal* 120 (6) (1990): pp. 1419–40.

43. P. Cotton, "Chaos, Other Nonlinear Dynamics Research May have Answers, Applications for Clinical Medicine," *Journal of the American Medical Association* 266 (1) (1991): pp. 13–14.

44. Cotton, "Chaos," pp. 17–18.

45. R. Ruthen, "Adapting to Complexity," *Scientific American*, Vol. 130 (1993): pp. 133–34. See also P. Bak and K. Chen, "Self-Organized Criticality," *Scientific American*, Vol. 46 (1991): pp. 46–53.

46. M. J. Wheatley, *Leadership and the New Science* (San Francisco: Berrett-Koehler, 1992). See also R. Stacey, *Managing Chaos: Dynamic Business Strategies in an Unpredictable World* (London: Kogan Page, 1992).

47. Denton, et al., *Fascinating Rhythm*, p. 1424.

48. Ibid.

49. Ibid., p. 1425.

50. R. Lindsay, "The Effect of Sex Steroids on the Skeleton in Premenopausal Women," *American Journal of Obstetrics and Gynecology* 166 (6, pt. 2) (1992): p. 1993.

51. N. Suganuma, T. Kitagawa, A. Nawa, and Y. Tomoda, "Human Ovarian Aging and Mitochondrial DNA Deletion," *Hormone Research*, Vol. 39 (1993): p. 16.

52. K. Arai and G. P. Chrousas, "Glucocorticoid Resistance," *Bailliere's Clinical Endocrinology and Metabolism* 8 (2) (1994): p. 317.

53. C. J. Adcock, L. A. Perry, D. R. Lindsell, A. M. Taylor, J. Jones, and D. B. Dunger, "Menstrual Irregularities Are More Common in Adolescents with Type 1 Diabetes," *Diabetic Medicine* 11 (5) (1994): p. 465.

54. A. K. Khella, "Epidemiologic Study of Premenstrual Symptoms," *Journal of the Egyptian Public Health Association* 67 (1–2) (1992): p. 109.

55. A. H. Whitaker, "An Epidemiological Study of Anorectic and Bulimic Symptoms in Adolescent Girls: Implications for Pediatricians," *Pediatric Annals* 21 (11) (1992): p. 752.

56. B. Runnebaum, "The Androgenicity of Oral Contraceptives: The Young Patient's Concerns," *International Journal of Fertility* 37 (Suppl. 4) (1992): p. 211.

57. A. L. Goldberger, D. R. Rigney, and B. J. West, "Chaos and Fractals in Human Physiology," *Scientific American* 262 (2) (1990): pp. 43–44.

58. Goldberger, et al., "Chaos and Fractals," p. 47.

59. Ibid.

60. Ibid., p. 49.

61. E. Martin, *Flexible Bodies: Tracking Immunity in America From the Days of Polio to the Age of AIDS* (Boston: Beacon Press, 1994).

62. F. Miyauchi, K. Nanjo, and K. Otsuka, "Effects of Night Shift on Plasma Concentrations of Melatonin, LH, FSH, and Prolactin, and Menstrual Irregularity," *Sangyo Igaku* (Japanese Journal of Industrial Health) 34 (6) (1992): p. 545.

63. T. Lloyd, J. M. Schaiffer, and L. M. Demers, "Urinary Hormonal Concentrations and Spinal Bone Densities of Premenopausal Vegetarian and Nonvegetarian Women," *American Journal of Clinical Nutrition* 54 (6) (1991): p. 1005.

64. W. R. Arney, *Experts in the Age of Systems* (Albuquerque: University of New Mexico Press, 1991), p. 51.

65. Cotton, "Chaos," p. 12.

66. Denton, et al., *Fascinating Rhythm*, p. 1425.

13

Menopause and the Great Divide
Biomedicine, Feminism, and Cyborg Politics

Kwok Wei Leng

In the literature on menopause, two models stand opposed: the biomedical and the feminist. The biomedical model defines menopause in hormonal terms. This definition can be traced to developments in sex endocrinology research during the 1920s and 1930s. According to this research, human sexual behavior, sexuality, and reproduction were understood through sex hormones. In the 1920s, *estrogen* was established as a female sex hormone, and although it was noted that the female body could supply estrogen in several forms, it was nonetheless *ovarian* estrogen that became the quintessentially female hormone. This move from estrogen to ovarian estrogen allowed sex endocrinology research to explain many functions of female sexual and reproductive life with respect to the fluctuation of hormonal secretions in one particular site: namely, the ovaries. This in its turn produced the biomedical view of menopause as the result of diminishing ovarian production of estrogen. So while some agreement was reached on the complexities of the physiology of menopause, the official interpretation of menopause came down to one cause: a decline in the production of ovarian estrogen. From here, it was a short step to the biomedical construction of menopause as a condition of ovarian estrogen "deficiency": against the younger woman with full-blown ovarian estrogen production, menopausal women could only be seen as lacking. And it was an even shorter step, in the history of sex endocrinology, to the definition of menopause as a "disease"; that is, as an illness with particular symptoms pertaining to ovarian functioning and estrogen deficiency and treatable through commercially prepared hormone replacement.[1]

The feminist model of menopause begins at this point. This is a particular strand in feminist politics that pits itself against the biomedical model to challenge the definition of menopause as a deficiency disease and the widespread cultural acceptance of this definition. This feminist position is quick to point out the link between the biomedical model of menopause—which developed together with the discovery of commercially prepared hormones as a cheap and readily available form of "treatment" of the symptoms of estrogen deficiency—and patriarchal attitudes towards women. According to the feminist argument, the biomedical model perpetuates patriarchal definitions of woman as a function of reproduction—as "the sex" or the sum of her body (ovaries). In patriarchal culture, the assumption is that women and their bodies (ovaries) would be completely unruly were it not for a medical gaze and masculine intervention. For feminists, the medicalization of menopause marks another frontier of natural and normal biological processes and experiences to be conquered by men. It expresses the latest effort to control all aspects of women's lives, thereby denying women any hope of an autonomous existence in their natural lives. The rejection of the biomedical model of menopause and the patriarchal foundations upon which it rests, and the creation of a separate, woman-centered perspective free of the ideology of patriarchy, are therefore central to a women's liberationary politics of menopause.

In this paper, I focus upon this particular kind of feminist response to the biomedical discourse on menopause. My discussion is based upon the following claim: in constructing an alternative interpretation to the biomedical definition of menopause, this feminist response posits a perfectly accessible and innocent experience, the experience of nature. Nature is taken as purely self-evident, and its taken-for-grantedness generates a series of binary opposites that are then excluded from the feminist position on menopause. "Nature" is thus pitted against "culture," "drugs," "high-technology," and other forms of patriarchal intrusions, and a feminist consciousness of the "natural body" is produced as the only antidote to such interventions. Now, this experience of nature functions as something quite foundational in the feminist discourse, so much so that the feminist model of menopause forecloses the possibility of the constructedness and partiality of its own position. In short, the feminist model becomes a thought system based upon the unassailable foundation of nature. But it could be argued that this same kind of metaphysical thinking has always inhabited the discourses of Man. For what else are the discourses of Man but systems of thought that place Man at the center as the unassailable foundation against whom all Others (chiefly Woman) are defined? If the feminist model of menopause shares in this same metaphysics of Truth, this same kind of logocentrism that has persisted in western philosophical thought, then it could be argued that the feminist response to the biomedical model of menopause is a troubling one indeed.

This becomes an even more troubling concern once we learn that such a metaphysics of Truth, in this case the Truth of Nature, is no longer sustainable in our times. Yet, a loss of these systems of first principles and totalities is not of itself such a bad thing. As Donna Haraway says, "We do not need a totality in order to work well."[2] What we *do* need to work well is a new way of coding politics and the embodiment of selves that might forge a way beyond metaphysical closures. In other words, if a politics built out of the Truth of Nature is no longer sustainable, then something else must replace it. I propose a different model and politics of menopause based upon Donna Haraway's cyborg myth, a myth for our times, a myth that eschews universals and grand claims to true experience in favor of partiality, irony, and perversity. It is proposed as a solution to the boundedness of feminist politics as it confronts the dominant medical model of menopause. A cyborg myth is a way of coding a new kind of politics of menopause that is also powerfully heretical of the western logos and its dominations.

The Feminist Challenge to the Biomedical Model of Menopause

Let me now look more closely at feminist critiques of the biomedical model of menopause through a selection of representative papers. We shall see how certain themes about women's experience of menopause and the misogyny of the medical establishment are replayed in the feminist literature. This classic feminist position on menopause has been most recently articulated by Renate Klein and Lynette Dumble in "Disempowering Midlife Women: The Science and Politics of Hormone Replacement Therapy." In the following discussion, I shall be commenting mostly upon this paper as well as on the writings of Germaine Greer, Kathlene MacPherson, Sandra Coney, and others.[3] Note that this feminist literature spans a period of some two decades.

The central argument in the feminist model is that the biomedical definition of menopause is an assault to the autonomy and integrity of women's normal bodily existence. This assault is carried out through what is known as a patriarchal conspiracy. It is argued that through a carefully orchestrated propaganda campaign conducted by the male-dominated medical profession, pharmaceutical industry, and media, the biomedical model of menopause extends its view of menopause as a deficiency disease and coerces women into buying its product: hormones.

> The menopause industry is about the colonization of a sex, the redefining of a normal life stage as a medical event. It is difficult for women to make choices freely when they have been subjected to a demoralizing propaganda campaign aimed at brainwashing them into accepting they are "estrogen deficient", in other words, defective in their normal state.[4]

For many feminists working within this model it is Dr. Robert Wilson and his book, *Feminine Forever*, that is the first instance of the biomedical propaganda campaign. Wilson, who had substantial backing from major drug companies that commercially prepared estrogen, also used the media to publish excerpts from his book. For instance, large sections of *Feminine Forever* appeared in major women's magazines, and the book itself sold 100,000 copies within its first seven months of publication.[5] In both his book and in the media, Wilson described the menopausal woman in withering, shrinking, wrinkling, and degenerating terms. He added, however, that the menopausal woman need not suffer through her biological destiny. Wilson promised women that they could be relieved of the menace of menopause and estrogen deficiency through estrogen replacement therapy (ERT): with the help of medicine the midlife woman could stay young and feminine forever. Not surprisingly, the popularity of Wilson's book and its message were matched by sales in "estrogen replacement therapy."

Klein and Dumble note that this idea of estrogen as a "solution" to menopause has persisted in the face of debate and controversy surrounding the treatment. For instance, the estrogen campaign continued with strength and vigor despite the alarm triggered in the 1970s by the endometrial cancer scare. In the process, a new formula for ERT—the presence of progestogens in the mix—was developed to offset women's fears of endometrial cancer, a move that also allowed the propaganda campaign to change the name of hormone replacement from ERT to HRT. For Klein and Dumble, this revival of estrogen therapy and its continuing existence as a form of therapy for menopause can only be read as strong proof of the efficacy of the propaganda campaign by the Masters of Menopause (the term belongs to Germaine Greer). Moreover, this revival has gone hand in hand with increasingly sophisticated marketing techniques that work to capture helpless women through new images of ERT. For instance, part of the rehabilitation of the image of ERT involves shifting the definition of menopause as a deficiency disease to that of a *deficiency syndrome*.[6] The revival of estrogen therapy, in other words, is seen by feminists as very much tied to the inclusion of new diseases in menopausal conditions. In this way, diseases that were once found to exist coincidentally *with* menopause have now become integral parts of a total syndrome *of* menopause. Osteoporosis is just one such disease that has become coterminous with menopause: its treatment or prevention has indeed become a prime target of medical menopausal management. Feminists such as Klein, Dumble, Coney, and others therefore argue that the inclusion of osteoporosis as part of "the menopausal syndrome" is in fact a major dimension in the revival of estrogen therapy for menopausal management.

Other feminists note that heart disease has been similarly included in the menopausal syndrome. Once again, the argument is that by playing on the fears of this terrible illness more women have become newly coerced into buying the estrogen propaganda.[7] But these strategies are dubious given that the successes of hormone replacement in the prevention of osteoporosis and heart disease remain unsubstantiated. It is still unknown, for example, whether the progestogen component of the combined therapy contradicts or overrules any gains made by the estrogen component in delaying the thinning of bone density.[8] And, as some feminists note, HRT can actually have the unintended consequence of putting women at risk of diseases even as it strives to prevent them (breast cancer is a disease that has most recently been linked to HRT).[9] With so little in the way of definite gains, the HRT campaign is a thin disguise for preying on an unsuspecting market and subjecting more and more women to the biomedical definition of menopause.

Some feminists go as far as to suggest that the HRT campaign is designed to rein women back into the sphere of male control precisely at a time when women are rethinking their relations with men. While the biomedical proponents of HRT say that they are rescuing women from the perils of their bodies, the feminist position sees the HRT campaign as a block to midlife women from taking control of their own destinies. As Greer writes, "The post-menopausal woman is not allowed to have no further need of men. She is defined as suffering from a deficiency disease, and men will once again demonstrate their superiority by supplying the remedy for her defect."[10] HRT is therefore seen as a violence against the bodily integrity and independence of all midlife woman: it is a means of complicating a completely *natural* process, and therefore ought to be resisted.

It makes sense, then, that resisting the medicalization of menopause restores power to women and to their bodies. For Nancy Worcester and Marianne Whatley, this consciousness is not new. They argue that feminists have for some time now been critical of the way in which natural processes of female reproduction have been colonized by the medical profession. This subjection of women's bodily processes to the medical gaze in its modern form dates back to the nineteenth century. Feminists today therefore promote resistance to medical interventions against a long history of modern medicine and its intrusion upon the female body. But for Worcester and Whatley, today's women must also recognize that menopause is a normal and healthy event, that it is not a problem requiring treatment and prevention through drugs or high technology. Today's women must be given the appropriate information about the workings of their bodies to resist the HRT campaign and its willful manipulation of menopause, osteoporosis, and heart disease—a manipulation that is simply the most recent expression of the imperialism of a patriarchal medical establishment.[11] Klein and Dumble agree: it is only by learning the lessons of the past—namely, the effects of medical interference on other normal female processes—that women become more cautious of the claims of HRT and shake off their passive status in relation to the Masters of Menopause. It is only through good "common sense" that women can resist the HRT campaign and prevent themselves from becoming, yet again, the victims of patriarchy and its medicalization of women's bodies:

> Will we personally resist HRT and politically expose the extraordinarily paralysing consequences if millions of women at the prime of their lives and ready to challenge the world instead become the Stepford Wives of the 1990s? . . . We trust that women's common sense will prevail, and that through exposing the "unethics" and real dangers of HRT, their resistance will be supported.[12]

In sum, according to the feminist model of menopause, women must learn the lessons of their own, normal bodies and return their experience of menopause to a bodily-centered and thus woman-centered perspective. Against the patriarchal medical establishment, feminists therefore argue for menopause as a time of spiritual awakening, rebirth, and rehabilitation. Menopause is a return to a true feminine self that challenges the requirements of patriarchy and the interventions of the medical gaze. Instead of others (men) naming the experience of menopause, women must be given a voice and a hearing; they must reclaim what is rightfully theirs. In Greer's evocative language: "The chrysalis of conditioning has once and for all to break and the female woman finally to emerge."[13]

Clearly there are only two options for midlife women. One position is to accept HRT and be duped by the HRT campaign, to be a victim of patriarchy once again. The other is to resist HRT, to believe in the body and to restore power to the crone. In the world of Klein and Dumble, however, the first position amounts to coercion; there is, in effect, only one *real* option for the "true" midlife woman. The first position is for the weak and weary and has no place on the feminist agenda and a woman-centered world.

The Great Divide? Or Two Sides of the Same Coin?

Thus far, I have detailed a particular feminist challenge to the biomedical interpretation of menopause. It is clear that in the literature on menopause the biomedical and feminist positions form a great divide, bitterly opposed to one another.[14] The question I now ask is: are these two models really that different?

In her paper, "Myth and the Menopause," Patricia Kaufert describes these two models as myths; that is, as ways of understanding and grasping phenomena in the world.[15] For Kaufert, the biomedical and feminist models are two interpretations of menopause. They both claim a validity and right to speak for menopausal subjects insofar as they build social realities for subjects; it is in creating a social reality for subjects that subjects are given a medium through which to act. In the case of menopause, the biomedical model and the feminist model are thus engaged in a battle to create a world, a social reality, for menopausal women. Through myth-making, their interpretations of menopause seek to shape and return to woman an authentic experience of menopause. According to Kaufert, neither the biomedical nor the feminist models have a greater claim to *the* truth. This is because both are equally myths, and the only thing either can offer is *an interpretation*. In other words, in the great divide between the biomedical model and the feminist model, the battle is not in the truth of menopause but rather in who controls the meanings of menopause, the medical profession or the feminists.[16] It is the *meanings* of menopause that have become the central political issue.

While Kaufert refers to the myths of menopause, Geri Dickson comments upon the *narratives* or *metalanguages* of menopause.[17] The biomedical model, for example, uses a particular style of thought that is not neutral but "filled with conscious and unconscious assumptions both about what the world is like and the nature of things."[18] For Dickson, metaphors or forms of thought create their own narratives or metalanguages that can themselves be examined, analyzed, and interpreted; they can be read symptomatically to reveal the motivations of their creators. The word "deficiency" in the biomedical model, for example, functions metaphorically. Other metaphors include "loss," "breakdown," and "failure." These are not neutral words but carry strong connotations that, as many feminists have argued, connect with dominant attitudes toward women and aging.[19] But in Dickson's account, the feminist position *also* works as a narrative or metalanguage, typically deploying positive metaphors to counter the negative, dominant medical paradigm. As we have seen, some popular metaphors include "renewal," "discovery," and "natural." According to Dickson, the biomedical model might well be criticized for reproducing reductionist notions of woman (woman as the sum of her ovaries); the feminist model, itself a narrative or metalanguage, is similarly embedded in a problematic mode of essentializing the natural woman, taking her to be the truth of experience.

> A foundational assumption in feminist menopause research is that women are not defined by their hormones. However, there is sometimes a tendency to develop essentialist assumptions about the nature of human beings (that there is an essential feminine or masculine nature) and the conditions for social life. . . . That is, in attempting to overcome the oppressive assumptions about women embedded in the traditional approaches, some feminist theorists have posited what they take to be (essentially) a feminine perspective.[20]

Implicit in Dickson's account is a deeper philosophical argument learned from Michel Foucault. Menopause, like any object of knowledge in the social sciences, is never simply given, always already in the real world for scientific method or theoretical work to "discover." Rather, menopause is animated by the discourses and practices that construct it as an object for study. These discourses and practices—whether biomedical or feminist—are themselves locked into particular social and historical conditions. When thinking about menopause, then, it is preferable to construct a genealogy of the *conditions* of its possibility as an object of biomedical or feminist knowledge.

One of the best known examples of the genealogical method is Foucault's own analysis of *The History of Sexuality*, which does not begin with the understanding of sexuality today. Instead, Foucault writes of the various discourses, practices, and historical conditions that allow for the possibility of sexuality as an object of study in the first place. According to his argument, sexuality as an object of knowledge is attached to nineteenth-century attitudes toward the body: the productive body, the clean and docile body, and so on. These attitudes emerged at a particular historical juncture: in the West, at least, sophisticated demographic and population studies became instrumental in governmental policy and decision making. Foucault identifies this as a new imperative in the history of the human species to manage and to administer biological existence. It represents the putting of biology or life into history, or "bio-power." Sexuality is located at the center of bio-power; it is its most crucial target. This is because the new biological imperatives of human existence could be most successfully achieved in the monitoring of sexuality. We see the emergence of specific categories of sexuality with specific pathologies to match. The fecund, heterosexual woman, for example, became vital to a healthy population and was held as the norm against the ill, frigid woman. Now, while Foucault's account of the emergence of sexuality as an object of knowledge is highly original, I believe that his most important point is that the numerous "reverse discourses" that emerge as a reaction to the norms of sexuality are also very much located within the network of bio-power. The sexual liberationary discourses of the 1960s, for instance—those discourses that tell us of our repressed sexuality—are mutually produced in the incitement to speak and know (and thus monitor, administer, and control) the empty truth of sex.[21]

Dickson's essay, "A Feminist Poststructuralist Analysis of the Knowledge of Menopause," details this foucauldian method of genealogy with respect to modern-day discourses on menopause.[22] As Dickson states, "Foucault's work provide[s] the direction for an unmasking approach to reveal the power and knowledge of the discourses of menopause."[23] As I read her, Dickson uses Foucault's notion of the normalizing technologies characteristic of the modern era to locate the emergence of the biomedical model on menopause and the feminist responses to it, and to avoid the trap of essentialism in both. In Dickson's account, the biomedical construction of the menopausal woman is located in Foucault's history of sexuality. Through the various techniques and technologies on the female body performed in the service of bio-power, a new category is produced: the menopausal subject, with a pathology to match, enters history. The menopausal woman is, from this moment on, regulated by the biological imperative. She lacks such an imperative and is consequently "deficient" and "ill," not a normal woman. Moreover, to add Foucault's second insight to Dickson's analysis, the existence of a reverse discourse on menopause is also an effect of this constellation of knowledge of and power over modern bodies. When feminists claim that their account is the true account of menopause, the natural or normal menopause free of patriarchal interventions, they too are incited to speak and to know more of the empty truth of the body of menopausal women.

This is not to say, however, that this poststructuralist method of discourse analysis cannot produce an oppositional account to the dominant model of menopause. Dickson's poststructuralism opposes not the biomedical model *per se* but rather the way a particular constellation of knowledge about bodies, sexuality, and menopause has become the truth, a serious "game of truth." Following Chris Weedon, Dickson posits that resistance inheres in contradictory subjectivity: the dominant model of menopause can never account for the *entire* experience of menopause, and these feelings in excess of the official truth can introduce new constructions of menopause and new possibilities of subjectivity. In short, there is nothing outside of discourse, least of all the possibility for resistance to dominant representations of menopause: "It is acknowledged that the 'knowledge' of menopause . . . represents a moment in history; the discourses and meaning of menopause are already changing."[24] In this way, Dickson calls her model of menopause a "feminist poststructuralist" model:

> The feminist questions . . . grappled with in this study were (1) how the "scientific truth" has set the standard for the "truth" for menopausal women, (2) how the "games of truth" that take on the form of science can be used to control women, and (3) how women exercize power and knowledge in resistance to the scientific form of control. . . . The feminist poststructuralist framework of this study assures women that they need not take for granted the established knowledge, power, and meaning of menopause: They are humanly produced and therefore bear the potential to be humanly altered.[25]

The strength of this feminist poststructuralist account over the feminist challenge to the biomedical model discussed earlier is that it does not pit an essential and eternal *content* of menopausal femininity against patriarchy. There is no natural menopausal body outside or beyond patriarchy that can counter the evils of male domination; there is no pure resource for feminist consciousness. Like Kaufert's use of the notion of myths, the discourses of the feminists' normal body and the partriarchs' medicalized body are equally constructed forms of discourse. What I like about Dickson's paper and Kaufert's notion of myth is that they both remind us that any knowledge—especially feminist knowledge—is a production, an "artefact of the first importance," to use Donna Haraway's expression. The biomedical "truth" of menopause cannot exist in some ready-made form any more than can the feminist call to the experience of menopause outside of patriarchal culture. As such, neither position stands still in an acultural or ahistorical vacuum. I think it is important to remember this with respect to the feminist model, for the feminist responses to menopause point to the constructedness of the biomedical model while allowing their own discourse to become metaphysically closed, a "truth" based upon a first principle of women's experiences of bodies. "Truth," no matter who utters it, is always constructed, relational, partial; moreover, the "experience" of "nature" as the basis of "truth" has no inherent claims to the grounding of political practice.

> "Women's experience" does not pre-exist as a kind of prior resource, ready simply to be appropriated into one or another description. What may count as "women's experience" is structured within multiple and often inharmonious agendas. "Experience", like "consciousness", is an intentional construction, *an artefact of the first importance.* "Experience" may also be re-constructed, re-membered, re-articulated.[26]

To put it bluntly, it seems that the classical feminist writings on menopause have thus far contained fundamental similarities to the biomedical writings on menopause. Both models, it seems, operate as closed thought-systems. In the classical feminist literature on menopause, it is the "natural" that becomes the basis of a closed narrative, a narrative that believes itself to be entirely self-evident. So the feminist model shares with the biomedical model the same philosophical assumption about "truth." It seems that the great divide between the two positions turns out to be no divide at all, but rather two sides of the same coin.

Now, it could be argued that one variation of this fantasy of self-evidence in the history of philosophy in the West is the discourse of Man; the self-evidence of Man as the (natural) human agent against which all Others (Woman, Native, Orient) are defined. Upon this principle, great ideologies and institutions are built—colonialism and phallocentrism, to name but two. It makes a lot of sense that resisting such metaphysical closures is crucial to dismantling the philosophical economy of Man and his dominations. But when the feminist model on menopause puts such great stock in "nature," it offers very little by way of this kind of deconstruction. At this point, I would be very interested in expanding the feminist agenda to include an assault upon metaphysical privileging.

For Jacquelyn Zita, feminism *can* resist metaphysical closures as part of the strategy I call for. Zita thinks of menopausal bodies as texts, sites for what she refers to as competing "rhetorics" of the body. The biomedical model reads the body as a text that unfolds a universally negative meaning or interpretation of menopausal experiences. It is a monolithic model because its location of authority, necessarily narrow and specific, is passed off as the truth. Shifting the biomedical rhetorics of the body is thus crucial to remaking and to renegotiating definitions of menopause. According to Zita, the feminist appeal to women's authority on menopause does just this: it produces a competing rhetorics of the body that might gain a privileged reading in the account of menopause. Feminists question the authority of the biomedical model to interpret the status and meaning of menopausal bodies. They demonstrate that such rhetorics of the body are tied to "a masculinist gerontocracy invested in the penultimate disempowerment of the female sex."[27] In response, they produce another interpretation of the body, one that valorizes female experiences of menopause. But for Zita this is not essentialist, for the feminist position stresses the multiplicity and variety of possible bodies, experiences, and voices, thereby avoiding the kinds of closures typical of the biomedical model:

> Diversity, multiplicity, possibility, and power emerge against the background of a medically monolithic and essentialized menopausal body. When these new voices escape diagnostic closure, they support oppositional and alternative readings of the body and the sense we make of our embodied experience. Menopause becomes a personal, physical, cultural, and political event, located

both inside and outside the physical boundaries of the body and inside a larger body politic.[28]

In other words, for Zita the feminist position is less likely to become a closed narrative on menopause, because it never presumes the body or experience as simply given. The feminist position is more attuned to the "discursively consti-tuted body," a body that is "as much a product of its biology as it is a product of institutional forces and cultural meanings imposed upon and disciplined into the flesh of our experience." So, in its valorization of the "transforming landscapes of the female flesh," the feminist position implicitly resists closure.[29]

In surveying the feminist literature above, however, I am not convinced of the success of feminist writings in resisting metaphysical closures and boundedness. I do not think that the feminist literature has necessarily resisted the monolithic menopausal body—not yet, anyway. Instead, the feminist literature reproduces a version of that monolithic body. As I have argued, the feminist valorizations of which Zita speaks obscure their own closed readings of the menopausal body under the banner of feminist consciousness or politics of menopausal experience. As we have seen, there are two positions available to menopausal women in the feminist literature: they can either submit to the biomedical paradigm (accept HRT) or resist it (reject HRT). But these two positions quickly reduce to one real position: the subjectivity proper to menopause is resistance, since to accept HRT and medicalization implies passivity and victimization. This resisting menopausal body then becomes the privileged site of feminist discourse and in this privileging, feminist politics itself becomes a totalizing narrative of menopause. My point is that this menopausal body, a body uncontaminated by patriarchal intervention, is no less constructed than the biomedical definition of menopause as deficiency or syndrome. Nature, and the normal body, are quite simply not to be trusted as foundations for anything.

Strange Couplings: Of Cyborgs and Other Monstrous Impossibilities

How, then, might a politics on menopause resist metaphysical closures of "truth" and its "experience" of "nature"? I suggest that the key lies in problematizing the "nature" upon which the classical feminist model is built. The classical feminist literature, for instance, tells us to learn from our nature and to restore the nor-mal body to menopausal experience. The trouble is, when we go to look for nature and its normal body, it is sometimes not there. For one thing, the menopausal body itself is not as fixed as it is hoped to be. It has been known to wander about, as in the case of the woman of times past, who bred more and bled less, often moving smoothly from her last pregnancy or state of lactational amen-orrhoea to menopause. For such a woman, menopause as the last bleed never comes. Second, the menopausal body can inhabit the young woman: "ovarian resistance syndrome," as it is known, can occur in women in their twenties (the earliest case was in a woman of seventeen).[30] But third, and most importantly, the message from Dickson (following Foucault) is that there is no innocent natural bedrock that observation or theory can "discover." There is no natural body and by extension no natural menopause: "nature" is as constructed as anything else of human thought. Or, to borrow from Judith Butler's formulation of the sex/gender divide, nature turns out to be culture all along.[31]

But in saying this, I am making a point that is quite different to the social-constructionist model. For if nature turns out to be culture all along, it is not because nature *is* culture; it is not because all that can be said of nature is cultural. Nature is not simply the passive object, the blank page to be written upon or etched, that the social-constructionist position takes it to be. But neither is it the completely untheorized, self-evident, and innocent object that the classical feminist model of menopause takes it to be. I do not want to play a game of restoring emphasis to one side or other of a new divide between essence and social-construction: of saying, like the classical feminist position, that there can be an innocence of nature; or of saying, like the social-constructionists, that there is no nature, only culture. As much as I like Dickson's Foucauldian approach (it reminds the classical feminist position about its own situatedness), I believe that the answer to metaphysical closures does not rest in social-constructionism. *What I wish to do, instead, is dismantle the divide between nature and culture itself, to render the divide as simply impossible.* And this is what I mean by problematizing "nature" as a way out of metaphysical closures. Let me thus shift the discussion *beyond* the social-constructionist critique of the classical feminist position on menopause.

For Donna Haraway, it is the blurring of the divide between nature and culture that is the basis for a reconstruction of ontology and politics beyond metaphysical closures. In this context, she introduces the figure of the cyborg. Haraway says that the cyborg is a myth for our century, a century built out of the *uncertainties of nature*. For Haraway, our time is late capitalism and the information era. Our time has a corresponding philosophical and aesthetic register as well, namely postmodernism. On both registers, cyborgs figure everywhere.[32] This is because we live in a world where all kinds of boundaries are becoming increasingly blurred. The "leakiest" distinctions or boundaries are those between the human and the animal, the human and the machine, and the physical and the nonphysical. For example, intelligence these days is "artificial" and our machines surprisingly animated. And since the cyborg is a cybernetic organism, "a hybrid of machine and organism, a creature of social reality as well as a creature of fiction," it is the cyborg, furiously heretical of boundaries, that best figures our "reality" and "experience" in the late twentieth century.[33]

Cyborgs haven't the time for western epistemological demands upon the innocence of nature. As Haraway notes: "The certainty of what counts as nature—source of insight and promise of innocence—is undermined, probably fatally. The transcendent authorization of interpretation is lost, and with it the ontology grounding 'Western' epistemology."[34] In another essay, Haraway continues:

> Women do not find "experience" ready to hand any more than they/we find "nature" or the "body" preformed, always innocent and waiting outside the violations of language and culture. Just as nature is one of culture's most startling and non-innocent products, so is experience one of the least innocent, least self-evident aspects of historical, embodied movement.[35]

For Haraway, then, "nature" has never been so slippery as in our time, but what difference has there ever been between nature and culture? The human body is naturally social, naturally cultural. The human subject is always already a prosthetic being: through its capacity to incorporate and to signify the social, cultural, and historical spaces that surround it, the body cannot be laid bare, as it were. For Haraway, this is the "truth" (can one really call it a truth?) in the twilight of truths of the twentieth century. This can only have shattering implications for a feminism—or indeed any other unified thought system—built upon the experience of nature. The postmodern omnipresence of cyborgs spells the death of any politics built upon "nature," as the classical feminist politics of menopause most often is. If we are living through a reconstruction of our basic ontology, then a reconstruction of *feminist politics* must follow. This is why the cyborg—itself a fabrication of organism and machine—best captures not only a new ontology but also a new political imagination for the hybridized realities of contemporary times as well. For Haraway, the cyborg myth is a way of building a politics upon partiality, hybridity, multiplicity, and contradiction:

> The cyborg is our ontology; it gives us our politics. . . . The cyborg is resolutely committed to partiality, irony, intimacy, and perversity. It is oppositional, utopian, and completely without innocence. . . . Nature and culture are reworked; the one can no longer be the resource for appropriation or incorporation by the other.[36]

Following Haraway, if a feminist discourse on menopause is to make up for the epistemological lag between a politics of nature and postmodern culture, it must address its own recourse to the experience of the innocence of "nature." Our thinking as feminists needs to be freed from these modernist constraints of essentialism, foundationalism, and nature, constraints that have grounded an entire generation of feminist politics on menopause and indeed the social-constructionist response to vault nature through culture. *Our thinking as feminists must become cyborg thinking.*[37] I suggest that this cyborg myth affords new kinds of menopausal subjectivities and politics previously unimagined and unimaginable in the old world of first principles, binary thought, totalities, and the problematics of nature or culture, essence or social-construction. Using the cyborg myth, I would like to reconstitute, or at least to begin to reconstitute, the feminist politics of menopause.

In the time of the cyborg, it seems no longer sensible to speak of pure bodies that stand opposed to the masculinist deployment of drugs and high technology on female reproductive processes. A cyborg politics will have nothing to do with any "natural matrix of unity." "Innocence, and the corollary insistence of victimhood as the only ground for insight, has done enough damage."[38] Rather, for cyborg politics, the way to theorize and to take control of the relation between women and menopause is to *reconstruct* the problem. For the quarrel is no longer between nature and technology/science—but was it really ever about this? The boundaries are just too fuzzy. Rather, the quarrel is between a cyborg will that might shape new understandings and the old metaphysical closures that produce closed narratives. In the time of the cyborg we must think through our relations to science and technology from the point of view of selves who might use them.

If we begin from this notion of rethinking through relations between science/technology and menopause, then a very different picture of a feminist politics on menopause emerges. Insofar as cyborg politics refuses closures and totalities, it could oppose drugs and high technology, but only if drugs and technology reproduced metaphysical closures. In this case, it is possible for a feminist cyborg politics to reject the promotion of HRT, but it is important to note here that this rejection would not be the same kind of rejection as the classic feminist position on HRT. If drugs and high technology, however, embraced cyborg thinking, then they could be important tools for embodiments and subjectivities of the future. In this case, a feminist cyborg politics could oppose the classical feminist position and encourage HRT and technology, but once again this siding with technology and medicine takes place on very different grounds from that of the biomedical model or according to classical feminist narratives. What is important to note, then, is that the field of politics, and what counts as for or against any issue of menopause, is radically reconstituted in postmodern culture and its cult of the cyborg. To put it another way, in this reconstituted field of ontology and politics, the binaries of nature or culture and the models proposed by biomedicine and classical feminism no longer hold up. As Alison Caddick writes, what we are talking about is "a more general transformation in the cultural setting within which choice is constructed, and its meaning radically altered."[39] Or, to sum up with Haraway herself:

> Cyborg imagery can help express two crucial arguments. . . . [F]irst, the production of universal, totalizing theory is a major mistake that misses most of reality, probably always, but certainly now; and second, taking responsibility for the social relations of science and technology means refusing an anti-science metaphysics, a demonology of technology, and so means embracing the skilful task of reconstructing the boundaries of daily life, in partial connection with others, in communication with all of our parts. . . . Cyborg imagery can

suggest a way out of the maze of dualisms in which we have explained our bodies and our tools to ourselves. This is a dream not of a common language, but
of a powerful infidel heteroglossia.[40]

My cyborg model of menopause is the illegitimate offspring of an unusual
coupling: that between the biomedical and classical feminist interpretations of
menopause. My cyborg model transforms the feminist and biomedical
HRT/drugs and technology debate beyond the alternatives of submit or resist. It
alone allows for a vision of menopausal women as always already culturally,
socially, and historically manipulated, which means that their "natural" bodies
cannot become the resource for "truth" and "experience"; nor, by extension, can
they become the repository for metaphysical closures, the playthings of feminism
or biomedicine. But the cyborg model of menopause most importantly allows
what there can be of nature to enter the discussion closed off by the social-constructionist response to the classical feminist mode. *For the very blurring of nature
and culture enters the field of menopause politics to reconfigure its terrain and the ontology that grounds it.* In this model, there is no room for simply being feminist or
antifeminist, resister or victim, pro- or anti-technology and drugs. Against the
heritage of metaphysical thought systems, there is only room for the powerfully
heretical; there is only room for the cyborg.

Notes

1. See Susan Bell, "Changing Ideas: the Medicalization of Menopause," *Social Science
   and Medicine*, 24 (6) (1987): pp. 535–42; Anne Fausto-Sterling, *Myths of Gender:
   Biological Theories about Men and Women* (New York: Basic Books, 1985), chapter 4;
   Ruth Formanek, "Continuity and Change and 'the Change of Life': Premodern
   Views of the Menopause," in *The Meanings of Menopause: Historical, Medical and
   Clinical Perspectives*, ed. Ruth Formanek (Hillsdale, NJ: The Atlantic Press, 1990).

2. Donna Haraway, "A Cyborg Manifesto: Science, Technology, and Socialist-feminism in the Late Twentieth Century," *Simians, Cyborgs, and Women* (New York:
   Routledge, 1991), p. 173.

3. Renate Klein and Lynette J. Dumble, "Disempowering Midlife Women: The
   Science and Politics of Hormone Replacement Therapy (HRT)," *Women's Studies
   International Forum* 17 (4) (1994): pp. 327–43; Germaine Greer, *The Change:
   Women, Ageing and the Menopause* (London: Penguin Books, 1992); Kathlene I.
   MacPherson, "Osteoporosis and Menopause: A Feminist Analysis of the Social
   Construction of a Syndrome," *Advances in Nursing Science* 7 (4) (1985): pp. 11–22;
   Kathlene I. MacPherson, "Menopause as Disease: The Social Construction of a
   Metaphor," *Advances in Nursing Science* 3 (2) (1981): pp. 95–113; Kathlene I.
   MacPherson, "Osteoporosis: The New Flaw in Woman or in Science?" *Health
   Values* 11 (4) (1987): pp. 57–61; Sandra Coney, *The Menopause Industry: A Guide to
   Medicine's "Discovery" of the Mid-life Woman* (North Melbourne: Spinifex, 1993);
   Nancy Worcester and Marianne H. Watley, "The Selling of HRT: Playing on the
   Fear Factor," *Feminist Review*, No. 41 (1992): pp. 1–26; Frances B. McCrea, "The

Politics of Menopause: The 'Discovery' of a Deficiency Disease," *Social Problems* 31 (1) (1983): pp. 111–23; Bell, "Changing Ideas"; Ann M. Voda and Mona Eliasson, "Menopause: The Closure of Menstrual Life," in *Lifting the Curse of Menstruation: A Feminist Appraisal of the Influence of Menstruation on Women's Lives*, ed. Sharon Golub (New York: The Haworth Press, 1983); Marlyn Grossman and Pauline Bart, "Taking the Men out of Menopause," in *Women Looking at Biology Looking at Men*, ed. Ruth Hubbard, Mary Sue Henifin, and Barbara Fried (Cambridge, MA: Schenkman Publishing Co., 1979); Fausto-Sterling, *Myths of Gender;* Janice Delaney, Mary Jane Lupton, and Emily Toth, *The Curse: A Cultural History of Menstruation*, rev. ed. (Urbana and Chicago: University of Illinois Press, 1988); Catherine R. Stimpson, "The Fallacy of Bodily Reductionism," and Alice J. Dan "The Interdisciplinary Society for Menstrual Cycle Research: Creating Knowledge From our Experience," both in *Changing Perspectives on Menopause*, ed. Ann M. Voda, Myra Dinnerstein, and Sheryl R. O'Donnell (Austin: University of Texas Press, 1982). See also the essays by Joy Webster Barbre, Patricia Smith, Kathleen I. MacPherson and Ann M. Voda in Joan C. Callahan, ed., *Menopause: A Midlife Passage* (Bloomington and Indiana: Indiana University Press, 1993).

4. Coney, *The Menopause Industry*, p. 20.

5. Klein and Dumble, "Disempowering Midlife Women," p. 330.

6. According to MacPherson, a disease presents a fixed set of symptoms peculiar to it, whereas a syndrome is a combination of symptoms occurring together. See MacPherson, "Osteoporosis and Menopause," pp. 11–12 and passim.

7. See Worcester and Whatley, "The Selling of HRT."

8. The feminist literature also points out that osteoporosis is a sociocultural disease. It seems that the high incidence of osteoporosis in the West is related to industrialized life styles and diets that prevent a good peak bone density in earlier years. Prevention in these earlier years might be a much better strategy than the wholesale prescription of HRT among one portion of the community. Moreover, a person has to fall and fracture before osteoporosis occurs, and the reason for falling may have nothing whatsoever to do with menopause or postmenopause. For example, the consumption of debilitating drugs or the lack of exercise, both of which diminish basic motor skills necessary to *avoid* falling, are common among the elderly. When these factors are taken into account, it is clear that the incidence of low bone density need not necessarily lead to the disease of osteoporosis. In conclusion, while HRT tends to delay the loss of bone density in menopausal and postmenopausal women, the disease of osteoporosis itself is more complex than the connection between low bone density, the lowering levels of ovarian estrogen, and menopausal and post-menopausal women. See Coney, *The Menopause Industry*, Part 3.

9. See, for instance, Ann M. Voda, "A Journey to the Centre of the Cell: Understand-ing the Physiology and Endocrinology of Menopause," in Callahan, *Menopause*, pp. 180–83.

10. Greer, *The Change*, p. 20.

11. See Worcester and Whatley, "The Selling of HRT," passim.

12. Klein and Dumble, "Disempowering Midlife Women," pp. 339–40.

13. Greer, *The Change*, p. 440.

14. There is one other model of menopause that is not discussed in this paper: the sociocultural model, which constructs menopause as a universal biological event and experience that nonetheless has quite different cultural and historical expressions.

These different expressions of menopause then lend meaning to the experience. Any problems related to menopause are therefore reactions to the cultural and historical constructions of the meanings of menopause and are to be addressed on the level of the cultural and historical. Many sociocultural writers cite ethnographic evidence of cultures with positive attitudes toward aging and the aged woman, which show a corresponding diminishing or absence of menopausal symptoms. See, for example, Yewoubdar Beyene, *From Menarche to Menopause: Reproductive Lives of Peasant Women in Two Cultures* (Albany: State University of New York Press, 1989). See also the papers in Formanek, *The Meanings of Menopause*.

15. Patricia A. Kaufert, "Myth and the Menopause," *Sociology of Health and Illness* 4 (2) (1982): pp. 141–61.

16. Ibid., p. 153.

17. Geri L. Dickson, "Metaphors of Menopause: the Metalanguage of Menopause Research," in Callahan, *Menopause*.

18. Ibid., p. 37.

19. See Emily Martin, "Medical Metaphors of Women's Bodies: Menstruation and Menopause," *International Journal of Health Services* 18 (2) (1988): pp. 237–54. See also her book, *The Woman in the Body: A Cultural Analysis of Reproduction* (Boston: Beacon Press, 1987).

20. Dickson, "Metaphors of Menopause," p. 44.

21. Michel Foucault, *The History of Sexuality*, Vol. 1: *An Introduction*, trans. by Robert Hurley (Harmondsworth: Penguin Books, 1981).

22. Geri L. Dickson, "A Feminist Poststructuralist Analysis of the Knowledge of Menopause," *Advances in Nursing Science* 12 (3) (1990): pp. 15-31.

23. Ibid., p. 21.

24. Dickson, "Metaphors of Menopause," pp. 54–55. See Chris Weedon, *Feminist Practice and Poststructuralist Theory* (Oxford: Basil Blackwell, 1987).

25. Dickson, "A Feminist Poststructuralist Analysis," pp. 22, 30.

26. Donna Haraway, "Reading Buchi Emecheta: Contests for 'Women's Experience' in Women's Studies," in *Simians, Cyborgs and Women*, p. 113; my emphasis.

27. Jacquelyn Zita, "Heresy in the Female Body: The Rhetorics of Menopause," in Callahan, *Menopause*, p. 60.

28. Ibid., p. 68.

29. Ibid., pp. 69–72.

30. Delaney, et al., *The Curse*, p. 214.

31. Judith Butler, *Gender Trouble: Feminism and the Subversion of Identity* (New York: Routledge, 1990), p. 7.

32. Two of Haraway's privileged examples are the women (usually of color) of the homework economies and integrated circuits—whose identities are fractured, contradictory, cutting across gender, race, and class—and the creatures who inhabit the world of feminist science fiction. See "A Cyborg Manifesto."

33. Ibid., p. 149.

34. Ibid., pp. 152–53.

35. Haraway, "Reading Buchi Emecheta," p. 109.

36. Haraway, "A Cyborg Manifesto," pp. 150–51.

37. It is for this reason that Patricia Mann has recently suggested that cyborgean ontology and politics is postfeminist. That is, the discussions of menopause, in our case, and the new reproductive technologies (specifically concerning abortion), in Mann's case, exceed the kinds of positions and identities offered by feminism. "Postfeminism" does not mean postpatriarchal, nor does it consist in a patriarchal "backlash" against the gains made by the second wave of feminism. "Postfeminism" simply means that agency and politics in the late twentieth century are no longer accommodated by the universalizing and naturalizing tendencies of the second wave of feminism. Feminism must today learn to expand to account for these new identities and politics. See Patricia S. Mann, *Micro-Politics: Agency in a Postfeminist Era* (Minneapolis: University of Minnesota, 1994), chapter 3.

38. Haraway, "A Cyborg Manifesto," p. 157.

39. Alison Caddick, "Feminist and Postmodern: Donna Haraway's Cyborg," *Arena*, Vol. 99/100 (1992): p. 120, and see pp. 121–22. Patricia Mann also writes: "We need to rethink our relationships to machines quite radically so as to expunge the antitechnological biases that have become hypocritical and misleading at this point" (*Micro-Politics*, p. 111).

40. Haraway, "A Cyborg Manifesto," p. 181.

Index